READINGS IN
CANADIAN LIBRARY
HISTORY 2

Edited by
PETER F. McNALLy

cla

CANADIAN LIBRARY ASSOCIATION / OTTAWA

Canadian Cataloguing in Publication Data

Main entry under title:

Readings in Canadian library history 2

Includes some text in French.
Includes biographical references and index.
ISBN 0-88802-269-7

1. Libraries--Canada--History. I. McNally, Peter F.
II. Canadian Library Association.

Z735.A1R43 1996   027.071   C96-900458-3

Front cover:
Two stills from *Library on Wheels* (National Film Board of Canada, 1945),
depicting the Fraser Valley Union Library in operation. The beginnings of
library service in the Fraser Valley are outlined in "Bringing Librarianship to
Rural Canada in the 1930s," page 241.
Photos courtesy the National Film Board of Canada. Reproduced with permission.

Printed on recycled paper

The paper used in this publication meets the minimum requirements of
American National Standard for Information Sciences—Permanence of
Paper for Printed Library Materials, ANSI Z39.48-1984 ∞

Contents

Preface

Although the Canadian library tradition stretches back to the sixteenth century, its historical study begins only in the second half of the nineteenth century. During the present century, Canadian libraries and their supporters have directed so much energy twoards the development of one of the world's great systems that little time has remained for studying how and why it developed. Of course, this begs the question: why should libraries be studied anywhere, especially in Canada?

To this question there are many possible answers. First, historical thinking and approaches constitute a legitimate way of looking at institutions and issues; indeed, many events can be properly understood only within an historical context. Second, it is important for Canadians and people from other lands to appreciate both the underlying similarities between the development of libraries in Canada and other countries and the unique elements that characterize Canadian library development. Third, anglophone and francophone Canadians should be aware of their differing traditions of library development. Fourth, librarians, library trustees, library and information instructors, historians and the general public will benefit by knowing better Canada's heritage and how it fits into larger social/cultural contexts. Finally, mapping the mind of the human past, in Canada or elsewhere, demands that we understand the vagaries of fortune that have affected the single most important institution yet devised for storing, organizing, and making accessible the graphic records of human experience.

This volume represents the third collection of essays to be published by the Library History Interest Group of the Canadian Library Association. The two previous collections are "Theme Issue on Canadian Library History," edited by Peter F. McNally, *Canadian Library Journal* 38, no. 6 (December 1981), and *Readings in Canadian Library History*, edited by Peter F. McNally (Ottawa: Canadian Library Association, 1986). Together with the current volume, they represent one of the most significant concentrations of scholarly writing ever to appear on our nation's library heritage; it is hoped that they will assist researchers and curious novices everywhere.

The Library History Interest Group was established in 1980 at the Canadian Library Association Annual Conference in Vancouver, B.C. The following year, in Hamilton, Ont., and at every subsequent annual conference of the association, the Library History Interest Group has held sessions at which scholarly papers have been presented. The group's statement of purpose is as follows:

This Group, which has been formed on the assumption that librarianship requires an understanding of its historical and philosophical foundations in order to face intelligently the challenges of the future, has four major aims:

1. To adopt, as its areas of concern, library history, philosophy and comparative librarianship, particularly as they relate to Canada.

2. To encourage awareness and discussion of the history of libraries and librarianship and of the place of libraries in a changing society.

3. To promote research and publication on library history and related areas.

4. To develop communication between librarians and other members of the academic community, relevant to the history and philosophy of librarianship.

As compiler and editor of this volume, I would like to thank the authors and anonymous referees, who together ensured its scholarly nature. I would also like to thank the CLA office staff and local arrangements committees across the country for their support and indulgence in organizing our annual sessions. Particular thanks are due to Elizabeth Morton, CLA's monographs editor, for her efforts in bringing this project through to successful completion, and to Melanie Fogel, who compiled the index. Although most of the papers were first presented before the Library History Interest Group, a few came from other sources. Due to unforeseen publication delays, some of the papers received initial publication elsewhere. We acknowledge with gratitude the permission of the publishers and authors to reproduce them here.

In reviewing this collection, and its two predecessors, I am struck by their widely ranging concern: most parts of the country are discussed; most types of libraries and library activities are mentioned; and both anglophone and francophone traditions are considered. Although these three collections do not constitute a synthesis, they make an essential contribution towards one.

As 1996 marks the fiftieth anniversary of the Canadian Library Association, this collection should be seen as a birthday tribute from the Library History Interest Group to the Association, and by extension to all of Canadian librarianship.

Peter F. McNally
Associate Professor
Graduate School of Library and Information Studies
McGill University
Montreal, Quebec

and

Co-Convenor
Library History Interest Group
Canadian Library Association

1 Guides to the Literature

Canadian Library History
in English and French to 1964:
A Survey and Evaluation

Peter F. McNally

Abstract

The literature of Canadian library history during its first one hundred years to 1964 reveals a wide range of intellectual and methodological trends. Anglophone publications emphasized professional process, few research fronts, and a lack of significant synthesis. Francophone publications emphasized research fronts and syntheses, an overwhelming concern with Quebec, and relatively little concern for professional process. The differing concerns of the two linguistic communities are reflected in the types of libraries studied: public libraries, academic libraries, and library associations were the three areas most studied by anglophones; personal, specialized and academic libraries were the most studied by francophones. No obvious historiographical links can be discerned between library history and Canadian history in general. This may be due either to the lack of social and cultural history during this period or to the failure of recent studies to discern its existence. In either case, this essay may serve as a guide to both library and social historians.

Résumé

La littérature sur l'histoire des bibliothèques canadiennes, jusqu'à 1964, révèle toute une gamme de tendances intellectuelles et méthodologiques. Les publications anglophones mettent principalement l'accent sur la démarche professionnelle et on y retrouve peu de pistes de recherche et peu de synthèses importantes. Les publications francophones mettent l'accent sur les pistes de recherche et les synthèses, accordent une grande importance au Québec et se préoccupent peu de la démarche professionnelle. C'est dans le type de bibliothèques étudié que s'illustre cette différence entre les deux groupes linguistiques. Les anglophones ont étudié principalement les bibliothèques publiques, les bibliothèques académiques et les associations de bibliothécaires tandis que les francophones se sont concentrés sur les bibliothèques personnelles, les bibliothèques spécialisées et les bibliothèques académiques. On ne peut identifier de lien historiographique évident entre l'histoire des bibliothèques et l'histoire du Canada en général. Cela s'explique peut-être par le peu d'histoire sociale et culturelle sur cette période ou par le fait que les études récentes n'en révèlent pas l'existence. Dans les deux cas, cet article peut servir de guide aux chercheurs en histoire des bibliothèques ou en histoire sociale.

The study of Canadian library history is best undertaken within the context of our nation's historiographical tradition.[1-9] Serious discussion of the Canadian past is generally considered to have begun with F.-X. Garneau's *Histoire du Canada* (Quebec: Aubin, 1845-52. 4 vols.). Garneau's work underlines the existence of separate anglophone and francophone historiographical traditions which predate it and continue to the present but which share a common concern with survival and nation-building.

In Quebec's francophone historiographical tradition before 1960, this concern manifested itself as clerically based French-Canadian nationalism and, since 1960 as secularly based Québécois nationalism. In the country's anglophone tradition, this concern manifested itself before 1960 as either localism or pan-Canadian nationalism and since 1960 as regionalism or provincialism, and in a certain decline of nationalism. In both traditions, great emphasis was placed in the earlier period upon political, constitutional and biographical studies. In addition, there developed an important school of English-language economic history during the 1920s and 1930s, called Laurentianism, and a small but significant school of French-language social and cultural history. Since the 1960s, however, social history has become a dominant element in both language communities.[6, 7, 8]

The practice of Canadian history in the nineteenth and early twentieth centuries was carried out largely by amateurs, whose efforts were frequently characterized by an energetic antiquarianism. Amongst anglophones, pragmatic "promoters, patriots and partisans" were the order of the day[9]; amongst francophones, priests or men trained by priests dominated the field until after World War II. In the 1880s and 1890s there began the gradual professionalization of Canadian history when the University of Toronto and McGill University appointed the country's first full-time history professors. *Bulletin des recherches historiques* (1895-1968) appeared as the first historical journal, to be followed by *Review of Historical Publications Relating to Canada* (1896-1918) and the *Canadian Historical Review* (1920-). The professionalization and secularization of history departments in francophone universities occurred only after 1945; the appearance of *Revue d'histoire de l'Amérique française* (1947-) marked a new level of maturity in francophone Canadian historiography.

Given this context, can one discern any obvious parallels or influences linking Canadian library history before 1965 with the country's general historiographical trends? To this question no clear and unequivocal answer can be given. On the one hand, all of the general historiographical studies in either English or French have so far overlooked the existence, during this period, of social and cultural history, including library history. On the other hand, the general studies provide suggestive interpretative frameworks which are useful for evaluating library history, such as the following: chronological divisions, classificatory subdivisions, amateur and professional distinctions, methodological and theoretical approaches, and linguistic traditions.

This article is intended, therefore, to fulfil two major functions: first, to assist practising and would-be library historians in identifying important and representative publications and in appreciating the major intellectual and methodological trends in their discipline; second, to alert a larger audience to a body of writing on Canadian library history that may provide an important clue in discerning the existence of a social-cultural historiographical tradition that has previously been overlooked.

TABLE 1

An Analysis of Publication on Canadian Library History to 1964

	English-Language	French-Language	Total
General Topics	50	10	60
Public Libraries	40	7	47
Specialized Libraries	16	25	41
Academic Libraries	20	14	34
Personal Libraries	2	26	28
Library Associations	19	2	21
National, Provincial, and Legislative Libraries	6	4	10
Biography	7	2	9
Adult Education	4	0	4
Library Education	2	2	4
School and Children's Libraries	1	0	1
Library Cooperation	0	0	0
Total	167	92	259

Noted in Table 1 are 259 publications encompassing over one hundred years of writings on Canadian library history to 1964. Although their quality is uneven, their numbers are impressive. Also impressive is the less than 2 to 1 ratio of English-language to French-language publications, reflecting the relatively greater concern about library history among francophones. Tables 2 and 3 show the very different concerns of francophones and anglophones during this period. In English-language publications, the top two categories are General Topics and Public Libraries; in French-language publications, they are Personal Libraries and Specialized Libraries. These variations reflect a preoccupation not only with different types of libraries but also with different methodological approaches and intellectual assumptions.

TABLE 2

English-Language Publications to 1964

General Topics	50
Public Libraries	40
Academic Libraries	20
Library Associations	19
Specialized Libraries	16
Biography	7
National, Provincial, and Legislative Libraries	6
Adult Education	4
Library Education	2
Personal Libraries	2
School and Children's Libraries	1
Library Cooperation	0
Total	167

English-Canadian library history began in the nineteenth century as an effort by Canadian, British and American investigators to promote the development of libraries in Canada. Their efforts were frequently little more than descriptive and statistical compilations of data with brief attempts at historical perspective carried out as part of the Anglo-American public library and public school movements. The study and development of libraries in Canada were part, therefore, of a much larger movement encompassing the entire English-speaking world. As there was no Canadian library journal before 1916, articles were frequently published in American professional journals, where they may still occasionally appear. Some

TABLE 3

French-Language Publications to 1964

Personal Libraries	26
Specialized Libraries	25
Academic Libraries	14
General Topics	10
Public Libraries	7
National, Provincial and Legislative Libraries	4
Biography	2
Library Associations	2
Library Education	2
Adult Education	0
Library Cooperation	0
School and Children's Libraries	0
Total	92

appeared also in Canadian historical journals, general magazines, and encyclopedias; some histories appeared as pamphlets and a few as monographs. Canadian, British and American government reports provided vehicles for publication as well; non-governmental agencies also published reports.

The overwhelming majority of anglophone authors were librarians or library supporters. They were writing works of partisan patriotism for other librarians, library supporters and local communities, pointing out the achievements of the past and challenges of the future. Only a handful of studies were written by professional or academic historians. From the 1900s to the early 1960s, a number of theses were produced, with all but a few being submitted to American library schools. By the time Canadian library education had developed a continuing commitment to research in the 1960s and 1970s, an ideological stance against historical studies had taken a firm hold. At no point was any awareness shown amongst anglophones of the French-Canadian tradition of library history. The inescapable conclusion must be that Canadian English-language library history in the century or so to 1964 emphasized professional process, showed only a few research fronts, and lacked any significant attempts at synthesis. That said, the publications of this period, taken *in toto*, constitute a formidable body of knowledge and information which students of the discipline ignore at their peril. Many of the individual studies are of a continuing value that transcends their historiographical interest.

French-language library history presents a very different face during the period to 1964. From the beginning, it was a research-based activity carried out by historians, archivists and clerics, among others. While some librarians were involved, their approach was shaped by the historiographical standards prevailing in francophone Quebec during the first 60 years of this century. It is unfortunate, therefore, that Serge Gagnon has largely ignored this period in his studies.[4, 5] Of particular importance is the role of the *Bulletin des recherches historiques* and its two editors, Pierre-Georges Roy (1870-1953) and his son Antoine (born 1905), who also served successively as Archivists of the Province of Quebec. The role of these two men and their journal in the historiographical development of Quebec history in general and of its library history in particular is too crucial to go unnoticed. In keeping with the scholarly priorities of the time, they placed great emphasis upon New France and the first half-century or so of the British régime.

A number of characteristics typify francophone publications of this period: the important syntheses of research by Fauteux[28] and Antoine Roy[29]; the overwhelming concentration upon francophone Quebec to the virtual exclusion of other communities such as anglophone Quebec or other francophone sections of the country; the brief, antiquarian and uninterpretive nature of most of the articles in the *Bulletin des recherches historiques*; the appearance of longer interpretive studies in other journals, theses or monographs; and, finally, the appearance of studies in the 1940s and 1950s reflecting the professional process approach typical of anglophone Canada.

[1] Berger, Carl, ed. *Contemporary Approaches to Canadian History*. Toronto: Copp Clark, 1987. 259p.

[2] ——. *The Writing of Canadian History: Aspects of English-Canadian Historical Writing since 1900*. Toronto: University of Toronto Press, 1976. x, 300p.

[3] ——. ——. 2nd ed. Toronto: University of Toronto Press, 1986. x, 364p.

[4] Gagnon, Serge. *Quebec and its Historians: 1840 to 1920*. Montreal: Harvest House, 1982. 161p.

[5] ——. *Quebec and its Historians: the Twentieth Century*. Montreal: Harvest House, 1985. 205p.

[6] Ouellet, Fernand. *The Socialization of Quebec Historiography since 1960*. Toronto: ECW Press, 1988. 66p.

[7] Phillips, Paul T. *Britain's Past in Canada; the Teaching and Writing of British History*. Vancouver: University of British Columbia Press, 1989. xi, 187p.

[8] Schultz, John, ed. *Writing about Canada: a Handbook for Modern Canadian History*. Scarborough, Ont.: Prentice-Hall, 1990. xiii, 282p.

[9] Taylor, M. Brook. *Promoters, Patriots, and Partisans: Historiography in Nineteenth-Century English Canada*. Toronto: University of Toronto Press, 1989. x, 294p.

General Studies

The English-language general studies are notable for their wide range of concerns, methodologies, and motivations. A number of general characteristics can be ascribed to them: their high concentration of American authors, publishers and sponsors; their relatively few and undeveloped research fronts and syntheses; and their apparent isolation from francophone scholarship. Perhaps they are best characterized as statistical surveys and general historical overviews, attached frequently as background to contemporary analyses meant to garner support for current and future library development.

Rhees is an essential starting point with his invaluable statistics.[10] James Bain appeared regularly in Canadian and American publications.[11, 12, 13] As with Rhees, the source of his statistics is uncertain, and his use of the phrase "public libraries" usually encompassed other types of libraries. The superficial historical analyses by Rhees and Bain reflect the malaise that accompanies studies undertaken solely to bolster present and future objectives. Burpee's "Canada Number" is an important starting point for early twentieth-century attitudes; historical and contemporary studies intermingle with one another.[14] His ALA article was for several generations probably the best general survey in English.[15]

From 1921 to 1958, the Dominion Bureau of Statistics provided essential and sometimes overlapping statistics deserving of much closer attention than they have hitherto received.[16, 17] Forsyth[18] and Holmes[26] undertook the first overviews in English of library development for a specific province, reflecting no doubt the early prominence of public libraries in British Columbia. Despite its concentration upon public libraries, the Ridington Report commissioned by the Carnegie Corporation covers various types of libraries and possesses an historical dimension; it is an essential starting point for studying the early decades of the century.[19] Lomer's brief survey reflects the general level of scholarship prevailing at the time.[20] Wolfenden did important primary research on a topic deserving further investigation.[21] Gundy undertook one of the first inventories of libraries in a Canadian city.[22] Harrop's thesis is cursory and superficial but of historiographical interest.[23] Morton's two short articles give a taste of her later efforts.[24, 25] Wees provides an elementary but helpful introduction to Quebec City and Montreal libraries.[27]

Unlike those in English, the general items in French are more scholarly but less numerous and lack concern for professional process. Fauteux provides an admirable synthesis of French-Canadian scholarship of the day and is still worth reading despite its brevity, its exclusive concern with Quebec, and its great concentration upon the personal libraries of the French régime.[28] Roy's book is actually his doctoral thesis for Université de Paris.[29]

9

This pioneering work in Canadian cultural history discusses libraries —
particularly personal libraries — within the context of his chapter on "la vie
intellectuelle, ce qu'on lisait, ce que l'on pensait, les bibliothèques". As
such, it is a precursor of the late twentieth-century *histoire du livre* school in
francophone Quebec. Trudel makes great use of the scholarship on library
history for his important study in intellectual history.[30] Massicotte undertook what is probably the first inventory of libraries in a specific community.[31]
Galarneau's article is an early example of his discussion of libraries within
the context of print culture.[32]

[10]Rhees, William J. *Manual of Public Libraries, Institutions and Societies in the United States, and British Provinces of North America.* Philadelphia: Lippincott, 1859. xxviii, 678p. (See pages 528-665.)

[11]Bain, James. "Public libraries of the Dominion of Canada." In *Statistics of Public Libraries in the United States and Canada,* by Weston Flint. Washington: Bureau of Education, Government Printing Office, 1893. xiii, 213p. (See pages 205-13.)

[12]——. "The public libraries of Canada." *Canada: an Encyclopedia of the Country,* 5: 207-11. Toronto: Linscott, 1899.

[13]——. "Canadian Libraries." *Library Journal* 25, no. 8 (August 1900): 7-10.

[14]Burpee, L.J., ed. "Canada Number." *Public Libraries* 9, no. 5 (May 1904): 195-235.

[15]——. "Canadian libraries of long ago." *American Library Association Bulletin* 2, no. 5 (September 1908): 136-43.

[16]Canada. Dominion Bureau of Statistics. *Survey on Education in Canada, 1921-1954.* Ottawa: King's Printer, 1923-1956. (Title and frequency vary; most volumes contain a section on libraries.)

[17]——. *Survey of Libraries in Canada, 1931-1958.* Ottawa: King's Printer, 1933-1959. (Title varies)

[18]Forsyth, John. "The Library Movement in British Columbia." In *Pacific Northwest Libraries: History of Their Early Development in Washington, Oregon, and British Columbia,* 32-40. Seattle: University of Washington Press, 1926. (Reprinted from the *Washington Historical Quarterly* for October 1926.)

[19]Carnegie Corporation. Commission of Enquiry. *Libraries in Canada: a Study of Library Conditions and Needs.* John R. Ridington, Chairman. Toronto: Ryerson Press; Chicago: American Library Association, 1933. 153p.

[20]Lomer, Gerhard. "Libraries." In *The Encyclopedia of Canada,* 4: 76-81. Toronto: University Associates of Canada, 1935-37.

[21]Wolfenden, Madge. "Books and Libraries in Fur-trading and Colonial Days." *British Columbia Historical Quarterly* 11, no. 3 (July 1947): 159-86.

[22]Gundy, H. Pearson. "Libraries in Kingston, 1811-1949." *Ontario Library Review* 33, no. 1 (February 1949): 7-11.

[23]Harrop, E.G. "Some Early Canadian Libraries." MSLS thesis, Western Reserve University, 1950. ii, 63p.

[24]Morton, Elizabeth. "Library Associations and Education for Librarianship." In *Encyclopedia Canadiana,* 6: 138. Toronto: Grolier, 1957.

[25]——. "Libraries." In *Encyclopedia Canadiana,* 6: 132-38. Toronto: Grolier, 1957.

[26]Holmes, Marjorie C. *Library Service in British Columbia: a Brief History of its Development.* Victoria, B.C.: Public Library Commission of British Columbia, 1959. 82p.

[27]Wees, Ian C. "Early Libraries in Quebec City and Montreal." *ALA Bulletin* 54, no. 4 (April 1960): 303-8.

[28]Fauteux, Aegidius. *Les bibliothèques canadiennes: études historiques.* Extrait de *La revue canadienne.* Montréal: Arbour et Dupont, 1916. 45p.

[29]Roy, Antoine. *Les lettres, les sciences, et les arts au Canada sous le régime français. Essai de contribution à l'histoire de la civilisation canadienne.* Paris: Jouve, 1930. 16, 292p. (See pages 58-87.)

[30]Trudel, Marcel. *L'influence de Voltaire au Canada.* 2 vols. Montréal: Fides, 1945.

[31]Massicotte, E.Z. "Bibliothèques d'autrefois à Montréal." *Bulletin des recherches historiques* 36, no. 10 (octobre 1930): 589-94.

[32]Galarneau, Claude. "Les échanges culturels franco-canadiens depuis 1763." *Recherches et débats* 34 (1961): 68-78.

Public Libraries

Nowhere are the strengths, weaknesses and vitality of anglophone library history of this period more evident than in the discussion of public libraries. The vitality is clearly seen in the large number and range of publications: theses, articles, pamphlets, monographic studies, and various reports of enquiry. The weakness manifests itself in the large number of brief amateur studies and the lack of either research fronts or syntheses for either the country or most of the provinces. The strength is seen in the numbers of scholarly studies and the development of research fronts and syntheses for Ontario and British Columbia.

Todd, in his promotion of public libraries for Ontario, gives some historical background.[33] Bain's statistics and light historical analyses in support of public libraries are always worthy of attention,[34] and Carnochan, a well-known chronicler of the Niagara district, undertook one of the first histories of a Canadian public library, in an attempt to prove it was the first in Ontario.[36] Hardy's doctoral thesis was the first in Canada to deal with librarianship; its opening chapter provides an historical survey of Ontario public libraries.[35] The development of public libraries in British Columbia was promoted and chronicled in the public library surveys,[37, 40] studied in works such as Des Brisay's,[46] and synthesized in overviews by Holmes[26] and Kroll.[49] Nora Bateson, one of the great, unappreciated figures in Canadian library history, chronicled her efforts to develop regional libraries in the Maritimes in the 1930s.[38, 39]

The pioneering role of Canada in the development of regional libraries has never been adequately acknowledged, but Wilson's bibliography was an early effort at doing so.[42] Mary Duncan Carter's 1942 thesis is a scholarly landmark, being the first doctorate devoted solely to Canadian libraries in one city; it includes an historical dimension.[41] Grad's important but much-criticized thesis was a pioneering attempt to provide a synthesis of Ontario's public library history; her research lacked depth due, in part, to there being an insufficient number of other serious studies to provide satisfactory contexts and perspectives.[43] Wark[48] and the Sudbury[50] history are good examples of the interesting, helpful, but slim histories of individual libraries which typify this period. Noble[44] and Riley[45] are painfully brief surveys of developments in Manitoba and Alberta. The statistics from the Dominion Bureau of Statistics are a continuation of numbers 16 and 17.[47]

Public libraries in Quebec's francophone community were notoriously underdeveloped during this period. It is all the more significant, therefore, that Chabot's work was undertaken in the professional process style common in English-speaking Canada at this time.[52] Historical background is presented within the context of urging current and future support for libraries. Marquis surveys various types of libraries in addition to public libraries.[51]

[33]Todd, Alpheus. "On the Establishment of Free Public Libraries in Canada." *Transactions of the Royal Society of Canada* vol. 1, Section 2 (1882): 13-16.

[34]Bain, James. "Public libraries in Canada." *Proceedings of the Canadian Institute.* New series, vol. 1, pts. 4-5 (May 1898): 95-100.

[35]Hardy, Edwin Austen. "The Public Library; its Place in Our Educational System." DPaed thesis, University of Toronto, 1912. 223p. (Published under the same title title: Toronto: Briggs, 1912. iii, 223p.)

[36]Carnochan, Janet. "Niagara Public Library." In her *History of Niagara,* 214-18. Toronto: William Briggs, 1914.

[37]British Columbia. Public Library Commission. *British Columbia Library Survey, 1927-28.* Victoria, B.C.: Banfield, 1929. 103p.

[38]Bateson, Nora. *The Carnegie Library Demonstration in Prince Edward Island, Canada, 1933-1936.* Charlottetown, P.E.I.: Prince Edward Island Libraries, 1936. 52p.

[39]——. *Library Survey of Nova Scotia.* Halifax: Department of Education, 1938. 40p.

[40]British Columbia. Public Library Commission. *Libraries in British Columbia, 1940; a Reconsideration of the Library Survey of 1927-28.* Victoria, B.C.: Public Library Commission, 1941. 31p.

[41]Carter, Mary Duncan. "A Survey of Montreal Library Facilities and a Proposed Plan for a Library System." PhD thesis, Graduate Library School, University of Chicago, 1942. v, 111, 217p.

[42]Wilson, Roberta. *Regional and County Library Service in Canada: a Bibliography.* Ottawa: Canadian Library Association, 1949. [13p.]

[43]Grad, Tamara E. "The Development of Public Libraries in Ontario, 1851-1951." MSLS thesis, School of Library Science, Drexel Institute of Technology, 1952. iv, 67p.

[44]Noble, George C. *Public Library Service in Manitoba: a Report and Recommendations.* Winnipeg: Manitoba Dept. of Education, 1955. 63p.

[45]Riley, Louise. "Fifty Years of Library Service in Alberta." *Canadian Library Association Bulletin:* 12, no. 3 (December 1955): 109-10.

[46]Des Brisay, Geoffrey Rex. "A Historical Survey of the Fraser Valley Regional Library, Abbotsford, British Columbia." MLS thesis, University of Washington, 1956. 110, [20] p.

[47]Canada. Dominion Bureau of Statistics. *Part I. Public Libraries, 1958-1974*. Ottawa: Queen's Printer, 1960-1974. (Title varies)

[48]Wark, Edmund T. *Middlesex County Library Co-operative; the First Twenty-five years, 1934-1959*. London, Ont.: Hunter Printing, 1959. 24p.

[49]Kroll, Morton, ed. *The Public Libraries of the Pacific Northwest Library Association*. Pacific Northwest Library Association, Library Development Report, vol. 1. Seattle: University of Washington Press, 1960. xv, 461p.

[50]Sudbury, Ontario. Public Library. *A Half-Century of Continuous Service; Sudbury Public Library, 1912-1962*. Sudbury: The Library, [1962] [16p.]

[51]Marquis, Georges-Émile. *Nos bibliothèques publiques*. Québec: Imprimerie du Soleil, 1925. 16p. (Les éditions du "Tiroir.")

[52]Chabot, Juliette. "La Ville de Montréal et ses bibliothèques publiques." MLS thesis, School of Library Science, McGill University, 1959. vi, 160p. (Published as *Montréal et le rayonnement des bibliothèques publiques*. Montréal: Fides, 1963. 189p.)

Specialized Libraries

Some of the most important library history in English has been done on this topic, with particular emphasis placed upon precursors of the public library. Despite its being prepared as a government report, May's important study of Ontario's Mechanics' Institutes is sufficiently historical for it to enjoy the distinction of being the first Canadian monographic library history.[53] Wurtele[54] and Carnochan[55] wrote notable histories of two precursors of public libraries. Harvey's two essays may be the most sophisticated library histories in English of this entire period; their titles to the contrary, they deal primarily with the social-cultural context of the proto-public library.[56, 57] The studies of Mechanics' Institutes in Montreal[58] and Nova Scotia[60] remain important starting points for both topics. Pearce's thesis is an outstanding and insufficiently appreciated study of the development of business, industrial and government libraries.[59]

French-language studies reveal their usual concern for scholarship and a lack of concern for professional process, with occasional exceptions. A major preoccupation was with the great nineteenth-century battle between the liberal l'Institut canadien and the parish libraries controlled by the Roman Catholic Church. Roy's brief note on an early Quebec City library may well be the first of his many articles on library history to appear in *Bulletin des recherches historiques*.[61] Robillard[62] and Bruchési[63] deal with Instituts canadiens in Montreal and Quebec City. Jean[64] and Maurault[65] deal with parish libraries in Quebec City and Montreal. The works by Jean[64] and Drolet[66] are particularly intriguing; written before the start of Quebec's quiet revolution, they are very critical of parish libraries and by implication the Church. Their emphasis upon professional process is a precursor of future trends.

[53]May, S.P. *Report on the Mechanics' Institutes.* Ontario Sessional Papers no. 46, 1881. 208p.

[54]Wurtele, Frederick C. "Our Library." *Literary and Historical Society of Quebec Transactions* New series, no. 19 (1889): 29-73.

[55]Carnochan, Janet. "Niagara Library, 1800 to 1820." *Niagara Historical Society Notes* no. 6 (1900): 4-30.

[56]Harvey, D.C. "The Intellectual Awakening of Nova Scotia." *Dalhousie Review* 13, no. 1 (April 1933): 1-22.

[57]——. "Early Public Libraries in Nova Scotia." *Dalhousie Review* 14, no. 4 (January 1935): 429-43.

[58]Montreal Mechanics' Institute. *The Mechanics' Institute of Montreal, 1840-1940.* Montreal, 1940. 54p.

[59]Pearce, C.A. "The Development of Special Libraries in Montreal and Toronto." MSLS thesis, University of Illinois, 1947. ix, 216p.

[60]Fergusson, C. Bruce. *Mechanics' Institutes in Nova Scotia.* Bulletin of the Public Archives of Nova Scotia, no. 14. Halifax: Public Archives, 1960. 47p.

[61]Roy, Pierre-Georges. "Bibliothèque circulante." *Bulletin des recherches historiques* 6, no. 5 (mai 1900): 142.

[62]Robillard, Charles. "La bibliothèque de l'Institut canadien." *Bulletin des recherches historiques* 41, no. 2 (février 1935): 114-22.

[63]Bruchési, Jean. "L'Institut canadien de Québec." *Cahiers des dix* 12 (1947): 93-114.

[64]Jean, Luce. "Les bibliothèques paroissiale de la ville de Québec." Thèse de MA (service social), Université Laval, 1949. x, 106, [3]p.

[65]Maurault, Olivier. "Saint-Sulpice et Montréal." In *Canadian Historical Association, Annual Report,* 55-62. 1956.

[66]Drolet, Antonio. "La revalorisation des bibliothèques paroissiales par les bibliothèques régionales." In *ACBF,* 57-61. Congrès. 1959. Rapport.

Academic Libraries

Discussion of academic libraries in English reveals a refreshingly higher level of scholarship than that found in many other categories. Although the audience remains primarily librarians and the aim of most of the publications is invariably professional process, one can see the emergence of a research front. Van Patten provides a brief introduction to Ontario's college and university libraries.[67] Barber,[68] Lomer[70] and Foreman[72] discuss library developments at Victoria College (Toronto), McGill University, and the University of Toronto. The theses by Hamilton[69] and Redmond[71] are invaluable in understanding the origins and development of libraries in institutions of higher learning in the West and the Maritimes. The statistics from the Dominion Bureau of Statistics are a continuation of numbers 16 and 17.[73]

In French, little was published on post-secondary libraries during this period. Tanghe provides a disappointingly brief introduction to the library at the Université de Montréal.[74] Drolet's article is one of a series he wrote on the library at Laval and its predecessors, including the Jesuit College.[75]

[67]Van Patten, N. "College and University Libraries of Ontario." *Library Journal* 52, no. 9 (May 1, 1927): 457-61.

[68]Barber, F. Louis. "The Treasure Room; Victoria University Library." *Canadian Bookman* 20, no. 1 (April-May 1938): 13-14.

[69]Hamilton, Dorothy. "The Libraries of the Universities of Alberta, British Columbia, Manitoba, and Saskatchewan. A Report." MA thesis, Department of Library Science, University of Michigan, 1942. 2, 2, 137, 2p.

[70]Lomer, G.R. "The Redpath Library; Half a Century, 1892-1942." *McGill News* 24, no. 1 (Autumn 1942): 9-13.

[71]Redmond, D.A. "Some College Libraries of Canada's Maritime Provinces: Selected Aspects." MSLS thesis, University of Illinois, 1950. v, 267, [20]p. (An abridged version was published as "Five Canadian College Libraries." *College and Research Libraries* 11, no. 4 (October 1950): 355-62.)

[72]Foreman, P.L. "University of Toronto Libraries." *Ontario Library Review* 35, no. 1 (February 1951): 9-13.

[73]Canada. Dominion Bureau of Statistics. *Part II. Academic Libraries, 1958-1971.* Ottawa: Queen's Printer, 1960-1972. (Title varies)

[74]Tanghe, R. "La bibliothèque de l'Université." In *Gala universitaire*, 19-25. Montréal: Université de Montréal, 1944.

[75]Drolet, Antonio. "La bibliothèque du Collège des Jésuites." *Revue d'histoire de l'Amérique française* 14, no. 4 (mars 1961): 487-544.

Personal Libraries

From the beginning, this topic has been largely overlooked by Canadian English-language historians. Perhaps the anglophone preoccupation with professional process and using history as a means of promoting libraries left no time or energy to deal with such a scholarly topic. The lack of knowledge of and interest in francophone scholarship on this topic is striking. Winsby's brief article is one of the few publications in English.[76]

Francophone preoccupation with this topic underlines a fundamentally academic approach to library history which has little regard for professional process. The close attention paid to personal libraries by the Roys, father and son, and by the *Bulletin des recherches historiques* is significant. The elder Roy's interest was an outgrowth, it would seem, of his studying the notarial records of the French régime.[79] Indeed, most of the articles in the *Bulletin des recherches historiques* are frequently little more than brief listings of the books found in the notarial records of various individuals' possessions at the time of death.

The focus on New France typifies francophone history at this time. The study of private libraries has been a major engine propelling French-language library history, even if most of the articles have been very brief and antiquarian in approach, with little or no commentary or interpretation. In any case, an important research front developed which has received synthesis on several occasions, most notably in this period by Fauteux[28] and Antoine Roy.[29] It should be mentioned that the study of personal libraries has been seen by some commentators as a way of proving that books and culture existed in New France and in French-Canadian society despite a paucity of libraries. The selection of articles presented here illustrates the fact that individuals and journals other than the Roys and *Bulletin des recherches historiques* dealt with this topic.[77, 78, 80, 81] Antoine Roy's article provides a comparative analysis of four nineteenth-century private libraries.[82]

[76]Winsby, Elizabeth. "The Treasure Room; Robie Reid, Book Collector." *Canadian Bookman* 21, no. 2 (June-July 1939): 19-21.

[77]Roy, Regis. "Claude-Thomas Dupuy." *Bulletin des recherches historiques* 16, no. 3 (mars 1910): 89-90.

[78]Massicotte, E.-Z. "Le juge Pierre Raimbault et sa famille." *Bulletin des recherches historiques* 21, no. 3 (mars 1915): 78-81.

[79]Roy, Pierre-Georges. "Jean Deshayes, hydrographe du roi." *Bulletin des recherches historiques* 22, no. 5 (mai 1916): 129-38.

[80]Maheux, Arthur. "La bibliothèque du missionaire Darion au dix-huitième siècle." *Le Canada français* 27, no. 7 (mars 1940): 650-61.

[81]Lefebvre, Fernand. "La bibliothèque des Frères Charon." *Bulletin des recherches historiques* 64, no. 3 (juillet-septembre 1958): 67-77.

[82]Roy, Antoine. "Sur quelques ventes aux enchères de bibliothèques privées." *Cahiers des dix* 26 (1961): 219-33.

Associations

Canadian library associations are a twentieth-century phenomenon, the first being founded in 1900. Given the body of literature appearing on them in this period, it is surprising that greater efforts towards synthesis did not occur. Three publications chronicle the development of the Ontario Library Association from 1900 to 1951.[83, 84, 85] The history of the Canadian Library Association from its founding in 1946 to 1960 is covered in two theme issues of the association's *Bulletin*.[88, 89] It is regrettable that these milestone chronicles were discontinued. The one overview of early library associations is lamentably brief.[87] The publications on the Saskatchewan Library Association[86] and the Institute of Professional Librarians[90] are helpful.

Martin's article on the Association canadienne des bibliothécaires de la langue française (the predecessor of the Association pour l'avancement des sciences et des techniques de la documentation) is one of only two articles in French.[91]

[83]*The Ontario Library Association: an Historical Sketch, 1900-1925.* Toronto: University of Toronto Press, 1926. 189p.

[84]Hardy, E.A. "The Ontario Library Association: Forty Years, 1900-1940." *Ontario Library Review* 25, no. 1 (February 1941): 9-13.

[85]"Second Quarter Century, 1926-1951." *Ontario Library Review* 36, no. 2, pt. 2 (May 1952). Issue.

[86]Wood, J.S. "The Saskatchewan Library Association, a Brief History." *Saskatchewan Library Association Bulletin* 8, no. 2 (May 1955): 2-13.

[87]"Library Associations in Canada, 1900-1946." *Canadian Library Association Bulletin* 11, no. 6 (June 1955): 270-72.

[88]"Tenth anniversary conference number." *Canadian Library Association Bulletin* 11, no. 6 (June 1955). Issue.

[89]"1955-1960. These Years of C.L.A.-A.C.B." *Canadian Library* 17, no. 6 (May 1961). Issue.

[90]Kent, Charles Deane. *A Short History of the Institute of Professional Librarians.* London, Ont.: London Public Library and Art Museum, 1962. iii, 57p.

[91]Martin, Paul-Aimé. "Les origines de l'ACBF." *ACBF Bulletin* 1, no. 2 (juin 1955): 4-6.

National, Provincial and Legislative Libraries

Serious study of these libraries has occurred throughout the century. It should be noted that shortly after the conclusion of this paper's period of study a major synthesis appeared. In English a number of important articles have been published dealing with Ontario,[92] Nova Scotia,[93] the Library of Parliament,[94] and the National Library of Canada.[95]

In French, Dionne's[96] article and Marquis's[97] book are still relevant.

[92]Wilgress, A.T. "Legislative Library of Ontario." *Ontario Library Review* 18, no. 1 (February 1934): 5-8.

[93]Harvey, D.C. "The Contribution of the Nova Scotia Historical Society to the Legislative Library." In *Nova Scotia Historical Society Collections,* 26: 115-30. Halifax: The Society, 1945.

[94]Hardy, F.A. "The Library of Parliament." *Dalhousie Review* 37, no. 2 (Summer 1957): 175-80.

[95]Lamb, William Kaye. "The National Library of Canada." *Canadian Geographical Journal* 64, no. 4 (April 1962): 124-25.

[96]Dionne, N.E. "Historiques de la Bibliothèque du Parlement à Québec, 1792-1892." *Royal Society of Canada, Proceedings and Transactions* Ser. 2, sect. 1, vol. 8 (1902-03): 3-14.

[97]Marquis, Georges-Émile. *La Bibliothèque de la Législature: son passé, son présent, son avenir.* Québec: L'Auteur, La Bibliothèque, 1946. 31p.

Biography

Canadian librarianship has never shown much interest in its pioneers and leaders. Aside from entries in biographical dictionaries and the occasional obituary, there is little to show for this period. In English, these are two examples of collective biography, by Wolfenden[98] and Benjamin[101]; the obituaries are on Nora Bateson[99] and Alexander Calhoun.[100]

No biographies were observed in French.

[98]Wolfenden, Madge. "Outstanding Personalities in the Library History of British Columbia." *Canadian Library Association Bulletin* 3, no. 5 (June 1947): 131-33.
[99]Chandler, H. Bramwell. "Miss Nora Bateson." *Maritime Library Association Bulletin* 20, no. 2 (Winter 1955-56): 20.
[100]Thomson, Georgina. "Alexander Calhoun." *Canadian Library Journal* 12, no. 3 (December 1955): 117-18.
[101]Benjamin, Martha. "The McGill Medical Librarians, 1829-1929." *Bulletin of the Medical Library Association* 50, no. 1 (January 1962): 1-16.

Adult Education

The role of libraries in the development of this important field has been crucial, as the British Columbia[102] and Kidd[103] studies make clear. Although the sections on libraries are brief, descriptive and current, they do give some sense of historical process.

No studies in French were noted.

[102]*A Preliminary Study of Adult Education in British Columbia, 1941: a Contribution to the Problem.* Victoria, B.C.: Public Library Commission, 1944. 77p. (See pages 31-34.)
[103]Kidd, J.R. *Adult Education in Canada.* Toronto: Canadian Association for Adult Education, 1950. xii, 249p. (See pages 88-99.)

Library Education

Canada's important tradition of library education was largely ignored during this period. In English, the theme issue of *Canadian Library* is an important, if dated, starting point.[104] These are the only published statistics from the Dominion Bureau of Statistics on library education ever to appear.[105]

Tanghe's history is the only monograph on this topic in either French or English and deals with the period up to the time the Université de Montréal upgraded its school from an affiliated to an integral department and hired its first full-time director and faculty.[106]

[104]"Library Education." *Canadian Library* 14, no. 5 (April 1958). Issue.
[105]Canada. Dominion Bureau of Statistics. *Survey of Libraries, Part III. Library Education, 1960-65.* Ottawa: Queen's Printer, 1961-1965.
[106]Tanghe, Raymond. *L'École de bibliothécaires de l'Université de Montréal, 1937-1962.* Montréal: Fides, 1962. 69p.

School and Children's Libraries

The only relevant study uncovered for this period was a brief section on Upper Canada in an 1866 British Royal Commission report on education.[107] The statistics from the Dominion Bureau of Statistics are somewhat fugitive.[108] No publications in French were noted.

[107]*Report of the Commissioners Appointed by Her Majesty to Inquire into the Education Given in Schools in England, not Comprised within her Majesty's Two Recent Commissions, and to the Commissioners Appointed by Her Majesty to Inquire into the Schools of Scotland, on the Common School System of the United States and of the Provinces of Upper and Lower Canada,* by the Rev. James Fraser. London: Eyre and Spottiswoode, 1866. v, 435p. (See pages 273-77.)
[108]Canada. Dominion Bureau of Statistics. *High School Libraries in Canada.* Ottawa: King's Printer, 1931. 2p.

Library Co-operation

No historical studies in English or French were found on the topic during this period.

Conclusion

In bringing this selective survey to its conclusion, I must mention six additional publications, even though they stray somewhat beyond the paper's terms of reference. Five are survey reports, three of which were published after the 1964 cut-off date. That all six titles are important and constitute an integral part of the historically significant literature of this period is beyond question. Although the Massey report provides limited historical background, its section on libraries laid the intellectual foundation for many developments of the 1950s, 1960s and beyond.[109] The reports of Williams,[110] Simon,[111] Bonn[112] and Downs[113] also provide limited historical background but do offer a snapshot of library conditions in the 1960s. They are particularly important for revealing the impetus and blueprints by which our libraries reinvented themselves to support the newly emerging research activities of Canadian universities, government agencies, and other types of institutions.

As for Drolet, his study is the first and only monographic synthesis of both English- and French-language Canadian library history and, as such, was highly dependant upon pre-1964 publications.[114]

[109]Canada. Royal Commission on National Development in the Arts, Letters, and Science. *Report ... 1941-1951*. Ottawa: King's Printer, 1951. xxi, 517p. (See chapter IX.)

[110]Williams, E.E. *Resources of Canadian University Libraries for Research in the Humanities and Social Sciences: Report of a Survey for the National Conference of Canadian Universities and Colleges*. Ottawa: The Conference, 1962. 87p.

[111]Simon, Beatrice V. *Library Support of Medical Education and Research in Canada: Report of a Survey of the Medical College Libraries in Canada, Together with Suggestions for Improving and Extending Medical Library Service at Local, Regional, and National Levels*. Ottawa: Association of Canadian Medical Colleges, 1964. xvii, 132p.

[112]Bonn, G.S. *Science-Technology Literature Resources in Canada: Report of a Survey for the Associate Committee on Scientific Information*. Ottawa: Associate Committee on Scientific Information, National Research Council, 1966. iv, 80p.

[113]Downs, Robert B. *Resources of Canadian Academic and Research Libraries*. Ottawa: Association of Universities and Colleges of Canada, 1967. xi, 301p.

[114]Drolet, Antonio. *Les bibliothèques canadiennes, 1604-1960*. Montréal: Cercle du livre de France, 1965. 234p.

Canadian Library History
in English and French, 1985-1991:
A Survey and Evaluation

Peter F. McNally

Abstract

The quantitative and qualitative growth of Canadian library history between 1985 and 1991 reflects the growing maturity of this area of study. One of the surest signs of this maturity is the unprecedented number of master's and doctoral theses that appeared. Another is the growing number of monographic studies and scholarly articles in academic journals. Research fronts are emerging in a number of areas, but few syntheses have appeared. Francophone publications continue to be strongly influenced by *histoire du livre*, and anglophone publications show a growing concern for social context. Otherwise, the two language groups show an unexpected degree of convergence: public libraries are the most studied topic for both, and francophones are increasingly apt to emulate anglophone research models by concentrating upon professional process. Noted also are the sharp decline in francophone publications on personal libraries and the number of topics, in both languages, in need of synthesis.

Résumé

Le développement quantitatif et qualitatif de l'histoire des bibliothèques canadiennes entre 1985 et 1991 reflète la maturation croissante de ce domaine d'études. Un des signes les plus évidents de cette maturité c'est le nombre sans précédent de thèses de maîtrise et de doctorat qui en traitent. Le nombre de monographies et d'articles dans les revues académiques augmente lui aussi. De nouvelles pistes de recherche apparaissent dans certains domaines, mais il existe encore peu de synthèses. Les publications francophones demeurent influencées par « l'histoire du livre » et les publications anglophones s'intéressent de plus en plus au contexte social. Par contre, les deux groupes linguistiques semblent converger de façon inattendue. Tous les deux étudient principalement les bibliothèques publiques et les francophones sont de plus en plus en mesure d'exploiter les modèles de recherche anglophones en étudiant la démarche professionnelle. Notons que les francophones s'intéressent de moins en moins aux bibliothèques personnelles et qu'un grand nombre de sujets auraient besoin de synthèses et cela dans les deux langues.

The years 1985 to 1991 saw a maturation and strengthening of Canadian library history in both quantity and quality. Although a number of names from the pre-1984 period — such as Donnelly, Galarneau, Lajeunesse, Lamonde, McNally and Wiseman — continued to appear, a host of new names also emerged. Many of these names may never be heard from again, but the fact that a core of Canadian library historians with a continuing interest in the field has emerged is beyond question.

Amateur histories continue to be a significant — and frequently valuable — characteristic of the field. What is even more significant, however, has been the growth of scholarly histories. Whether these histories are undertaken by academics, librarians or others, an appreciation for the scholarly apparatus of primary research, background reading, footnoting, factual accuracy, and relevant interpretive and contextual frameworks is becoming widely accepted. Monographic publications are much more prevalent than they were 20 years ago. Articles are appearing in a wide range of library and historical journals as well as in important collections of essays. Bibliographical and historiographical studies are becoming more prominent; a major retrospective study is awaiting completion. The overwhelming majority of all the studies were undertaken or published in Canada.

It is difficult to comment upon ideological or interpretive schools within Canadian library history for few, if any, exist. That said, a number of large-scale or macro-historiographical trends bear inspection. Few works of synthesis appeared during this period. There are, however, a number of topics where syntheses are being attempted, or should be attempted, given the large number of secondary studies that have appeared in recent years. Research fronts are becoming more plentiful and concentrated than previously. Public, academic and legislative libraries are showing particular vitality.

Master's and doctoral theses constitute one of the surest ways of maintaining research fronts. The number of master's theses and research projects was, however, too large for more than a few to be listed in this study. As for doctoral theses, eight were completed, two of which, by Gallichan and Bernhard,[56, 76] were in history and education for French-language institutions; two, by Dolan and Wiseman,[19, 36] were in librarianship for foreign universities; two, by MacDonald and Cummings,[22, 62] were in librarianship for the University of Western Ontario; and the remaining two, by Howarth and Mudge,[70, 73] were in librarianship for the University of Toronto. These last two along with Bernhard are included because of their coverage of recent chronological periods, even though they lack the normal interpretive and contextual frameworks usually employed by historians.

A similar non-historical approach to the study of recent historical phenomena is observable in the very important work of Mittermeyer and Auster.[30, 51] The study of Canadian library history by non-historians using non-historical techniques is potentially enriching, if the alternative techniques are appropriate and if the conclusions can eventually be synthesized into historical contexts.

The major categories within Canadian library history continue to be language and type of library activity. Identifiable publications for the years 1985 to 1991 can be organized as follows:

TABLE 1

An Analysis of Publication on Canadian Library History, 1985-1991

	English-Language	French-Language	Total
Public Libraries	34	13	47
General Topics	29	7	36
Biography	25	-	25
Specialized Libraries	25	10	35
Academic Libraries	21	12	33
Library Co-operation	9	2	11
Library Education	9	4	13
Associations	7	6	13
National, Provincial and Legislative Libraries	6	10	16
School and Children's Libraries	4	4	8
Personal Libraries/Collections	3	8	11
Adult Education	1	2	3
	173	82	255

Several general observations can be made from this list. English-language publications continued to predominate. But given that the ratio of English-to French-language publications is 2.11 to 1, which is much narrower than the 4 to 1 ratio generally found between English and French publications, the vitality of French-language library history can be assumed. As might be

---

TABLE 2

English-Language Publications, 1985-1991

Public Libraries	34
General Topics	29
Biography	25
Specialized Libraries	25
Academic Libraries	21
Library Co-operation	9
Library Education	9
Associations	7
National, Provincial and Legislative Libraries	6
School and Children's Libraries	4
Personal Libraries/Collections	3
Adult Education	1
	173

TABLE 3

French-Language Publications, 1985-1991

Public Libraries	13
Academic Libraries	12
National, Provincial and Legislative Libraries	10
Specialized Libraries	10
Personal Libraries/Collections	8
General Topics	7
Associations	6
Biography	-
Library Education	4
School and Children's Libraries	4
Adult Education	2
Library Co-operation	2
	82

---

expected, minor shifts in ranking can be observed from previous periods. What is surprising, however, has been the decline among francophone studies of personal libraries from first place to fifth, and the forward movement of public and academic libraries to first and second place from the eighth and fifth places they held prior to 1985. These shifts may reflect a number of things, such as the growing strength of public and academic libraries in Quebec and the growing number of francophone librarians and library educators, as opposed to professional historians, who are now doing library history.

Canada's two language communities continued to display characteristic differences as well as some newly emerging similarities in their library history. French-language publications continue to come largely from Quebec and to be greatly influenced by France's *histoire du livre* tradition, in which libraries are seen as one element among many in the study of print culture and its social, cultural and intellectual contexts. English-language publications, by contrast, are still greatly concerned with internal institutional and administrative concerns, although a growing concern for social contexts is beginning to emerge. Up to 1991, however, there was little concern with the study of print culture among anglophones. Interestingly enough, a movement towards institutional and internal administrative concerns is beginning to emerge in some of the francophone studies. Perhaps convergence will occur in the future.

Inexorably, both anglophone and francophone library history are becoming integrated with social history: the study of minorities, of the everyday life of men and women, and of anonymous social forces, accompanied frequently by quantitative analysis. Library history is obviously amenable to feminist, family, native, ethnic, economic, labour, intellectual, political and rural interpretations — to mention a number.

The challenge facing Canadian library history is, therefore, to continue the efforts to end its ghettoization and isolation from the mainstream of Canadian history and to integrate the role of libraries within larger social, cultural and intellectual contexts. That a problem remains is exemplified by some recent publications: Caron,[2] which is the single best guide to Canadian history, and Gerson and Tippett,[4, 5] which are significant new studies on English-Canadian reading and cultural development, make only cursory references to libraries; Van der Bellen's[1, 3] two checklists, despite their titles, omit any reference to libraries. That said, it must also be conceded that academics from fields other than librarianship undertook library history during this period: Bernhard,[76] Kerr,[27] Harvey[37] and Lamonde,[44] amongst others.

[1]Van der Bellen, Liana. "A Checklist of Books and Articles in the Field of the History of Books and Libraries, 1." *Papers of the Bibliographical Society of Canada* 23 (1984): 84-99.

[2]Caron, Gilbert, ed. *Guide du chercheur en histoire canadienne.* Québec: Presses de l'Université Laval, 1986. xxxii, 808p.

[3]Van der Bellen, Liana. "A Checklist of Books and Articles in the Field of the History of Books and Libraries, 2." *Papers of the Bibliographical Society of Canada* 25 (1986): 139-52.
[4]Gerson, Carole. *A Purer Taste: the Writing and Reading of Fiction in English in Nineteenth-century Canada.* Toronto: University of Toronto Press, 1989. xiv, 210p.
[5]Tippett, Maria. *Making Culture, English-Canadian Institutions and the Arts before the Massey Commission.* Toronto: University of Toronto Press, 1990. xiv, 253p.

The following list is meant to be selective, including a mixture of important and representative titles which can serve as guide-posts to the literature. Additional studies can be discovered through standard library and historical bibliographies and indexes. A few titles published in 1984, but omitted inadvertently by the author from previous listings, have also been included.

Bibliography and Historiography

Enormous strides were made in the bibliographical control of Canadian library history during the seven years between 1985 and 1991. As part of a larger historiographical study which is nearing completion, McNally's[6, 7, 8] three articles provide a selective evaluation of the literature, placing it within various contexts. Palmer[9] refers to history, among other topics. Lamonde and Brunet[10, 11] are comprehensive bibliographies of Quebec intellectual history and *histoire du livre*, or the study of print culture, in which libraries constitute one of the elements; contextual and historiographical trends are provided implicitly rather than explicitly.

[6]McNally, Peter F. "Canadian Library History in English, 1964-1984: a Survey and Evaluation." In *Readings in Canadian Library History*, edited by Peter F. McNally, 19-30. Ottawa: Canadian Library Association, 1986.
[7]—. "Canadian Library History in French, 1964-1984: a Survey and Evaluation." In *Readings in Canadian Library History*, edited by Peter F. McNally, 31-39. Ottawa: Canadian Library Association, 1986.
[8]—. "The Historiography of Canadian Library History: or Mapping the Mind of the Canadian Past." *Journal of Library History* 21, no. 2 (Spring 1986): 445-55.
[9]Palmer, Joseph. "Where to Find Information on Canadian Librarianship." *Canadian Library Journal* 44, no. 3 (June 1987): 173-75, 177-79.
[10]Lamonde, Yvan. *L'histoire des idées au Québec, 1760-1960; bibliographie des études.* Montréal: Bibliothèque nationale du Québec, 1989. 167p.
[11]Brunet, Manon. *Bibliographie des études québécoises sur l'imprimé, 1970-1987.* Compilé par le Comité de l'Association québécoise pour l'étude de l'imprimé (AQEI). Montréal: Bibliothèque nationale du Québec, 1991. 134p.

Collections

The importance of collections of essays can never be underestimated, for they are frequently benchmarks of historiographical trends. In the French-language volumes, library history is only one of a number of themes: those edited by Bonenfant and Sirois[12, 15] deal with Quebec's Eastern Townships; Galarneau's[16] volume includes a number of fascinating articles on various aspects of *histoire du livre* in early nineteenth-century Quebec; and Rolland-Thomas[17] presents essays on topics associated with the late Professor Denis. McNally's[13] collection was the second issued by the Library History Interest Group of the Canadian Library Association and is the only one in this section to deal exclusively with library history (the first appeared in the December 1981 issue of *Canadian Library Journal*). Fraser[14] covers a wide range of issues within law librarianship, including its history.

[12]Bonenfant, Joseph, ed. *A l'ombre de DesRochers: le mouvement littéraire des Cantons de l'Est; 1925-1950; l'effervescence culturelle d'une région.* Sherbrooke, Que.: La Tribune, 1985. viii, 381p.

[13]McNally, Peter F., ed. *Readings in Canadian Library History.* Ottawa: Canadian Library Association, 1986. vi, 258p.

[14]Fraser, Joan M., ed. *Law Libraries in Canada, Essays in Honour of Diana M. Priestly.* Toronto: Carswell, 1988. x, 237p.

[15]Sirois, Antoine. *L'essor culturel de Sherbrooke et de la région depuis 1950.* Sherbrooke: Département d'études françaises, Université de Sherbrooke, 1986. x, 292p. (Cahiers d'études littéraires et culturelles, 10)

[16]Galarneau, Claude, ed. *Le livre et lecture au Québec (1800-1850).* Québec: Institut québécois de recherche sur la culture, 1988. 269p.

[17]Rolland-Thomas, Paule, ed. *Perspectives en bibliothéconomie et en science de l'information: mélanges dédiés à la mémoire de Laurent-G. Denis.* Montréal: ASTED, 1990. 150p.

General

Although no large-scale syntheses of Canadian library history appeared during our period of discussion, a number of works that advanced greatly the cause of synthesis were published. Woodland and Swanick[20, 23] in their collections of essays have provided essential starting points for any history of libraries in British Columbia and New Brunswick. Dolan and MacDonald[19, 22] in their dissertations have laid the groundwork for any future studies of the role of government and scientific information and collections in Canadian libraries. Rainville and Gallichan[18, 21] consider the role of clerical censorship and historical sensibility in the development of Quebec libraries — themes which deserve much greater attention.

[18]Rainville, Danielle-M. "Le monde de l'imprimé et l'église au Québec (1880-1960): considérations sur la censure." *Argus* 14, no. 3 (septembre 1985): 95-100.

[19]Dolan, Elizabeth Macdonald. "A Study of the Free Distribution of Canadian Federal Government Publications to Depository Libraries in Canada." Doctoral thesis (Library Service), Columbia University, 1986. 173p. (Published as: *The Depository Dilemma; a Study of the Free Distribution of Canadian Federal Government Publications to Depository Libraries in Canada.* Ottawa: Canadian Library Association, 1989. 121p.)

[20]Woodland, Alan and Ellen Heaney, eds. *British Columbia Libraries: Historical Profiles; a Project for the Celebration of the 75th Anniversary of the British Columbia Library Association.* Vancouver: British Columbia Library Association, 1986. iv, 178p.

[21]Gallichan, Gilles. "Les bibliothécaires et leur conscience historique." *Documentation et bibliothèques* 34, no. 3 (juillet-septembre 1988): 99-101.

[22]MacDonald, Bertrum H. "'Public Knowledge': the Dissemination of Scientific Literature in Victorian Canada as Illustrated from the Geological and Agricultural Sciences." Doctoral thesis (Library and Information Science), University of Western Ontario, 1990. x, 370p.

[23]Swanick, Eric L., ed. *Hardiness, Perseverance and Faith: New Brunswick Library History.* Occasional Paper, no. 52. Halifax: Dalhousie University, School of Library and Information Studies, 1991. xvi, 174p.

Public

Many publications appeared in recent years which are of enormous importance in understanding the development of Canada's public libraries. From Ontario, with the largest concentration, has come Wiseman's[36] synthesis of the forty years accompanying the first public library legislation. Bruce's[31] study is part of his ambitious project to synthesize the entire Ontario public library movement. Greenfield[34] recounts the story of one of Ontario's finest systems, and Marshall[24] shows the dynamism of the Toronto Public Library in the 1960s and 1970s. Gagnon and Lajeunesse[25, 35] outline the sad tale of Quebec's public libraries, which are the country's most undeveloped. The one exception have been those in the English-speaking sections of Montreal, which are being studied by Hanson[32] — this article being a first step. She may be able to provide the comparative evidence required for understanding better the very slow advancement of Quebec's public library movement. Studies of a number of specific libraries elsewhere in the province, of which Panneton[33] is an example, will assist in this process. Otherwise, the Prairies have shown the most concern for the history of their public libraries: Carnie,[26] Kerr,[27] Inskip[28] and Macdonald[29] have discussed various aspects of municipal and regional developments. In addition, Carnie provides an important case study of the sorts of documentary evidence required to carry out the history of a public library. Finally, Mittermeyer[30] has done a comparative analysis by province of public library statistics that will provide much helpful data for any future syntheses; Quebec's position in last place cannot be ignored.

[24]Marshall, John. *Citizen Participation in Library Decision-making: the Toronto Experience*. Metuchen, N.J.: Scarecrow, 1984. xxvii, 342p.

[25]Gagnon, Gilbert. "La politique d'aide au développement des bibliothèques publiques du Québec (1960-1985)." *Documentation et bibliothèques* 31, no. 1 (janvier-mars 1985): 9-25.

[26]Carnie, Betty. "Board Meetings as a Source of Library History, with Particular Reference to Saskatoon Public Library." In *Readings in Canadian Library History*, edited by Peter F. McNally, 43-52. Ottawa: Canadian Library Association, 1986.

[27]Kerr, Don. "The Battle of the Books: Saskatoon Public Library and the Rationalist Press Association — 1913." In *Readings in Canadian Library History*, edited by Peter F. McNally, 111-21. Ottawa: Canadian Library Association, 1986.

[28]Inskip, Robin. *The Marigold System: a Case Study of Community Planning Networks and Community Development*. Occasional Paper, no. 41. Halifax: Dalhousie University, School of Library and Information Studies, 1987. 117p.

[29]Macdonald, R.H. *Don't Cry Baby — We'll Be Back: the History of the Wheatland Regional Library, 1967-1987*. Saskatoon: Wheatland Regional Library, 1987. xvi, 172p.

[30]Mittermeyer, Diane. *Les bibliothèques publiques canadiennes de 1979 à 1983: analyse comparative de certaines données statistiques*. Montréal: L'Association des directeurs de bibliothèques publiques du Québec, 1987. vi, 78p.

[31]Bruce, Lorne, and Karen Bruce. *Public Library Boards in Postwar Ontario, 1945-1985*. Occasional Paper, no. 42. Halifax: Dalhousie University, School of Library and Information Studies, 1988. 149p.

[32]Hanson, Elizabeth. "Architecture and Public Librarianship in the Early Twentieth Century: the Westmount Public Library, 1899-1939." *Libraries and Culture* 23, no. 2 (Spring 1988): 172-203.

[33]Panneton, Jacques. "La bibliothèque municipale de Montréal: survol historique et perspectives d'avenir." *Documentation et bibliothèques* 34, no. 1 (janvier-mars 1988): 19-24.

[34]Greenfield, J. Katharine. *The Hamilton Public Library, 1889-1963; a Celebration of Vision and Leadership*. Hamilton: Hamilton Public Library, 1989. 139, 16p.

[35]Lajeunesse, Marcel. "L'Évolution des bibliothèques publiques du Québec vue par les études et les rapports." In *Perspectives en bibliothéconomie et en science de l'information: mélanges dédiés à la mémoire de Laurent-G. Denis*, edited by Paule Rolland-Thomas, 113-32. Montréal: ASTED, 1990.

[36]Wiseman, John. "Temples of Democracy: a History of Public Library Development in Ontario, 1880-1920." Doctoral thesis (Library and Information Studies), Loughborough University, 1989. xiv, 323p. (A summary was published as: "Temples of Democracy." *Canadian Library Journal* 47, no. 1 (February 1990): 37-39.)

Specialized

The study of specialized libraries — including precursors of public and other types of libraries — has been pursued vigorously in both English and French. In Quebec, the prolonged and agonizing fights, during the nineteenth century, over l'Institut canadien have attracted the particular interest of historians, as can be seen by the articles of Lamonde and Harvey.[37, 40, 44] There is a growing suspicion that the failure of a francophone public library movement to develop in Quebec in the nineteenth century may be due to this infamous case, which affected the political life of the province and the country for several decades. Lassonde[41] discusses the parish library of Montreal during its early years at its present site; the Sulpician Library is important because of its triumph over l'Institut canadien decades earlier and later transformation into the Bibliothèque nationale du Québec in the 1960s.

In English-speaking Canada, Mechanics' Institutes continued to attract much attention. Blanchard[38] has compiled a much-needed preliminary bibliography, and Hewitt[42] has discussed their role in the Maritimes during the nineteenth century. Curtis[39] discusses an Ontario alternative to the Mechanics' Institutes, the township libraries. The "Canadian Number" and Murphy[43, 45] look at the development of music and law libraries in particular environments. Little work was done on business libraries in Canada during this period. Mechanics' Institutes and l'Institut canadien are probably ready for works of synthesis.

[37]Harvey, Louis-George and Mark V. Olsen. "A Quantitative Study of Book Circulation: the Library of the Institut canadien de Montréal." *Historical Methods* 18, no. 3 (Summer 1985): 97-103.

[38]Blanchard, Jim. "A Bibliography on Mechanics' Institutes, with Particular Reference to Ontario." In *Readings in Canadian Library History*, edited by Peter F. McNally, 3-18. Ottawa: Canadian Library Association, 1986.

[39]Curtis, Bruce. "'Littery merrit', 'Useful knowledge', and the Organization of Township Libraries in Canada West, 1840-1860." *Ontario History* 78, no. 4 (December 1986): 285-311.

[40]Harvey, Louis-George and Mark V. Olsen. "La circulation de la bibliothèque de l'Institut canadien de Montréal, 1865-1875." *Social History* 19, no. 57 (mai 1986): 139-60.

[41]Lassonde, Jean-René. *La Bibliothèque Saint-Sulpice, 1910-1931.* Montréal: Bibliothèque nationale du Québec, 1986. 359p.

[42]Hewitt, Martin. "The Mechanics' Institute Movement in the Maritimes, 1831-1889." Master's thesis (History), University of New Brunswick, 1986. 312p.

[43]"Canadian Number." *Fontes Artis Musicae* 34, no. 4 (October-December 1987). Issue.

[44]Lamonde, Yvan. "La bibliothèque de l'Institut canadien de Montréal (1852-1876): pour une analyse multidimensionnelle." *Revue d'histoire de l'Amérique française* 41, no. 3 (hiver 1988): 335-61.

[45]Murphy, Cynthia Jordan. "Law Firm Libraries." In *Law Libraries in Canada, Essays in Honour of Diana M. Priestly*, edited by Joan M. Fraser, 33-38. Toronto: Carswell, 1988.

Academic Libraries

The years between 1985 and 1992 saw a marked improvement in the historical understanding of Canada's college and university libraries. Significantly more histories of Canadian institutions of higher learning are including sections on their libraries than did so previously. The monographic studies of the libraries at the University of Western Ontario and the University of Toronto[49, 50] are firsts for any Canadian academic libraries. Blackburn's analysis of how Toronto developed the largest academic library in Canada — and one of the largest in the world — is outstanding; it is the finest study ever to appear on the history of a Canadian academic library and one of the finest on any aspect of Canadian library history. Lajeunesse,[46] in studying Quebec's junior college libraries, has provided the only history of one type of academic library ever attempted in Canada. Savage, Brault and Auster[47, 48, 51] have addressed the greatest challenge facing Canadian academic libraries during the past twenty years: retrenchment in the face of growing demand. Auster is particularly thorough in her analysis.

[46]Lajeunesse, Marcel. *Bibliothèque des collèges d'enseignement général et professionnel du Québec: étude de leur évolution, 1969-1983.* Montréal: Université de Montréal, École de bibliothéconomie, 1985. 208p.

[47]Savage, Daniel A. "Steady-state Academic Libraries: Retrenchment Solution?" *The Canadian Journal of Higher Education* 17, no. 3 (1987): 67-72.

[48]Brault, Jean-Rémi. "Bibliothèques universitaires du Québec, 1980-1986." *Documentation et bibliothèques* 34, no. 3 (juillet-septembre 1988): 103-6.

[49]Banks, Margaret A. *Libraries at Western, 1970 to 1987: with Summaries of their Earlier History and a Postscript.* London, Ont.: University of Western Ontario, University Library System, 1989. xv, 146p.

[50]Blackburn, Robert. *Evolution of the Heart: a History of the University of Toronto Library up to 1981.* Toronto: University of Toronto Library, 1989. xviii, 375p.

[51]Auster, Ethel. *Retrenchment in Canadian Academic Libraries.* Ottawa: Canadian Library Association, 1991. xx, 230p.

National, Legislative and Provincial Libraries

A new synthesis is clearly required to update John Beard's *Canadian Provincial Libraries* (Ottawa: Canadian Library Association, 1967). Monographic histories of the legislative libraries of Saskatchewan, Lower Canada and New Brunswick[53, 56, 57, 58] have transformed our understanding of the field. Shorter studies of others, such as British Columbia,[55] have aided this understanding, as will the soon-to-be-completed study of the Ontario Legislative Library. The late Dolores Donnelly[52] capped her pioneering work on the National Library of Canada with this article. Kingston[54] provides a suggestive but flawed evaluation.

[52]Donnelly, F. Dolores. "The National Library of Canada: its History and Function." In *The ALA Yearbook of Library and Information Services,* vol. 10, 200-1. Chicago: American Library Association, 1985.

[53]MacDonald, Christine. *The Legislative Library of Saskatchewan: a History.* Regina: Saskatchewan Legislative Library, 1986. x, 109p.

[54]Kingston, Rebecca. "The National Library of Canada: a Study in the Growth of a Nation." *Canadian Library Journal* 45, no. 3 (June 1988): 165-70.

[55]Burton, Joan. "Evolution of the British Columbia Legislative Library." *Canadian Parliamentary Review* 13, no. 3 (Autumn 1990): 18-19.

[56]Gallichan, Gilles. "Le livre et la politique au Bas-Canada, 1791-1849." Doctoral Thesis (histoire), Université Laval, 1990. x, 599p. (Published as: *Livre et politique au Bas-Canada: 1791-1849.* Sillery, Qué.: Éditions du Septentrion, 1991. 519p.)

[57]*The Development of the New Brunswick Legislative Library, 1841-1991.* Fredericton, N.B.: Legislative Library, 1991. vi, 64p.

[58]*Évolution de la Bibliothèque de l'Assemblée législative du Nouveau-Brunswick, 1841-1991.* Fredericton, N.B.: Bibliothèque de l'Assemblée législative, 1991. vi, 62p.

Personal Libraries

Perhaps the most striking historiographical development within Canadian library history during this period was the relative decline of interest in the personal library amongst francophone historians. Since the historical study of libraries in Quebec began 100 years ago, French-Canadian research has been dominated by this topic. Perhaps there is nothing more to say on private libraries, or perhaps there are too many other issues that engage the attention of historians. Langlois and Labonté[59, 60] analyze private libraries in the late eighteenth and early nineteenth centuries. Lindsay's[61] article builds on previous studies of fur traders' libraries in the Canadian wilderness during the nineteenth century and earlier.

[59]Langlois, Egide. "Livres et lecteurs à Québec, 1760-1799." M.A. (histoire), Université Laval, 1984. xvi, 112p.

[60]Labonté, Gilles. "Les bibliothèques privées à Québec, 1820-1829." M.A. (histoire), Université Laval, 1986. xxvi, 301p.

[61]Lindsay, Debra. "Peter Fidler's Library: Philosophy and Science in Rupert's Land." In *Readings in Canadian Library History,* edited by Peter F. McNally, 209-29. Ottawa: Canadian Library Association, 1986.

Biography

Neglect of the men and women who designed, built and operated the Canadian library system continues to be a major historiographical weakness. Cummings[62] completed the most sophisticated work to date on any Canadian librarian in his study of the idiosyncratic Angus Mowat. Despite its slimness, the study of Calhoun by Lohnes and Nicholson[63] is very helpful; the lives of dozens of other Canadian library figures deserve equivalent treatment. McNally[66] provides a comparative analysis of McGill's three university librarians. Obituaries are notoriously elusive, but frequently provide the only published biographical information on librarians and library supporters; a bibliography of obituaries is greatly needed. Sylvestre's[64] eulogy of Donnelly is an excellent example of its genre. Thériault's[65] entry is one of a number on librarians in the *Dictionary of Canadian Biography/Dictionnaire biographique du Canada*; the inclusion of more such entries should be encouraged.

[62]Cummings, Stephen F. "Angus McGill Mowat and the Development of Ontario Public Libraries, 1920-1960." Doctoral thesis (Library and Information Science), University of Western Ontario, 1986. viii, 428p. (An abridged version was published as: "On the Compass of Angus Mowat: Books, Boats, Soldiers and Indians." In *Readings in Canadian Library History*, edited by Peter F. McNally, 245-58. Ottawa: Canadian Library Association, 1986.

[63]Lohnes, Donna and Barbara Nicholson. *Alexander Calhoun*. Calgary: Calgary Public Library, 1989. 69p.

[64]Sylvestre, Guy. "Sister Frances Dolores Donnelly (1914-1987)." *National Library News* 19, no. 3-4 (March-April 1987): 1.

[65]Thériault, Yvon. "François Romain." In *Dictionnaire biographique du Canada*, vol. 6, 726-28. Québec: Les Presses de l'Université Laval, 1987.

[66]McNally, Peter F. "Scholar Librarians: Gould, Lomer, and Pennington." *Fontanus: from the Collections of McGill University* 1 (1988): 95-104.

Library Co-operation

As co-operation, standards, and automation have emerged as the great totems of late twentieth-century librarianship, it is unfortunate that they have received so little historical study. Medical and law librarianship[67, 68] have produced a few minor studies; the impact of automation is considered by Brault and Howarth.[69, 70] Although it is not intended to be an historical study, Howarth's thesis provides much valuable historical information.

[67]Fraser, Bill. "B.C. Medical Library Service." *Bibliotheca Medica Canadiana* 7, no. 2 (1985): 57-58.

[68]Hu, Shi-Sheng. "Development of Library Standards, with Special Emphasis on the Canadian Courthouse and Law Society Libraries." In *Law Libraries in*

Canada, Essays in Honour of Diana M. Priestly, edited by Joan M. Fraser, 135-46. Toronto: Carswell, 1988.

[69]Brault, Jean-Rémi. "De la centrale de catalogage à la centrale des bibliothèques (1964-1969)." *Documentation et bibliothèques* 35, no. 3 (juillet-septembre 1989): 105-11.

[70]Howarth, Lynne. "The Impact of Automation on Operations and Staffing Configurations in Cataloguing Departments in Public Libraries; a Study of Four Public Library Systems in the Municipality of Metropolitan Toronto, Ontario, 1970-1986." Doctoral thesis (Library and Information Science), University of Toronto, 1990. xii, 239p.

Library Education

During the period under study, only a handful of articles and no monographs or syntheses appeared on the history of Canadian library education or individual schools. Technician programmes were virtually ignored. Lajeunesse's[71] study of the programme at the Université de Montréal is very helpful, as is Reade's[72] comparative study on the education of school librarians.

[71]Lajeunesse, Marcel. "L'École de bibliothéconomie et des sciences de l'information de l'Université de Montréal: un quart de siècle de formation des professionnels de l'information (1961-1986)." *Argus* 16, no. 1 (mars 1987): 3-8.

[72]Reade, J.C. "Training for School Library Professionals: Views from Both Sides of the Atlantic." *Canadian Library Journal* 44, no. 2 (April 1987): 97-101, 103-4.

Library Associations

Voluntary professional organizations, staff associations, and unions have all fulfilled crucial roles in the development of Canadian librarianship and in the improvement of working conditions of librarians. The comparative neglect of these groups has prevented an understanding of an important element in the evolution of Canadian librarianship. Mudge[73] provides a valuable introduction to unionization in Ontario libraries. Boisvenue[74] gives a brief introduction to Canada's major French-language library association, which is centred in Quebec. Banks'[75] study of the Canadian Association of Law Libraries should be replicated for scores of other associations.

[73]Mudge, Charlotte R. "Bargaining Unit Composition and Negotiation Outcomes: a Study of Academic and Public Library Personnel in Ontario." Doctoral thesis (Library Science), University of Toronto, 1984. 190, 72p. (A summary was published as: "Mixed Unit Bargaining: Are Librarians Losing?" *Canadian Library Journal* 43, no. 3 (June 1986): 193-94.

[74]Boisvenue, Marie-Josée. "ASTED: Promoting Information Science in Quebec." *Canadian Library Journal* 43, no. 3 (June 1986): 137-38.

[75]Banks, Margaret A. *The Canadian Association of Law Libraries/L'Association canadienne des bibliothèques de droit: a History*. Toronto: The Association, 1988. 32p. (Special Issue: *C.A.L.L. Newsletter*).

School and Children's Libraries

This is another area requiring much work; the basic facts of school and children's libraries in Canada remain virtually unknown. In a study that is contemporary in its focus, Bernhard[76] synthesizes the history of Quebec school libraries rather than providing additional information. Spring-Gifford[77] illuminates developments in Alberta as part of what, it is hoped, will be a larger study. Fasick[78] covers a wide variety of subjects, some of which are of historical interest.

[76]Bernhard, Paulette. "La bibliothèque/médiathèque: instrument d'éducation dans l'enseignement secondaire au Québec." Doctoral thesis (éducation), Université de Montréal, 1986. 2 v. (Summaries were published in the following journals: *Argus* 17, no. 4 (décembre 1988): 101-7; *Canadian Library Journal* 45, no. 1 (February 1988): 49-50; *Documentation et bibliothèques* 33, no. 1 (janvier-mars 1987): 19-24; *School Libraries in Canada* 8, no. 1 (Fall 1987): 45-51.)

[77]Spring-Gifford, Christine. "In Search of a Policy: the Development of School Libraries in Alberta." In *Readings in Canadian Library History*, edited by Peter F. McNally, 191-206. Ottawa: Canadian Library Association, 1986.

[78]Fasick, Adele M., ed. *Lands of Pleasure: Essays on Lillian H. Smith and the Development of Children's Libraries*. Metuchen, N.J.: Scarecrow, 1990. vii, 176p.

Adult Education

Selman's[79] book contains some interesting information on libraries and adult education. Otherwise, this is a field which has been largely neglected in recent years.

[79]Selman, Gordon R. *Alan Thomas and the Canadian Association for Adult Education, 1961-1970*. Occasional Papers in Continuing Education, no. 24. Vancouver: University of British Columbia, Centre for Continuing Education, 1985. 85p.

Conclusion

In both official languages, Canadian library history displays growing vitality and strength. Linkages between research fronts are beginning to emerge; syntheses are becoming feasible. Individual studies no longer stand so obviously in isolation, but are starting to fit into meaningful contexts. In other words, the foundation for a scholarly appreciation of Canada's library tradition is being laid; the task of completion is ongoing.

Social, cultural and intellectual history are necessary to provide the appropriate contexts for library history. Only in the past generation have they developed to the point of sophistication in Canada that our library history can make use of them. In Quebec, French-language studies have adopted the contexts of *histoire du livre*. In English-speaking Canada, social, cultural and intellectual contexts of a more varied nature are being considered.

A positive sign during this period was the appearance of doctoral theses with historical orientations from the library and information science programmes at the University of Toronto and the University of Western Ontario. The concern for recent library history is also positive. Still to be achieved is a general appreciation by the historical community of the significance of libraries to an understanding of Canada's past.

2 Library Education

Fanfares and Celebrations: Anniversaries in Canadian Graduate Education for Library and Information Studies

Peter F. McNally

Abstract

Canadian graduate education for library and information studies has a long and venerable history. Yet the anniversaries of a number of important events are being largely ignored. This paper looks at each major event in terms of the people, issues, and circumstances surrounding it: 1904, the first program; 1930, the first graduate program; 1951, the first master's program; 1965, the two-year master's program; and 1971, the first doctoral program. Particular attention is paid to the two-year master's program, which is considered to be Canada's unique contribution. Comparisons are made between the Canadian experience and that of the United States, Britain, and France. The crucial roles played by the two senior schools — McGill and the University of Toronto — are discussed. Similarities and differences among the seven Canadian graduate programs are considered.

Résumé

La formation des 2ᵉ et 3ᵉ cycles en bibliothéconomie et en sciences de l'information a un passé digne de mention. Pourtant, les anniversaires de plusieurs développements importants passent sous silence. Cet article présente chaqun des développements en fonction des gens, des problèmes et des circonstances qui les entourent : en 1904, le premier programme de bibliothéconomie dans notre pays ; en 1930 le premier programme de 2ᵉ cycle ; en 1951 le premier programme de maîtrise ; en 1965 le programme de maîtrise de deux ans ; et en 1971 le premier programme de doctorat. Nous examinerons sutout le programme de maîtrise de deux ans, ce qui est une contribution unique du Canada. Nous mettrons en comparaison les expériences canadiennes avec celles des États-Unis, de la Grande-Bretagne

Reprinted from *The Canadian Journal of Information and Library Science/Revue canadienne des sciences de l'information et de bibliothéconomie*, Vol. 18, No. 1, April 1993

et de la France. Nous discuterons du rôle critique joué par les deux écoles réputées — McGill et l'université de Toronto. De plus nous examinerons les ressemblances et les différences entre les sept programmes canadiens des 2ᵉ et 3ᵉ cycles.

Fanfares and celebrations are used by professions and institutions as much as by cities, provinces, and nations to mark the anniversaries of important events in their historical development. The popular attention which an anniversary generates may gain them a sympathetic hearing from the public at large; it can also lead to internal stock-taking with meditation upon the past and future, where one is coming from and where one is going. With these thoughts in mind, a highly important anniversary in the educational life of the Canadian library and information studies profession occurred and was largely overlooked in 1990: the twenty-fifth anniversary of the two-year Master of Library Science degree. As a result, a marvellous opportunity both for public attention and critical self-evaluation was lost. Yet this uniquely Canadian contribution to library and information studies education can only be discussed meaningfully within the context of four other significant events whose anniversaries are also upon us: the ninetieth anniversary in 1994 of the country's first library education program, the sixtieth anniversary in 1990 of the introduction of graduate library education into Canada, the fortieth anniversary in 1991 of our first master's program in librarianship, and the twentieth anniversary also in 1991 of the first doctoral program.[1] If ever an opportunity presented itself for the Canadian library and information studies profession to capture the attention of the public and to reconsider and re-evaluate its origins and directions, surely it is now.

It has been too easily assumed that librarianship in this country operates simply as an adjunct — a branch plant operation — to activities in the United States. That Canadian professional practice and conceptual understanding — theory and principles — have been greatly influenced by American precedent is beyond dispute. It is crucial, however, to understand that library and information studies in Canada, with the assistance of certain British and European influences, has also developed its own uniquely Canadian characteristics, procedures, and values. The interplay between Canadian and American approaches is particularly obvious in the development of our educational programs. Moreover, these programs have both preceded and accompanied our country's library development, thereby providing a framework for future growth.

In 1904, nearly ninety years ago, library education was quietly launched in Canada with a summer program at McGill University, Montreal.[2] As

Melvil Dewey was the consultant, the American influence upon the program's approach can be taken for granted. Of equal importance was its establishment within a university, thereby ensuring an academic tradition for Canadian library education. Formal library education having been inaugurated less than two decades earlier in 1887 by Dewey at Columbia University,[3] the McGill school is consequently one of the oldest in the world to be based in a university. By comparison, a Toronto summer program was founded in 1911 by the Ontario Department of Education,[4] and a francophone program was begun in 1937 as the École de bibliothécaires, which, although technically affiliated with the Université de Montréal, was located at the Bibliothèque municipale de Montréal. Library education programs in these non-academic milieus would ultimately prove unsatisfactory. As a result, in 1928 the Ontario Library School became a joint venture with the University of Toronto through the Ontario College of Education, and Montreal's francophone school became in 1961, after many vicissitudes, a fully integrated department of the Université de Montréal.[5]

These early programs with high school diplomas being the only prerequisite strike us today as very primitive and inadequate. Yet given the rudimentary state of Canadian libraries at the time, they are undoubtedly all that was needed. When the century opened in 1900, our libraries were reasonably numerous but relatively weak, numbering around 536 with total holdings of about two million volumes,[6] or .27 volumes per person in a population of 5.3 million. Only a bare few had holdings of one hundred thousand or more volumes. The only ones housed separately in their own buildings were the Library of Parliament, two university libraries, under a dozen Ontario public libraries, and a few others in Quebec and possibly some other provinces. The first public library legislation was passed in Ontario in 1882 followed by British Columbia in 1891 and Manitoba in 1899. In 1901 the Ontario Library Association became our first professional society for librarians. Also in 1901 Andrew Carnegie made the first of his 125 grants to build public libraries in Canada, of which 111 were in Ontario.[7] Montreal and Toronto were our largest and wealthiest cities — as they are still today — and were the hubs of by far the largest concentrations of libraries. Their schools would supply their own staffing needs and those of the rest of the country for many decades to come.

That McGill, and eventually the University of Toronto, should have initiated Canadian library education reflects their status as Canada's preeminent universities of the early twentieth century — and some would say of the late twentieth century as well. In the 1890s they had introduced the German-American approach to higher education into Canada, where by a liberalized undergraduate curriculum had grafted upon it graduate and professional education to create the modern university we still know one hundred years later. They also opened Canada's first separately designed academic library buildings: at Toronto[8] in 1892 and at McGill in 1893. The founder of the McGill school and University Librarian was Charles H. Gould (1855-1919), a friend of Melvil Dewey and an outstanding librarian, who developed the largest Canadian academic library of the day, hosted the American Library Association's 1900 conference in Montreal, and became its first Canadian president in 1908.[9] Between 1897 and 1904, he ran an apprenticeship training program in the McGill library.

Even in the United States librarianship was in a very confused state at this time with a mélange of summer and sessional educational and training programs located in universities, libraries, and other sorts of institutions, with widely varying entrance and graduation standards.[10] During the 1920s order emerged from this chaos thanks to the Carnegie Corporation of New York. Motivated by a desire to ensure education of the highest quality, it undertook major and widely publicized studies in the early years of this century of a number of professions such as medicine, law, engineering, teaching, and librarianship, which exposed the inadequacy of their educational systems and advocated university programs — usually at a graduate level — and greatly improved standards, so as to meet the needs of society. These powerful and well-done reports led invariably to the fundamental reorganization of education in the designated professions. Librarianship was no exception and Charles C. Williamson's *Training for Library Service*, published by the corporation in 1923, provided the basis for developments whose influence continues to the present.[11] That the Carnegie Corporation should have included librarianship among the professions whose education was investigated reflects a concern both for ensuring the quality of the libraries so generously funded by the Corporation and its founder, Andrew Carnegie, and also for promoting the vital role it foresaw libraries and librarians playing in future educational developments at all levels.

Williamson's advocacy of university-based graduate education for librarianship, with a bachelor's degree as the entrance requirement and accepted standards for curricula and teaching, was very much within the general philosophical principles of the Carnegie Corporation and was soon accepted as the norm for American library education. Of course, the financial support given by the corporation did much to hasten the enterprise along: $5,000,000 for the American Library Association to develop an accreditation system, for a number of existing library schools to upgrade themselves, and for the University of Chicago's Graduate Library School to serve as a prototype for the others.[12] In 1925 ALA produced its first accreditation standards; by 1933 all of the accredited schools were connected with degree-granting institutions; and by 1935 sixteen of the twenty-six accredited schools had graduate programs.[13]

Canada was immediately affected by these changes. In 1927 McGill's summer program was accredited under the new ALA standards. That same year the university received a Carnegie grant to upgrade its school and introduce a one-year sessional program (accredited in 1929), which required high school matriculation for entrance and awarded a diploma. The next year, 1930, still with the support of the Carnegie Corporation, McGill transformed the diploma program into Canada's first graduate program in librarianship, requiring a bachelor's degree for admission and granting a Bachelor of Library Science after one year of study; this program was accredited in 1931 and reaccredited in 1934 under ALA's 1933 standards.[14] The dual anniversary of sixty years of graduate library education and its accreditation in Canada occurred, therefore, in 1990-1991.

As for the Ontario Library School, the University of Toronto assumed joint responsibility for it in 1928 when the provincial Department of Education agreed to place it in the Ontario College of Education and have it develop a one-year diploma program, with high school graduation being the prerequisite. In 1936 the school introduced the one-year Bachelor of Library Science, with an undergraduate degree as prerequisite, which was accredited by ALA the following year.[15]

Several factors strike one immediately when contemplating these developments of the 1920s and 1930s. First is the American influence that was so powerfully felt not only upon library education but upon all aspects of Canadian professional education during this period. To be progressive and forward-looking was frequently equated with following American initiatives. In truth, there were few other readily available models at this time in Canada or elsewhere. In Europe, the preference was generally for apprenticeship training, or "learning by doing," in all the professions, including librarianship. In 1879 the French government[16] and in 1885 the Library Association of the United Kingdom[17] developed apprentice/study programs in librarianship for their respective countries, a model which never took hold in Canada. The introduction of library education by British and French universities occurred very slowly. In 1919, with a £7,500 grant from the Carnegie United Kingdom Trust, the University of London School of Librarianship was founded, but did not become a graduate program until 1946.[18] The study of librarianship in other British universities would only emerge in succeeding decades. In France, a wide range of educational programs would come and go before the establishment in 1963 of the École nationale supérieure des bibliothèques as a graduate program. Various thoughts come to mind in considering these developments: Canadians showed an early preference for the academic study of librarianship rather than for the apprenticeship approach of the British and French; the adoption of the academic model was generally later coming to France and Britain than

43

to Canada; but the very fact of Britain and France — the mother countries — concerning themselves with library education would help legitimize Canadian developments.

The second factor is the still weak but steadily growing state of libraries in our national life as the prosperity of the '20s gave way to the economic depression of the '30s: in 1921 there were 662 in the entire country, of which 248 were public.[19] In 1932 the first Canadian chapter of the Special Libraries Association was founded in Montreal.[20] In 1933, the first formal report on Canadian libraries was published; sponsored by the Carnegie Corporation and prepared under the chairmanship of John Ridington of Vancouver, it pointed out strengths, weaknesses, and future directions, and included this statement in its conclusion: "... four-fifths of Canada's population ... are utterly without library service of any kind. Only three of the nine provincial governments as yet give more than a pious, theoretical approval to the principle that the library is an integral part of a people's welfare and education ...."[21]

Although Canada possessed little more than the foundation of a library system at this time, the fact is that there was a foundation upon which a very large structure could be built, given proper support and direction. The graduate programs would supply the standards and professional staffs needed for direction. Only society could provide the support.

The third important factor in this inter-war period is the leading role assumed by McGill University. As Canada's only private university, existing as neither a religious nor a state foundation and receiving little or no government funding but living largely off its fees and endowments, it had a strong tradition of flexibility and initiative. Like virtually every other Canadian university, it benefited greatly from Carnegie grants; a previous principal, Sir William Peterson (1856-1921), had served for many years as chairman of the Carnegie Foundation for the Advancement of Teaching.[22] In giving the university money for the school — $139,500,[23] which was a very generous sum at the time — the corporation was clearly intending to create a prototype for Canadian library education, an intention which was largely fulfilled. The school's second director and university librarian during this period, Gerhard Lomer (1882-1970), was an eminent scholar, librarian, and educator who had received his doctorate from Columbia University and who deserves accolades for being not only a co-founder, with his predecessor Gould, of the McGill Library School but also the founder of graduate library education in Canada. In addition, he introduced or participated in a number of library education courses and programs in other parts of the country.[24] Lomer is undoubtedly the single most important individual in the history of Canadian library education.

Until the 1960s McGill and Toronto dominated Canadian library education. Programs of varying quality and longevity did emerge at universities such as Acadia, Laval, Mount St. Vincent, Ottawa, St. Francis Xavier, and Western Ontario but none was ever accredited or achieved enduring viability. The program at the Université de Montréal had no full-time faculty before 1961. The two senior schools set the tone, therefore, for Canadian librarianship, and from them would emerge any uniquely Canadian qualities.

The issue of American influence over Canadian library education came to a head in the 1940s with significant results. In 1940, the Carnegie grants for the McGill Library School ended — as they did for those in the United States — at which point the corporation's direct concern for Canadian library education ceased. The university, however, assumed full financial responsibility for the school, which continued along the American pattern. In 1947 the Canadian Library Association, which was founded the previous year, passed the first of many formal motions delegating the accreditation of the country's schools to the American Library Association. Despite periodic calls over succeeding decades to establish a Canadian accreditation system, no compelling reasons for it have ever been presented.[25] In 1947/48, the most significant split between Canadian and American education occurred when Columbia University's School of Library Service, along with some other schools, announced a fundamental restructuring and strengthening of its program: termination of its Bachelor of Library Science degree and the sixth-year master's — for which the BLS had been the prerequisite — and replacement of them both with a new Master of Library Science degree with a revised curriculum.[26] Within a few years all the accredited schools in the United States had adopted this new configuration, which would typically require three academic terms (or one calendar year) and thirty-six credits for completion. A fifth-year master's in librarianship had, in fact, been created.

That McGill and Toronto did not follow suit reflected the then prevailing attitude in Canadian universities of considering the master's to be a research degree for which a bachelor's in the same subject was a prerequisite. To be eligible for a master's in librarianship, therefore, a candidate was expected to have first completed a bachelor's in librarianship. As a result, the two schools responded by modernizing and updating their curricula and instituting sixth-year MLS degrees with the BLS as a prerequisite along the lines of the pre-1948 American pattern. It was in this atmosphere that some forty years ago, in 1951, Toronto introduced Canada's first MLS program with an optional thesis,[27] followed by McGill in 1956 with a required thesis.[28] Concern was expressed whether the Canadian programs would be eligible for accreditation under ALA's new 1951 standards, which stated that the fifth-year MLS was the "appropriate" first professional degree. As it happens, however, ALA concluded that the quality of the two-term Canadian BLS degrees was the equivalent of the three-term American MLS, and accreditation was granted to Toronto in 1956 and McGill in 1957. In 1958 a CLA-sponsored conference designated the BLS as Canada's first professional degree in librarianship. An important precedent had been established: graduate library education in Canada and that in the United States could develop separately from one another yet still be considered academically equivalent.

These events occurred within the context of the post-World War II economic and population boom when a new Canadian self-confidence emerged — cultural and otherwise. Libraries and librarianship shared in this optimism: in 1946 the Canadian Library Association was formed; in 1951 the Massey Royal Commission report on arts, letters, and science emphasized the importance of libraries;[29] and in 1953 the National Library of Canada was established by Act of Parliament.[30] Wide-ranging library growth and development of various sorts, particularly of public and regional libraries, was occurring throughout the country.

Toronto's introduction of the MLS in 1951 coincided exactly with the retirement from the school's directorship of Winifred Barnstead (1884-1985) and the succession of Bertha Bassam (1896-1989); between them they directed the school's fortunes for thirty-six years, 1928 to 1964. Forceful, energetic, and intelligent, they provided strong leadership and continuity in pursuing the school's three major goals of this period: the development of professional standards; the reorganization of the school as a department of the university with separate quarters; and the school's removal from the direct authority of the College of Education and, through it, the Ontario Department of Education.[31] Development of the master's degree assisted the fulfilment of all three goals over succeeding decades.

The 1960s were undoubtedly the most dynamic and innovative decade in Canadian educational history, particularly in higher education. Enrolments increased dramatically, new institutions and programs proliferated, ferment and change were in the air. Libraries academic and non-academic shared in this proliferation and change, and so by extension did their educational establishment. Growing concern developed, however, at the inability of our academic libraries to meet the country's greatly increasing research activities. In four major reports E.E. Williams (1962),[32] Beatrice V. Simon (1964),[33] G.S. Bonn (1966),[34] and Robert B. Downs (1967)[35] identified problems and made recommendations for improvement and strengthening that resulted in massive expenditures of money. Given this climate of opinion and activity, it is hardly surprising that during the decade four new graduate programs emerged which, as the dates in parentheses indicate, were soon accredited: University of British Columbia in 1961 (1962),[36] University of Western Ontario in 1967 (1969),[37] University of Alberta in 1968 (1970),[38] and Dalhousie University in 1969 (1973)[39] — two in the West, one in Ontario, and one in the Atlantic provinces. In

addition, the École de bibliothéconomie became a fully integrated department of the Université de Montréal in 1961 with a full-time director and
faculty; its program gained accreditation in 1969.[40] By comparison, twenty-
three new graduate programs began in the United States between 1961 and
1976.[41] Finally, but not incidentally, in 1962 the first Canadian program for
library technicians, or nonprofessional staff, was inaugurated in Winnipeg.[42]
These developments reflected several emerging trends: that libraries and
information were of growing concern for Canadians; that McGill and
Toronto were no longer able to meet the country's growing demand for
librarians; that neither the francophone community of Quebec nor the people of the Atlantic and Western provinces wished to depend further upon
the two senior schools for professional staff; that Canadian universities were
becoming sufficiently sophisticated and prosperous to afford accredited
programs; and that alternative ways of providing library education should be
investigated.

For the new graduate programs, an immediate issue was whether to opt
for the Canadian or American model of education. The results were, to say
the least, mixed: UBC and Alberta chose the by now traditional two-term
Canadian BLS, while Western Ontario and Dalhousie opted for master's
degrees which were interesting mixtures of Canadian and American practices.
As for the Université de Montréal, it introduced the one-year bachelor's
degree in 1961 and a unique two-year bachelor's degree in 1966, the first year
of which was devoted to general education.

It was in this environment of change and uncertainty, just over twenty-
five years ago during 1965, with little fanfare or publicity, but under the
sometimes encouraging and frequently hostile scrutiny of the entire
Canadian library community, that McGill University launched Canada's
unique contribution to library education: the two-year MLS degree. Both the
two-term BLS and the thesis MLS programs were replaced by this new degree;
the revised curriculum required four academic terms (unlike the three-term
American master's) but no thesis. In other words, McGill had created a new
standard of education for graduate professional librarians that soon became the
Canadian norm: a sixth-year master's as the first professional degree.

What were the factors that led McGill to take this daring and extraordinary leap of faith into an unknown future despite predictions of disaster
from many critics?[43] Within the Canadian library education community,
general concern was shared at the growing difficulty of including within the
one-year curriculum the steadily increasing body of knowledge, both theoretical and applied, that the discipline and profession of librarianship and
newly emerging information studies were creating. For instance, new fields
such as administration and automation had to be accommodated. Also
there was a felt need to ensure a distinct difference between a graduate

degree and a library technician's diploma; neither inside nor outside the universities was it generally appreciated that a BLS was a graduate degree. Within McGill University, maintaining and developing the quality and reputation of its many professional schools has long been a preoccupation, with particular emphasis placed upon innovation and leadership. There was a growing realization that programs such as library science, engineering, education, management, and social work needed a pattern of graduate education beyond the bachelor's but different from the traditional research master's with thesis. Encouraged actively by the Library School, the university developed the concept of the two-year master's programs without thesis for professional schools — that is, a professional master's degree.

Within the school itself, the architect and prime mover behind the two year MLS was its associate director and future director, Virginia Murray (1910-1983), a brilliant teacher endowed with a quick and intuitive intelligence. She along with the school's then director, Vernon Ross (1901-1977), and future directors Violet Coughlin and Effie Astbury, plus Beryl Anderson and Eleanor Magee, constituted a band of courageous and visionary women who walked very warily, always "polite, cautious but determined,"[44] in the male-dominated environment that typified McGill and other Canadian universities. They were closely in touch with developments in the profession and its educational establishments in both Canada and the United States, as well as with the prevailing standards of Canadian universities. That McGill's library school must eventually switch to the master's as a first professional degree became increasingly obvious to them during the late '50s and early '60s. To begin with, the two-term BLS was able to cover only the required curriculum; few electives with any depth of coverage could be offered. The sixth-year MLS permitted depth and specialization but attracted few students: by 1965 McGill had only seven graduates compared to Toronto's twenty-six.[45] At the same time, Ross, Murray, and Coughlin (who had all studied at Columbia University, where the latter two received their doctorates) realized the limitations of the three-term American master's which, they felt, did not permit the full development of either the required curriculum or electives. It is not clear whether they also realized that in a confidential report of 1921 to the Carnegie Corporation, shortly before the publication of his *Training for Library Services*, Williamson (who later became dean of Columbia's school) had recommended two years of graduate study for librarianship.[46] In any event, Columbia's introduction of a one-year post-master's diploma program, in 1961, may well have provided the salient clue for the future.[47] Working with McGill officials, particularly Stanley Frost, dean of the Faculty of Graduate Studies, the school developed a program that would be at once both professional and academic in character, meet the newly developing professional master's standards of McGill and other Canadian universities, permit both breadth and depth of coverage, and overcome the perceived shortcomings of the American three-term pattern. Two academic years, it was agreed, were needed to accommodate both the required and elective curricula — one year for each. An indigenous Canadian standard had been created.

The success of this new standard of education and its impact upon the other schools is best gauged by the resolution passed in April 1968 at a Toronto conference on library education that was attended by representatives of all the Canadian library schools: "that a four-term graduate program leading to a master's degree in library science [is] the basic preparation for the professional practice of librarianship in Canada; and that Canadian library schools attempt to implement the new basic master's program within five years, i.e. by 1973."[48]

Conversion to the new two-year MLS was very swift for some schools and much slower for others: Toronto and the Université de Montréal in 1970 and British Columbia in 1972. Dalhousie during its first two years, 1969-71, offered simultaneously both a three-term and a four-term MLS but in 1971 opted for the four-term degree as being more in line with Canadian academic practice. Alberta granted an MLS with the BLS as prerequisite from 1971 to 1976, when it discontinued both in favour of the two-year master's. Western Ontario continued with its unique hybrid of the Canadian and American pattern: a forty-five credit MLS awarded after three academic terms or one calendar year. As the school operates on a trimester system, there are three incoming classes per year. During its early years, Western's calendar always included the following passage or some variant: "The ... course of studies leading to the Master of Library Science degree can normally be completed in a minimum of three terms, i.e. eleven months."[49] It has been replaced in recent years by the following: "Since the School operates on the trimester system, the M.L.I.S. program can be completed in a minimum of twelve months by a full-time student, although the four-term, 16-month program is strongly recommended."[50] In other words, Western Ontario gives nearly the equivalent of a Canadian two-year master's, placed within a three-term American pattern, which is increasingly spread over four terms in the now typically Canadian pattern.

Another indication of the success of the two-year Master of Library and Information Studies is its adoption by at least three American universities: North Carolina at Chapel Hill, California at Los Angeles, and Washington. After nearly a century of borrowing from American practice, Canada has finally been able to repay the favour by developing an indigenous standard of education and sharing it with our southern neighbour.

In 1971, just over twenty years ago, the first Canadian doctoral program in librarianship was inaugurated at the University of Toronto, followed by the University of Western Ontario in 1973. Alberta and McGill accepted their first doctoral candidates in 1990 and 1991 respectively. The Université de Montreal has indicated its intention of introducing the world's first French-language doctorate in library and information studies during the 1990s. When compared with the United States, where the first doctoral program was begun at Chicago in 1928,[51] Canada has been very slow. Given the relatively undeveloped state of Canadian libraries and library education before the 1960s, however, neither the need nor the resources for such a program existed; American schools were able to fulfil all our doctoral needs. The development of doctoral programs by the two Ontario schools reflected their status as our largest schools of the time and Ontario's status as the largest and wealthiest province with the greatest concentration of libraries. To depend solely upon foreign doctoral programs was no longer feasible or acceptable, even if a 1972 report on the Canadian market for doctorates has proven overly optimistic.[52] In any event, the rate of production has been steady and moderate with fifteen graduates from Toronto by the end of 1991 and twenty-one from Western Ontario, an average of slightly fewer than two per year over twenty years.

That the University of Toronto should have introduced the first domestic doctoral program reflects the enormous increase in support given to the School during the 1960s and '70s. Its director between 1964 and 1972 was Brian Land, a worthy and effective successor to Barnstead and Bassam, long noted for his political adroitness, who brought to fruition their fight for standards, a distinctive identity, and separate quarters. In 1965 the school became an integral unit of the university, freed at last from the College of Education, the college's building, and the Ontario Department of Education; in 1970 the two-year MLS was introduced. Then in 1971, concurrent with the beginning of its doctoral program, it moved into the world's largest separately planned library school building, thereby reflecting a new prominence for library education in Toronto and all of Canada.[53]

From the perspective of the 1990s, one way of looking at Canada's seven graduate programs is to consider their parent institutions: all are large and prestigious with highly developed graduate and professional programs; all have medical and law schools; all are considered leaders in this country with several having significant international reputations. A recent highly criticized but widely read survey of undergraduate programs in forty-six Canadian universities ranked the seven as follows: McGill first, Toronto fourth, British Columbia seventh, Dalhousie ninth, Alberta tenth, Montréal eleventh, and Western Ontario sixteenth — all in the top twenty.[54] Another consideration is library collections, with the seven ranking among Canada's twenty-seven academic research libraries in terms of millions of volumes as follows: first Toronto (5,952), second British Columbia (3,653), third Alberta (3,399), fourth McGill (2,610), seventh Montréal (2,059), eighth Western Ontario (1,961), and nineteenth Dalhousie (1,343).[55] It is significant that four of the schools are in institutions with the country's largest collections. The implications are clear: the Canadian academic community has concluded that graduate library and information education belongs in a graduate/professional school environment and that the seven schools conform to the goals of the parent institutions. By comparison, in the United States its fifty-two accredited graduate programs are dispersed throughout a wide spectrum of institutions ranging from primarily undergraduate colleges to major universities emphasizing graduate and professional education.

Looked at among themselves, the seven schools reveal an intriguing mixture of uniformity and variation. All combine the words "library" and "information" in their titles in acknowledgment of the academic, technological and ideological changes which have transformed the discipline and profession over the past thirty years.* In their master's programs, all have strong cores of required courses that constitute approximately fifty per cent of their credit requirements and reveal blends of traditional subjects — selection, cataloguing and reference — plus newer subjects such as automation, research methods, and management. All offer a wide range of electives including the opportunity of undertaking a research project either as an optional or required aspect of the degree. Except for Western Ontario, all require completion of a minimum of forty-eight credits, so maintaining their status as four-term programs offering four courses per term to full-time students. Some schools require more credits, as many as sixty in one instance; Western Ontario at forty-five credits is only one course short of a minimal four-term program. Several schools offer alternative programs such as archival studies at British Columbia and Montréal, and a Master of Information Science at Toronto. A detailed analysis of the calendars over many decades is clearly required to reveal how the schools' curricula have adapted to academic and professional developments.

Accreditation continues to be a major concern for the seven schools. They have all been successfully reaccredited at six- or seven-year intervals under the ALA's 1972 standards; the conditional accreditations, which have occasionally been granted, have always been converted to full accreditations within one year. A Canadian is a member of any site team visit to a Canadian school; and the CLA is invited to send an observer on these visits. There is always a Canadian member of ALA's Committee on Accreditation. The schools are all intending to participate in the accreditation process under ALA's 1992 standards.

---

*In 1994, the Faculty of Library and Information Science at the University of Toronto changed its name to the Faculty of Information Studies.

51

Another concern is with the closing, between 1978 and 1991, of fourteen of the graduate schools in the United States.[56] That no Canadian programs should have been closed may simply reflect the good fortune of being able to keep the number of our schools to seven and of their being able to maintain moderate enrolments, thereby preventing an oversupply of graduates. There may be, however, other factors at work that deserve some attention. The apparent fusion, which our schools have accomplished, of library education and information studies education requires particularly close scrutiny. Was this fusion undertaken for marketing or substantive reasons? What have been the short-term and long-term effects upon the curricular and other activities of our programs? These questions are especially relevant given the current problems facing national organizations such as the CLA and the Canadian Association for Information Science. Do the delicate balancing acts performed by our schools between tradition and technology, professional formation and academic contribution, practice and theory, reflect vitality or aimlessness? Such questions need to be addressed but perhaps elsewhere at another time.

What is most striking in this history of the past ninety years is the integral role played by education in our national library development. Our educational programs have either anticipated or accompanied all the major advances in libraries and librarianship during this century. The McGill and Toronto schools began when Carnegie grants and pre-World War I prosperity were making libraries an important part of the Canadian scene. The inter-war transformation of the two senior schools into first sessional then graduate programs positioned them well to deal with the conflicting demands of the prosperous '20s, the depressed '30s, the war years, and the booming '40s and '50s. The emergence of new schools and the general strengthening of all the programs during the past thirty years or so have paralleled exactly Canada's development of one of the world's great library systems, containing over 5,000 libraries with annual expenditures of $1 billion.[57] With total holdings of approximately 250 million items, our libraries now have an average of ten items per Canadian, a very respectable figure by any criterion. Europe and the United States possessed a wide range of strong libraries before the introduction of formal library education. By comparison, Canada's library development has occurred largely within the context of the leadership and education provided by its graduate programs and their predecessors. This is a typically Canadian approach of providing a framework for development rather than relying upon unplanned growth and proliferation. The question is now, do our seven graduate programs plan to continue providing a framework for future Canadian development of its library and information activities?

Given that we are now in the midst of a cluster of significant anniversaries, is this not the perfect time for the Canadian library and information profession to reconsider and re-evaluate its origins and directions and to capture the attention of the public with fanfares and celebrations?

Notes

[1] Olga B. Bishop and Gerald Prodrick, *Canadian Association of Library Schools/Association canadienne des écoles de bibliothéconomie Handbook*, rev. ed. (Toronto: Association, 1982). Chapter VII; Robin S. Harris, *A History of Higher Education in Canada, 1663-1960* (Toronto: University of Toronto Press, 1976), 295, 416-417, 543; Mary E.P. Henderson, "Professional Library Education in Canada" in *Canadian Libraries and Their Changing Environment*, ed. Loraine Spencer Gary (Toronto: York University, 1977), 394-419; and "Library Education," *Canadian Library* 14, no. 5 (April, 1958). Issue. (These are the best general introductions, despite certain omissions and errors)

[2] Violet Coughlin, "McGill University. Graduate School of Library Science," *Encyclopedia of Library and Information Science* (New York: Dekker, 1976): 17, 304-11.

[3] William Z. Nasri, "Education in Library, and Information Science; Education for Librarianship," *Encyclopedia of Library and Information Science* 7 (1972): 414-65.

[4] Bertha Bassam, *The Faculty of Library Science, University of Toronto, and its Predecessors, 1911-1972* (Toronto: Faculty of Library Science, 1978). Chapter 2.

[5] Marielle Durand, "L'École de bibliothéconomie de l'Université de Montréal, 1937-1962" in *Livre, bibliothèque, et culture québécoise*, ed. Georges A. Chartrand (Montreal: ASTED, 1977), II: 485-507.

[6] James Bain, "Canadian Libraries," *The Canadian Magazine* 16, no. 1 (November 1900): 28-32.

[7] Margaret Beckman, *The Best Gift; a Record of the Carnegie Libraries in Ontario* (Toronto: Dundurn Press, 1984), 19, 28-29.

[8] Robert H. Blackburn, *Evolution of the Heart; a History of the University of Toronto Library up to 1981* (Toronto: University of Toronto Library, 1989), 92-93.

[9] Ritva Makela, *McGill University Library during the Tenure of Charles H. Gould as University Librarian, 1893-1919* (Montreal: Graduate School of Library Science, McGill University, 1974), vol. II, 37p.; and Peter F. McNally, "McGill University Libraries," *Encyclopedia of Library and Information Science*, 17 (1976): 311-20.

[10] Carl M. White, *A Historical Introduction to Library Education; Problems and Progress to 1951* (Metuchen, N.J.: Scarecrow, 1976). Chapters 3-6.

[11] Charles C. Williamson, *Training for Library Service; a Report Prepared for the Carnegie Corporation of New York* (New York, Merrymount Press at Boston, 1923). 165 p.; Sarah K. Vann, *The Williamson Reports: a Study* (Metuchen, N.J.: Scarecrow, 1971), xi, 212 p.

[12] White, 167, 231-32.

[13] Ibid., 197-98.

[14]Coughlin, 305.

[15]Bassam, 31-32, 41-43.

[16]Michel Merland, "The Education of Librarians and Documentalists," in *Library and Information Science in France: a 1983 Overview*, ed. William Vernon Jackson (Austin, Texas: Graduate School of Library and Information Science, University of Texas, 1984), 143-65.

[17]D.J. Grogan, "Education for Librarianship: Some Persistent Issues," *Education for Information* 1, no. 1 (March, 1983): 3-23; and D.D. Haslam, "The Library Association," *Encyclopedia of Library and Information Science* 14 (1975): 312-37.

[18]B.C. Vickery, "University College London. School of Library , Archive and Information Studies," *Encyclopedia of Library and Information Science* 16 (1975): 288-389.

[19]Canada. Dominion Bureau of Statistics, *Annual Report on Education Statistics in Canada, 1922* (Ottawa: King's Printer, 1924), 167.

[20]Peter F. McNally, "Fifty Years of Special Libraries in Montreal and Eastern Canada, 1932-1982," *Special Libraries, Eastern Canada Chapter, Bulletin* 47, no. 4 (May 1982): 26-29.

[21]*Libraries in Canada; a Study of Library Conditions and Needs; by the Commission of Enquiry, John Ridington, Chairman* (Toronto: Ryerson, 1933), 139.

[22]Stanley B. Frost, *McGill University; for the Advancement of Learning* (Montreal: McGill-Queen's University Press, 1984), 2: 107.

[23]Harris, 346; and McGill University Archives, RG2 Principal, Library School and Carnegie Corporation, 1938-1939, File 1221, C66.

[24]Peter F. McNally, "Scholar Librarians: Gould, Lomer and Pennington." *Fontanus: from the Collections of McGill University* 1 (1988): 95-104.

[25]"Accreditation," *Canadian Library Journal* 31, no. 2 (April 1974). Issue.

[26]White, chapter 9.

[27]Bassam, 45-46, 66-67.

[28]Coughlin, 305.

[29]Canada. Royal Commission on National Development in the Arts, Letters, and Science. *Report ... 1941-1951* (Ottawa: King's Printer, 1951). Chapter 9.

[30]F. Dolores Donnelly, *The National Library of Canada; a Historical Analysis of the Forces which Contributed to its Establishment and to the Identification of its Role and Responsibilities* (Ottawa: Canadian Library Association, 1977), 101.

[31]Bassam, 50-51, 76.

[32]E.E. Williams, *Resources of Canadian University Libraries for Research in the Humanities and Social Sciences: Report of a Survey for the National Conference of Canadian Universities and Colleges* (Ottawa: The Conference, 1962), 87p.

[33]Beatrice V. Simon, *Library Support of Medical Education and Research in Canada; Report of a Survey of the Medical College Libraries in Canada, Together with Suggestions for Improving and Extending Medical Library Service at Local, Regional, and National Levels* (Ottawa: Association of Canadian Medical Colleges, 1964), xvii, 132p.

[34]G.S. Bonn, *Science-technology Literature Resources in Canada; Report of a Survey for the Associate Committee on Scientific Information* (Ottawa: Associate Committee on Scientific Information, National Research Council, 1966), iv, 80p.

[35]Robert B. Downs, *Resources of Canadian Academic and Research Libraries* (Ottawa: Association of Universities and Colleges of Canada, 1967), xi, 301p.

[36]Samuel Rothstein, "University of British Columbia, School of Librarianship," *Encyclopedia of Library and Information Science* 3 (1970): 274-76.

[37]William J. Cameron, "University of Western Ontario. School of Library and Information Science," *Encyclopedia of Library and Information Science* 33 (1982): 124-29.

[38]Mary E.P. Henderson and Catriona de Scossa, "University of Alberta. Faculty of Library Science," *Encyclopedia of Library and Information Science* 37 (1984): 2-8.

[39]Norman Horrocks, "Dalhousie University. School of Library and Information Service," *Encyclopedia of Library and Information Science* 37 (1984): 65-70.

[40]Marcel Lajeunesse, "University of Montreal. School of Library and Information Science," *Encyclopedia of Library and Information Science* 18 (1976): 272-75; and "L'École de bibliothéconomie et des sciences de l'information de l'université de Montréal: Un quart de siècle de formation des professionnels de l'information (1961-1986)," *Argus* 16, no. 1 (mars 1987): 3-8.

[41]Deanna B. Marcum, "Library Education: A Challenge for the 1990s," *The Bowker Annual* 36 (1991): 83-89.

[42]Jean Riddle Weihs, "The Library Technician," *Canadian Libraries and Their Changing Environment*, 420-42.

[43]Henderson, "Professional Library Education in Canada," 400-1.

[44]Effie C. Astbury, "'Polite, cautious, but determined'," in *A Fair Shake; Autobiographical Essays by McGill Women*, ed. Margaret Gillett (Montreal: Eden, 1984), 260-67.

[45]Henderson, 401.

[46]Charles C. Williamson, *Training for Library Work: a Report Prepared for the Carnegie Corporation of New York* (New York, 1921). 276p.; and Vann, 89, 153.

[47]J. Periam Danton, *Between M.L.S. and Ph.D.; a Study of Sixth-year Specialist Programs in Accredited Library Schools* (Chicago: American Library Association, 1970), viii, 103p.

[48]Bishop, 36-37.

[49]University of Western Ontario. School of Library and Information Science, *Calendar 1968-1969*, 13.

[50]Ibid. (1990-1992), 15.

[51]Nasri, 424.

[52]Laurent-G. Denis and Lloyd J. Houser, "A Study of the Need for Ph.D.s in Library Science in Large Canadian libraries," *Canadian Library Journal* 29, no. 1 (January-February 1972): 19-27.

[53]Brian Land, "The University of Toronto. Faculty of Library Science," *Encyclopedia of Library and Information Science* 30 (1980): 472-91.

[54]"Ranking the Universities," *Maclean's, Canada's Weekly Newsmagazine* 104, no. 42 (October 21, 1991): 14-17.

[55]Canadian Association of Research Libraries, *Operating Expenses, 1989-90*. Table V.

[56]"Perspectives on the Elimination of Graduate Programs in Library and Information Studies: a Symposium," *Library Quarterly* 61, no. 3 (July 1991): 259-92.

[57]Donna J. Owens, "Statistics," *Canadian Library Yearbook, 1990* (Toronto: Micromedia, 1989): 47-63.

From: "Fanfares and Celebrations: Anniversaries in Canadian Graduate Education for Library and Information Studies / Fanfares et célébrations : anniversaires de la création des programmes des 2e et 3e cycles en bibliothéconomie et sciences de l'information au Canada" by Peter F. McNally in *The Canadian Journal of Information and Library Science/Revue canadienne des sciences de l'information et de bibliothéconomie* vol 18: 1 pp 6-22. Reproduced with permission.

Early Canadian Library Education:
The McGill and Ontario Experience,
1904-1927

Elizabeth Hanson

Abstract

This paper responds to the current lack of information on the history of library education in Canada and is an effort to promote a more informed appreciation of the development of Canadian librarianship. It focuses on the first two formal library education programs in Canada; these programs were were held as short courses in Montreal at McGill University and in Toronto between 1904 and 1927. Curricula, faculty, students, and pedagogical techniques are investigated using a variety of sources, including contemporary periodical articles, departmental annual reports, and personal correspondence. An effort is made to assess how well each program met the goals it seemed to set for itself. The courses are compared to each other, and their underlying philosophy is related to the thinking that sustained contemporary U.S. library education efforts. Finally, anecdotal evidence which suggests that the McGill and Toronto programs were successful and were much appreciated by their students is cited.

Résumé

Cet article vise à combler le manque d'information sur l'histoire de l'éducation en bibliothéconomie au Canada et à mieux faire connaître l'information sur le développement de la bibliothéconomie canadienne. L'article met l'accent sur les deux premiers programmes de bibliothéconomie au Canada, l'un à Toronto, l'autre a l'université McGill de Montréal, deux programmes courts offerts entre 1904 et 1927. L'article analyse les curriculums, la faculté, les étudiants et les méthodes pédagogiques en se basant sur des sources variées comme les périodiques de l'époque, les rapports annuels des départements et la correspondance personnelle. On tente d'évaluer jusqu'à quel point chaque programme rencontrait les objectifs qu'il s'était donnés. L'article compare les cours entre eux et associe leur philosophie à celle qui prévalait alors dans les établissements d'enseignement de la bibliothéconomie aux États-Unis. Finalement, on cite des anecdotes qui laissent supposer que les programmes de McGill et de Toronto furent un succès et qu'ils étaient fort appréciés des étudiants.

In his analysis of published research on Canadian library history in English from 1964 to 1984, Peter McNally identified library education as an area that "requires much work"; his subsequent review of the years 1985 through 1991 repeated this assessment.[1] For example, the University of Toronto is the sole library school with an entire monograph devoted to it, and McNally could point only to summaries of graduate and technical library education by Henderson and Weihs as other notable works.[2] And yet a deeper understanding of the educational tradition of librarianship in Canada would contribute considerably to Canadian librarians' appreciation of how their profession has developed.

This paper seeks to add to that understanding by looking at the two short library courses held at McGill from 1904 through 1927 and in Toronto between 1911 and 1927 — courses that marked the very beginnings of formal library education in Canada.

Informal Library Education

We know comparatively little about Canadian libraries and librarianship in the late nineteenth and early twentieth centuries, and one of the gaps in our knowledge is how informal library education was carried out during this time. We do know, however, that one approach used in the United States was adopted in Canada: apprenticeship training. When Charles Gould, the first university librarian at McGill University, wrote to university officials in late December 1903 or early 1904, he explained that "our own library, for 7 or 8 years past, has been obliged to receive a certain number of 'students in training.' Had this course not been followed it would have been impossible either to enlarge our staff or to fill vacancies in it without sending away from home to do so."[3]

Two glimpses of what it was like to be an apprentice in the McGill Library come from Sydney Mitchell, founder and dean of the School of Librarianship at Berkeley, and Mary Saxe, chief librarian of the Westmount Public Library and one of Canada's most prominent public librarians in the first third of the twentieth century. As Mitchell described his experience as an unpaid apprentice in the fall of 1901, he noted that

> My advent as the first male McGill graduate to become an apprentice in the Library was not so momentous a matter to anyone but myself that any special preparations had been made for my reception or instruction. I was simply given a desk in the general workroom which housed the head cataloger and her staff.[4]

There he began the study of cataloguing but also, "As Mr. Gould was a scholar and his interest was in scholarly libraries, I was given a good deal of background reading, such books as Putnam's *Libraries in the Middle Ages*, and was introduced to Cutter's *Rules for a Dictionary Catalogue* and to his *Expansive Classification*."[5] After Mitchell had served as an apprentice for three or four months, he was offered and accepted the paid job of supervising the reading room and circulation at McGill's Redpath Library.

Saxe served for 10 months as an apprentice at the Redpath in 1899, and in several letters to Gould she referred to this experience. In July 1899 she wrote to say that after her return in the fall, she "... would like it if you would let me keep at one branch of the work, until I feel I have mastered it. Now I have a good general idea of the whole but I cannot do anyone [sic] thing perfectly."[6] She also indicated in the same letter that over the summer she would practise writing, presumably the "library hand" which was then used for library records. In another letter she also asked if she could be paid for her work. This request indicates that she, too, received no salary.[7]

Mitchell's and Saxe's seemingly very different experiences while working under Gould may be due to the varied amounts of time they served as apprentices. It could also be the result of different assumptions about how men and women librarians should be trained, in accordance with stereotyped expectations of them. Another possibility is that Gould may simply have approached each one based on his sense of their interest and potential.

At the turn of the century, the University of Toronto Library under the leadership of H.H. Langton also accepted some women apprentices. However, Blackburn's comprehensive history of that library cites no exceptional librarians who emerged from that group.[8]

Beginning of the McGill Summer School

Partly as an outgrowth of his apprentice class, Gould initiated formal library education in Canada at McGill in June of 1904.[9] Prior to this, in December 1903, Gould had written to his good friend Melvil Dewey, "I have a plan in mind which I want to talk over with you and the earlier I can do it the better, but, as I have said, I should like very much to see the Library School in operation when I go to Albany."[10] The reference to Dewey's New York library school suggests that this plan related to establishing a library school at McGill. In a letter dated a week later, Dewey encouraged Gould to do just that:

> There is a growing demand for a high grade professional school for the training of public librarians in the Dominion .... It ought to be in the Metropolis. It ought to be connected with the strongest university. It ought to be under the man most closely identified with successful work in Canada, and that is yourself. McGill and Montreal fill the other conditions.[11]

Dewey went on to emphasize that although U.S. library schools were accepting Canadians,

> No American school can fully supply your needs. Your teaching must regard Canadian conditions. You must work from the standpoint of your laws, customs and popular interests and prejudices, must teach your public documents instead of ours and must lean more to English publications than we do. While there is much in common, there is difference enough to demand a school on your side.

Later that month or early in 1904, Gould, on behalf of the Library Committee, petitioned the McGill administration to establish a library school. He explained that the best way to train librarians was through "a combination of school training with practical work in a good library," and he went on to make a strong case for the need to establish such a school:

> Notwithstanding the increase in the number and size of libraries in Canada during the past 10 or 15 years, and the correspondingly increased demand for trained librarians, there has hitherto been no Canadian school in which such training might be obtained .... But .... the requests which we have received for admission to our library on the footing of apprentices have been sufficiently numerous and frequent to show that a very considerable desire for library training exists in this country and has existed for years.[12]

He emphasized that a yearly course of eight or nine months, supplemented by a summer course of about six weeks, was needed and that "such a course would not only supply a real demand but ... it could hardly fail to make the McGill Library the chief centre of library influence in the Dominion."[13] However, while asserting that the committee "feels that nothing less should be looked upon as desirable or permanent," Gould acknowledged that such a school might not be an immediate prospect. Therefore, he went on, "in order to make a beginning and to be of some assistance to a number of smaller libraries, your Committee recommends that a short course in Library Economy be given this summer."

In early April 1904, Gould wrote to Dewey, "I want you to know as soon as anyone that we are to start a summer course in Library science this year at McGill, and I hope that before the course is over we shall be in a position to speak definitely in regard to a school."[14] He was never able to achieve an academic-year school, but the decade during which he maintained the summer program should be seen as the foundation on which the sessional course was eventually built.

The first formal training in librarianship in Canada took place from June 4 to July 6, 1904. Gould was assisted by three instructors. Sydney Mitchell came directly from completing his studies at the New York State Library School, and Hanna Rodgers travelled up from the Pryn Library in Albany. A graduate of the New York State Library School and formerly a staff member of the New York State Library, Rodgers was recommended for the position by Mary S.C. Fairchild, vice-director of the New York State Library School. Dewey himself seems to have initially approached her about teaching at McGill. The third faculty member is identified only as a graduate of the Pratt Institute Library School.

The curriculum consisted of "classification, cataloging, accessioning, shelf-listing, charging and order system [*sic*], desk work and reference work, including elementary bibliography."[15] At least three pedagogical approaches were used: lectures, field trips (to a bindery, a printing office and various Montreal libraries), and special lectures. The last included talks by James Bain (Chief Librarian of the Toronto Public Library), Mary S.C. Fairchild, Mary W. Plummer, W.R. Eastman (Inspector of Public Libraries for New York), and Melvil Dewey (who wrote Gould, "I can talk as much Tuesday as they can stand").[16] The course included 108 hours of instruction and was in session from 9 a.m. to 5 or 6 p.m., Monday through Friday. Twenty-two students completed the full course and four finished part of it.

This summer program specifically focused on librarians already working in small, presumably public, libraries, but it also encouraged those who wanted to become librarians to attend. Indeed, in a 1906 article Gould presented a very wide sweeping perspective on the goal of the course:

> Its aim is to help. To help librarians already in active service to do better and more earnest work: to improve their methods, and quicken their enthusiasm. To help, train and interest those who would like to be librarians, but have as yet had neither experience nor instruction. To help Trustees and others entrusted with the conduct of libraries by enabling them, through more efficient librarians, to obtain results commensurate with the money invested in their libraries, and to help the public to appreciate more thoroughly than it does at present, the power for good lying as yet all but dormant, in the libraries present and prospective of the country.[17]

The summer school retained the same structure through 1914, when it was discontinued for the duration of the war. Indeed, so consistent was the course that for several years the brochure advertising the school remained unchanged. Throughout the period, tuition remained at $5.00, with essential supplies at $3.00.

In 1905 the course was extended to six weeks, but this proved impracticable and subsequently it seems to have been shortened to four weeks, seven hours daily with (at least after 1906) a half day on Saturday.[18] For at least the first few years, the staff remained quite stable. Sidney Mitchell taught for the first four years, Hanna Rodgers taught for the first three, and Harriet Peck of the Gloversville (New York) Public Library (and a graduate of the New York State Library School) taught in 1906 and 1907.

By at least 1906, practice work in McGill's Redpath Library had been added. Class work was revised daily and returned to the students to serve as a permanent guide. Also, readings were assigned which students then discussed at round tables.

No entrance requirements were mentioned until 1907, when the prospectus stated:

> No entrance examinations are required, and anyone who is actually filling a library position will be admitted. But it must not be forgotten that a most important qualification for success in a library is a good general education, and no one who has not already begun is advised to undertake such work without having obtained at least a High School diploma.[19]

This position remained unchanged until 1914, when the advertisement stated, "there is no entrance examination, but applicants for admission who are not actually filling library positions, are expected to hold at least a High School diploma."[20]

In terms of the curriculum, the only additions were made in 1906, when "Binding and Repairing Books" and "Library Buildings" were added, and in 1907 when "Travelling Libraries and Extension Work" and "Work with Schools and Children" were added. However, the second and fourth of these courses marked a significant augmentation of the offerings. The 1914 curriculum was exactly the same as for 1907.

Ontario Library School, 1911-14

During its early years, the McGill program served as an incentive for the development of library education in Ontario. In 1908, T.W.H. Leavitt, inspector of public libraries for Ontario, strongly urged the Minister of Education to establish a summer library school in the province. He argued:

> As the efficiency of a library depends in a great measure upon the librarian no means should be neglected for improving the knowledge of librarians concerning the work to be done. To this end it has been found necessary in the United States to establish Library Schools ....

For several years past Mr. C.H. Gould, B.A., librarian of McGill University, Montreal, has been conducting a summer school in that city .... The work done in the school has been excellent.[21]

However, as Leavitt went on to explain, this school clearly would not meet the needs of Ontario librarians:

The attendance from Ontario has been limited .... Experience having demonstrated that the librarians of Ontario cannot be induced to attend a school located in Montreal it becomes necessary to provide facilities for their instruction in Toronto. I therefore recommend that provision be made for establishing a Summer Library School.[22]

Leavitt clearly had something immediate in mind, for he spoke of the next summer when Toronto Public Library's new reference building might be available to the school.

The following year Leavitt died and the campaign was taken up by his successor, Walter R. Nursey. In his annual report for 1909, Nursey encouraged Ontario librarians to attend the McGill school, but also indicated that "the time has nearly arrived when facilities, similar to those provided in Montreal, should be extended to Toronto for the special instruction of Ontario's librarians."[23] Like Leavitt, he suggested that the school be held in the new Toronto Public Library building, and he concluded with the statement, "I respectfully recommend that initial steps be taken to provide for a Summer Library School in Toronto."[24]

In his 1910 report, Nursey pointed out that "the demand and need for a Summer Library Training School in Ontario is increasing" and stated that only four Ontario students had attended McGill's 1909 school.[25] He then went on to write, "I would respectfully suggest that provision be made in the estimates for a small sum sufficient to hold a library school at some suitable place this summer."

The efforts of these two successive inspectors were finally successful. In May 1911, Nursey received authorization to organize a provincial library school. He quickly issued a prospectus for the first summer session but still, "only two weeks remained ... in which to secure competent instructors, prepare a syllabus, select quarters, and correspond with prospective students," all with only minimal funding available.[26]

No provision for this school had been made in the legislative estimates for the Department of Education, so "the appropriation available was sufficient only to meet bare expenses. It was a question of not how much was wanted, but how little we could get along with."[27] However, despite the substantial difficulties, Mabel Dunham, instructor in charge, registered students for Ontario's first formal library education opportunity on June 14, 1911.

It is important to realize that the school was sponsored by the department for a very specific reason. Nursey stated in the prospectus that "The primary purpose of the Ontario Summer Library School is the raising of the standard of librarianship in the smaller libraries of the Province, the interests and needs of which will receive special attention."[28]

With this in mind, practising librarians were the preferred students for the school, as Nursey explained: "The special object of the Minister of Education is to extend facilities to those librarians who have expressed their desire to take such a course, and to give them an opportunity to generally enlarge their knowledge of literature, of library methods and administration."[29]

This focus shaped every aspect of the school. Since it was aimed at individuals who were currently working in Ontario public libraries, strong incentives were provided to encourage attendance by these librarians: "Books and bibliographical and other material for working purposes will be provided by the Department .... together with cards and stationery .... There is no Entrance or other fee. All expenses of conducting the school will be paid by the Department."[30] The department even paid the transportation costs of all students who completed the course.

The goal of training Ontario librarians also strongly influenced the selection of faculty, which

> was composed entirely of Canadians, residents of the Province, it being thought best in inaugurating the school to depend upon native talent exclusively, the endeavour being to follow the excellent advice of Mr. Gould, of McGill, and to "teach thoroughly what was taught," with special emphasis on cataloguing and classifying.[31]

Instructors were recruited from the Ontario Department of Education Library, the Toronto Public Library, and the University of Toronto Library; Dunham was from the Berlin (now Kitchener) Public Library (Ontario). Literature was taught by Professor L.E. Horning of Victoria University. Among those giving special lectures were E.A. Hardy, secretary of the Ontario Library Association and a key figure in the development of Ontario libraries; W.O. Carson, then librarian of the London Public Library; H.H. Langton, University of Toronto librarian; George Locke, chief librarian, Toronto Public Library; and Nursey himself.

The school ran for four weeks and met in the Department of Education's Model School. The curriculum included literature, library methods, classification and cataloguing, administration, reference work, travelling libraries, and work with children. The emphasis on small libraries resulted in one unexpected broadening of the curriculum. Lectures on literature were included because the Inspector felt that "there are many to-day engaged in library work who have never acquired the culture conferred by wide, general reading that should be a qualification even in the case of the ordinary librarian."[32] The classification system taught was the Dewey Decimal system, surely because it was "the one recommended by the Department of Education for use in Ontario."[33]

Pedagogical techniques included lectures, practical demonstrations, practice work, visits to branch libraries, and the special lectures. Classes ran from 9 a.m. to 4 or 5 p.m., Monday through Friday, with some Saturday sessions.

That first year, entrance examinations were not administered but "candidates are supposed to have a High School course or its equivalent."[34] Among the women students, who comprised all but two of those enrolled, four had college degrees from the University of Toronto or "affiliated colleges."[35] Final exams were not given; students were instead evaluated on the basis of their attendance, notebooks and practice work.

Twenty-three students completed the 1911 course. The wide interest that the school generated was reflected in the broad geographic distribution of the communities from which these individuals came. One of them later wrote:

> That it was appreciated was shown by the attendance, librarians being present from Brockville and Peterborough in the East, and from as far North-West as Fort William and Sault Ste. Marie, North from Owen Sound and Bracebridge and West from Windsor, Chatham, Sarnia, South from the Niagara peninsula, and from Morrisburg, on the St. Lawrence.[36]

Dunham commented:

> They came too, with as many different grades of qualifications and as many varied degrees of experience in library work. Twelve were chief or only librarians, seven were assistants, seven others had had absolutely no experience in library work, four were ex-librarians and one was the official classifier and cataloguer of the Education Department.[37]

For the next few years, the school retained much the same approach.[38] From 1912 to 1914 the classes were held at the University of Toronto but were still sponsored by the provincial department of education. Each year between 24 and 30 students, most of whom were from small libraries, completed the course.

One 1913 addition to the staff was particularly noteworthy. In September 1912, Miss Lillian Helena Smith came to the Toronto Public Library to organize its children's services. A graduate of the training school for children's librarians at the Carnegie Library in Pittsburgh, Smith (a Canadian by birth) "became the first trained children's librarian in the British Empire."[39] She subsequently became an internationally known authority in children's services and was a tremendous addition to the Ontario library school's faculty.

The year 1914 signified the close of the first phase of development for both programs discussed here. When each resumed after at least a year's hiatus it was under different leadership.

Ontario Library School, 1916-27

In 1916 the Ontario Library School re-opened under the direction of W.O. Carson, the newly appointed inspector of public libraries and former librarian of the London Public Library. That year the program changed from a one-month summer school to a one-month fall course. Classes were held in the Dovercourt Branch of the Toronto Public Library.

As before, the course was designed for practising librarians. Carson wrote that "persons without experience or library positions were not encouraged to take the course, as such a course is not a short-cut to a library position for those without experience in the work," and 30 out of the 31 students did have library experience.[40] They came from across the province: "from Fort William and Port Arthur on the west, to Kingston and Kemptville on the east."[41] Also attending were the librarian of the Saint John Public Library (New Brunswick) and a Canadian who had worked in a Cleveland, Ohio, library. Certificates for completion of the course were given to 26 people.

The focus of the curriculum was on "the first essentials that are difficult to learn without a teacher," and these were approached from a public library perspective.[42] The curriculum included Book-selection, Elementary bibliography, Evolution of modern prose literature, Reference work, Classification, Cataloguing, Shelf-listing and accession work, Circulation and Readers' Advisory work, Work with children, Public library and community welfare, Administration and secretarial work, and Simple routine.[43]

As before, no entrance exams were required, although students "were advised that they should have at least four years' high school training and a liberal education gained through general reading."[44] Evening practice work in the Toronto Public Library branch libraries was incorporated into the course, and exams now tested practical as well as written performance.

The teaching staff was composed of five instructors. This session saw the first involvement of Winifred G. Barnstead in library education when she became chief instructor; previously she served as Chief of the Cataloguing Department at the Toronto Public Library. Dorothy Bray, who had just graduated from Western Reserve University Library Training School in Cleveland, came from the Thamesford Public Library (Ontario). Two of the other instructors, Lillian Smith and Gertrude Boyle, were from the Toronto Public Library, while the last one, Marion Baxter, was from the London Public Library. Special lectures were also given by George Locke; W.J. Sykes, librarian of the Ottawa Public Library; and E.A. Hardy, among others.

After 1916, the school (known as the Training School for Librarianship from 1919 on) could be considered a partnership between the Department of Education and the Toronto Public Library. Every year between 1916 and 1922, Carson gave thanks to the Library Board and Locke for providing classroom space, instructors and special lecturers and facilities for practice work. Between 1919 and 1927 the course was held in the Toronto Public Library's main building.

Between 1917 and 1927, the reports of the Inspector of Public Libraries to the Ontario Department of Education indicate that while the school retained the same basic structure, it was decidedly upgraded in several areas and its focus shifted somewhat.

The first area to be upgraded was the length of the course. The 1917 session was extended to two months "after consultation with the instructors, a few of the librarians that were likely to send students, and then with the Department."[45] In spite of this extension, however, Carson indicated that although "the results were very satisfactory ... the time was still very short."[46]

A portent of the further extension of the course had actually come in the previous year's report, in which Carson argued strongly that

> A short course library training school of one month is of some value, and of considerable value to those who have had experience in the use of modern methods, but efficiency on the part of librarians generally cannot be expected until a longer and more thorough course is established. A standard library school course covers one, and sometimes two academic years of about eight months each. No adequate course has been established as yet in Canada, and the need for something better than a one month course is apparent.[47]

He went on to argue for a three-month course. The first part would be

> a short course, similar to the one held in 1916 ... in order to provide
> a one month's course for those who may desire it or cannot spend a
> greater length of time in Toronto. The candidates who wish a three
> months' course will remain for the second and third months, which
> time will be devoted to an elaboration, extension and more inten-
> sive study of the subjects and practice dealt with in the first month
> or shorter course.

The achievement of just such a three-month course in 1919 was the biggest
advance that the school had made up to 1927.

It is interesting to note that the curriculum remained virtually
unchanged, despite the extra time allowed. The relative weight probably
shifted, however. In 1917 Carson wrote,

> The principal subjects taught were: Book-selection, Cataloguing,
> Classification, Children's Work, Reference Work, and Circulating
> Work. Other subjects upon which a few lectures were given were:
> Administration, Community Welfare, Modern Literature, Shelf-
> listing and Accession Work, and Simple Routine.[48]

"The Evolution of Modern Prose Literature" became the topic of several
"literary lectures."[49] Among the principal subjects, cataloguing "received
more time than was given to any other subject," presumably because it "is a
technical branch of the work that is difficult either to teach or learn."[50] An
Ontario Library Review article by students of the school gives additional
insight into the structure of the curriculum. Their information can be tab-
ulated thus:

Topic	Number of Lectures	Practice Sessions
Book selection	7	several sessions
Cataloguing	16	48 hours
Classification	17	34 hours
Reference	7	20 hours
Children's Work	10	4 or 8 sessions
Circulation	5	8 sessions[51]

Interestingly, the 1919 curriculum as presented in the promotional
brochure was word for word the same as the 1917 curriculum, except that the

latter also included "Public Library and Community Welfare." The feeling seemed to be, then, that the depth rather than the breadth of the course needed attention.

In addition to the length of the course, the qualifications of the students also changed between 1916 and 1927. Carson was still committed to training practising librarians, but he gave a doleful assessment of the students attending between 1916 and 1918:

> we assumed that each student would, through experience, have gained an insight into librarianship, but the great majority of the students had little or no experience, and a number of them had a kind of experience that was of little value to them in the study of modern librarianship. The ones that had had experience that was really worth while were very few in number.[52]

While there is little evidence that the students' level of experience improved, it seems certain that their level of education did. In 1917 an article in the *Ontario Library Review* explained, "no educational test is required, but candidates from town and city libraries should have junior matriculation standing or its equivalent"; this statement is repeated in the 1919 brochure.[53] In the latter year, competition developed for places in the school. Carson reported that "forty-three students attended the school, and several applicants could not be admitted for want of accommodation."[54] The next year, 41 students attended, 37 from Ontario, one each from Prince Edward Island, Nova Scotia and New Brunswick, and even one from as far away as China.

In 1921 Carson explained that applicants without university degrees or honors matriculation standing "were required to pass an entrance examination which included questions on history, literature and current events."[55] The class was limited to 30 students. In 1922

> ... the average educational and other qualifications of the students were the highest we have had. We had fifteen university graduates, and the remainder of the class had matriculation standing or something higher. Following the principle adopted last year an entrance examination was required of those who were not university graduates. The applications we receive for entrance greatly outnumber the maximum we can accept."[56]

Along with the curriculum, the teaching faculty remained much the same through 1927. The position of instructor in charge was filled by four different women during the period — Miss A.P. Dingman of the Cleveland

Public Library (but originally from Stratford, Ontario) in 1917, Louise Gahan of the London Public Library in 1918, and Gertrude Boyle in 1919. After that, Dorothy A. Thompson of the Ontario Public Libraries Branch took over through 1927.[57]

With the longer course came a shift in the goals of the school. Carson was as convinced as Nursey that the school should focus on educating practising librarians. But whereas up until 1918 the school emphasized librarians from small public libraries, with the lengthening of the course it subtly shifted to librarians from larger institutions. In 1919 the school was divided up into two programs, with the first one-month session labelled a "small libraries" course.[58] In *The Faculty of Library Science, University of Toronto, and its Predecessors, 1911-1927*, Bertha Bassam explains, however, that "only five students from small libraries chose to take the one-month short course and this experiment was never repeated."[59]

In the years that followed, there were definite indications that the focus was shifting. In 1919, a decidedly varied class came for training: "five types of libraries were represented in the class of 38 members: public, normal school [teacher training], university, social service, and government department."[60] A second indication that attention was moving away from the small public library came in Carson's 1921 prognostication that "the time has come when we should have a special course for training the librarians of the smaller towns."[61] He continued to push for this "special course" in subsequent years but to no avail.

Carson's push for two short courses of varying length was only part of a complete restructuring of the provincial library education offerings. In his 1918 report he wrote,

> Conditions in Ontario really require three types of library training schools (1) a short course covering one month for the training of librarians in small towns and general assistants in town and small city libraries; (2) a course similar to the one given in 1918 but extended over three months; (3) a full course covering an academic year .... I have good reason to believe that a full-term course covering approximately eight months, would be highly appreciated by the libraries of Ontario, and would be patronized to an extent that would justify the establishment of such a school.[62]

Eventually, the Ontario school did give way to a full academic-year course in library science. In 1928, at the urging of the provincial department of education, the University of Toronto established its library school under the leadership of Winifred Barnstead.

McGill Library School, 1920-27

In 1920 the McGill Library School was re-opened under the direction of Dr. Gerhard Lomer, Gould's successor as McGill University Librarian and graduate of the first library school session at that university. Peter McNally has acknowledged Dr. Lomer as the co-founder of the McGill library school and has argued that Lomer made his greatest mark on librarianship as a library educator.[63]

The school met for the four weeks of June and included 150 hours of lectures and practice work. The much more detailed curriculum was laid out in four parts as follows:

Technical courses
> Elementary cataloguing
> Classification
> Book numbers
> Accessioning
> Shelf-listing
> Binding and repairs
> Alphabeting [sic], filing, and indexing
> Library handwriting and typewriting

Bibliographic courses
> Reference work
> Book selection and subject bibliography
> Trade bibliography and ordering
> History of books and printing
> Periodicals and serials

Administrative courses
> Introduction to library routine
> Library administration
> Library buildings, equipment and supplies
> Printed forms and printing
> Loan administration

Special lectures
> Publicity and extension work
> Travelling libraries
> The school library

As to faculty, Harriet Peck returned from the Rensselaer Polytechnic Institute in Troy, New York, and Mary M. Shaver, cataloger at the Vassar

College Library, was the second instructor who assisted Lomer. Special lectures were given by the heads of McGill's Circulation and Travelling Libraries departments; Mary Saxe, chief librarian of the Westmount Public Library; and Charlotte Houston, librarian at the Montreal High School.

The school met 9 a.m. to 5 p.m., Monday through Friday, and Saturday morning. On most mornings an hour-long lecture on cataloguing was followed by practice work in this area. The afternoon sessions also included lectures and practice work on other topics.

Lomer gave no specific indication of an aim for the school in the official 1920 prospectus. But in the promotional material he developed to advertise the school's re-opening, he explained that in the earlier "decade of its activity it trained numbers of library assistants who have since filled positions in various parts of the country. The School has also provided additional training for librarians in active service who have wished to become acquainted with the best methods of library routine."[64] By evoking this particular mission, Lomer presumably intended to suggest that the school would retain the same thrust.

According to the prospectus, "particular attention is paid to the study of reference books and to practical aspects of work in a small library."[65] The prospectus also emphasized that both the "Library Administration" and "Library Buildings" courses focused on the small library. Likewise, the "Reference" course was designed to give "the student practice in looking up the miscellaneous information generally asked for in public libraries," and in the "Periodicals and Serials" course "Lists of periodicals suited for public libraries are supplied."[66] Thus, as in the school's earlier embodiment, the emphasis was on students who were already or would be working in small public libraries.

Information about the McGill summer school in the post-World War I years is sparser than for the Ontario Library School, but it basically tells the story of a school whose mould was set in 1920 and was in many ways adhered to throughout the rest of its existence. The school met in the Redpath Library. In 1922 the school was able to move into a new wing that considerably improved its facilities.

In terms of curriculum, the offerings for 1920 and 1921 were exactly the same — even down to the wording in the brochure — except that three courses offered in 1920 and listed for 1921 were not actually offered during 1921. The 1922 schedule showed all the 1921 offerings except for three special lectures. The three 1920 courses not offered in 1921 were reinstated in 1922, however.

In 1923 three of the topics which had previously been the subject of special lectures became listed as regular courses, and "Literature for Children" and "Museums and Their Use" were added as courses. The 1924 offerings mirrored those of 1923; there was no school in 1925. The 1926 brochure was almost verbatim that of 1924, except for "Book Selection," "Medical Libraries" and "Business Libraries" being added as lectures. In 1927 several notable additions were made to the curriculum, including "Subject Headings," "Public Library Work," and two reference courses, "Use of Reference Books" and "Study of Selected Reference Books and Assigned Problems." That year, "Library Handwriting and Typing" was dropped.

A daily schedule for 1922 that survives gives insight into the relative weight assigned to the various subjects covered and the emphasis given to practice work. That year, 21 hour-long lectures were devoted to cataloguing alone, while 31 hours were devoted to all other topics combined. Many subjects received only an hour's attention with one or two hours of practice attached. In regard to practice hours, 39 hours were spent on cataloguing and a total of 30 on all other topics.

Two distinct features of the program that were considerably emphasized were the special lectures and the Saturday afternoon excursions. In 1924, the latter included tours to the Art Association of Montreal, the Art Book Binding and Loose Leaf Company, the Bibliothèque Saint-Sulpice, the Château de Ramezay, the David Ross McCord National Museum, the Dominion Press and Mercury Press, the Fraser Institute Free Public Library, the Mechanics' Institute of Montreal, the McGill Medical Library, the Montreal Public Library, and the Westmount Public Library.

The list of libraries may be less illustrious than it would appear, however. When Lomer wrote to Mary Saxe, chief librarian of the Westmount Public Library, in 1922 in reference to the school's visit to her library, he termed it "one of the few live libraries here from which we can learn anything."[67]

The special lectures, while still an important part of the school, had lost the international lustre with which Gould had imbued them. In 1922 all the speakers were from Montreal and virtually all from McGill. The prospectuses from 1924 through 1927 reflect the addition of several lecturers from Queen's University and the Public Archives of Canada, but no international figures were included.

In regard to the faculty, Lomer served as chief instructor every year. Before 1923 or 1924, however, the other two instructors varied considerably but were usually Americans. Harriet Peck came back for the first two years, and in 1920 and 1922 Mary M. Shaver, a cataloger at Vassar College, assisted. Katherine M. Christopher, librarian at Julia Richman High School in New York City, taught in 1921, and the following year Blanche McCrum, Washington and Lee University Library, also served. After at least 1924, E.V. Bethune, assistant cataloger at the University of Toronto Library, and Mary Duncan Carter, assistant librarian at Skidmore College, consistently taught.

The school seemed proud of the fact that its graduates held positions across Canada and in the United States. Its 1924 and 1926 prospectuses include a list of libraries in Montreal, the rest of Canada, and the U.S. in which graduates had worked or continued to work. These included public, academic, provincial, federal, school and special libraries.

From the beginning, Dr. Lomer worked to replace the summer school with a full sessional course. In December 1921 he presented to Sir Arthur Currie, principal of McGill, a detailed proposal to this effect. In early 1922 the governors approved it, and Lomer anticipated that the new course would begin the next fall. But this did not occur, probably due to lack of funding, and the summer sessions remained the only offering until 1927. That year Lomer was able to secure a Carnegie grant through the American Library Association Board of Education for Librarianship, and in the fall he initiated the sessional course, which became the first such offering in Canada.

Evaluation

These, then, were the two short programs through which Canadians were first introduced to library education in the early twentieth century. In order to evaluate them, we first need to frame the goals the schools sought to accomplish. The first of these goals was to establish a new standard of professionalism for Canadian librarianship. The founders of both schools argued that libraries were important institutions that deserved good leadership; this leadership, in turn, required a sound education. In a 1906 article about the McGill program, Gould wrote,

> If it [the library] ... is to yield adequate returns, it needs to be administered with great ability. The business men who act as trustees of libraries can no more afford to employ untrained librarians than they can afford to put inexperienced or incompetent heads over commercial undertakings .... [The library] ... is probably able to reach and influence a larger proportion of the population than any other single agency. Surely then, the librarian who directs and applies this influence ought to possess not only natural qualifications, but a thorough preparatory training.[68]

In his first annual report as Ontario Inspector of Libraries, Nursey wrote,

> The vital need for competent librarians in the furtherance of library work ... was never more speakingly demonstrated than in the conditions ... that to-day confront us .... A library ... is a great temple of educational possibilities, employment in which means a tribute to superior attainments and special fitness.[69]

The second goal was to implement this standard among present and prospective public librarians.

How well did these programs succeed in achieving their goals? The question needs to be answered in light of the development of public libraries in Canada, but at this point we know comparatively little about this process beyond the fact that most early twentieth-century Canadian public libraries were in Ontario. However, a number of observations can still be made.

The barriers that lay in the way of achieving the first goal were considerable, and were both attitudinal and financial. First, in many communities the position of librarian held few expectations among either those who hired for or held the job. In 1909 Nursey lamented,

> Not only have rural, but even urban libraries, been turned into asylums for pensioners on the mere good will of a municipality. Many an unsuitable tenant has been pitch-forked into a responsible library position .... The trouble is that after a library has been turned into a "haven," the ratepayer who might have courage enough to suggest a change, would be anathema. The library is the least suitable place in the world as a dry-dock for derelicts.[70]

Sydney Mitchell had run into this reality in 1907 when he began to look for a new position. He became interested in applying for one in the public library of Winnipeg where his sister had moved but "after investigation my brother-in-law told me that the job was promised to a previously displaced schoolman on the condition that he keep sober."[71]

The problem, then, was that library positions were seen as jobs for which no training was needed and therefore for which a local untrained person could well be appointed. In late 1904 Lawrence Burpee, later to be appointed librarian of the Ottawa Public Library, ruefully wrote to Gould, "I fear there is no hope of persuading the committee to appoint anyone outside of Ottawa. There are too many applicants already in sight."[72]

In 1908 Leavitt described what could be considered the result of this policy:

> I find that the great majority of small libraries, suffering from dry rot, are afflicted with the following evils:
> (a) An incompetent librarian who neglects to attend Library Institutes — who does not read the literature upon library problems prepared by the Education Department and the Ontario Library Association — who possesses no knowledge of modern library methods — who is opposed to all changes which would involve additional work and activity — who resists every attempt made to abolish

absurd restrictions and clings with tenacity to a policy long since discarded and worthless.

(b) A Library Board guided and influenced by an incompetent librarian.[73]

A major financial barrier to the adoption of the proposed new standard for librarians arose from the fact that in the early twentieth century Canadian public libraries served and were supported by individual communities. County libraries were many years in the future. Many libraries therefore had too small a financial base to afford a trained librarian. In 1918 Carson indicated that 286 of the 425 free and association libraries in Ontario subsisted on an annual income under $500.[74]

On the other hand, the resources of the schools were such that only a comparatively small number of individuals could be trained each year. Therefore, if the two programs had widely succeeded in promoting the need to hire trained librarians, they would not have been able to keep up with the demand.

In regard to the second goal, how well were these programs able to train the students they did enrol? In both cases, the length of the program was dictated by the options available to the potential students. Hanna Rodgers explained that in 1906 the McGill program was cut back from six weeks to four "because of the difficulty facing librarians who wished to attend, of leaving their work for a greater length of time."[75] In 1917 Carson, despite the previous year's call for a three-month program, lengthened the course to only two months. He compromised because he came to feel that the cost for students to remain in Toronto for that time "would prevent many librarians and assistants from attending. Until more liberal salaries are paid by public libraries, two months will be as much time as can be given to a short course with reasonable prospects of securing a good attendance."[76] Bassam enlarged on the low salaries Ontario librarians earned:

> In the 175 free public libraries only five librarians received salaries of $2000 or more, while 65 were paid in the $700 to $1000 range. In the face of these facts Mr. Carson and his advisers considered that the Department was not justified in offering a three months' course. Until larger salaries were paid, it was agreed that a two months' course was all the libraries and librarians could afford.[77]

Both schools recognized that the time limitations on their sessions severely restricted what they could accomplish. In describing a summer school such as he had in mind, Leavitt wrote, "schools of the class suggested are primary in character,"[78] and in the 1911 prospectus for the Ontario Library School's first session Nursey explained,

This short course is not expected to provide a full training, but to extend an opportunity to acquire a fundamental knowledge of library economy and modern library methods, care being taken to confine demonstrations, laboratory work and problems to those conditions and phases of work ordinarily met with in the daily routine of the average library .... It is not expected that a four weeks' course would enable any one not thoroughly familiar with library work to qualify as an expert, but to the ambitious student should prove of great benefit.[79]

In 1906, after arguing the case for the McGill program, Gould wrote, "Such facts speak loudly for the value of the training given — elementary though it is."[80] In the same issue of the *Canadian Municipal Journal* Hanna Rodgers, one of the early McGill instructors, wrote that the duration of the 1904 session "was too short for effective work" and went on to explain:

No attempt has been made to cover, even in a smattering fashion, the full course of a professional library school ... and little comparative work in methods has been even suggested. One simple but effective method of classifying and cataloguing the books and keeping the other necessary records with the greatest clearness and least expenditure of time and money, has been taught ... and the scope of the reference books and bibliographies most valuable to a small library impressed upon the students' attention by the very practical questions.[81]

Such limitations prompted both schools to focus on practical skills. As Alice Millard wrote of McGill in 1906, "The teaching is eminently practical, [with] every facility being given the students to gain a working knowledge." And, as has been noted in connection with the 1922 daily schedule, considerable time was allocated to practice work.[82]

Carson in Ontario criticized the one-month course in that it "allowed very little time for practice work."[83] With the expansion of the course in 1918 to two months, however, it was promised that "one half of the time will be devoted to lectures and instruction and one half to practice."[84] But the brochure advertising the 1919 Training School for Librarianship told another story, stating that "about forty per cent of the time will be devoted to lectures and instruction and about sixty per cent. to practice."[85]

Of the two schools, McGill always had the broader vision. This was largely due to the setting, the individuals involved, and the specific outlook of the program. The international scope of the McGill program was at its apex under Gould, who recruited largely American librarians as instructors and drew his special lecturers from among the most prominent U.S. librarians. He placed considerable stress on the latter:

> A feature of the summer course on which strong emphasis is laid, consists in the lectures on special topics which have been delivered each year by a number of the most noted and successful librarians of Canada and the United States. The students derive much knowledge and great inspiration from these lectures.[86]

Also, the Saturday afternoon excursions that Lomer developed gave the students a cursory acquaintance with a wide variety of libraries. In addition, Lomer continued Gould's tradition of drawing faculty largely from among U.S. librarians.

Finally, the school's affiliation with a well-known university probably prompted a greater emphasis on academics. This was certainly true for Gould, who in 1915 wrote to a prospective student that

> the better one's general education, the better librarian — other things being equal .... Very few librarians have time to read during their working hours; but every librarian should do reading out of hours, and should have a special line of study apart from his regular library work, which he can pursue independently.[87]

Prospective as well as practising librarians were always encouraged to enrol at McGill. By at least 1913, its prospectus included a section that specifically discussed the benefits the school could provide to the librarian, the library assistant, the school teacher, the business woman and the college student. Thus they were successful in attracting a variety of students. In 1906 Hanna Rodgers wrote,

> The students of the three classes have included not only those already in library work who felt the need of more technical training in modern methods and wished a broader outlook of the whole field, but also some who wished to have an intelligent idea of modern library work from the educational point of view; and a larger number who sought active service without realizing definitely what they wanted.[88]

Both Gould and Lomer wanted to transform the summer school into an academic-year program. In his initial letter to the McGill administration, Gould portrayed the summer school as just a starting point. In a 1906 *Public Libraries* article, he wrote under "Plans for future":

An eight months' course, complete in one year, with an independent summer course of four to five weeks, the latter especially intended for librarians and assistants of smaller libraries and for teachers …. It is hoped that the full course can be so framed as to be especially useful to Canadians, while at the same time broadening the outlook of the student.[89]

In fact, Sidney Mitchell indicated that he was lured back to McGill in 1904 by Gould's indication that "he had hopes of the endowment of a library school at McGill; that, if and when this was obtained, he wanted me on hand to take charge of it."[90]

For the most part, however, observations regarding McGill's broader scope do not reflect negatively on the Ontario Library School, because the latter had a somewhat different focus. Ontario pursued the same broad goals as McGill but always with specific reference to the public libraries of its province. Whereas McGill wanted to promote library education as an end in itself, Ontario considered library education a tool to improve public libraries in the province. This difference is important, for it could be said that while Gould and Lomer were most interested in librarianship, Nursey and Carson were more concerned with libraries.

Additionally, the restrictions the Ontario Library School placed on itself were less limiting than they might at first seem. For example, the policy of limiting its faculty and special lecturers to Ontario librarians still gave them the pick of some of the most prominent librarians in the country. H.H. Langton, George Locke, and Lillian Smith were among the cream of Canadian librarians. Also, the limitation of field trips to Toronto Public's branch libraries was not only appropriate for a school that focused on producing public librarians, but also gave students a chance to observe the workings of one of Canada's truly outstanding public libraries. A 1916 *Ontario Library Review* article touted the Dovercourt Branch, where the school was held, as "one of the best modern branch library buildings on the continent, where the most approved methods are in use, and splendid work is being accomplished."[91]

Bassam suggests, however, that the policy of discouraging prospective librarians from attending the Ontario school may well have undermined to a certain extent the school's ultimate goal of improving public librarianship in the province. Yet given the school's emphasis on upgrading the present public libraries, it might have seemed reasonable to focus on upgrading the skills of those already working in these libraries. Also, the school was funded by provincial money and, as Nursey wrote, "I am unable to discover any Library School either in Canada, the British Empire, the

United States, or any other country in the world, which extends such generous privileges."[92] Finally, in 1922 Carson justified his stance in light of the current job market:

> Ontario should have about seventy vacancies annually for qualified librarians and assistants, but the absence of regulations reduces the number called for to about thirty-six and nearly half of them are for the city of Toronto. The great majority of our students come to us with some position in view; they are prospective appointees for some library. We do not feel safe in encouraging even the best type of candidates who have nothing in view and want to become trained in the hope of obtaining a good position.[93]

Bassam observes, however, that he took this position even further:

> This was no idle statement as Mr. Carson neither encouraged able young university graduates to take a full course of professional training in the United States where good, varied public library experience was available to them, nor did he try to place in Ontario public libraries those who, at their own expense had qualified in this way for library service.[94]

And in her opinion, this stance created future problems for Ontario libraries: "This was a surprising attitude for the professionally minded Mr Carson to take and the shortage of fully qualified librarians for senior positions in Ontario in the late 1920's seems to indicate that it was also an unfortunate decision."[95]

Comparison with U.S. Library Education

In the United States what Carl White has termed a "popular summer school movement" began at Amherst College in 1891 when William I. Fletcher began his one-man library school.[96] By the early twentieth century, when the two short courses at McGill and Toronto had a monopoly on library education in Canada, in the United States summer schools were but one of many library education efforts. This was largely because the period between 1887 and 1920 was, in White's words,

> a period of experimentation and the library school was only one of the institutional forms tried out. It gained and held first place in professional respect, but the head of one school estimated as of 1917 that competing agencies were turning out two to three times as many librarians each year as the library schools were.[97]

White explains that shortly after the beginning of the twentieth century, however, "the competition narrowed to library schools, apprentice and training classes, and summer schools."[98] In 1920 ALA's Committee on Library Training enumerated twelve summer schools, sponsored by Albany, Colorado Agricultural College, Columbia, Illinois, the Indiana Public Library Commission, Iowa State University, University of Michigan, Minnesota State Board of Education, University of North Carolina, Pennsylvania Free Library Commission, Simmons, and the Wisconsin Free Library Commission.[99]

White commented on the variety among the sponsors, pointing out that "four of the twelve ... were conducted by state library commissions, seven by colleges, only three by regular library schools."[100] In commenting on the character and clientele of the summer school, he wrote, "Its greatest service lay in providing training that dealt as thoroughly as the time allowed with the essentials of running a small library. Its natural clientele were those who were tied to their communities by bonds not loosened by their library interests."[101]

White also explains that after World War I the summer schools never gained back their early popularity. He indicates that while some simply closed, others became regular library schools.[102]

The fact that the stamp of the U.S. programs is clearly visible on the Canadian ones is not surprising, since Gould worked so closely with Dewey, and Nursey acknowledged that the Ontario program was modelled on the McGill school: "It seems hard, after the Province has benefited by Mr. Gould's enterprise, to steal his powder, but as imitation is the sincerest form of flattery, he will forgive."[103] In terms of specific similarities, the Canadian emphasis on educating public librarians was also apparent in the United States, where "courses as well as placement records show a dominent [sic] interest in public libraries."[104] Several of the same pedagogical approaches were also emphasized on both sides of the border. For example, special lectures — which were such an important part of both Canadian programs — figured prominently in the New York Library School and therefore probably in other schools as well. Surely the most important function of these lectures was to inspire students. As White wrote in making a different point,

> What student could work with Dewey, an imaginative innovator in the organization and management of libraries, with a man of Dana's insight into the library's service potential, with Frances Jenkins Olcott as a founder of children's library work, and gain no more than a technician's grasp of what the library movement is all about?[105]

In the area of curriculum, it has already been noted how much emphasis was placed on cataloguing (and classification) in both the Canadian programs. The 1900 report of ALA's Committee on Library Schools established that at the turn of the century cataloguing also dominated the curriculum of most of the U.S. library schools. Vann summarized the statistical data presented in the report:

> at Drexel ... 40 per cent of the hours were allocated to it, and also at Albany ... 35.5 per cent of the hours were allocated to the subject. When cataloging and classification are considered as one subject ... Drexel allocated 42.9 per cent; Albany, 41.7 per cent; Illinois, 26.5 per cent; Pratt, 22.4 per cent.[106]

But the most telling indication that Canadian and U.S. library education were from the beginning rooted in the same thinking is reflected in what White holds up as ten "specific norms of educational thought that gained acceptance during the period. They stand alone as presented, but together formed a single, well integrated system."[107] These included statements such as these two: "Professional learning is practical, not theoretical, and as such is separate and distinct from the aims, methods and results of academic scholarship;" and "The professional curriculum should provide the practical instruction that is needed to acquaint the student with library work and how to do it."

The Ontario Library School program would have supported all but two of the ten statements, namely, "Basic preparation for a career as librarian should consist of a course of study concentrated into a single academic year" and "Manning the profession with capabilities beyond those of the good craftsman is a recruiting responsibility"; the McGill program would have agreed with them all.[108] The Canadian programs therefore shared much the same educational philosophy as the U.S. programs.

Conclusion

How successful were these two Canadian programs? A thorough evaluation must await a fuller sense of how librarianship developed in Canada during the early twentieth century. But, based on student testimonials and other anecdotal evidence, both programs seem to have been effective.

In adjoining articles in the *Canadian Municipal Journal* in 1906, both Gould and Hanna Rodgers tried to enumerate the benefits which had accrued from the first three sessions at McGill. Rodgers wrote,

> The course has served as an eye-opener to many in showing the vast scope and possibilities of a library's usefulness in a community,

and its integral part of the whole educational system. It has taught some to so systematize and develop the resources of a small library as to double and even treble its influence. It has been an intellectual treat to many more ... in the ability acquired to use and open up ... knowledge by an intimate acquaintance with a few good tool-books of reference and bibliography.[109]

In his article, Gould related the story of one graduate:

The librarian of a medium sized library in a town several hundred miles from Montreal came to the school. She had been doing her best unaided, but had accomplished less than she wished to accomplish. On her return from the school, she was able to re-organize the whole library. Her work grew so fast that her trustees raised her salary, then secured her an assistant. Now her library is an assured success, she has a well-filled children's room and the work is extending rapidly.[110]

In the same year in *Public Libraries*, Alice Millard, a librarian at the Galt Public Library (Ontario), wrote about her experiences at McGill:

Although I had been in the work for some years I never had before such an insight into or true idea of what a librarian's work was, or what a library means to the people who come to read or borrow books .... in my work every day I realize how much benefit the school has been and is now to me.[111]

Subsequent student interest in the school also spoke well of McGill. Nursey indicated of it that "in order to test the hold this school had taken on its constituencies all advertising was omitted and no circulars issued in 1909" and it still had a successful school.[112] The absence of prospectuses for 1910 to 1912 in the archives of the school suggests that this might have been the policy for several years.

Lomer discovered how popular the school was in 1922 when he planned to discontinue it in anticipation of an academic-year course beginning that fall. In late March he wrote to Mary Shaver, "we have had so many applications for a summer course that I am writing to ask whether you could possibly teach here again this summer."[113]

The Ontario Library School also received high marks from its students. After completing the first session, a number of them expressed their appreciation, including two who wrote,

"I found the course of the Summer School very practical and helpful. I know my work as assistant librarian in our library will prove more efficient in the future."

"I feel that I owe my appointment to the library here in a great measure to the letter of recommendation the Inspector gave me and my course of study at the Library School."[114]

In 1917 a group of Ontario Library School students published an article in *Ontario Library Review* describing and evaluating the school. One individual gave an assessment of its overall value:

The importance to a librarian of the training afforded in such a course ... cannot be overestimated .... in a course covering so wide a field as that of the Departmental library school, the student is given a larger vision of librarianship, and training in every branch of it; in this way her value to the institution is greatly increased and to the assistant herself fresh fields of usefulness are opened up.[115]

The school's continuing popularity is reflected in the fact that, beginning in 1919, more individuals made application to the school than could be admitted.

Praise also came from several other quarters. In 1913 Nursey wrote, "Strong expressions of approval of ... [the school] have been voiced by representative speakers at every Library Institute," and a 1920 article in *Public Libraries* commented on its favourable reception:

Professional training in librarianship has taken hold splendidly. It is encouraging to all who are interested in library advancement to see the response that is being made to all that has been said and done about library training. Library boards are acknowledging the necessity for trained service and librarians and assistants are promoting it. The future is bright.[116]

Such evidence is too fragmentary to be the basis of a thorough evaluation; however, the evidence suggests that the two short programs at McGill and Toronto were quite successful in introducing library education into Canada. Certainly, these two schools were the direct progenitors of the country's first two academic-year library schools and as such they played an important role in the development of librarianship in Canada. Their spirit is summarized in the 1917 article written by an Ontario Library School student, who wrote,

We value to a high degree the tuition received, but the greatest and most lasting influence of the school was the inspiration and the broader outlook that the class received .... the outstanding influence was that which impressed one that it is grand and glorious to be a librarian, and that librarianship offers limitless opportunities for useful service to people.[117]

Acknowledgements

I would like to gratefully acknowledge the advice and assistance of Professor Peter McNally of the McGill University Graduate School of Library and Information Studies in the researching and writing of this paper and to thank him for the opportunity to deliver an earlier version to the Canadian Library Association Library History Interest Group at the CLA Conference in Halifax in June 1988. Professor George Whitbeck of the Indiana University School of Library and Information Sciences is also to be thanked for his encouragement of my research in library education. Finally, Dr. Robert Michel and Mr. Gordon Burr of the McGill University Archives provided much-appreciated assistance in connection with my archival research on Canada's first library school.

Notes

[1] Peter McNally, "Canadian Library History in English, 1964-1984: a Survey and Evaluation," in *Readings in Canadian Library History*, ed. Peter McNally (Ottawa: Canadian Library Association, 1986), 26; and Peter McNally, "A Review of Canadian Library History: 1985-1991," in this volume.

[2] McNally, "Canadian Library History in English, 1964-1984," cited above.

[3] C.H. Gould, *Report of the Library Committee re Establishment of a Summer School of Library Training*, University Archives, McGill University, Montreal, Quebec, 1. Undated but certainly written between December 1903 and April 1904.

[4] Sydney B. Mitchell, *Mitchell of California* (Berkeley: California Library Association, 1960), 103.

[5] Ibid., 104.

[6] Mary Saxe to Charles Gould, July? 1899, Charles Gould Papers, University Archives, McGill University.

[7] Mary Saxe to Charles Gould, undated but probably September 17, 1899, Charles Gould Papers, University Archives, McGill University.

[8] Robert H. Blackburn, *Evolution of the Heart: A History of the University of Toronto Library up to 1981* (Toronto: University of Toronto Library, 1989), 103-4.

[9] C.H. Gould, "McGill University, Montreal," *Public Libraries* 11, no. 3 (March 1906): 133.

[10] Charles Gould to Melvil Dewey, December 16, 1903, Charles Gould Papers, University Archives, McGill University.

[11]Melvil Dewey to Charles Gould, December 23, 1903, Charles Gould Papers, University Archives, McGill University.

[12]Gould, *Report of the Library Committee*, 1.

[13]Ibid., 2.

[14]Charles Gould to Melvil Dewey, April 4, 1904, Charles Gould Papers, University Archives, McGill University.

[15]See note 9 above.

[16]Melvil Dewey to Charles Gould, May 9, 1904, Charles Gould Papers, University Archives, McGill University.

[17]C.H. Gould, "McGill University Library School," *Canadian Municipal Journal* (July 1906): 251.

[18]Detailed information is not available for the years 1909 through 1912.

[19]McGill University, *Summer School for Librarians*, Fourth session, Montreal, June 3 to 29, 1907 (Montreal: McGill University, 1907), [1].

[20]McGill University, *Summer School for Librarians* (Montreal: McGill University, 1914), 2.

[21]Ontario, *Report of the Minister of Education, Province of Ontario, for the Year 1908* (Toronto: L.K. Cameron, 1909), 162.

[22]Ibid.

[23]Ontario, *Report of the Minister of Education, Province of Ontario, for the Year 1909* (Toronto: L.K. Cameron, 1910), 400.

[24]Ibid.

[25]Ontario, *Report of the Minister of Education, Province of Ontario, for the Year 1910* (Toronto: L.K. Cameron, 1911), 540 and 541.

[26]Ontario, *Report of the Minister of Education, Province of Ontario, for the Year 1911* (Toronto: L.K. Cameron, 1912), 547.

[27]Ibid., 552.

[28]Ibid., 545.

[29]Ibid.

[30]Ibid., 546, 552.

[31]Ibid., 553.

[32]Ibid., 545.

[33]Mary T. Butters, "Paper by Miss Mary T. Butters," in Ontario, *Report of the Minister of Education, Province of Ontario, for the Year 1911* (Toronto: L.K. Cameron, 1912), 554.

[34]Ontario, *Report ... 1911*, 545.

[35]"Library Schools and Training Classes," *Library Journal* 36 (August 1911): 434.

[36]Butters, 554.

[37]B. Mabel Dunham, "The Ontario Library Summer School 1911," in *Proceedings of the Ontario Library Association*, 12th Annual Meeting (Toronto: L.K. Cameron, 1912), 65.

[38]Information in this paragraph comes from Bertha Bassam, *The Faculty of Library Science, University of Toronto, and its Predecessors, 1911-1972* (Toronto: Faculty of Library Science in association with the Library Science Alumni Association, 1983), 10.

[39]Margaret Penman, *A Century of Service: Toronto Public Library, 1883-1983* (Toronto: Toronto Public Library, 1983), 30.

[40]Ontario, *Report of the Minister of Education, Province of Ontario, for Year 1916* (Toronto: A.T. Wilgress, 1917), 105-6.

[41]"Short Course Training School for Librarianship," *Ontario Library Review* 1 (September 1916): 35.

[42]Ontario, *Report … 1916*, 105.

[43]"Library Training School for 1917," *Ontario Library Review* (May 1917): 91-92.

[44]Ontario, *Report … 1916*, 106.

[45]Ontario, *Report … 1917*, 93.

[46]Ibid.

[47]Ontario, *Report … 1916*, 112.

[48]Ontario, *Report of the Minister of Education, Province of Ontario, for the Year 1917* (Toronto: A.T. Wilgress, 1918), 93.

[49]"The Training School for Librarianship," *Ontario Library Review* (November 1917): 56.

[50]Ontario, *Report … 1917*, 93.

[51]"The Training School for Librarianship," 53-57.

[52]Ontario, *Report of the Minister of Education, Province of Ontario, for the Year 1918* (Toronto: A.T. Wilgress, 1919), 132.

[53]"Library Training School for 1917," 91; and *Training School for Librarianship, 1919* (Toronto: A.T. Wilgress, 1919), 3.

[54]Ontario, *Report of the Minister of Education, Province of Ontario, for the Year 1919* (Toronto: A.T. Wilgress, 1920), 76.

[55]Ontario, *Report of the Minister of Education, Province of Ontario, for the Year 1921* (Toronto: C.W. James, 1922), 76.

[56]Ontario, *Report of the Minister of Education, Province of Ontario, for the Year 1922* (Toronto: C.W. James, 1923), 86.

[57]Bassam, 17.

[58]Ontario, *Report … 1920*, 105.

[59]Bassam, 17.

[60]"Province of Ontario", *Public Libraries* 25, no. 1 (January 1920): 46.

[61]Ontario, *Report … 1921*, 77.

[62]Ontario, *Report … 1918*, 132.

[63]Peter McNally, "Scholar Librarians: Gould, Lomer and Pennington," *Fontanus* 1 (1988): 99.

[64]"Summer Library School at McGill," attachment to letter to Miss Young, May 5, 1920, from Lomer, 2.

[65]McGill University, *Summer Library School* (Montreal: McGill University, 1920), [2].

[66]Ibid., [3]-[4].

[67]Gerhard Lomer to Mary Saxe, April 13, 1922, Gerhard Lomer Papers, University Archives, McGill University.

[68]C.H. Gould, "McGill University Library School," 251.

[69]Ontario, *Report … 1909*, 398.

[70]Ibid.

[71]Mitchell, 148.

[72]Lawrence Burpee to Charles Gould, November 23, 1904, Charles Gould Papers, University Archives, McGill University.

[73]Ontario, *Report ... 1908*, 151.

[74]Ontario, *Report ... 1919*, 79.

[75]Hanna H. Rodgers, "The Summer Library School at McGill University, Montreal," *Canadian Municipal Journal* (July 1906): 252.

[76]Ontario, *Report ... 1917*, 93.

[77]Bassam, 15.

[78]Ontario, *Report ... 1908*, 162.

[79]Ontario, *Report ... 1911*, 545.

[80]C.H. Gould, "McGill University Library School," 252.

[81]Hanna H. Rodgers, "The Summer Library School at McGill University, Montreal," 252-53.

[82]Alice G. Millard, "Letters from Librarians Who Have Been in the Schools," *Public Libraries* 11, no. 3 (March 1906): 138.

[83]Ontario, *Report ... 1917*, 93.

[84]"Library Training School for 1917," *Ontario Library Review* 1 (May 1917): 91.

[85]*Training School for Librarianship, 1919*, 3.

[86]C.H. Gould, "McGill University Library School," 252.

[87]Charles Gould to Marion Casselman, October 4, 1915, Charles Gould Papers, University Archives, McGill University.

[88]Rodgers, "The Summer Library School at McGill University, Montreal," 252.

[89]Gould, "McGill University, Montreal," 133.

[90]Mitchell, 140.

[91]"Short Course Library Training School," *Ontario Library Review* 1 (June 1916): 13.

[92]Ontario, *Report ... 1913*, 755.

[93]Ontario, *Report ... 1922*, 86.

[94]Bassam, 19.

[95]Ibid.

[96]Carl M. White, *A Historical Introduction to Library Education: Problems and Progress to 1951* (Metuchen, N.J.: Scarecrow Press, 1976), 93.

[97]White, 62.

[98]Ibid., 116-17.

[99]Ibid., 93-94.

[100]Ibid., 94.

[101]Ibid.

[102]Ibid.

[103]Ontario, *Report ... 1909*, 399.

[104]White, 88.

[105]Ibid., 144.

[106]Sarah K. Vann, *Training for Librarianship before 1923* (Chicago: American Library Association, 1961), 93-94.

[107]White, 139.

[108]Ibid., 148, 149 and 150.

[109]Rodgers, "The Summer Library School at McGill University, Montreal," 253.

[110]Gould, "McGill University Library School," 251.

[111]Alice G. Millard, "Letters from Librarians Who Have Been in the Schools," 138.

[112]Ontario, *Report ... 1909*, 399.

[113]Gerhard Lomer to Mary Shaver, March 23, 1922, Gerhard Lomer Papers, University Archives, McGill University.

[114]Ontario, *Report ... 1911*, 552.

[115]"The Training School for Librarianship," 53.

[116]"Province of Ontario" *Public Libraries* 25, no. 1 (January 1920): 46.

[117]"The Training School for Librarianship," 57.

3 Public Libraries

The Aims of the
Public Library Movement
in Late Victorian Ontario

Lorne D. Bruce

Abstract

The fundamental encouragement of free public library service in Ontario stemmed from late nineteenth-century reform liberals, who believed that government should undertake more positive action to improve society. Public library advocates developed important assumptions about local self-government and the nature of public control, finance and accessibility that gave their movement a distinctive character and an attractive political aura. To secure the passage of local library bylaws, the movement formulated a variety of successful arguments to justify the need for free public libraries. These explanations defined the public library's place within the emerging educational sphere, emphasized its economic advantages, identified social and cultural roles by which the library could improve society, and associated the public library with the advance of democratic principles in local government. During this process Victorian reformers created a lasting public institution that offered circulating adult and juvenile collections, reading rooms, and reference service to the entire public.

Résumé

Le mouvement réformiste libéral de la fin du dix-neuvième siècle est à l'origine du concept des bibliothèques publiques « gratuites » en Ontario. Les réformistes croyaient fermement que les gouvernements devaient agir pour améliorer la société. Les défenseurs de la bibliothèque publique firent valoir d'importants principes sur la gestion locale, la nature du contrôle public, les finances et l'accessibilité qui donnèrent à leur mouvement son caractère distinct et un aura politique assez attrayant. Pour faire passer les lois sur les bibliothèques locales, le mouvement proposa toute une gamme d'arguments positifs qui justifièrent les besoins. Ces explications définirent la place de la bibliothèque publique dans l'éducation, mirent l'accent sur ses avantages économiques, identifièrent les rôles sociaux et culturels que devait jouer la bibliothèque pour améliorer la société, et associèrent la bibliothèque publique au progrès de la démocratie dans le gouvernement local. En fait, les réformistes victoriens créèrent une institution publique solide qui prêtait des livres aux adultes et aux jeunes, disposait de salles de lecture et offrait un service de référence à toute la population.

There are numerous references to the concept of a public library movement in Ontario throughout the late Victorian era. In his *Address to the Board of Management of the Toronto Free Library*, John Hallam spoke glowingly of a "far reaching movement [that] is likely to extend to every city and considerable town in this Province."[1] Eighteen years later, in April 1901, James Bain's presidential address at the first Ontario Library Association conference was appropriately entitled "The Library Movement in Ontario." Bain enthusiastically outlined an ambitious agenda for action:

> The time is propitious. With the beginning of a new century we venture to look forward to new lines of work, to vast increase in the number and sizes of our libraries, and to extension in every direction which aims at the development of their true end — the mental advancement and culture of the people of this province.[2]

Clearly, Hallam and Bain believed there were important tasks for public libraries to fulfil; they were certain it was proper for government to supply libraries at public expense. Library growth between 1882 and 1901 indicates people in many Ontario communities were in agreement.[3]

It can be said that the public library movement was a positive influence on library development in late Victorian Ontario. The movement contributed to an underlying general consensus of liberal-democratic ideals that proposed the creation of a more literate, prosperous, devout and knowledgeable society.[4] Ontarians were prepared to accept that publicly funded and governed free libraries offered individuals the opportunity to improve their social well-being and, at the same time, helped to cure a number of social ills — poverty, ignorance, irreligion, alcoholism and crime — besetting society. Library enthusiasts of all political persuasions were inspired by the Utilitarian social doctrine of the greatest happiness of the greatest number.

In the area of social reform, most Victorians concentrated on the self-improvement of the individual rather than attempting to determine causes within the broader social structure. They assumed individual changes would aggregate to societal changes. Naturally, some of the movement's well-to-do upper-class members or conservatives were convinced that free libraries encouraged social stability through educational means rather than fostering radical political change.[5] However, the fundamental impetus to encourage support for libraries stemmed from the late nineteenth-century liberal creed that allowed government to undertake a more positive role to improve society and the lives of citizens from all classes.[6]

Free Public Libraries: An Agenda for Change
There were some appealing characteristics of free public libraries that facilitated the mobilization of public support for change in Ontario at the government level. In principle, as it developed in North America and Britain after 1850, free library service could be used by all community members without direct payment because the library transcended the divisions of social class. The library was locally managed by a public corporation, and library staff (normally few in number) strove to render the collection more accessible to those who used its resources. The movement's founders in Ontario emphasized that these democratic features distinguished free public libraries from libraries in Mechanics' Institutes or public schools.[7] Collections in these two agencies had been open to the public; however, they were only one part of each institution's activities and had not attracted extensive patronage.

Mechanics' Institutes were proprietary bodies with an ambitious educational program to teach artisans and skilled workers the scientific principles underlying manufacturing, crafts, and natural phenomena. But many people were becoming sceptical of the potential to reach individuals on a subscription basis, as Dr. Samuel May's landmark *Special Report of the Minister of Education on the Mechanics' Institutes (Ontario)* demonstrated in 1881.[8] The provincial government also acknowledged that Egerton Ryerson's public libraries in schools were "practically abandoned" by 1880; one commentator stated that they were prematurely forced upon ratepayers and that book selection was too rigidly centralized to suit many tastes.[9]

Free public library service exemplified important underlying liberal-democratic assumptions about local self-government and the nature of public control, finance and accessibility that gave the movement a distinctive character and an attractive aura within the political arena. After 1882, the authority and legitimacy for establishing libraries rested in a provincial enabling act whereby political activity was necessary at the municipal level to secure majorities for library bylaws.

At this time, educational concerns in Ontario were controlled locally; upon establishment, libraries were administered by an independent board of citizens appointed by school boards and municipal councils. Libraries were also publicly funded by an established rate of taxation, a maximum 1/2 mill on ratable local assessment, which the library board could request from council each year. Finally, public access was maintained in terms of local proximity and availability of standard resources: reading rooms, circulating collections, reference departments, and adequate accommodation were considered necessary by most advocates. To secure passage of local library bylaws, the movement had to develop persuasive arguments to justify the need for free libraries within the emerging structure of local government activities.[10]

Educational Qualities: The "Caliban of the Nineteenth Century"

Voters who approved free library bylaws[11]; supporters who signed petitions, attended or spoke at meetings, wrote letters to newspapers, or helped organize local committees; and the movement's directors were all attracted by a variety of reasons advanced for establishing libraries. Many of the arguments were familiar ones that had been current when Mechanics' Institutes were introduced in the 1830s.

At the forefront of these arguments were educational considerations. Most contemporaries, especially those of Scottish extraction, thought that better education led to more intellectual progress and taught people respect for the nature of social relationships. Libraries diffused knowledge; thus, they helped to communicate and to make accessible ideas to the general populace.

Victorians were confident that educational bodies could help forge a stable culture and political life. Writing in 1881, John G. Bourinot concluded, "Here there is no ancient system of social exclusiveness to fix a limit to the intellectual progress of the proletariat. Political freedom rests on a firm, broad basis of general education."[12] Because books were regarded as an essential part of education, Bourinot regretted to say that Canada was behind other countries in the formation of public libraries.

A decade later, the historian William Kingsford was more optimistic. He wrote, "The whole hope of the future of Canada lies in the sound sober sense of community, by which opinion is influenced" and he added, "it is by reading and thought that men of this character are moulded." Kingsford concluded with a confident prediction that the Toronto Public Library was destined to be one of the foremost institutions on the continent.[13] Most Victorians would have agreed with Hamilton Public Library's chief librarian, Richard Lancefield, who stated at a lecture that, given an educated public, "there is little doubt but that many grave social problems which now threaten us with disaster would be peaceably and speedily resolved."[14]

Within this educational context the circulation of accepted literature, including fiction, was regarded as a public good. Graeme Mercer Adam wrote that a central city library in Toronto should supply "the advantage which the wide-spread dissemination of wholesome literature" provided.[15] In Brantford, the editor of the *Daily Expositor* spoke glowingly on the subject of a free library for Brantford: "The cost is so small in comparison with the general diffusion of knowledge, and its great usefulness to every man, woman and child in the city so apparent that the vote upon it will doubtless be unanimous in its favor."[16]

Victorians ordinarily agreed that ideas should be communicated as widely as possible and believed that a unified common culture could be shaped. Cultural accessibility was highly esteemed. Few would have disagreed with Ontario's deputy minister of education, John Millar, who wrote, "This popularizing of knowledge has, no doubt, increased the demand for higher education. The effect is a national gain, in spite of what the aristocrat may believe or of what the demagogue may proclaim."[17]

Some advocates viewed libraries as an extension of the public school system and universities or as useful repositories for teaching labourers the skills and crafts needed in the work force. At the formal opening of Toronto's library, William Henry Withrow, editor of the *Canadian Methodist Magazine*, described libraries as "the people's colleges where the poorest lad or the toiling artisan shall enjoy the best teaching in the world."[18]

Similarly, in 1895, Mary Klotz, whose family was active in the movement, wrote in a special library issue of the *Ottawa Evening Journal*, "The Public Library is an extension of our schools and even of our universities. We may truly call it the people's university, where rich and poor, old and young, may all drink at its inexhaustible fountain."[19]

Indeed, promoters like John Taylor felt the library was an essential government service:

> Every year hundreds of youths graduate at the Public Schools and go out upon the world, drifting about like a rudderless ship upon a treacherous sea — without any link between giddy youth and sober mankind. That missing link is the public library. It is the caliban of the nineteenth century, and the only practical adult school which the State can supply us.[20]

The *Palladium of Labor* echoed this view by applying popular Darwinian terminology: "The Public Library is as truly an integral part of our educational system as the public school, supplementing and turning to account the work of the latter, which, for lack of such an agency in times past, has often resulted in what the scientists term 'arrested development'."[21]

The question of technical education was raised at times. John Hallam referred to "the works of John Ruskin, the Grammar of Ornament, or Smith's Dyeing, or any other of the expensive publications so necessary in the technical education of the artizan" at a Hamilton meeting.[22] Emmanuel Essery, a London barrister and later city mayor, told a small pro-library audience: "Unless the mechanics of Canada were enabled to cope with those of

Germany — where they have every facility afforded for a sound technical education — the former would become secondary."[23] As early as 1883, the provincial government permitted free libraries to acquire assets or property from Mechanics' Institutes and continue to receive the legislative grant that the institute had earned (46 Vic., c. 19).

Eventually, the government formalized the link with technical education in 1889 to allow libraries to offer evening classes "in such subjects as may promote a knowledge of the mechanical and manufacturing arts" (52 Vic., c. 38). This additional power intruded further on the work of Mechanics' Institutes, but by this time their reputation had declined precipitously. At a December 1888 meeting organized by the Minister of Education, George Ross, the following exchange took place:

> Mr. A.F. Jury said that a feeling prevailed in Mechanics' Institutes that mechanics are not wanted there.
> Mr. Ross — I never thought they were created for aristocrats. (Laughter)[24]

At a subsequent assembly on university extension, Queen's University Principal, George Munro Grant, quipped, "if you want to go to a place where you are certain not to find mechanics, go to a Mechanics Institute."[25] From the education department's perspective, therefore, after 1889 public libraries were evidently in the ascendant.

The Economic Rationale for Free Public Libraries

The case for technical education overlapped other claims for free libraries based on economic arguments. An Ingersoll newspaper editor stated that "Intelligence and virtue, ignorance and vice are so ultimately connected that the parent, the town and the nation really economize when they spend for the intellectual advancement of those committed to their care."[26]

Reform liberalism originating in the later part of the nineteenth century held that the common welfare was improved if government assistance was provided for those who wished to improve themselves beyond what private enterprise and markets could operate efficiently. On the other hand, traditional liberals, accustomed to the Manchester School of thought, believed in limited government activity and maximum individual freedom. They emphasized the need for new services to be demonstrated in economic terms and were less likely to approve government expenditures for libraries because the doctrine of *laissez-faire* still loomed large: the decisions of individuals and Adam Smith's "invisible hand" remained the surest guide to economic success and social stability. One Hamilton citizen complained, "Don't you know that this so called free library act emanated from the same villainous source — a conspiracy to deprive people of their liberties."[27]

To counter this fundamental difference, library promoters pointed out that previous forms of public libraries had failed for lack of a suitable financial basis or that the work force required educational materials on changing technological conditions to update their knowledge and skills. John Hallam insisted, "The movement being a rate-supported one will render it independent and permanent, and not liable to fluctuations which too often beset many institutions which have to depend for their support on voluntary and charitable contributions."[28] The *Toronto Globe* likewise justified its support of tax-supported public libraries:

> In default of private endowments furnishing an income sufficient to pay the salaries of curators, etc., there has never been found any practical way of supporting public libraries except out of the rates. As the libraries are resorted to almost entirely by the poorer classes, there need be no dread of the "poor man's vote" to stand in the way of improvement.[29]

Modified Utilitarian philosophy and John Stuart Mill's writings were cited to vindicate the library movement. A provincial MLA, John M. Gibson, paraphrased Jeremy Bentham's dictum when Hamiltonians voted in 1889: "The by-law was a measure which promised the greatest good to the greatest number."[30] At the opening of the new library in London, Robert Reid referred to Mill's efforts to broaden the individualistic bent in Utilitarian thought in terms of a more harmonious integration of economic activity:

> As John Stuart Mill had put it, in his essay on Socialism, the uncultivated masses and their employers must learn to practice to labor and combine for public and social purposes, and not, as hitherto, solely for narrowly interested ones. If our public libraries were conducted on proper principles they could not fail ....[31]

Reid, like many people, assumed that the working classes would gain materially by access to texts and manuals. The Chatham Board of Trade circulated a library advertisement to voters, maintaining, "The more intelligent the mechanic or laborer, the higher his wages, and the more comfortable his home. Crude labour is at a discount. Skilled labour is at a premium."[32] Augustus T. Freed, one of the chairmen of the Royal Commission on the Relations of Labour and Capital in Canada (1886-1889), "was glad to learn that the workingmen are alive to their interests and are taking up this free library movement."[33]

Ratepayers and other electors, of course, remained to be convinced libraries were worthwhile institutions. Even though the principle of utility provided a powerful rationale for government to establish public services,[34] local private interests and men of enterprise often rallied to the call of economy. At the close of his influential pamphlet, *Notes by the Way on Free Libraries and Books*, John Hallam, the principal leader of the movement prior to 1900, best expressed the view that free libraries were profitable investments. He declared libraries "must necessarily diminish the ranks of those two great armies which are constantly marching to gaols and penitentiaries, and in the same ratio they must decrease the sums of money which ratepayers have to provide for the maintenance of those places" and concluded, "I want Toronto to pay for intelligence — for popular education in the free library sense. If she does so fairly and fully, her bill for poverty and depravity will be materially lessened."[35]

Social and Cultural Roles

Intertwined with subjective educational and economic claims about libraries were diverse social and cultural ones. Victorians for the most part believed in progress, believed that technological and intellectual change would probably continue indefinitely to enrich society by advancing knowledge, providing economic prosperity, and improving the human spirit.

Alpheus Todd told the Royal Society of Canada, "In the machinery of modern progress now in operation, whether in Europe or America, free libraries, accessible to all classes, occupy a conspicuous place."[36] Windsor's library chairman, John Curry, opened a renovated building, Lambie Hall, in 1894 on a confident note: "You are aware that our city is a progressive one. We are blessed with all the modern conveniences which tend to make life happy and this evening we add still another — a Public Free Library."[37]

Opposing viewpoints could be associated with unprogressive ideas or unbusinesslike practices. Hamilton opponents of the 1889 library bylaw were labelled "mossbacks," an American reference to political reactionaries, and Edwin Hardy wrote, "it is true of towns as of business men, that they must be progressive and up-to-date" when he urged the foundation of a rate-supported library at Lindsay.[38]

Religious considerations stood alongside the progressive faith. Evangelical Protestants — strict observers of the sabbath, believers in scripture reading and the virtues of trust, piety and charity — presumed libraries should embody a strong moral tone. Liberal Protestants believed the salvation of souls and the moral regeneration of society were important tasks for the Christian ministry.[39] A Toronto minister advocated a library in *Rose-Belford's Canadian Monthly and National Review* by asking, "How much might it do here to attract young men from the 400 dram shops that infest this city? How much to quicken frivolous young women to the perception of somewhat better than silks and jewellery, parties, and flirtations?"[40] William Cochrane, a well-known Presbyterian minister and long-time director of the Brantford Mechanics' Institute, asserted, "In order to remove existing temptations, there must be counter attractions provided, and none better can be found than in the rooms of a free public library."[41]

The temperance issue was always close at hand, for public houses were plentiful. A Baptist minister, Robert G. Boville, warned,

> Hamilton, it is said by some, cannot afford to support a free library; and yet the people of Hamilton can spend at least $500,000 for alcoholic drink every year. Depend upon it, there will be many an alcoholic vote cast against a free-library by-law; and therefore every temperance vote in the city should be cast in favor of the by-law.[42]

A *Brampton Conservator* editorial in 1895 concluded that the library would "keep some, at least, out of the barroms [sic], who are now on the road to ruin through barroom influence."[43]

Literature and book learning were considered worthwhile pursuits because people could learn Christian doctrines or liberal virtues such as industry, tolerance, duty, self-help, thrift, liberality and temperance. Libraries could help to reinforce religious faith by lessening atheistic and agnostic influence.

It is not surprising that T.K. Henderson, a compositor, received first prize on the subject "Free Libraries from a Workman's Standpoint," when he wrote, "the perusal of good books would also strengthen and build up his religious character, and as man is a religious animal, it is of no small consequence of what sort his religion may be."[44]

Conservatives, as well as upper/middle-class liberals, were conscious of the need to foster respectability and deference to authority.

The public library offered the prospect of assisting in the continuing struggle against worldly temptation and corruption while contributing to an orderly society. The *Ottawa Evening Journal* cited British statistics to show that vice and crime in the streets might be reduced.[45]

Finally, the nuclear family would be safeguarded: both the *Guelph Daily Mercury* and the *Toronto Globe* were emphatic on this score in editorials published simultaneously in both papers:

> When once such a library is established he [a labourer] will not be forced to spend his evenings in listless idleness, or be tempted, in order "to pass away the time," to go to the bar-room to have a chat and hear the news. The entertaining book from the free library, read aloud by himself, his wife, or one of the children, will interest the whole family, and make the hours pass innocently and pleasantly.[46]

Edwin Hardy also appealed to the sense of family unity in a letter to the *Canadian Post* in 1898.[47]

The Democratic Faith

Liberalism at its noblest extolled the free competition of opinions and writings as well as free interplay in disseminating and propounding them. The potential for free libraries to enlighten citizens was a powerful inducement, because libraries were viewed by Victorians as an instrument to strengthen the liberal-democratic basis of the whole nation or community.[48] Libraries also gave some measure of reassurance to those who feared the advent of socialism during the rapid extension of the franchise. Again, T.K. Henderson's prize essay is instructive: "By and by the working classes of Canada will be the actual rulers of the country, and universal suffrage will take its place among our laws. Into whose hands will this power be entrusted?"[49]

A second-prize essay by another typesetter noted the desirability of workers' having access to books on politics and political economy: "This would enable them readily to see through the specious, threadbare arguments of pothouse politicians and the sophistries of self-constituted but ignorant wire pullers, and would do much to create a more healthy tone in political life ...."[50] In Stratford, an Anglican minister said that free libraries were essential: "whatever statesmen might do the people were the real rulers. The people should, therefore, have the highest possible intelligence."[51] As the *Hamilton Spectator* put it succinctly, "It [the library] will make the people better able to govern themselves."[52]

Associated with this democratic commitment was the blossoming of a stronger, more united Canada and local civic pride. For some, the nationhood and a higher cultural attainment were virtually synonymous. George Ross, the minister of education, closed a memorable speech at the opening of a library in London in this idealistic vein:

> We hope, round the altar here, that young Canadians will worship with a pure heart loftier ideals of national life; that a broader patriotism will be quickened by higher conceptions of duty, and that in the long hereafter, as was said in the brave days of old, it will be said that there were Canadians made better and stronger men because it entered into the hearts of the citizens of London, in the closing years of this wonderful century, to place at their disposal the treasurehouse of knowledge (Loud and continued applause).[53]

Shortly after 1900, the assimilation of immigrants into Anglo-Protestant culture assumed greater prominence in the quest for national unity. Libraries provided resources to educate "our young, our various nationalities, foreign emigrants and social strata" into the "fibrous metal of a unified Canada, a homogeneous greater Britain."[54]

Local boosterism, moreover, promoted the cause of libraries; public spirit and the provision of civic amenities were evident during the growth of municipal government in late nineteenth-century Ontario. The American term "booming" appears on occasion with reference to the clamour and vigour favouring library bylaws.[55]

A number of public-spirited people contributed property and funds for libraries before the Carnegie program swept the province after 1900. In Uxbridge, a former member of Parliament left money for the town to build the "Joseph Gould Institute" at a cost of $5,000. It functioned for a decade as a Mechanics' Institute library until January 1898, when the provincial library superintendent, Dr. Samuel May, encouraged a public meeting to petition the town council to make it free.[56]

In Napanee, a library building was erected after three prominent men donated money and land. When the library board undertook a general subscription for equipment, books and furnishings, the *Napanee Express* supported the activity by suggesting, "Some public spirited citizen may wish to add to the beauty of the building by the gift of a memorial window to the Canadians who fell in South Africa, or some liberally disposed gentleman may wish to show his loyalty by a gift commemorating the reign of Victoria the Good ...."[57]

James Stavely, a wealthy Clinton merchant, died in 1892 without heirs; consequently, his estate reverted to the Province. The local council made several appeals to secure some of the proceeds of the estate; eventually, in 1896, a provincial statute gave $10,000 to the town to be used for a public building (59 Vic., c. 6). A library was the main feature of "Stavely Hall," and, when it was completed, the ratepayers voted 225 to 121 in January 1900 to create a free library on the strength of an endowment that helped finance operations.[58]

In Streetsville, in 1901, a resident gave part of a two-storey shop "to the Library Board and its successors in office forever" for a small sum of $200. Bolstered by the donation, the board pressed council for free status, which came into effect on July 1, 1902.[59] Some offers did not materialize. In 1895, the estate of William G. Perley offered a home for a library in Ottawa; however, Ottawa's first free bylaw was rejected by the ratepayers shortly afterwards, even though reports in the press indicated that the home was quite suitable for library purposes.[60]

Progress of the Movement before 1900

How successful was the library movement in putting forth its ideas and achieving its goals in local elections? Prior to 1895 only twelve free public libraries were established in Ontario. Local library bylaws were characterized by comfortable majorities and low voter turn-outs. Normally, less than 15 per cent of the total population cast ballots, and even the number of rate-payers voting was not substantial (see Table 1). It was not until 1895, after the provincial legislature decided to reconstitute Mechanics' Institutes as public libraries by allowing libraries to be formed by council bylaw without elections and also by dispensing with the necessity for the 1/2 mill rate that the number of free public libraries increased significantly.

TABLE 1

Free Public Library Bylaws, 1883-1895, by Year

Date	Place	Population	Ratepayers	Votes For	Votes Against	Majority	Total
1883	Guelph	10,190	2,486	646	137	509	783
1883	Toronto	94,755	27,981	5,405	2,862	2,543	8,267
1884	London	25,792	6,713	1,583	942	641	2,525
1884	Simcoe	3,000	N/A	328	47	281	375
1884	Berlin (Kitchener)	4,473	N/A	376	167	209	543
1884	St. Thomas	10,811	2,433	N/A	N/A	N/A	-
1884	Brantford	11,783	2,165	1,086	275	811	1,361
1885	Hamilton	41,280	10,640	1,358	1,547	-189	2,905
1888	London	26,960	8,356	838	245	593	1,083
1888	Waterloo	2,664	N/A	N/A	N/A	N/A	-
1888	St. Catharines	10,080	3,452	N/A	N/A	N/A	-
1889	Hamilton	44,653	11,774	3,697	2,030	1,667	727
1890	Ingersoll	5,200	N/A	486	232	254	718
1890	Chatham	8,730	1,835	540	500	40	1,040
1893	London	33,427	8,400	3,522	1,279	2,243	4,801
1894	Windsor	11,468	11,468	919	254	665	1,173

Population given is provincially assessed. Ratepayers excludes tenants and other qualified electors.
The 1888 London bylaw repealed the 1884 bylaw.

Sources: Ontario. Bureau of Industries. *Annual Report*
Newspapers, local reports, bylaw results

This beneficial public policy change demonstrated the broader, more relevant community appeal of public library services compared with the narrower individualism of Mechanics' Institutes. On the political front, the merging of the two perspectives on library service also made the formation of public library boards easier: by 1901 there were 132 boards scattered across the province serving about a quarter of the total population. However, in the critical area of finance, some new free libraries became dependent on the bounty of municipal councils unless the electors passed a local bylaw to secure the 1/2 mill rate.

The important 1895 legislative changes were brought about, in part, by the movement's persistence in promoting its political agenda and aims and the education department's insistence on closer supervision. As well, the legislative changes reflected public opinion, which was slow to accept rate-supported libraries as an integral part of government but was receptive to the less expensive voluntary alternative that had sustained Mechanics' Institutes. Even with legislation more conducive to the passage of bylaws in support of free libraries, such bylaws were not easy to secure. Dr. May summarized his experience over two decades at an Ontario Library Association meeting in 1902:

> ... our adult population did not seem to appreciate the benefits to be derived from municipalities providing good reading for themselves and for their children; another reason which retarded the progress of Free Libraries was that many members of Mechanics' Institutes were very conservative, and preferred paying membership fees, so that they might to a certain extent be exclusive in enjoying the privileges of the Library and Reading Room ....[61]

The education minister also identified the substantial cost of "suitable buildings and premises" as a major drawback.[62] Of course, from a financial standpoint, libraries were not free, as one Hamilton citizen angrily declared: "It was nonsense to call the library 'free,' because the citizens would have to pay for it in taxes. You might as well call groceries 'free' that you have to pay for."[63]

Obviously, civic economy was a dominating factor confronting supporters who pondered the chances of passing a rate-supported bylaw. Financial motives influenced liberal as much as conservative or non-partisan citizens, who realized municipal funding formed the basis of operations. This obstacle, as well as the disinclination of the Ontario government to improve its own incentives for forming free libraries, contributed to the more relaxed legislation. Before 1895, Mechanics' Institute directors, who were empowered to transfer assets to free libraries, realized there was usually little financial gain resulting from a library bylaw because most communities were reluctant to levy the maximum mill rate or because the rate was insufficient to provide adequate services.[64] Added to this, the reading public continued to accept payment of small fees for library services.

After 1895, many institutes simply changed their title to "public library" without making an immediate effort to achieve rate-supported free status. In Dundas, for example, the directors approached council to pass a bylaw and to increase the municipal grant to $300 in return for reducing the membership fee to one dollar. The *Dundas Star* agreed: "One dollar is within the reach to any person and the volumes at their command cost many thousands besides the magazines and newspapers on file in the reading room."[65]

The movement's adherents had to rebut a range of practical objections related to the costs involved in library services. A Hamilton lawyer protested: "There will not be a book in the library that can be read as a substitute for food, clothing or a warm house. If a public library is not a necessity, it is in the nature of a luxury. The same economy and prudence shown in a family should be practiced in the management of the affairs of a community."[66] The *Hamilton Times* believed the 1885 bylaw failed because "when trade is dull and employment is precarious ... it would be cruel to delude people into expenditures that were not absolutely necessary."[67]

Cost-consciousness extended to the 1/2 mill rate, which some communities found excessive. For this reason, supporters sometimes predicted that a newly appointed board would not demand the full rate, notably in Hamilton.[68] Eventually, in 1892, the province reduced the rate to 1/4 mill in cities over 100,000 population (52 Vic., c. 24) to ease these concerns.

Inexpensive literature also emerged as a reason for not forming free libraries. Goldwin Smith was among the first to state that cheap printing allowed the public to buy plentiful reading "for a few cents"; he suggested a reference library would suffice for Toronto's purposes.[69] John Hallam corresponded with William F. Poole in Chicago about Smith's remarks, which Poole replied were a bit old-fashioned.[70] Normally, the presence of low-priced literature was not a persuasive objection, and a Conservative *Toronto Mail* editorial is illustrative: "We wonder if those who say so ever put themselves in the artisan's place, and calculated how much he could spare in a year, after supporting his family, for books. For a quarter of a dollar in taxes, or less, the library will give him the use of, or choice from, thousands of volumes."[71] William Briggs, a well-known publisher, agreed, adding, "all that many readers want is the reading, not the owning, of certain classes of books."[72]

Occasionally, in the heat of debate, financial issues could be turned to good advantage against antagonists. The following exchange took place at a Hamilton meeting:

Mr. Anthony Rowan protested that the by-law should not be carried.
He said "I can buy a book for 10 cents and read it."
A voice — a dime novel.

Mr. Rowan said that the library would impose a heavy tax on property owners.

A voice — Serves you right, for having so much property.[73]

In fact, financial considerations cut both ways. At Thorold, the town council inspected the Mechanics' Institute and took it over as a free library, primarily because it was a "valuable asset."[74] The ratepayers at Simcoe approved an 1884 bylaw for similar reasons. Here, the town was already paying $200 rent annually for use of part of the Institute and stood to gain after a few years after the debt on the building was paid off.[75] Chatham residents voted for a free library in 1890 partly because they believed the provincial grant to its Institute would not be available for library purposes if the directors were forced to close down.[76]

Another major issue that bedevilled library followers was the fiction question. One observer noted:

> Probably the chief argument advanced against the adoption of the Free Libraries Act is that because the circulation of fiction is from 50 to 75 per cent of the whole, therefore free public libraries are a snare, a fraud and a delusion, and the general body of ratepayers should not be asked to provide foolish girls and beardless young men with novels to read wholesale.[77]

Library supporters met the issue directly by justifying quality novel reading and including it in collections. John Hallam told a meeting: "I can get more true knowledge and real good from such books as the Vicar of Wakefield, Silas Marner, Jane Eyre, Caleb Williams, Adam Bede, and the works of Walter Scott, Thackeray, Dickens, some of Bulwer Lytton's, and those of other great novelists, than I could from nine-tenths of the sermons that were ever preached or published."[78]

Quality recreational fiction, as well as fiction with a purpose, was acceptable to most library enthusiasts, who did not accept rigid evangelical strictures. From the outset, then, the library's mission was widely defined in terms of literature, a fact that often drew criticism from a vocal constituency that felt public morality rested on private virtue.

The debate extended for many decades, with fiction gradually gaining acceptance. John Taylor revealed the course of public preference by stating the public was "too advanced in the nineteenth century to underrate the benefits of good healthy fiction."[79] While dime novels, penny dreadfuls, shilling shockers, romances, and melodramas were obviously frowned upon, serious novels were considered a source of moral and social instruction.[80] As long as libraries exercised discretion in book selection, critics might concur with one Toronto bookseller who said libraries would tend to lead readers in a "proper direction."[81] For selection purposes the *Toronto Evening News* proposed using the American Library Association's catalogue of "best books" for general readers.[82] By 1902, John Davis Barnett could say, "Until I find a non-novel reading community (past or present) which in reforming energy or morals, in manners or charity [sic] of judgement, is superior to the novel using community, I intend to claim novel circulation as one of the values the P.L. confers."[83]

Non-fiction could also pose problems. Liberals, of course, believed in freedom of expression, but on occasion free-thinking literature, especially atheist tracts, could damage the case for libraries. When the London Ministerial Association protested about "infidel books" after it learned the Workingmen's Free Library had requested $500 from council to provide free services in 1892, it was protesting the writings of atheists like the British Member of Parliament Charles Bradlaugh. In this case, the *London Advertiser* helped resolve the dispute. It published the complete contents of the Workingmen's library with the scrupulous opinion that the books were "a very fair nucleus for a free library." The newspaper also advised that the Mechanics' Institute library should be added to form a free public library.[84]

There was also persistent criticism that the working classes would not be able to use libraries in their leisure hours or that alternate public bookstocks existed. One person complained that books, newspapers, and libraries abounded and that "few of us are disposed to yield to the tempter's charms to desert our homes after a day's work to absorb an extra taxed literature collected by a conclave of any designing body of men, whether aldermen alone or in collusion with others."[85] The *Hamilton Times* explained:

> About the usefulness of a library and reading room as a place of resort for workingmen in the evenings we are inclined to doubt. The workingman, who has to be at his place in the shop at 7 o'clock in the morning, is not going to have much time to loaf in the evening after he has got his supper and read the daily paper. Professional and commercial men may make the library a place of resort, but mechanics and factory operatives, as a rule, will not.[86]

Sometimes support from organized labour could offset this criticism; trade unions were active in local politics and interested in securing social benefits for workers.[87] Other libraries were put forward as substitutes in some instances. In Toronto and Ottawa, the parliamentary libraries were mentioned[88]; however, neither the collections nor the hours of operation were suitable. Hamilton's Central School library, dating to Ryerson's administration, became an issue during one unsuccessful free bylaw campaign.[89]

Conclusion

All these challenges presented serious obstacles to the passage of free library bylaws, especially when liberal assumptions postulated by library reformers either failed to match the reality of library service as it existed in communities or conflicted with interests influencing other supporters. Nevertheless, the movement's encounters with other groups or divergent viewpoints helped shape and define its activities and goals. When the provincial government consolidated legislation pertaining to Mechanics' Institutes and free libraries in 1895, it broadened the political course. After this time, the ranks of the library movement, until then small in number, grew steadily as Institute directors were drawn into the public library cause.

One exceptional new member was Edwin Hardy from Lindsay; like James Bain, Jr., in Toronto, he recognized the need for more vigorous organization and additional goals and purposes for the movement. By 1900, Bain was already advocating larger units of service and the inclusion of art galleries and museums in libraries, as well as better library funding and organization.[90]

Hardy initiated another change in a letter to George Ross in the summer of 1899. He asked for more centralized direction from the education department; for the publication of library directories, new book bulletins, and manuals on management; for a better classification system; and for other improvements. Ross encouraged Hardy, suggesting a conference of leading librarians and those interested in public libraries be convened.[91] The formation of the Ontario Library Association followed in 1900, and a firmer organizational basis for provincial cooperative action was finally established. Library promotion no longer depended on articulation by steadfast individuals and small local support groups.[92]

The nineteenth century was drawing to a close. New technological, managerial and organizational changes were advancing across North America. Names familiar in the early work of Ontario libraries — John Hallam, John Taylor, William Edwards,[93] Emmanuel Essery, William Cochrane, and Richard Lancefield — were less active now in the movement. New leaders were more visible.

In 1902, Lawrence Burpee enthusiastically outlined progress in cataloguing, classification, circulation systems, and the role of the librarian to the Royal Society of Canada in his paper, "Modern Public Libraries and Their Methods."[94] Circulation and volumes added to collections grew more steadily after 1900. New services and techniques, which contemporaries labelled "modern," were emerging, especially from the United States.[95]

Dr. May, a traditional Victorian favouring orthodoxy and possessing a healthy scepticism about these ideas, was dispatched by the education department to tour larger American libraries in New York, Philadelphia and Buffalo in 1901. He reported it was "gratifying to state that the Public

Libraries in Ontario are conducted at much less cost than the Libraries in the United States" and that the new system of open access to the shelves would not be successful in Ontario because "it would require too many assistants." Yet even May was not entirely opposed to new ideas, because he approved heartily of children's departments.[96]

By about 1900, therefore, the public library movement in Ontario was beginning to develop along new "modern" directions with a stronger level of organization. The formation of more public libraries at the polls or at council sessions gave a vigorous expression to a community enterprise that identified strongly with a sense of place, a vital consideration in Ontario politics.

The democratization of reading seemed assured, for on a provincial scale there was a growing cohesiveness and structural base in local communities where supporters felt comfortable furthering the interests of the movement. Their program of action to establish a publicly funded institution that offered circulating adult and juvenile collections, reading rooms, and reference service to the entire public on a free basis continued to provide a unifying process around which collective action and supportive arguments could be organized.

Carnegie philanthropy, better organized cooperative efforts, an expanded range of functions, and modern methods would invigorate the movement after 1900 by adding a broader range of organizational tasks. Nonetheless, the fundamental spirit of Victorian liberal reform and its optimistic rationale would remain the guiding light for library development in Ontario well into the first half of the twentieth century.

Notes

[1] John Hallam, *Address to the Board of Management of the Toronto Free Library* (Toronto:, n.p., 1883), unpaged. The early development of the movement is studied by Eric C. Bow, "The Public Library Movement in Nineteenth-Century Ontario," *Ontario Library Review* 66 (1982): 1-16. Eugène Rouillard, *Les Bibliothèques populaires* (Quebec: L.-J. Demers & Frère, 1890), 45-46 noted Ontario's enthusiasm at an early date.

[2] James Bain, Jr., "The Library Movement in Ontario," *Public Libraries* 6 (1901): 349. Different versions of his speech appear in *Library Journal* 26 (1901): 269-70 and in the Archives of Ontario, Ontario Library Association, MU 2239. He includes other types of libraries in the movement, but he is primarily concerned with public libraries.

[3] The evolution of library service during this period is studied in detail by John Wiseman, "Temples of Democracy: A History of Public Library Development in Ontario, 1880-1920," (PhD thesis, Loughborough University of Technology, Library and Information Studies, Loughborough, U.K., 1989), 1-76.

[4]I am using the term "movement" in the sense that people and groups organize formally or informally to support and produce change in society. At its core a movement should have a set of values and beliefs, a structure, and program to effect change. For the general intellectual climate, I follow Ann Robson, "The Intellectual Background of the Public Library Movement in Britain," *Journal of Library History* 11 (1976): 187-205; and Sidney Ditzion, "The Anglo-American Library Scene: A Contribution to the Social History of the Library Movement," *Library Quarterly* 16 (1946): 281-301.

[5]I do not consider social control, that is, the regulation of society by acceptable behaviour to attain desirable social values, to be the major explanation for the growth of free libraries in Ontario during this period. It is a useful causal element, but the heterogeneous nature of library resources available to the public, the permissive feature of enabling legislation which regulated the establishment of libraries, the extent of public use of libraries, and general public acceptance of library-promoted "ideology" are all limitations.

[6]One of the Ontario Liberal Party's governing principles was based on "progressive changes in government as from time to time may be developed": see Adam Crooks, *Reform Government in Ontario; Eight Years Review* (Toronto: Hunter, Rose & Co., 1879), 33. Naturally, he was concerned that government reform should respond to public demand and foster public consent.

[7]According to Tamara Grad, "The Development of Public Libraries in Ontario, 1851-1951" (M.A. thesis, Drexel Institute of Technology, School of Library Science, Philadelphia, 1952), 25, "The libraries of Ontario from now on entered a new stage of development."

[8]See Jim Blanchard, "Anatomy of Failure: Ontario Mechanics' Institutes, 1835-1895," *Canadian Library Journal* 38 (1981): 393-98; John Wiseman, "Phoenix in Flight; Ontario Mechanics' Institutes, 1880-1920," *Canadian Library Journal* 38 (1981): 401-5; and Foster Vernon, "The Development of Adult Education in Ontario, 1790-1900," (Ed.D. thesis, Ontario Institute for Studies in Education, Toronto, 1969), 473-523.

[9]Ontario, Department of Education, *Educational Statement of the Hon. Adam Crooks, Minister of Education, on Moving the Estimates for 1880, in Committee of Supply, House of Assembly, Province of Ontario* (Toronto: C.B. Robinson, 1880), 12; and Alpheus Todd, "On the Establishment of Free Public Libraries in Canada," *Proceedings and Transactions of the Royal Society of Canada* Series 1, 1, Sec. 2 (1882-83): 14. Bruce Curtis, "'Littery Merrit', 'Useful Knowledge', and the Organization of Township Libraries in Canada West, 1840-1860," *Ontario History* 78 (1986): 285-311 explores Ryerson's libraries in the context of the "politics of literacy." His analysis does not include alternate interests that sought to influence the state form of public libraries, such as the unsuccessful bills to establish free libraries introduced by William Boulton in 1852 and by Alexander Morris in 1866, or continued legislative support for Mechanics' Institute libraries after 1851.

[10]American and British texts furnished ample explanations, e.g., William I. Fletcher, *Public Libraries in America* (Boston: Roberts Brothers, 1894) and Thomas

Greenwood, *Public Libraries: A History of the Movement, and a Manual for the Organization and Management of Rate-Supported Libraries*, 4th ed. (London: Cassell & Co., 1898). According to Fletcher (p. 113), a librarian from the United States "would feel quite at home" in the Toronto Public Library.

[11] Throughout this period in Ontario, widows, unmarried women and males who were 21 years of age who met certain basic property qualifications and who were British subjects were eligible to vote for library bylaws. This issue was raised during the Hamilton vote in 1885.

[12] John G. Bourinot, *The Intellectual Development of the Canadian People; An Historical Review* (Toronto: Hunter, Rose & Co., 1881), 128 and 119-21. He is speaking about the Victorian convention of "high culture," the appreciation of what constitutes the "best" in intellectual, moral and social life.

[13] William Kingsford, *The Early Bibliography of the Province of Ontario, Dominion of Canada, with Other Information* (Toronto: Rowsell & Hutchison, 1892), 128-29.

[14] "Studies in Sociology," *Hamilton Daily Spectator*, February 24, 1893. Lancefield served as chief librarian from 1889 to 1902: see Katharine Greenfield, *Hamilton Public Library 1889-1963: A Celebration of Vision and Leadership* (Hamilton: Hamilton Public Library, 1989), 16-34.

[15] "A Dufferin Public Library," *Toronto Mail*, October 1, 1878. Adam later applied for the post of chief librarian at Toronto: see *Testimonials in Favor of the Candidature of Mr. Graeme Mercer Adam for the Position of Librarian of the Free Public Library, Toronto* (Toronto: n.p., 1883).

[16] "A Free Library," *Brantford Daily Expositor*, November 30, 1883.

[17] John Millar, *Books: A Guide to Good Reading* (Toronto: William Briggs, 1897), 64. Popularization was particularly evident in the field of science, where local societies proliferated and natural scientists were linked with colleagues in Britain and the United States.

[18] "Public Library Formal Opening by the Lieutenant-Governor," *Toronto Globe*, March 7, 1884.

[19] Marie Klotz, "A Public Library," *Ottawa Evening Journal*, April 13, 1895. Also, Anita Rush, *The Establishment of Ottawa's Public Library, 1895-1906* (Ottawa: n.p., 1981), 3. Newspaper publishers and editors, like Philip Ross of the *Journal*, consistently supported libraries, partly because many of the ideas both were promoting were similar: see Paul Rutherford, *A Victorian Authority: The Daily Press in Late Nineteenth-Century Canada* (Toronto: University of Toronto Press, 1982), 156-89.

[20] John Taylor, *Toronto's Free Library; Facts for the Citizens* (Toronto: n.p., 1881), unpaged. The Caliban metaphor had been popularized by Robert Browning's poem and served as the subject matter of a Canadian publication by Daniel Wilson, *Caliban: The Missing Link*, in 1873. See A.B. McKillop, *A Disciplined Intelligence: Critical Inquiry and Canadian Thought in the Victorian Era* (Montreal: McGill-Queen's University Press, 1979), 129-32.

[21] "The Free Library," *Palladium of Labor*, April 25, 1885.

[22] "For a Public Library," *Hamilton Evening Times*, May 2, 1885. Hallam served as the Toronto library's first chairman.

[23]"To Be or Not To Be," *London Advertiser*, June 9, 1888. Essery was an ardent library enthusiast who had served as a director of the Mechanics' Institute and Workingman's Library before becoming a public library trustee.

[24]Ontario, Department of Education, *Report of the Minister of Education on the Subject of Technical Education* (Toronto: Warwick & Sons, 1889), 167. Also published in *Ontario Sessional Papers*, no. 22, 1889.

[25]Ontario, Department of Education, *Supplement to the Report on the Minister of Education, 1892; University Extension* (Toronto: Warwick & Sons, 1892), 12. Also published in *Ontario Sessional Papers*, no. 58, 1892.

[26]Editorial observation in *Ingersoll Weekly Chronicle and Canadian Dairyman*, December 26, 1889.

[27]"Principle versus Fraud," *Hamilton Daily Spectator*, December 26, 1888. William D. Grampp, *The Manchester School of Economics* (Stanford: Stanford University Press, 1960) stresses that the School's members held divergent views on a variety of social issues and were not strictly doctrinaire.

[28]"The Proposed Free Library," *Toronto Globe*, December 18, 1882.

[29]"Wanted a Public Library and Reading Room," *Toronto Globe*, January 27, 1881.

[30]"A Public Meeting in Favor of the Free Library," *Hamilton Evening Times*, May 9, 1885. At a previous meeting Gibson had urged, "If for no utilitarian object, the fact that Hamilton was singular in being without a public library of any kind should urge its citizens to move in favor of such a project." See "The Library Question," *Hamilton Daily Spectator*, May 7, 1885.

[31]"Dedicated to the Citizens," *London Free Press*, November 27, 1895. J.S. Mill's "Chapters on Socialism" reprinted in *Essays on Economics and Society*, ed. John M. Robson (Toronto: University of Toronto Press, 1967), vol. 2, 703-53. Of course, Utilitarians of the narrower Benthamite legacy objected to raising taxes for libraries: see a letter to the editor by "Utilitarian" in the *Ottawa Free Press*, January 3, 1896.

[32]"Citizens of the Municipality of the Town of Chatham," *Chatham Tri-Weekly Planet*, December 27, 1889.

[33]"Booming the By-Law," *Hamilton Daily Spectator*, December 20, 1888. The Commissioners heard testimony from Hamilton workers after the proceedings began in November 1887. For Freed's role, see *Canada Investigates Industrialism*, ed. Gregory S. Kealey (Toronto: University of Toronto Press, 1973), xv-xix.

[34]As a noted British economist put it, libraries led to "an enormous increase of utility which is thereby acquired for the community at a trifling cost": see W. Stanley Jevons, "The Rationale of Free Public Libraries," *Contemporary Review* 39 (1881): 385-402.

[35]John Hallam, *Notes by the Way on Free Libraries and Books with a Plea for the Establishment of Rate-Supported Libraries in the Province of Ontario* (Toronto: Globe Printing Co., 1882), 31-32.

[36]Alpheus Todd, 13. Todd was Parliamentary Librarian between 1867 and 1884: see *Dictionary of Canadian Biography* (Toronto: University of Toronto Press, 1967-   ), vol. 11, 883-85.

[37]"The Library Opened," *Windsor Evening Record*, December 5, 1894. Curry's speech is reprinted in Gladys Shepley, "60 Years of Service — Windsor Public Library 1894-1954," *Ontario Library Review* 38 (1954): 231-32.

[38]"Rough on Mossbacks," *Hamilton Daily Spectator*, December 27, 1888. The *Spectator's* editorial of January 8, 1889, welcomed the passage of the bylaw: "The result is evidence that mossbackism is losing its grip upon Hamilton, and that there really is some ambition in the ambitious city." Also, "The Free Library; Some Reasons Therefor," *Lindsay Canadian Post*, December 2, 1898.

[39]However, the more active liberal Protestant social reformers studied by Ramsay Cook, *The Regenerators: Social Criticism in Late Victorian English Canada* (Toronto: University of Toronto Press, 1985) were not part of the public library movement.

[40]W.R.G. Mellen, "Wealth and its Uses," *Rose-Belford's Canadian Monthly and National Review* 2 (March 1879): 349.

[41]"The Free Library By-Law; Letter from Dr. Cochrane," *Brantford Daily Expositor*, January 5, 1884. Cochrane served as a director of the Mechanics' Institute and library for many years. He died in 1898.

[42]"Mr. Boville's Census," *Hamilton Daily Spectator*, December 29, 1888.

[43]"Free Library," *Brampton Conservator*, September 5, 1895.

[44]T.K. Henderson in *Free Public Libraries for Canada; Working-men's Prize Essays* (Toronto: "The Citizen," 1882), 3.

[45]"Education, Crime and Free Libraries," *Ottawa Evening Journal*, December 30, 1895. The editor was using Thomas Greenwood's influential *Public Libraries*.

[46]The editorials are identical: "Vote for the Free Library," *Toronto Globe*, December 30, 1882, and "The Vote for the Free Library on Monday," *Guelph Daily Mercury*, December 30, 1882.

[47]"The Free Library," *Lindsay Canadian Post*, December 2, 1898.

[48]The democratic role of the public library is emphasized by John Wiseman, "Temples of Democracy," especially pages 306-8.

[49]*Free Public Libraries for Canada; Working-men's Prize Essays*, 4.

[50]H.M. Evans in *Free Public Libraries for Canada; Working-men's Prize Essays*, 14.

[51]"A Free Library," *Stratford Evening Beacon*, November 5, 1895.

[52]"The Free Library By-Law," *Hamilton Daily Spectator*, December 27, 1888.

[53]"London's Library," *London Advertiser*, November 27, 1895.

[54]Archives of Ontario, Ontario Library Association, MU 2239, John Davis Barnett, "The Value of Public Libraries to the Community," 3. The work of library reading camps in Ontario's timberland was helpful in this regard: see George L. Cook, "Alfred Fitzpatrick and the Foundation of Frontier College (1899-1922)," *Canada: An Historical Magazine* 3 (1976): 15-39; and Alfred Fitzpatrick, *Library Extension in Ontario; Travelling Libraries and Reading Camps* (Toronto: n.p., 1901).

[55]For example, at Ottawa, "Getting a Move On," *Ottawa Evening Journal*, December 23, 1895.

[56]"Free Library Question," *Uxbridge Journal*, January 20, 1898.

[57]"The Public Library," *Napanee Express*, November 1, 1901. But on this occasion a free library was not created.

[58]"Will the Library be Free?" *Clinton News Record*, December 7, 1899; and "Municipal Elections," January 5, 1900.

[59]A *Village Library Grows*, 2d rev. ed. (Streetsville, Ont.: Streetsville Public Library Board, 1973), 19-20.

[60]"Just the Place," *Ottawa Evening Journal*, January 4, 1896.

[61]Archives of Ontario, Ontario Library Association, MU 2239, Dr. May, "How to Secure the Passing of a Free Public Library By-Law," 2. May superintended public libraries until three years before his death in 1908.

[62]George W. Ross, *The School System of Ontario (Canada); Its History and Distinctive Features* (New York: D. Appleton, 1896), 159.

[63]"Singular Objections," *Hamilton Daily Spectator*, May 13, 1885.

[64]James Bain, Jr., "Brief Review of the Libraries of Canada," *Library Journal* 12 (1887): 408-9. Bain proposed either enlarging the service area for taxation purposes or altering the Act to increase the maximum rate. "Hamilton's Public Library," *Toronto Globe*, September 16, 1890, stated that the mill rate was "utterly inadequate for small places," giving Seaforth as an example.

[65]"The Public Library," *Dundas Star*, September 26, 1895. Of course, not every approach to council was successful. At Newmarket the Mechanics' Institute directors were rejected in 1896: see *Newmarket Era*, February 7, 1896; February 2, 1896; and February 28, 1896. At Stratford the directors were also disappointed: see *Stratford Evening Beacon*, November 19, 1895.

[66]"A Public Library," *Hamilton Evening Times*, May 6, 1885.

[67]"The Library By-Law," *Hamilton Evening Times*, May 16, 1885.

[68]See especially "Booming the By-Law," *Hamilton Daily Spectator*, December 20, 1888, where the meeting organizers carried a motion advising 1/4 of a mill on the dollar.

[69]"Ontario Education; Third Day of the Provincial Teachers' Association," *Toronto Globe*, August 11, 1882.

[70]Metropolitan Toronto Public Library, John Hallam Papers, vol. 2, correspondence with W.F. Poole, April 2, 1883, and April 6, 1883.

[71]"The Free Library," *Toronto Mail*, December 25, 1882.

[72]"A Free Library for Toronto," *Toronto Mail*, December 30, 1882.

[73]"In Favor of the Library," *Hamilton Evening Times*, May 7, 1885. In the *Hamilton Daily Spectator* account of this meeting, Thomas Brick is identified as the "voice." He was a spokesman for labour and a city alderman at this time: see Gregory S. Kealey and Bryan D. Palmer, *Dreaming of What Might Be; The Knights of Labor in Ontario, 1880-1900* (Cambridge, Mass.: Cambridge University Press, 1982), 206-7.

[74]"The Council Takes Over the Library," *Thorold Post*, October 18, 1895.

[75]"The Free Library By-Law," *Norfolk Reformer*, January 3, 1884; and *Simcoe Public Library; An Historical Sketch* (Simcoe, Ont.: n.p., 1978), 1.

[76]The Board of Trade promoted the free library on this basis: see "Board of Trade," *Chatham Tri-Weekly Planet*, December 20, 1889.

[77]"Hamilton Public Library," *Toronto Globe*, September 16, 1890.

[78]"Books Without Buying," *Hamilton Daily Spectator*, May 2, 1885.

[79]"The Free Library," *Hamilton Daily Spectator*, March 28, 1885. Taylor, who had been a director of the Toronto Mechanics' Institute and an alderman who promoted Toronto's free library, was active in the early years of the movement, especially in transferring the Toronto institute's assets and property to the free library.

[80]For a broader context see Robert A. Colby, *Fiction with a Purpose; Major and Minor Nineteenth-Century Novels* (Bloomington: Indiana University Press, 1968).

[81]"Books That Are Read; Public Literary Taste Steadily Improving," *Toronto Globe*, January 10, 1884. Many Canadian literary critics and public library spokesmen did not have a high regard for the trend to realism, i.e., works that portrayed everyday life and its consequences. *Catalogue of Books Recommended for Public Libraries* produced by the Department of Education (Toronto: Warwick & Rutter, 1895) contained a small section for "standard" novels.

[82]"Public Libraries," *Toronto Evening News*, December 17, 1881. However, publication of the ALA catalogue was delayed for more than a decade.

[83]Archives of Ontario, Ontario Library Association, MU 2239, Barnett, "Value of Public Libraries," 8. Barnett collected a valuable private library on Shakespeare that was later given to the University of Western Ontario: see "Noted Bibliophile Passes in London," *Toronto Globe*, March 22, 1926.

[84]"The Free Library; Books which the Workingmen Have on Their Shelves," *London Advertiser*, May 26, 1892, and "People's Forum" (Walter M. Roger), May 25, 1893. Also, Eleanor Shaw, *A History of the London Public Library* (London, Ont.: London Public Library and Art Museum, 1968), 32-33.

[85]"Arguments Against the Free Library" (Citizen), *Toronto World*, December 30, 1882.

[86]"The City Library By-Law," *Hamilton Evening Times*, May 8, 1885.

[87]At Toronto: "Trades and Labour Council," *Toronto Globe*, December 16, 1882. At Hamilton: "Free Library," *Hamilton Evening Times*, May 11, 1885 (Central Labor Union). In general, labour leaders were not prominent in the library movement.

[88]At Toronto: "Public Library," *Toronto Evening Telegram*, December 15, 1882; and "Provincial Library," *Toronto Evening Telegram*, February 3, 1883. At Ottawa: editorial observation in *Ottawa Free Press*, February 5, 1895.

[89]"A Public Library Already," *Hamilton Evening Times*, May 8, 1885.

[90]James Bain, Jr., "Public Libraries in Canada," *Proceedings of the Canadian Institute*, New series, 1 (1897-98): 95-100; and "Lectures, Museums, Art Galleries, etc., in Connection with Libraries," *Library Journal* 18 (1893): 214-16.

[91]Archives of Ontario, Ontario Library Association, MU 2239, George Ross correspondence to E.A. Hardy, July 20, 1899.

[92]Prior to 1900, some Ontarians had attended ALA conferences; for example, in Buffalo in 1883 Hallam and Bain lobbied successfully to have the succeeding ALA meeting in Toronto, but the meeting was subsequently relocated. See "Librarians in Council," *Toronto Globe*, August 15, 1883, and August 17, 1883.

[93]For William Edwards' continued efforts to promote a general classification ledger scheme after the Association of Mechanics' Institutes ceased to exist after 1886, see the Archives of Ontario, Association of Mechanics' Institutes of Ontario, MU 2021, Miscellaneous Memoranda, Circular Letters 1880-1896.

[94]Lawrence J. Burpee, "Modern Public Libraries and Their Methods," *Proceedings and Transactions of the Royal Canadian Society*, 2d series, 8 (1902): 3-47.

[95]One influential American publication that later emphasized this point is *The American Public Library* by Arthur E. Bostwick (New York: D. Appleton, 1910).

[96]Ontario, Department of Education, *Report of the Minister of Education (Province of Ontario) for the Year 1901, Part II* (Toronto: L.K. Cameron, 1902), 197. May, like many other Victorians, recognized that change was a necessary part of progress, and I have not used the term "Victorian" as a stereotype for rigid conformity.

Local Government and Library Boards
in Ontario, 1882-1945

Lorne D. Bruce

Abstract

The original model for board governance of public libraries in Ontario was established by the Free Libraries Act, 1882. This act ensured that locally controlled and financed boards would be representative and responsible bodies by requiring community petitions and the successful passage of referendums before municipal bylaws created appointed boards of management; by sharing appointments among three elective bodies; by limiting appointments to two to three years on an overlapping basis; and by empowering boards to raise a mill rate on local rateable assessment after approval of annual estimates by the municipal council. Between 1882 and 1945 there were numerous disputes between boards and councils, disagreements about provincial direction set by the Department of Education, and conflicts with other boards or citizens. However, throughout this period library boards retained their independence because appointed trustees satisfied the preference for citizen participation in local affairs. This fundamental belief persisted until local government structures underwent considerable reassessment and enlargement after 1945.

Résumé

Le premier modèle ontarien de conseil d'administration de bibliothèques publiques fut établi par le *Free Libraries Act* de 1882. La loi stipulait que les membres des conseils d'administration, contrôlés et financés localement, seraient nommés, mais que la bibliothèque devait d'abord obtenir de la population les signatures nécessaires et que les règlements municipaux, créant les conseils d'administration, devaiet être sanctionnés par des référendums. La loi précisait que les nominations devaient se partager entre trois groupes d'élus et que les mandats seraient limités à deux ou trois ans, en alternance. Elle permettait également aux conseils d'administration d'imposer une taxe basée sur le rôle d'évaluation après avoir obtenu du conseil municipal, l'approbation des dépenses annuelles. Entre 1882 et 1945, les conseils d'administration se disputèrent régulièrement avec les conseils municipaux., Il y eut de fréquentes mésententes avec le Ministère de l'éducation au sujet des directives provinciales et plusieurs conflits éclatèrent entre les différents conseils d'administration et avec les citoyens. Toutefois, tout au long de cette période, les conseils d'administration gardèrent leur indépendance parce que les administrateurs favorisèrent toujours la participation des citoyens aux affaires locales. Ces valeurs eurent cours jusqu'en 1945 alors que les gouvernements locaux furent réorganisés et devinrent plus importants.

Local library authorities in Ontario are special-purpose bodies, a fact deeply rooted in history. It is often repeated in public administration texts that free library boards developed rapidly in Canada's larger urban centres during the three decades of urban reform between 1890 and 1920 (better known in the United States as the Progressive Era) as part of a general response to political patronage and increasing requirements for professionalization in municipal government.[1]

The municipal reformers aimed at establishing local government systems based on administrative values of economy and efficiency, free from political interference. In this historical approach, the growth of library boards is usually regarded as part of an urban reform experiment with special-purpose bodies in government at the turn of the last century, an experiment which contributed to fragmentation in local government.

But, in fact, the reform trends in cities that seemed to remove boards from "politics" simply strengthened the established form of governance that boards had already achieved throughout Ontario and in the United States at a time when responsible and representative local self-government was rapidly developing.[2] In the second half of the nineteenth century, local government — that is, the activities of the municipal corporation and numerous local agencies and boards serving a community — had not yet come to be generally identified with municipal government, the affairs of the municipal corporation alone. Elected local councils satisfied the common democratic need for self-determination as the franchise was extended; however, there was less enthusiasm for strong centralized control within localities where elected public school trustees, appointed high school trustees, or other officials coexisted with councils.

In the nineteenth century library boards were more than administrative bodies; they served a broader political purpose. Boards were representative and responsible entities that helped share community power by satisfying the growing public preference for non-partisanship at the local level, by offering positions for people who eschewed the elective process, by giving substance to the idea that local public service could provide training in the process of

government, and, more pragmatically, by providing positions for appointments in a political culture that was mostly influenced by upper- and
middle-class visions and permeated by patronage.[3] These ideas and practices
concerning local government were especially prevalent in the delivery of
educational services long before the influence of the American Progressive
Era commenced in Canada, and these ideas and practices continued to have
political as well as administrative significance after 1900.

The Development of Boards Prior to 1882

The predecessors of free libraries in Ontario were social libraries (also
known as association libraries), Mechanics' Institutes, and common school
libraries. Association libraries dedicated to a variety of cultural interests
flourished in eastern Canada after 1800. Like Mechanics' Institutes, most
associations provided a meeting place for lectures, discussions and programs
as well as a circulating library for members. Association libraries,
Mechanics' Institutes, and common school libraries were usually governed
by committees of management or independent school boards. The pattern
was established first at Newark (Niagara-on-the-Lake) in 1800, where the
subscription library here was administered by a six-member board of
management.[4]

In the first half of the nineteenth century, local library corporations that
needed financial assistance petitioned the House of Assembly of Upper
Canada directly. It began granting aid to small groups of directors in
Kingston and Toronto as early as 1835.[5] Subsequently, after 1850, Egerton
Ryerson began to supply a multitude of school section board libraries with
books and supplementary grants from his Educational Depository in
Toronto, a system the Governor General, Lord Elgin, described in 1854 as a
"new era" in the colony's educational and intellectual history. In September
1852, a Conservative from Toronto, William Henry Boulton, introduced a
bill in the Canadian Parliament authorizing cities and towns to establish and
maintain public libraries, but it was discharged at second reading.[6]

Perhaps Boulton's bill did not gain backing because the Province of
Canada had passed legislation the year before, in 1851, to permit local
boards of Mechanics' Institutes or literary associations to vary in size and
authorized generous legislative grants for book purchases. The rationale
behind the enabling legislation was stated by James Young, a Liberal
member of the Ontario legislature, at an Association of Mechanics'
Institutes meeting in 1880:

> But it is a mistake to suppose that the Institutions were created
> and legislative grants given for one class of the community alone,
> and in the interest of these institutions, and even of the mechanical

classes themselves, it is of the utmost importance, in consideration of the intelligent and consequently limited constituency in each community from which they draw support, that our Mechanics' Institutes should continue to be open to all classes on terms of perfect equality.[7]

In this formative period of urban growth following passage of the Municipal Corporations Act of 1849 (also known as the Baldwin Act after its sponsor, Robert Baldwin) which allowed for municipal government, the modern distinction between "private" service agencies (e.g., Mechanics' Institutes) and "public" governmental institutions (e.g., common school libraries) remained casual. There were two acceptable ways to develop local services: local government bodies supported by taxes on municipal property, or supplemental provincial funding for philanthropic civic associations that claimed to serve a broad spectrum of the community.

This was an important distinction. Local initiative, directed in great part by the well-heeled, was fundamental in identifying community needs and responding to those needs within the growing economic marketplaces of Canada West. Even during a period of economic recession in 1859, when the Cartier-Macdonald government decided to eliminate grants for literary associations and Mechanics' Institutes, many politicians continued to support the concept of disbursement of grants. During parliamentary debate on the 1859 government estimates, Thomas D'Arcy McGee argued in support of continuing the grants:

> He [McGee] believed that the grants which had been customary to vote to Mechanics' Institutes had called into existence many societies which had been got up chiefly for the purpose of receiving the Government aid. But the remedy for that evil was not to cut of[f] all literary institutions. There should be some system of discrimination adopted, so as to provide for aid being given to those institutions which were the most useful, and, therefore, the most deserving of such assistance.[8]

Thus, the pattern of local library corporations — public or private — supported by provincial legislative revenue and supervised from a provincial department in Toronto had appeared by mid-century; this dichotomous scheme continued for another century until association libraries were abolished in Ontario in 1966.

After 1860, when enthusiasm for Ryerson's centralized scheme of tax-based public library service in schools began to wane, a new effort was made to integrate libraries into the evolving framework of local government.

Alexander Morris, a prominent Liberal-Conservative representing the constituency of Lanark near Ottawa, presented a bill in August 1866 to authorize the formation of free libraries in communities larger than 5,000 population.[9] He proposed forming a library board of management composed of nine members: six to be directly elected by ratepayers at an annual public meeting, and three to be selected by "those who have made donations to the Corporation." The interests of property were quite evident in Morris' arrangement and reflected the dominance of local propertied elites in municipal corporations throughout this period.

Although his bill was introduced too late in the legislative session for serious consideration (it was discharged at second reading), Morris' effort illustrated the appeal of direct elections for boards — among the owners of real estate at least — apart from the municipal council and the perceived need for voluntary service by wealthier people in many of Ontario's emerging urban centres. In this type of decentralized local government, the power to tax for certain educational purposes, administration of some services, and public accountability often rested outside the municipal council.

Legislation for Free Libraries, 1882

For the founding of free libraries these conditions were very important. Writing in 1881, John G. Bourinot, a leading expert on Canadian government and history, eloquently stated the case for philanthropic aid for libraries:

> ... but what we want, above all things are public libraries, to which all classes may have free access, in the principal centres of population. The rich men of this country can devote a part of their surplus wealth to no more patriotic purpose than the establishment of such libraries in the places where they live ....[10]

In larger cities, such as London and Toronto, the idea of a free library, already a popular feature in the United States, began to attract more attention about 1880. The Rev. W.R.G. Mellen wrote in *Rose-Belford's Canadian Monthly and National Review*,

> Just now, in the City of Toronto, is an opportunity for some rich man to supply an imperious need, and to secure for himself a fragrant memory as enduring as the city. For how pressing is the need here of a free public library, worthy the rapidly growing metropolis of this great and wealthy Province![11]

When Toronto seriously considered a free library in autumn 1881, the mayor, William B. McMurrich, arranged a meeting at which "liberal offers of subscriptions" were made by some leading citizens.[12] At the same time, library promoters, such as Toronto aldermen John Hallam and John Taylor, were adamant that the proposed board of management be independent of council. Although the two men advocated slightly different schemes of composition for a board, Taylor succinctly stated the case for independence at a meeting in late 1881: "He held that the proposed Board of Maintenance for the Toronto library — being of a representative and responsible character — would be as competent to handle the city funds with due economy as any other Board of an educational nature."[13]

Naturally, civic-minded benefactors like John Hallam, who advocated rate-supported libraries in Toronto and later made substantial book donations as well, often expected a voice in administration. It was a given that local self-government in Ontario revolved around the issue of property and the prerogatives of property holders. A pragmatic solution was to enact provincial legislation for appointments to independent boards of management. This provision fitted nicely with a broad range of liberal, conservative, and radical democratic ideas about decentralized self-government.

Generally, local institutions were considered to be "schoolrooms of democracy," where men gained valuable education in the administration of public affairs, and in this process there was also room for non-elective offices where "men of stature" could be selected to direct and shape community progress.[14] Some of the basic propositions advanced for special-purpose library boards, repeated many times for many decades, are familiar to us today:

1) Because appointed boards are to some degree insulated from immediate political concerns, library trustees are freer to act in the long-term interests of the entire community and its general values.

2) Appointed boards are non-sectarian, so a better balance can be struck among religious groups in the community since one group does not have a preponderance of library appointments.

3) Trustees can devote their full energy to a library to ensure its prominence and efficient operation, thus relieving aldermen of an added duty.

4) Voluntary public participation on boards is valuable because citizens should share, in a significant way, in the decision-making process and public policies of local government.

5) Trustees, partly selected on the basis of knowledge and expertise, can provide better judgement and continuity in expanding library services to a community.

6) Public accountability is ensured by means of legislative provisions regarding the elected appointing bodies that ultimately control the selection process and financing of services.

7) Appointments to library boards allow more flexibility for representing the varied community characteristics than the electoral process permits.

Although all these arguments are important and cut across party lines or political doctrine, when the Free Libraries Act was proclaimed by Oliver Mowat's Liberal government in 1882, the primary concern was likely accommodating the tradition of voluntary service by prosperous persons on independent boards in relation to the structure of city, town and village municipal councils that had developed rapidly after passage of the Baldwin Act of 1849. Provincial legislatures were concerned that local self-government should embody the principles of responsibility and representation.

However, the legacy of voluntary bodies in the field of education, such as literary societies and Mechanics' Institutes, which dealt directly with the legislature and its departmental officials, worked against the centralization of authority at the local level. The existence of legislative grants for library purposes reinforced this tendency: aid for educational purposes normally was administered outside the domain of councils.[15] The "working out" of local government was undertaken with the knowledge that the people legislated and governed through their direct representatives, who were qualified to appoint a wide range of officials. To ensure the independent library board would be a responsible and representative body, the legislature enacted four essential legal provisions in the Free Libraries Act, 1882.[16]

First, the circulation of a petition and the approval of a majority of eligible electors in a municipal referendum was necessary before a library board could be created by council bylaw: in effect, a board was created by direct expression of popular sovereignty. In fact, a clause to ensure community support was added to the bill when it initially passed through the legislature. Second, appointments to boards were shared by three elective bodies: the municipal council and two school boards. In theory, this practice, together with the absence of property qualifications for holding a position on the board of management, safeguarded the board from domination by sectarian, property, or party interests that were present in local government. Third, appointments were for limited two- or three-year periods on an overlapping arrangement patterned on school board practice to allow for stability and continuity, an important planning consideration at a time when municipal terms of office were normally one year. Finally, the library board was legally empowered to levy a Public Library Rate — a maximum 1/2 mill on taxable assessment — and was obligated to submit yearly estimates to council for approval.

The adoption of enabling legislation that specified independent board status for single municipalities seemed to serve the library community in Ontario reasonably well for about half a century, especially in city jurisdictions, which grew rapidly during this period. The legislation satisfied the accepted liberal-democratic belief that local government was an educative process, the more radical (or egalitarian) position that believed the extension of significant public participation in local administration was a democratic necessity in conjunction with a more liberal franchise, and the established (or elitist) preference for non-elective office in which prominent persons could exercise a degree of social control. In the United States and Great Britain, independent boards of management were also popular: Edward Edwards' 1869 publication, *Free Town Libraries*, touted the success of boards and made persuasive arguments on this point.[17]

Library trustees, in theory, were non-partisan representatives of their constituencies at a time when ethnic, religious, and party pressure was a common feature that urban reformers wished to remove from annual municipal elections in Ontario. The non-partisan nature of library governance was attractive to many high-minded citizens and advocates of free libraries, such as John Taylor, who emphasized, "The scheme of a free library has special claims upon the public on account of its non-sectarian character. Within its walls the Jew and Gentile, Catholic and Protestant, may fraternize, and on its shelves their various views will have a place."[18]

Appointments also presumably helped to secure a measure of prestige for an educational institution because members had usually achieved a respected place within the hierarchy of their communities, even though library legislation did not dictate property or residence qualifications for serving in office. The liberal-minded *Toronto Globe* enthusiastically endorsed this point in an editorial on January 19, 1883:

> There is no reason to doubt that each of the selecting bodies will do its best to choose the best men, and there appears to be every probability that the Library Board will be distinguished above all other municipal bodies for the literary and commercial talent that will be represented on it.[19]

This situation was reinforced when the directors of Mechanics' Institutes were empowered to transfer their assets and legislative grant to free libraries after 1883; naturally, many directors did continue as library trustees. When the Guelph library board was created, the editor of the *Guelph Dairy Mercury* commented, "We think it would be a wise and prudent course ... to select as many as practicable from the present Directors of the Mechanics' Institute."[20]

However, in practice there were some shortcomings. The self-styled "people's daily" published by John Ross Robertson, the *Toronto Evening Telegram*, printed a withering commentary on February 16, 1883, about the selection process for the first Toronto board:

If the citizens of Toronto had known what they know at present the by-law lately submitted for the founding of a free library would have been defeated. No sooner was the poll which decided the matter closed, than the ward politicians, wire-pullers, aldermen and school trustees put their heads together and proceeded to create a political machine for the distribution of party pap to the needy ones. The free library board is to-day as strong a party lever as there is in Ontario.[21]

The perceived quality of municipal aldermen no doubt was the essential factor in wise appointments. When the Mechanics' Institute at Collingwood changed to free public library status in January 1896, the *Collingwood Enterprise* observed, "whether or not the educational and literary forces of the Library will be strengthened by placing the appointment of managers in the hands of such Councils as we have at present, for instance, is a debatable question."[22]

Another difficulty in the plan for creating free libraries in the province was the community infrastructure and political environment upon which it was based — the municipality. In the late 1800s, incorporated small towns and villages were still regarded as well-managed and self-sufficient local systems that could reasonably provide for the growing demand for public services. The reports of the Ontario Commission on Municipal Institutions in 1888-89 were particularly self-congratulatory.

Because Ryerson's scheme for school-based public libraries had been "practically abandoned" by 1880, in the words of the Minister of Education, Adam Crooks,[23] potential library development was centred on the small library collections that existed in many towns and villages where Mechanics' Institutes were established. A statistical analysis of institute libraries derived from Samuel May's *Special Report of the Minister of Education on the Mechanics' Institutes (Ontario)* published in 1881 reveals that these libraries were relatively small scale operations with limited resources.

Figure 1 indicates that the vast majority of institutes were located in places of fewer than 5,000 people with fewer than 200 regular members. To better compare and rank these institute collections, I converted the statistics from Dr. May's study into per capita figures. Figure 2 shows that about 85 per cent of the institutes held only one book or less per capita, that almost 90 per cent circulated two books or less per capita, and that 98 per cent operated on less than $1.00 per capita.

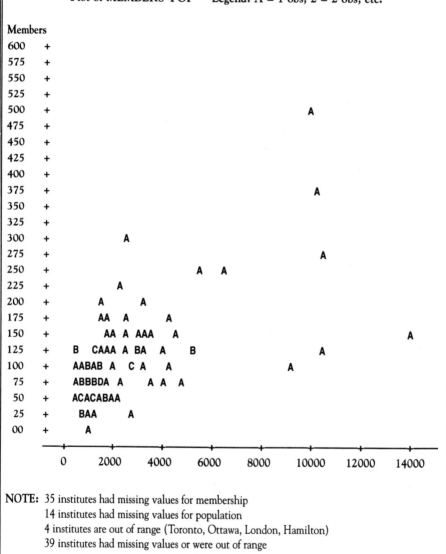

FIGURE 1

Population and Membership of Mechanics' Institutes
in Ontario, 1879-80

Plot of MEMBERS*POP   Legend: A = 1 obs, 2 = 2 obs, etc.

NOTE: 35 institutes had missing values for membership
       14 institutes had missing values for population
       4 institutes are out of range (Toronto, Ottawa, London, Hamilton)
       39 institutes had missing values or were out of range

Source: *Special Report of the Ministry of Education on the Mechanics' Institutes (Ontario)* (Toronto, 1881)

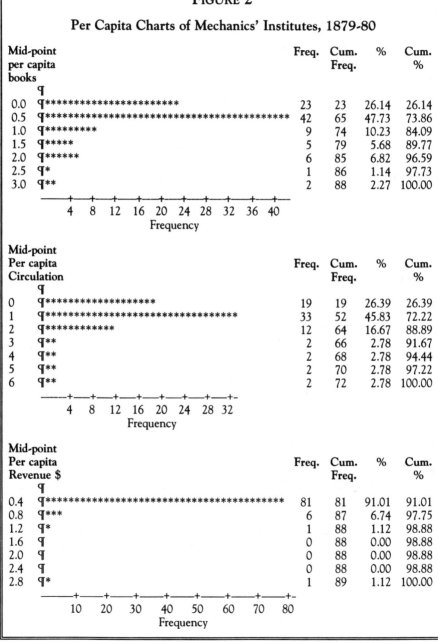

FIGURE 2

Per Capita Charts of Mechanics' Institutes, 1879-80

Mid-point per capita books ꟼ		Freq.	Cum. Freq.	%	Cum. %
0.0	ꟼ*********************	23	23	26.14	26.14
0.5	ꟼ***	42	65	47.73	73.86
1.0	ꟼ*********	9	74	10.23	84.09
1.5	ꟼ*****	5	79	5.68	89.77
2.0	ꟼ******	6	85	6.82	96.59
2.5	ꟼ*	1	86	1.14	97.73
3.0	ꟼ**	2	88	2.27	100.00

```
        +—+—+—+—+—+—+—+—+—+—+—
        4   8  12  16  20  24  28  32  36  40
                    Frequency
```

Mid-point Per capita Circulation ꟼ		Freq.	Cum. Freq.	%	Cum. %
0	ꟼ******************	19	19	26.39	26.39
1	ꟼ*******************************	33	52	45.83	72.22
2	ꟼ************	12	64	16.67	88.89
3	ꟼ**	2	66	2.78	91.67
4	ꟼ**	2	68	2.78	94.44
5	ꟼ**	2	70	2.78	97.22
6	ꟼ**	2	72	2.78	100.00

```
        +—+—+—+—+—+—+—+—+-
        4   8  12  16  20  24  28  32
                    Frequency
```

Mid-point Per capita Revenue $ ꟼ		Freq.	Cum. Freq.	%	Cum. %
0.4	ꟼ*************************************	81	81	91.01	91.01
0.8	ꟼ***	6	87	6.74	97.75
1.2	ꟼ*	1	88	1.12	98.88
1.6	ꟼ	0	88	0.00	98.88
2.0	ꟼ	0	88	0.00	98.88
2.4	ꟼ	0	88	0.00	98.88
2.8	ꟼ*	1	89	1.12	100.00

```
        +—+—+—+—+—+—+—+—+-
       10  20  30  40  50  60  70  80
                    Frequency
```

Source: *Special Report of the Minister of Education on the Mechanics' Institutes (Ontario)* (Toronto, 1881)

TABLE 1

Percentage Decrease in Population by Ten-Year Periods in Rural Counties or Census Divisions, 1881-1921

Region	1881-91	1891-1901	1901-11	1911-21	Total
Bruce	-0.94	-8.64	-15.23	-11.49	-36.30
Dufferin	1.12	-5.80	-15.67	-13.11	-33.46
Dundas	-2.26	-1.86	-8.06	-4.71	-16.89
Durham	-10.58	-14.98	-4.20	-6.75	-36.51
Glengarry	1.02	-1.41	-3.94	-3.49	-7.82
Grenville	-4.98	-2.72	-16.54	-5.14	-29.38
Grey	0.96	-2.28	-5.32	-10.38	-17.02
Haldimand	-6.16	-9.42	1.55	-1.28	-15.31
Huron	-12.73	-7.43	-14.29	-11.13	-45.58
Lanark	11.04	-1.31	-7.67	-4.02	-1.96
Leeds	2.20	-3.32	-3.22	-5.02	-9.36
Lennox & Addington	-6.55	-5.67	-12.68	-6.83	-31.73
Norfolk	-7.56	-5.95	-6.99	-2.74	-23.24
Northumberland	-7.51	-9.35	-2.09	-7.33	-26.28
Ontario	-7.08	-10.91	1.48	13.38	-3.13
Oxford	-0.62	-2.90	-2.13	-1.29	-6.94
Peel	-4.98	-13.65	2.92	8.12	-7.59
Perth	-3.68	-3.57	-1.38	3.38	-5.25
Prince Edward	-10.24	-5.43	-4.00	-2.01	-21.68
Victoria	-1.97	-3.15	-5.55	-7.93	-18.60
Wellington	-8.19	-6.24	-2.07	-0.61	-17.11
Ontario (Prov.)	9.73	3.25	15.77	16.08	44.83

Source: *Census of Canada, 1931*

Many of the counties and regions where these communities were situated underwent a serious long-term population decline after 1882, while the provincial population increased by about 45 per cent (see Table 1). Local revenue sources were also constrained during this period. Thus, the evolving infrastructure for free libraries was to be confined in many respects to a small number of cities, which had more revenue and could better adapt to the changing demands for library service.

The Political Dynamics of Library Boards, 1882-1920

Political power vested in boards of management was significant. Policy-making, site selection and erection of buildings, raising operating and capital funds, budgeting, and personnel management were all potentially important local issues. In practice, a system of checks and balances operated to ensure boards could not act arbitrarily. At the provincial level prior to 1896, the Department of Education had *de facto* supervision of free libraries through its legislative grant process and correspondence with local directors by Superintendent Samuel May. The "management and control" of public library legislation by the department was formalized by statute in 1896 (59 Vic., c. 69, s. 3), and when Dr. May resigned in 1905 the library official's title was changed to Inspector.

Inspections were supposed to be made on a regular basis to ensure boards were operating in accordance with legislative provisions. However, the government was not always satisfied with the extent of this power. In March 1907 Premier James Pliny Whitney complained in the legislature that small libraries were charging out too many "slushy novels." When he suggested the education department might try to remedy conditions, the *Toronto Daily Star* lead editorial said he was taking "too narrow a view" and defended public reading tastes. Although he did garner some support for modifications, Whitney allowed the issue to subside.[24]

Normally a visit by the Inspector of Libraries was a routine affair, although disagreements did occur. In one incident, Inspector William Carson criticized the Hamilton board publicly. Carson startled many at the end of 1920 when he wrote to the Hamilton Board of Control:

> the Hamilton public library as an institution for serving the people of the city is below the reasonable level of merit as judged by modern library standards. It is capable of giving its patrons a fair amount of satisfaction, but it is only realizing a small fraction of its possibilities. A reorganization is desirable. The weakness and defects of the library were so manifest as to be obvious to anyone well versed in librarianship.[25]

But this type of confrontation was the exception, not the rule.

It does not appear, from surviving evidence, that Dr. May's small bureau kept extensive files on each library,[26] but was content rather to answer requests and monitor the annual legislative grants. This often involved the process of interpreting legislation. For example, at Goderich the legality of a local referendum on free status was challenged in January 1900, and the Deputy Minister, John Millar, who reviewed the evidence, replied:

... it may be presumed that the vote of the ratepayers gives sufficient authority to the council to take such action as is provided by section 4 [i.e., to pass a bylaw establishing a free library board funded by a 1/2 mill rate]. Should the council not wish to pass the necessary bylaw, it still has the power to make a grant for the purpose of a library, and section 18 (part II) has in view this authority [i.e., to grant optional sums from general revenue].[27]

Apparently, routine instruction and direction from the provincial office absorbed much of the inspectors' available time.

In the legislature opposition members sometimes tried to introduce changes. On two occasions, in 1888 and again in 1894, the member from the constituency of Brant, William Wood, requested that the education department table a return in the Assembly concerning the distribution of grants to Mechanics' Institutes and free libraries for library purposes.[28] Wood was attempting to demonstrate that departmental policy did not adequately serve rural Ontario because the province did not permit grants for Farmers' Institutes, but he was unsuccessful. (However, in 1895 the government abolished grants to Mechanics' Institutes and instituted a full-scale public library system.)

Later, in 1902, the member from Hamilton East, Henry Carscallen, presented a bill which proposed a restriction on the power of boards to raise municipal taxes for building purposes in cities of less than 100,000 population. He too was unsuccessful, largely because departmental officials in the education office, such as Deputy Minister John Millar, objected that "Library Boards would be seriously hampered if the Bill were to pass."[29] Consequently, Carscallen's effort was stymied at second reading during the legislative session.

Local disputes between councils, aldermen, library promoters and boards also arose from time to time, especially in larger urban communities. All the trustees of London's new free library resigned in 1884 after the council refused to authorize the levying of the public library rate because the board's estimates had not been submitted in time. Judge William Elliott, the board chairman, wrote, "In this situation of matters we have either to engage in litigation with the Council, or remain powerless members of the Board, or resign."[30] Although the original bylaw establishing a library remained in existence, no more members were appointed to the board until 1888. In this year, the council, despite some opposition, submitted a bylaw to the electors in mid-year to repeal the 1884 bylaw and successfully dissolved the board.[31] London remained without free public library service until another bylaw was subsequently passed and a new building was erected in 1895.

In Hamilton a bylaw to establish a free library was unsuccessful in 1885 due, in part, to the opposition of several aldermen, who insisted that the power to levy rates should reside with council alone and that the library board should be elected in order to be held properly accountable. One alderman, who disagreed with his colleagues, wrote:

> The provisions of the act as to the control of the library are, I think, the very best that could be devised. Representation is secured to both Protestant and Catholic members of the community, which would not likely be the case were the trustees elected by the people directly. It will plainly be seen, however, from the above that the people have a direct control over the members of the library board through their representatives in the council and in the school board, and these bodies, together with the press and public opinion, will be able to keep the trustees, even if inclined to be refractory, within the proper limits both as regards management and expenditure.[32]

Nevertheless, the bylaw failed by a good margin.

On some occasions library boards of management were successful in disputes with council. The Toronto board found its budget estimates trimmed by council from time to time until, in 1900, Toronto aldermen attempted to question and reduce both the capital estimates and the current expenditures submitted by the board. The board sought a court ruling in this circumstance, and the council was rebuffed by a court decision.[33] However, in terms of public relations this action may not have been particularly astute. In its report on the decision, the *Toronto Globe* observed,

> Had the members of that board been responsible directly to the people, as the aldermen are, it is a matter for conjecture whether they would have resorted to the courts and incurred the additional expense which such a course involves, even though they may have been within their rights under the law in demanding the full amount of their estimates.[34]

Ultimately, councils could approach the legislature to enact a bill in specific cases to resolve local problems. Municipal councils in Ottawa and Lindsay exercised this option in 1902 and 1903, respectively. When a Carnegie grant of $100,000 was offered to Ottawa in March 1901, the city council was not disposed to allow a semi-autonomous board to assume any control. The *Ottawa Evening Journal* concurred. It printed a piece calling boards "a municipal curse in this province" and concluded:

If we are to have a public library board let it be one that the council can control. Make the basis of two or three aldermen, then appoint competent citizens to act with them, but make the appointments terminable at any time by the council, and require the annual estimates of expenditure to be approved by the council before being acted on.[35]

Otto Julius Klotz, one of the leading advocates for a free library in Ottawa, protested that continuity would be sacrificed if council made all nominations on an annual basis. He felt alternating appointments among three bodies was a necessary factor in library administration:

Under such a system men who had made a special study of library matters could be obtained to act on the Board, and a general scheme involving perhaps years for its evolution could be carried out, while under the proposed method, the library committee might be composed of wholly new members every year.[36]

Nevertheless, the Ottawa council submitted a bill to the Ontario legislature that established a local board appointed by council composed of the mayor, eight aldermen, and three citizens. The term of office for all members was limited to one year.[37]

At Lindsay, when the board and council could not agree on a site for the new Carnegie library, the legislative route was also used. During the course of the controversy, labour leaders from the Central Committee of the Allied Organizations criticized the board for not being "directly responsible to the people." In response, the board secretary, Edwin Hardy, who was also a prominent figure in the Ontario Library Association, wrote to the editor of the *Lindsay Weekly Post* about the "principle that some part of our governing bodies should be elected and some appointed."[38] A few alderman proposed that three more council appointees be added to gain control of the board. One alderman complained:

It seems to me that anybody can be elected to the Council, but according to the present arrangement they are not good enough to be associated on the Library Board. I would consider that a slur on the Council. I certainly think the council should appoint three [more] members. The Socialist vote may be small, but their influence is great.[39]

However, on this occasion the proposal to change the composition and size of the board was not adopted.[40]

Even private citizens could present legal challenges if they were dissatisfied with local arrangements. At Palmerston one individual challenged the right of the municipal council to transfer a one-time grant of $650 to the library to purchase land because a section of the Free Libraries Act seemed to prevent this kind of grant without a vote of the ratepayers in the community. However, an Ontario Division Court ruling handed down in December 1902 allowed the transfer and clarified the legal relationship among the acts pertaining to libraries and municipal corporations: "Held, that the power to grant aid to free libraries was absolutely in the hands of the local municipality under the general provision of the Municipal Act, and that the by-law was valid notwithstanding section 18 of R.S.O. 1897, ch. 232 ...."[41] The municipal contribution was used to buy a site, where a Carnegie building was eventually erected.

Throughout the province there were groups interested in making improvements in board structure and operating procedures. In rural Ontario there was a lingering dissatisfaction with library grants to Mechanics' Institutes, the education department's regulations, and its system of inspection. In the 1870s an organization known as the Grange had spread into central Canada from the United States. The Dominion Grange worked to educate farmers to cope with changes in the national economy and political life. As early as 1882 the Dominion Grange's committee on education decided to press the provincial government for "a grant to Granges establishing libraries the same assistance as is now extended to other bodies."[42] On another occasion, on March 13, 1896, the Grange presented a petition to the legislature praying for certain amendments to the Public Libraries Act, specifically that boards in unincorporated villages "shall not be required to have more than fifty members, and that only twenty five [sic] of these shall necessarily be twenty one [sic] years of age."[43]

The Grange realized that many small libraries could not easily qualify for a legislative grant because a statutory section required boards to have at least 100 members, of whom 50 had to be 21 years of age or older. However, the petitioners were not successful. The membership problems encountered by small association libraries were destined to continue for many decades.

Another prominent group, the Ontario Library Association (OLA), also began to make requests after its formation in 1900. The most audacious proposal came in 1902-03 when the association pressed for the establishment of a provincial library commission composed of five or six appointed citizens to replace the Department of Education as the central library authority in Ontario. Of course, the education department had no intention of relinquishing its powers by creating a independent commission to coordinate the activities of local boards, and it turned aside the request in December 1902.[44] In the following year OLA President Hugh H. Langton

135

elaborated upon the advantages of the American commission style of library governance at the annual OLA conference, but his campaign was unsuccessful because the government held that OLA's proposition was not in keeping with "the genius of the constitution."[45]

Occasionally, there were substantive challenges or alterations to the original legislative arrangements for financing and board composition. In 1892, Toronto city council approached the Ontario legislature to curtail the financial power of the library when it felt the board had become overly ambitious. Ironically, the alderman who spearheaded this move was John Hallam. It was not without some humour that he made the city's case to the legislature's Municipal Committee chaired by the Attorney General, Arthur S. Hardy:

> Ald. Hallam made a vigorous speech in favour of the bill, saying: —
> "The Property Owners' Association is in favor of the bill. The Trades and Labor Council is in favor of the bill. I am in favor of the bill." (Laughter)
> "All the great bodies are," said Mr. Hardy, amid renewed laughter.
> "Carried," "carried," shouted the committee.[46]

The result was an amendment pertaining specifically to cities of more than 100,000 population: the amendment reduced the tax levy to 1/4 mill and compelled boards to receive council approval to establish a museum.[47]

More than two decades later, in 1913, efforts by the provincial government to reduce council appointments on library boards by increasing the number of public school board positions for teachers, ostensibly to help in book selection, failed due to strong opposition and a successful lobby for the status quo.[48] A determined Toronto delegation that met with the Minister of Education, Robert Pyne, to protest the proposed amendments said the changes would "destroy the representative nature of the board." They were willing only to make a modest concession to the intent of the bill:

> It is quite possible that this legislation in some modified form might be suitable for rural localities, but not at all for cities. There the business matters formed the larger part of discussions and the purchase of books was a minor matter and left almost entirely to the staff. In the villages and smaller towns the custom was for the boards to purchase the books and the idea of the amendments might be worked out to meet those conditions.[49]

At this time, the chief direction for educational affairs was in the hands of the Superintendent, John Seath, who personally preferred to have school boards in charge of libraries. He shared the lingering sentiment that school boards could better direct library progress. In his presidential address at the 1903 Ontario Educational Association convention, Seath had suggested that "One board should control the public libraries as well as the schools. They were all parts of the Provincial system of education."[50]

But Seath was unable to give schools more control over libraries. In 1913, trustees directly pressured members of the legislature, the department, and even the premier with resolutions or letters similar to one from Belleville which protested that the proposed change "would not insure a proper representation of the general public" and one from North Bay that observed that school principals were "not regarded as having so much interest in town affairs" because they usually were not property owners or long-term residents.[51] As a result, the particular clause in question never received royal assent.

After 1900 the success of county library authorities in the United States began to raise the possibility of structuring library services in rural areas on a broader, multi-jurisdictional basis. But, although contractual arrangements for service between boards were first introduced in 1896, the Ontario legislature continued to prefer single jurisdictions. The successful growth of free libraries in cities was held to be evidence that the existing system worked reasonably well (see Table 2).

Amending legislation that allowed police villages (1898) and townships (1916) to form free library boards essentially replicated the original model for board governance, except for the number of trustees.[52] The police village system of local government in Ontario predated Confederation; the original purpose was to establish a local body in a village to maintain public order. Police villages were not incorporated but were created by a bylaw of the particular county council.

The 1/2 mill rate was retained, despite the knowledge that low assessments in smaller communities produced about the same revenue as voluntary contributions. An increased mill rate was not considered, for, as one observer noted, "serious opposition would arise in cities, where the feeling exists that it would be dangerous to permit a body not directly elected, power to enforce a higher taxation."[53] But it was evident some modifications were needed to adjust to conditions in rural Ontario, because libraries in many communities (especially unincorporated ones) could not or would not adopt free status; they remained voluntary association libraries organized under a separate part of the revised 1909 Act.

In police villages, townships, and school sections, the usual balance between council and school boards was not easily attained because their authority often did not coincide territorially. It was becoming obvious that the promotion of free public library service outside urban areas was more

TABLE 2

Public Library Boards in Cities, 1919

City	1919 Population	Circulation	Volumes	Expenses $
Belleville	12,345	34,823	9,978	4,563
Brantford	28,725	113,913	29,352	11,919
Chatham	15,030	58,539	11,060	4,140
Fort William	19,523	109,903	30,560	20,674
Galt	12,558	45,043	10,516	4,757
Guelph	16,974	75,847	19,553	6,000
Hamilton	110,137	419,655	58,083	70,283
Kingston	23,737	74,047	12,419	5,369
Kitchener	19,767	58,969	15,697	6,841
London	58,421	308,892	49,126	20,998
Niagara Falls	12,434	61,563	16,212	5,134
Ottawa	104,007	286,546	74,990	36,169
Peterborough	20,904	67,049	16,645	6,885
Port Arthur	15,100	81,290	15,632	10,654
St. Catharines	19,189	51,591	12,233	6,862
St. Thomas	17,209	71,796	16,745	4,640
Sarnia	12,178	47,735	12,797	4,437
Sault Ste Marie	20,529	72,425	10,110	10,301
Stratford	17,143	61,798	15,479	3,660
Toronto	489,681	1,755,079	343,363	187,105
Welland	9,876	13,012	5,298	526
Windsor	29,344	95,510	28,330	10,681
Woodstock	10,051	47,009	12,446	3,646
City total	1,094,862	4,012,034	826,624	$446,244
Ontario total	2,621,785	6,180,705	1,906,942	$619,903
City % of total	41.8	64.9	43.3	72.0

Sources: Ontario. Department of Education. *Annual Report 1920*
Ontario. Bureau of Municipal Affairs. *Bulletin 1919*

TABLE 3

Provincial Expenditures for Libraries, 1910-24

Year	Public Library Grants	Travelling Libraries	Rural School Library Grants
1909-10	$ 33,743	$ 1,843	$ 6,060
1910-11	37,764	2,515	5,847
1911-12	38,483	2,789	8,060
1912-13	37,168	2,810	8,241
1913-14	38,644	2,257	7,962
1914-15	38,008	1,543	8,294
1915-16	37,747	1,859	8,201
1916-17	36,793	2,714	8,272
1917-18	38,343	2,997	8,397
1918-19	38,435	3,236	7,895
1919-20	42,543	3,661	8,274
1920-21	38,854	3,309	8,453
1921-22	53,601	4,998	8,360
1922-23	53,964	4,262	8,343
1923-24	54,037	4,753	8,276

Source: Ontario. Provincial Auditor. *Public Accounts.*

difficult than in urban centres because lower educational levels and geo-graphical distances made petition referendums more difficult to carry through successfully. In rural communities, where the heritage of volunteerism continued to manifest itself in the existence of more than two hundred association libraries, the apolitical nature of boards (an important feature in cities) was less relevant.

Assistance for smaller libraries began to appear in the consolidated Act of 1895 which allowed Teachers' and Farmers' Institutes to affiliate with boards in providing service; provision was also made to have one represen-tative from a Teacher's Institute sit on boards.[54]

Two programs the Department of Education put more emphasis on after the Act was revised in 1909 — a travelling library system and grants for rural school libraries — were somewhat popular in rural Ontario, as Table 3 shows. However, the problem of the small association library persisted because depopulation had occurred in many rural counties (see Table 4) along with a simultaneous transfer of economic activity to more urbanized centres.

TABLE 4

New Library Boards in Counties
Recording Population Losses between 1880 and 1919

County	New Boards in 1919	Board Status	Municipal Status	Population 1880	1919	Percent Change
Bruce	Cargill	Assn.	-			
	Chesley	Free	town	740	1,703	130.1
	Glamis	Assn.	-			
	Hepworth	Assn.	village	-	410	
	Kincardine	Free	town	2,648	2,139	-19.2
	Lucknow	Free	village	1,068	907	-15.1
	Mildmay	Assn.	village	-	671	
	Parkhead	Assn.	-			
	Pinkerton	Assn.	-			
	Riversdale	Assn.	-			
	Southampton	Assn.	town	1,108	1,500	35.4
	Tara	Free	village	-	520	
	Teeswater	Free	village	909	824	-9.4
	Tiverton	Assn.	village	727	260	-64.2
	Underwood	Assn.	-			
	Westford	Assn.	-			
Dufferin	Grand Valley	Free	village	-	558	
	Honeywood	Assn.	-			
	Mono Centre	Assn.	-			
	Shelburne	Free	village	660	976	47.9
Dundas	Iroquois	Assn.	village	872	818	-6.2
	Matilda	Assn.	-			
	Morrisburg	Assn.	village	1,797	1,318	-26.7
	Winchester	Assn.	village	-	1,047	
Durham	Millbrook	Free	village	1,119	746	-33.3
	Solina	Assn.	-			
Glengarry	Lancaster	Free	village	-	574	
	Martintown	Assn.	-			
	Williamstown	Assn.	-			
Grenville	Cardinal	Free	village	800	1,147	43.4
	Merrickville	Free	village	781	792	1.4
	Oxford Mills	Assn.	-			

Table 4. New Library Boards (*cont.*)

County	New Boards in 1919	Board Status	Municipal Status	Population 1880	Population 1919	Percent Change
Grey	Badjeros	Assn.	-			
	Chatsworth	Assn.	village	-	257	
	Dundalk	Assn.	village	-	700	
	East Linton	Assn.	-			
	Elmwood	Assn.	-			
	Flesherton	Assn.	village	-	378	
	Hanover	Free	town	-	3,225	
	Holstein	Assn.	-			
	Kemble	Assn.	-			
	Markdale	Free	village	-	925	
	Thornbury	Assn.	town	-	733	
	Thorndale	Assn.	-			
Haldimand	Canfield	Assn.	-			
	Cayuga	Free	village	-	737	
	Cheapside	Assn.	-			
	Hagersville	Free	village	-	1,058	
	Jarvis	Assn.	village	-	490	
	Nanticoke	Assn.	-			
	Victoria	Assn.	-			
Huron	Auburn	Assn.	-			
	Bayfield	Assn.	village	632	391	-38.1
	Beechwood	Assn.	-			
	Brucefield	Assn.	-			
	Dungannon	Assn.	-			
	Ethel	Assn.	-			
	Fordwich	Assn.	-			
	Gorrie	Assn.	-			
	Hensall	Free	village	-	715	
	Kirkton	Assn.	-			
	St. Helen's	Assn.	-			
	Walton	Assn.	-			
	Zurich	Assn.	-			
Leeds	Athens	Assn.	village	-	597	
	Delta	Assn.	-			
	Gananoque	Assn.	town	2,781	3,434	23.5
	Lyn	Assn.	-			

Table 4. New Library Boards (*cont.*)

County	New Boards in 1919	Board Status	Municipal Status	Population 1880	1919	Percent Change
Lennox & Addington	Bath	Assn.	village	542	327	-39.7
	Newburgh	Assn.	village	723	426	-41.1
	Odessa	Assn.	-			
	Strathcona	Assn.	-			
Norfolk	Delhi	Free	village	-	654	
	Port Dover	Assn.	village	1,046	1,319	26.1
	Port Rowan	Free	village	-	618	
	Waterford	Free	village	1,052	985	-6.4
Northumber -land	Campbellford	Free	town	1,292	2,866	121.8
	Cobourg	Assn.	town	5,118	4,835	-5.5
	Colborne	Assn.	village	1,009	939	-6.9
	Gore's Landing	Assn.	-			
	Grafton	Assn.	-			
	Warkworth	Assn.	-			
Ontario	Beaverton	Free	village	-	932	
	Brooklin	Assn.	-			
	Cannington	Assn.	village	919	818	-11.0
	Claremont	Assn.	-			
	Pickering	Assn.	-			
	Zephyr	Assn.	-			
Peel	Alton	Assn.	-			
	Brampton	Free	town	3,128	4,238	35.5
	Caledon	Assn.	-			
	Clarkson	Assn.	-			
	Inglewood	Assn.	-			
	Lorne Park	Assn.	-			
	Mono Road	Assn.	-			
	Port Credit	Assn.	village	-	1,100	
Perth	Atwood	Assn.	-			
	Millbank	Assn.	-			
	Milverton	Free	village	669	929	38.9
	Monkton	Assn.	-			
Prince Edward	Bloomfield	Assn.	village	-	500	

Table 4. New Library Boards (*cont.*)

County	New Boards in 1919	Board Status	Municipal Status	Population 1880	1919	Percent Change
Victoria	Bobcaygeon	Assn.	village	717	844	17.7
	Cambray	Assn.	-			
	Kinmount	Assn.	-			
	Kirkfield	Assn.	-			
	Little Britain	Free	-			
	Manilla	Assn.	-			
	Norland	Assn.	-			
	Oakwood	Free	-			
	Omemee	Assn.	village	774	467	-39.7
	Victoria Road	Assn.	-			
	Woodville	Assn.	village	-	400	
Wellington	Alma	Assn.	-			
	Belwood	Assn.	-			
	Clifford	Free	village	660	516	-21.8
	Drayton	Free	village	764	622	-18.6
	Erin	Free	village	-	480	
	Glen Allan	Assn.	-			
	Moorefield	Assn.	-			
	Morriston	Assn.	-			
	Mount Hope	Assn.	-			
	Speedside	Assn.	-			
	Stevensville	Assn.	-			
	Palmerston	Free	town	1,759	1,815	3.2

Table 4 Synopsis
- 124 new boards in 1919 (95 association libraries, 29 free libraries)
- 124 communities in 19 counties (10 towns, 43 villages, and 71 unincorporated places)
- 109 libraries in incorporated and other places under 1,000 population in 1919

Sources: Ontario. Department of Education. *Report of the Minister 1920*
Ontario. Bureau of Industries. *Annual Report 1886*
Ontario. Bureau of Municipal Affairs. *Bulletin 1919*

The Public Libraries Act, 1920

To remedy some of the problems that had arisen during four decades, the education department introduced some innovations in the thoroughly revised 1920 Act, which served as the basis for legislation until the late 1950s.[55] More specific clauses allowed an association library to request that council assume its assets and create a free public library in the usual manner:

143

in this case no bylaw would be necessary. Provision for school section boards was allowed in rural areas. Councils or school trustees could become the sole appointing bodies for township, police village, or school section boards, and the size of these boards could vary between five and nine members. Union libraries were also permitted and contractual situations clarified.[56]

As a result of these changes, boards in police villages, townships, and school sections began to diverge from the traditional urban prototype developed after 1882. The most notable feature of the 1920 Act was a strengthening of the financial position of free boards. A per capita Public Library Rate of fifty cents, an entirely new formula, was unveiled by Inspector William Carson. Generally, legislators were satisfied these modest changes would allow boards to fulfil their program needs, although the Ontario Library Association went on record at its 1923 convention as saying that the new per capita rate was inadequate.[57]

The 1920 Act is usually regarded as a landmark, a reinforcement along progressive lines of the statutory authority trustees had possessed for four decades. Inspector Carson, who had served previously as an alderman in London, was instrumental in fortifying and promoting this perspective: "A free public library, according to the statute, is essentially the property of the electors of the municipality or other community in which the library is situated. It is legally qualified to support by tax-levy, and is under the management of a board appointed to serve on behalf of the electors."[58]

Carson's views were a classic restatement of the concept of trusteeship eloquently put forward in the last quarter of the nineteenth century. The traditional distinction in Ontario between political and educational matters[59] could be rationalized in cities where boards might justify their position vis-à-vis councils by referring to the detailed nature of their deliberations, but the policy of retaining boards as separate entities also suited the Department of Education's perspective, accustomed as it was to dealing with school boards and learned associations. During Carson's years as Inspector (1916-1929), the departmental library component expanded considerably.[60] In fact, its size, duties, and budget were not surpassed until after 1945.

Additionally, before 1920, some ideas associated with the American Progressives had contributed to the independence of library boards. Urban reformers had successfully introduced sound business methods in the administration of many local services. The tenets of scientific management or Taylorism (named after its founder, Frederick Winslow Taylor) and praise for the role of urban professionals were now embracing libraries: efficiency, economy, and technical expertise were becoming bywords in the public library lexicon.[61] From the 1890s to the Great War, the semi-autonomous position of library trustees was tested and defined in a series of legislative and judicial decisions. Trustees received their authority from the Province, they were usually perceived to be representative of the social fabric of their communities, to be above the strife of local politics, and to be participating in a broader educational movement to improve society. These qualities complemented the philosophy of good government espoused by American Progressives. Consequently, the status of boards within local self-government seemed secure; indeed, the vitality of local government and its prospects for serving the needs of Ontario's growing population appeared to be quite favourable at the end of the First World War.[62]

But by this time a few troublesome issues had come to the surface, issues the 1920 Act did not address directly. By the 1920s, some commentators on local government, notably Horace Brittain and William Munro, were openly questioning the rationale and need for special-purpose bodies; they believed a strong general-purpose council could efficiently administer services such as libraries and parks.

Munro, from Almonte in eastern Ontario, taught public administration at Harvard University between 1904 and 1929; he decried what he felt to be American populist preferences for independent boards at the municipal level.[63] Brittain, the director of the Toronto-based Bureau of Municipal Research, believed special-purpose bodies were detrimental because they fragmented decision making and increased expenditures: "In the same way, the library board. I believe this earmarking revenues for boards is an absolutely wrong proposition."[64]

Checks and balances in municipalities, especially independent boards, were no longer so attractive from a political standpoint. Municipal politics had become less factional; the influence of lodges and political parties was less evident.[65] Indeed, the inexorable growth of provincial and federal governments was beginning to overshadow the concerns of local government. A greatly expanded electorate had come to accept the municipal council as the primary local authority or to rely upon ratepayer groups and Home and School Associations to guard their interests rather than "establishment" bodies, such as library boards, that were frequently composed of reappointed representatives[66] and on some occasions acted irresponsibly. The rationale for boards had changed subtly during the era of urban reform: the need for appointed boards was now couched in administrative terms, not political ones.

At the same time, planning for regional library service began to be seriously considered. After a lengthy debate, one which had begun 20 years before, the formation of county library associations began in Lambton County during the early years of the Great Depression. The purpose of these county library associations was stated by the 1933 national Ridington Commission library report: "the pooling of resources, in funds, in books and in personnel, of these little libraries into a unified regional library system, soundly financed, ably led, competently staffed, and efficiently administered."[67]

In 1936, amendments were finally introduced to allow library associations on a county basis to contract with other boards.[68] Prior to 1939 the Department of Education encouraged the establishment of five independent county associations in Lambton, Middlesex, Oxford, Elgin, and Simcoe, but the approach of war did not allow for more effective legislation to be enacted or for the formation of regional system boards.[69]

Thus, after 1920, trustees continued to rely upon their statutory authority and were reluctant to develop new ideas that would alter the traditional pattern of local control. The apparent unsuitability of the prototypical board in rural areas, the possibility of larger units of service, and the renewed interest in delegating more power to stronger urban municipal councils did not seem cause for serious concern. Even during the depression years of the 1930s, when municipalities were hard pressed financially, the board form of governance continued. Only when Windsor, East Windsor, Walkerville and Sandwich were amalgamated to resolve financial problems was a library directly administered by a city council (between 1935 and 1937).[70]

Debate about changes in the form of boards, their composition and size, the value of special-purpose bodies as administrative entities, trustee accountability, library financing, the relationship between trustees and aldermen, and the centralization of library services at the county or regional level remained unresolved at the outset of World War II. As a result, ambiguity about the traditional paradigm of lay board governance enacted in 1882 existed even before the entire structure of local government in Ontario began to undergo reassessment after 1945.[71]

Notes

[1] For example, C.R. Tindal and S. Nobes Tindal, *Local Government in Canada*, 3d ed. (Toronto, 1990), 55-58 and 198-99; and T.J. Plunkett and G.M. Betts, *The Management of Canadian Urban Government* (Kingston, 1979), 100-25.

[2] By the late nineteenth century, the term "responsible government" had evolved to mean self-government and included the municipal level: see John G. Bourinot, *How Canada is Governed* (Toronto, 1895), 24-25. The representative aspect, rights of the people, and local politics are outlined by Dennis A. O'Sullivan, *Government in Canada: the Principles and Institutions of Our Federal and Provincial Constitutions*, 2d ed. (Toronto, 1887), 232-44.

[3] Patronage is used in terms of the power to make appointments based on many considerations. For example, Otto Klotz, the founder of the Preston Mechanics' Institute, wrote to John A. Macdonald for a Senate seat because he was the "father of German Conservatives": see Jeffrey Simpson, *Spoils of Power; the*

Politics of Patronage (Toronto, 1988), 316. For biographical information on Klotz, see Jesse Middleton and Fred Landon, *The Province of Ontario — a History, 1615-1927* (Toronto, 1927-28), vol. 3, 171-72. For patrons and clients in this era see Sidney J.R. Noel, *Patrons, Clients, Brokers: Ontario Society and Politics, 1791-1896* (Toronto, 1990), 275-93.

[4]Janet Carnochan, "Niagara Library, 1800 to 1900," reprinted in her *History of Niagara (In Part)* (Toronto, 1914), 49. This library is studied in detail by Chung S. Kim, "The Development of the First Library in Ontario, 1800-1900" (M.A. thesis, University of Toronto, Faculty of Education, ca. 1985).

[5]See "Petition from the Mechanics' Institution, Kingston" in *Journals of the House of Assembly of Upper Canada* (Toronto, 1835), vol. 1, appendix 57; and "Report of Select Committee on Petition of Richard Murphy and Others" in *Journals* (Toronto, 1836), vol. 3, appendix 119.

[6]James Bruce Elgin, *Condition and Prospects of Canada in 1854* (Quebec, 1855), 20. A number of township corporations directly administered some of these libraries: see Bruce Curtis, "'Littery Merrit', 'Useful Knowledge', and the Organization of Township Libraries in Canada West, 1840-1860," *Ontario History* 78 (1986): 285-311. For Boulton's bill see Canada (Province). Legislature, *Debates of the Legislative Assembly of United Canada, 1841-1867* (Montreal: Presses de l'École des hautes études commerciales, 1970-), vol. 11, pt. 1, 606, September 20, 1852.

[7]Reprinted in the *Toronto Globe*, September 24, 1880.

[8]The entire debate is recorded in the *Toronto Daily Globe*, March 20, 1859.

[9]The bill is reprinted in J. George Hodgins, ed., *Documentary History of Education in Upper Canada* (Toronto, 1907), vol. 19, 207-10.

[10]John G. Bourinot, *The Intellectual Development of the Canadian People; an Historical Review* (Toronto, 1881), 122-23.

[11]W.R.G. Mellen, "Wealth and its Uses," *Rose-Belford's Canadian Monthly and National Review* 2 (1879): 349. For London see "A Public Library," *London Advertiser*, October 12, 1881.

[12]See "Free Library Question," *Toronto Globe*, December 13, 1881.

[13]"Free Public Library," *Toronto Globe*, November 24, 1881.

[14]J.G. Bourinot, "Local Government in Canada: an Historical Survey," *Proceedings and Transactions of the Royal Society of Canada* Series 1, vol. 4, section 2 (1886): 73. Bourinot questioned the need for election of all public officials in his influential "Elected or Appointed Officials? A Canadian Question," *Annals of the American Academy of Political and Social Science* (Philadelphia, 1895), vol. 5, 674-75.

[15]See in particular John Millar, *Canadian Citizenship; a Treatise on Civil Government* (Toronto, 1899), 111-12.

[16]Free Libraries Act, 1882, 45 Vic., c. 22, s. 2, pp. 3, 8. See the editorial on changes in the *Toronto Evening Telegram*, March 9, 1882. For the original handwritten amendments to the act see Archives of Ontario, Records of the Office of Legislative Assembly, RG 49, Series I-7-H, Bill 104, February 28, 1882. Previously (in 1985) I suggested that the Ontario law resembled an earlier 1872

Illinois state law and I have since had the opportunity to read a similar conclusion by Jean Eileen Stewart, "The Public Library in Canada in Relation to the Government" (Report to the Fellowships and Scholarships Committee of the American Library Association) (Chicago, 1939), 28.

[17]Edward Edwards, *Free Town Libraries, their Formation, Management, and History* (London, 1869), 22-30.

[18]John Taylor, *Toronto's Free Library; Facts for the Citizens* (Toronto, 1881), 1.

[19]"The Free Library," *Toronto Globe*, January 19, 1883.

[20]"Free Library Carried in Guelph," *Guelph Daily Mercury*, January 2, 1883. Of course, most directors were well-to-do and cautious to guard privilege and property. As one advocate noted, Mechanics' Institutes were managed by "gentlemen of influence and wealth" and those "possessing enterprise, education and intelligence": see Otto Klotz, *A Review of the Special Report of the Minister of Education on the Mechanics' Institutes Ontario* (Toronto, 1881), 7.

[21]"The Free Library," *Toronto Evening Telegram*, February 16, 1883. The *Globe* subsequently agreed with Robertson's opinion in a later editorial, "The Free Library By-Law," April 3, 1883, but still supported the appointive system for boards instead of the elective process.

[22]"Free Public Library," *The Enterprise and Collingwood Messenger*, October 24, 1895.

[23]Adam Crooks, *Educational Statement of the Hon. Adam Crooks, Minister of Education on Moving the Estimates for 1880 in Committee of Supply, House of Assembly, Province of Ontario* (Toronto, 1880), 12.

[24]*Toronto Daily Star*, March 7, 1907, and "Public Libraries," March 9, 1907. Archives of Ontario, Sir James Pliny Whitney Papers, MU 3122, letter from W.H. Ferguson (Secretary of the London Real Estate Owners' Association) to Whitney approving an amendment to improve "trashy" or "unwholesome reading" in libraries, March 30, 1907. The Association also suggested reducing the free library rate to one-quarter mill for all places over 50,000 population.

[25]"Public Library is Below Level Demanded Here," *Hamilton Spectator*, November 22, 1920. Also "Hamilton Library Severely Criticized," *Toronto Globe*, November 22, 1920, and November 24, 1920. The incident is reviewed by J. Katharine Greenfield, *Hamilton Public Library 1889-1963; A Celebration of Vision and Leadership* (Hamilton, 1989), 50-54.

[26]For example, very little information — correspondence, memos, circulars — survives from this period. In the case of Port Rowan, where local records were destroyed by fire, the Department responded to a request for information on the establishment of free status by the library in 1897 by saying it had "some evidence" (a printed annual report of the Minister) that Port Rowan had passed a local bylaw, but no actual documentation: see Archives of Ontario, Dept. of Education, RG 2, Series P-3-DM-7-K37, Box 203 #3, Director of Public Library Service, letter from Deputy Minister to F.G. Killmaster, Secretary of Port Rowan Library, February 17, 1937.

[27]"The Free Library," *Goderich Signal*, January 18, 1900.

[28]*Return to an Order of the Legislative Assembly, dated 15th March, 1888*, printed as *Ontario Sessional Paper* vol. 20, part 6, 1888, no. 76. *Return to an Order of the*

House, dated the 23rd April, 1894, not printed as a sessional paper, but the original is at the Archives of Ontario, Records of the Office of Legislative Assembly, RG 49, Series I-7-B-2, 1894, no. 125.

[29] Archives of Ontario, Records of the Dept. of Education, RG 2, Series D-7, box 18, memorandum of February 18, 1902, John Millar to the Minister of Education. Carscallen's proposed legislation, Bill 150, is attached to Millar's correspondence.

[30] "The Library Board," *London Advertiser*, March 11, 1884.

[31] Eleanor Shaw, *A History of the London Public Library* (London, 1968), 30-31 covers this period.

[32] "Public Library," *Hamilton Daily Spectator*, May 13, 1885. The aldermanic opposition occurred mostly at public meetings: see *Hamilton Daily Spectator*, March 31, 1885; May 8, 1885; and May 9, 1885; as well as *Hamilton Times*, May 8, 1885, and May 9, 1885.

[33] "Toronto Public Library Board v. City of Toronto" in *Ontario Practice Reports* (Toronto, 1899-1901), vol. 19, 329-32.

[34] *Toronto Globe*, December 17, 1900.

[35] "As to the Library," *Ottawa Evening Journal*, March 13, 1901.

[36] Otto Klotz, "The Public Library," published as Appendix A in Ottawa. Council, *Annual Departmental Report for the Year 1905* (Ottawa, 1906), 29.

[37] An Act Respecting the Establishment of the Carnegie Library in the City of Ottawa, 2 Edw. VII, c. 55. This act was later repealed: see An Act Respecting the City of Ottawa, 1911, 1 Geo. V, c. 98.

[38] See "Labor and the Library," *Lindsay Weekly Post*, February 20, 1903; and *Lindsay Weekly Post*, February 27, 1903.

[39] "The Public Library Bill is Approved," *Lindsay Weekly Post*, March 20, 1903.

[40] The town council submitted a petition and bill that later received royal assent: see An Act Respecting the Lindsay Public Library, 3 Edw. VII, c. 61; and Archives of Ontario, Legislative Assembly, RG 49, Series I-7-F-2, 1903, petition no. 82, received March 25, 1903.

[41] "Hunt v. The Corporation of the Town of Palmerston and the Palmerston Public Library Board" in *Ontario Law Reports* (Toronto, 1903), vol. 5, 76-80.

[42] See *Canadian Farmer and Grange Record* 4, no. 32 (April 12, 1882): 511. Also, "Farmers' Institutes," *The Rural Canadian* 9, no. 2 (February 1886): 33 subsequently criticized the department's inspection of Mechanics' Institutes and the failure of the institutes to properly serve the mechanical classes.

[43] Archives of Ontario, Records of the Legislative Assembly, RG 49, Series I-7-F-2, 1896, petition no. 354, received March 11, 1896.

[44] The immediate reply of the Minister of Education was negative: "It is not likely that he [the Premier] will be able to appoint one in the immediate future": see Archives of Ontario, Records of the Dept. of Education, RG 2, Series D-7, box 7, letter of Richard Harcourt to H. Langton, December 19, 1902.

[45] Hugh H. Langton, "A Provincial Library Commission," presidential address delivered at the third annual meeting of the Ontario Library Association, April 13, 1903. Also, *Toronto Globe*, April 15, 1904. The failure of the state library

commission form of government to reach Ontario indicates the difficulty of identifying this province's library movement with all the elements of the Progressive movement which influenced American libraries.

[46]"Legislative Notes," *Toronto Globe*, April 6, 1892.

[47]An Act to Amend the Free Libraries Act, 1892, 55 Vic., c. 48.

[48]Statute Law Amendment Act, 3-4 Geo. V, c. 18, s. 38; and George Locke, "Recent Legislation Affecting Public Libraries in Ontario," *Proceedings of the Ontario Library Association 1914* (Toronto, 1914), 69-72.

[49]See "Strong Protest against Library Board Change," *Toronto Daily Star*, April 30, 1913.

[50]See *Toronto Globe*, April 15, 1903; and Archives of Ontario, Ontario Library Association, MU 2239, letter from Norman Gurd to E.A. Hardy, February 10, 1904. During the 1913 controversy Seath maintained a discreet silence: see "Radical Change of Personnel of Library Board," *Toronto Daily Star*, April 28, 1913.

[51]Archives of Ontario, Sir James P. Whitney Papers, MU 3135, letter from H.J. Clarke (Secretary of the Corby Public Library at Belleville) to Whitney, May 2, 1913; and Archives of Ontario, RG 2, Series P-3, box 2 1913, PM-7, no. 1, letter from H.A. Beattie, Esq. (Secretary of the High School Board at North Bay) to R.A. Pyne, Minister of Education, December 26, 1913.

[52]An Act Respecting Public Libraries in Police Villages, 61 Vic., c. 27; and An Act to Amend the Public Libraries Act, 6 Geo. V, c. 45. Two bills introduced in 1906 and 1908 to establish libraries in townships and to permit police villages to acquire a township library that had become part of the village were never enacted. See Archives of Ontario, Legislative Assembly, RG 49, Series I-7-H, Bill 127, March 8, 1906, and RG 49, Series I-7-H, Bill 111, February 28, 1908.

[53]James Bain, Jr., "Brief Review of the Libraries of Canada," *Library Journal* 12 (1887): 409. He also suggested an enlarged service area for rural libraries.

[54]The Public Libraries Act, 1895, 58 Vic., c. 45, s. 14-15. Women's Institutes were permitted to affiliate later in 1909: see The Public Libraries Act, 1909, 9 Edw. VII, c. 80, s. 16.

[55]For the immediate background to this act, see John Wiseman, "Temples of Democracy: a History of Public Library Development in Ontario, 1880-1920" (PhD thesis, Loughborough University of Technology, Library and Information Studies, Loughborough, U.K., 1989), 192-211. (Summary published as "Temples of Democracy," *Canadian Library Journal* 47, no. 1 (February 1990): 37-39.)

[56]The Public Libraries Act, 1920, 10-11 Geo. V, c. 69, s. 10, 17-20, 39(1).

[57]*OLA Proceedings 1923* (Toronto, 1923), 45-46 [typescript].

[58]"The Public Libraries Act of 1920," *Ontario Library Review* 5 (1920): 11.

[59]For this dichotomy see the handbook by George Fraser, *How We Are Governed* (Toronto, 1899), 35-42.

[60]Ontario's leadership role in library service at this time is discussed by Stephen F. Cummings, "Angus McGill Mowat and the Development of Ontario Public Libraries, 1920-1960" (PhD thesis, University of Western Ontario, School of Library and Information Science, 1986), 43-47.

[61]For Taylor's impact on American libraries, see Marion Casey, "Efficiency, Taylorism, and Libraries in Progressive America," *Journal of Library History* 16 (1981): 265-79.

[62]Paradoxically, the autonomy and power of municipal corporations began to erode rapidly after this time: see John Taylor, "Urban Autonomy in Canada: Its Evolution and Decline," in *The Canadian City: Essays in Urban and Social History*, ed. Gilbert Stelter and Alan Artibise, rev. ed. (Ottawa, 1984), 478-500.

[63]William Munro, *American Influences on Canadian Government* (Toronto, 1929), 118.

[64]H.L. Brittain, "The Relation of Outside Boards and Commissions," *Municipal World* 32 (1922): 210.

[65]For example, see W.D. Lighthall, "The Elimination of Political Parties in Canadian Cities," *Canadian Municipal Journal* 12 (1916): 616. However, some contemporary views were less optimistic: "Our Municipal Conscience," *Canadian Forum* 4 (1923-24): 105-06 still complained about the power of ward associations or lodges in cities and the danger of extravagant expenditures.

[66]Lengthy tenure on boards was common, e.g., at Waterloo Jacob G. Stroh served for 40 years between 1879 and 1919. At a banquet held in his honour when he retired, he received a "luxurious 'easy' chair to spend his leisure hours": see *The Waterloo Public Library Golden Jubilee, 1876-1926* (Waterloo, c. 1926), 12.

[67]John Ridington, Mary J.L. Black, George H. Locke, *Libraries in Canada; a Study of Library Conditions and Needs* (Toronto, 1933), 61-62.

[68]The School Law Amendment Act, 1936, 1 Edw. VIII, c. 55, s. 19.

[69]Gordon Wragg, "Library Service in Ontario and Some Possible Improvements, Especially in Rural Library Service" (B.A. thesis, Ontario Agricultural College, Guelph, 1943), discusses this process in more detail. The Inspector of Public Libraries, Angus Mowat, finally got the opportunity to prepare detailed amendments for the Act shortly after the war. However, a number of proposals (e.g., centralized regional or metropolitan boards) were not implemented: see Archives of Ontario, Records of the Dept. of Education, RG 2, Provincial Library Service Branch, Recommendations for the Revision of the Public Libraries Act R.S.O. 1937, unprocessed material, accession no. 11785, received May 10, 1977.

[70]The City of Windsor (Amalgamation) Act, 1935, 25 Geo. V, c. 74, s. 13; and The City of Windsor (Amalgamation) Amendment Act, 1936, 1 Edw. VIII, c. 66, s. 3.

[71]See Lorne Bruce and Karen Bruce, *Public Library Boards in Postwar Ontario, 1945-1985*, Occasional Paper, no. 42 (Halifax: Dalhousie University, School of Library and Information Studies, 1988) for this period.

From Mechanics' Institute to Corby Public Library: The Development of Library Service in Belleville, Ontario, 1851-1908

Elizabeth Mitchell

Abstract

The first Mechanics' Institute in Belleville was established in 1851 and later closed due to financial difficulties. Public support led to its re-establishment in 1876, with funding largely from subscriptions, private donations, and the provincial grants available at the time. Evening classes, public lectures, and a gymnasium were promoted at the beginning, but interest in these aspects of the Mechanics' Institute declined, and eventually the directors left these to other institutions. Focus was placed on the library, as the Mechanics' Institute came to be seen, not just as a means for improving young working men, but also as a resource for life-long self-education for all people. The generosity of Gilbert Parker and Henry Corby in their support for a free public library, as well as a great increase in financial support from Belleville city council after the turn of the century, resulted in the new Corby Public Library being opened to the public in January 1909.

Résumé

La première École technique de Belleville s'établit en 1851, ferma ses portes à cause de difficultés financières, et reprit ses activités en 1876. Le financement venait principalement de cotisations, de dons privés et des quelques subventions provinciales disponibles à cette époque. Au début, il y eut des classes du soir, des conférences publiques et un gymnase, mais l'intérêt pour ces activités déclina et les directeurs de l'École technique les laissèrent peu à peu à d'autres institutions. La bibliothèque devint rapidement le centre d'intérêt et avec le temps, on considéra l'École technique non seulement comme un moyen de « polir » les jeunes gens, mais comme une ressource de perfectionnement personnel pour tout le monde. La Bibliothèque Corby, une bibliothèque publique, ouvrit ses portes en janvier 1909 grâce à la générosité de Gilbert Parker et de Henry Corby, grands défenseurs de la bibliothèque publique et à l'appui financier du conseil municipal de Belleville.

An examination of newspaper accounts of and surviving documents about the Belleville Mechanics' Institute and its development as a public library provides an interesting study of a part of Belleville's social history and of a representative Mechanics' Institute and library in Ontario. The attitudes and expressed purposes of its founders, the fluctuations in its fortunes, and the development of its collections and facilities are typical of many such institutes in towns and small cities in the mid- to late nineteenth century.

First Mechanics' Institute in Belleville

Mechanics' Institutes began in Great Britain in the early nineteenth century for the purpose of educating young working men and promoting their moral and social improvement. The idea soon spread to Canada, the first institute being opened in Ontario, at York, in 1831.[1] A Mechanics' Institute existed in Belleville as early as 1851, when it is recorded as having received $200 after an act was passed to provide for incorporation and better management of Mechanics' Institutes.[2] The correspondence of William Hutton,[3] a Belleville pioneer and educator, includes the text of a lecture he delivered, "The World We Live In," at the Belleville Mechanics' Institute on March 9, 1851.

There is no further evidence of the activities of the Belleville Mechanics' Institute until a small advertisement, dated October 5, 1857, appeared in local newspapers advising members that "the Mechanics Institute Reading Room is now opened every evening, (Sunday excepted) from 7 o'clock to 9 1/2, [signed] W. Tilley, Librarian."[4]

In an age of progress, the acquisition of knowledge by the labouring classes was of great importance. Thus, at the official opening of the Reading Room in November 1857, Benjamin Beddome took as his lecture topic "The Pleasure and Advantages of Mental Cultivation." He spoke first of the history and purpose of Mechanics' Institutes, describing the English Mechanics' Institutes as "the means of education, of moral and social improvement, to thousands of families who otherwise would be almost destitute of such advantages."

Turning to the Belleville institute in particular, Beddome said that such a reading room had long been needed, a place

> in which young men may be able to read the newspapers and light literature of the day without the necessity of resorting to places in which pernicious habits and customs are imbibed or indulged in .... Learning, knowledge, education (both secular and religious), will drive out, or subdue, the desire for low, animal gratifications. "The pleasures and advantages of mental cultivation" will then become ... a part of the personal experience of those who practice it.[5]

Beddome outlined his view of what the Belleville Mechanics' Institute should be: open to both men and women, both old and young, supported by all classes in the community. Those who had unused books or spare money should donate to this worthy cause. Instructional classes and lectures on all subjects should be important activities of the Institute.

Beddome then described the sort of books worth reading in order to cultivate the mind. His choice of good literature and his dismissal of much light fiction as "literary garbage" would be echoed in the high standards of the directors of the Mechanics' Institute in Belleville, as in other places. First in his list were the Greek and Latin classics, in translation — Homer, Herodotus and Tacitus — and the writings of the early Church Fathers, such as St. Augustine. Shakespeare he regarded as the first and greatest writer of dramatic poetry in English, Milton as the greatest epic poet, and Byron as the greatest descriptive poet.

Though some people disapproved of novels, Beddome felt that some writers, such as Sir Walter Scott and James Fenimore Cooper, were worth reading because of the way they brought history to life. Dickens, however, was suited only for young people; his stock characters and predictable plots, which ended with the hero and heroine getting married and living happily ever after, were rather trivial for people with mature reading interests and a taste for more important things. "It is much to be regretted," said Beddome, "that there should be such a general demand for novels, in all libraries, and so little demand for works of a more useful, substantial, or instructive character."

Beddome foreshadowed future difficulties for the Belleville Mechanics' Institute when he mentioned that they had about 100 members, but that there should be at least 300. Recurring themes until the beginning of the twentieth century were to be the need for more members (i.e., more subscription money) and the question of why more people did not take advantage of the educational benefits offered to them at such a low cost.

An article in the *Hastings Chronicle* in December 1859 outlined the difficult financial circumstances into which the Mechanics' Institute had fallen in only two years:

> There is no doubt that this town is large enough, and that the people of Belleville are liberal enough, to sustain a Mechanics' Institute, with Library and Reading Room, but the number of members at present is not large enough, with so very small an annual subscription, to enable the Directors to meet the current expenses.[6]

If members could not find some way of meeting expenditures, the Reading Room would have to be closed.

At a meeting on December 14, 1859, members were opposed to the idea of having to close the Reading Room. It was pointed out that the amount of their debt ($223.55) was only a few dollars over the usual government grant, showing that it was discontinuance of the $200 grant that put them so far behind (1858 was the last year in which government grants were paid to Mechanics' Institutes in Upper Canada until 1868, when the Mechanics' Institutes Association was incorporated, and grants were again available).[7] Several members were appointed to canvas all areas of the town to collect subscriptions. They were unsuccessful; the Library and Reading Room were closed soon after, and the Mechanics' Institute ceased operations.

However, the desire for a public library did not die. A letter to the editor of the *Hastings Chronicle* in May 1863 asked why Belleville, "one of the largest and most flourishing towns of Canada," had no public library when almost every town and frontier township of the country had one: "Scores of young men who are now fast losing their moral and intellectual manliness and energy, by spending their evenings and earnings in the saloon or on the street, might be saved and elevated by the companionship of a good, interesting, and instructive book."[8]

The writer, a Mr. Burwash, suggested that $500 could be appropriated by the school board or raised by subscription to purchase about 1,000 books, which would form the nucleus of a library collection. "The expense," he wrote, "is a mere trifle compared with the amount of benefit conferred on all classes of the community. Will not the intelligent, public spirited, and progressive people of Belleville immediately act in this matter?"

Second Mechanics' Institute

Despite Mr. Burwash's plea, action was not taken until 1876. By October of that year a large group of citizens had become interested in establishing a Mechanics' Institute, and they had raised almost $1,000 in donations and pledges. The list of 88 subscribers published in the newspaper includes the names of many prominent business and professional men.[9]

A public meeting was called for November 28, 1876, to consider forming a "Belleville Mechanics' Institute and Library Association." A newspaper report the following day expressed the gentlemen's ideas about the purposes and benefits of a Mechanics' Institute. It would be "a place where young men could spend their time profitably and pleasantly …. Valuable and instructive books would be bought, lectures would be given, a museum would be established and a gymnasium would be connected with the institute."[10]

All those attending the meeting were in favour of establishing a Mechanics' Institute in Belleville. The question of financing it formed a large part of their discussions that evening. They realized that they would need at least $1,000 above the $1,000 which had already been raised. A motion was made to ask the town council to appropriate $1,000 to aid the enterprise. In seconding the resolution, the Hon. Billa Flint said that "the Council could give that sum to the institute, and by doing it they would confer a greater benefit than had been made by some of the sums they had given away."

Others, including Professor John Macoun and Mackenzie Bowell, felt that the project should be supported by individual enterprise rather than municipal funding. Bowell optimistically said that when financial aid was required, "he had no doubt but that assistance would be rendered .... Belleville has a reputation for liberality, and we should obtain a subscription of $2,000 over and above the annual subscriptions." Macoun said that "Mechanics, lawyers' clerks, and dry goods clerks needed knowledge, but the men with means should come forward to aid this scheme."

The resolution to ask the town council for aid was withdrawn. One wonders what the result would have been if they had decided otherwise and had been able to persuade the council to give substantial support to the Institute from the beginning. It might have paved the way for further annual appropriations and to the Institute's becoming a free public library, supported by public funds, much earlier than 1903. Between 1876 and 1902, the council would usually give an annual grant of $200, far less than what was needed to maintain the library. For the next quarter century, the library would have to rely on subscriptions from members.[11]

Following the inaugural meeting in November 1876, the members immediately set to work. At their December meeting, three gentlemen were appointed to select books for the library. Committees were set up for the Reading Room, Lectures, Gymnasium, and Finance.[12] The committee formed to find a suitable building for the Institute quickly got a location for a library, and a brief report published in the *Weekly Intelligencer*, January 11, 1877, stated, "The rooms are being prepared as rapidly as possible and in a short time the reading room will be ready for visitors."[13]

By January 1878, at the end of a satisfactory first year of operation, they were occupying rented rooms on Campbell Street, had 383 members, and had 830 volumes in the library, as well as a large number of daily and weekly newspapers and leading English, U.S. and Canadian magazines. Classes had been organized for mechanical drawing, arithmetic, elocution, French, and German, with satisfactory attendance. Seven lectures had been given, which, the annual report said, "were but meagrely attended, showing that the literary taste of the people of Belleville in this particular has yet to be cultivated."

In order to encourage more young people to use the library, the directors had reduced membership fees to allow apprentices and youths under seventeen to belong for $1.00 a year and to allow clubs of workmen in any establishment, of not less than four persons, to use the Library and Reading Room for $1.50 per annum. The directors had hoped to have a gymnasium erected, but this had not been accomplished, resulting in "a material loss to the Association and a disappointment to the members."[14]

Despite the good start, they had liabilities of $699.60, which, the president said, could be covered by the still-unpaid 1877 fees of some present members, plus members' fees now due for 1878. Unpaid fees were to be a recurring problem, as was the need for acquiring new members in order to meet expenses. However, Belleville was doing well, and the *Intelligencer* exaggerated only a little in proclaiming that after only one year in existence the Belleville Institute ranked third in the list of 68 Institutes in Ontario, and was exceeded only by Toronto and Hamilton in terms of membership and equipment.[15]

By May 1880, membership had increased to 505, and there were over 1,000 volumes in the library.[16] Assets exceeded liabilities by a healthy sum. However, of the five evening classes that had been advertised the previous October,[17] only three were given: French and German, by the Rev. Mr. Schuster (who gave his services gratuitously), and English branches by Mr. McKeown. Attendance at Mr. Schuster's classes averaged twenty-two, and at Mr. McKeown's, six. The long-awaited gymnasium had been built, and a Mr. E.W. Johnston was employed as instructor in gymnastics, his services doing much to render the gymnasium a success.

The year 1880 marked the beginning of a temporary decline in the Institute's fortunes. The annual report presented in May 1881 showed that membership had dropped to 351 and the gymnasium had been so poorly attended that it had been closed in March. Only two classes were taught, one in English branches with nine pupils, and the other in mechanical drawing, with five pupils, and only one lecture was given. The directors reported that an effort was being made to "enlist the active support of the lady members."[18] During the next two decades, the ladies were to become an important force in supporting the Institute so that it could continue.

Circulation statistics for 1880 showed that works of biography, history, miscellaneous literature, science, and art had been taken out an average of twice each, books on travel nine times, and novels an average of thirteen times each. The directors were concerned with these statistics: "The proportion between the issue of novels from the library and those of other books is suggestive, and teaches a practical lesson as to the necessity of a strict supervision in the selection of works of this nature."

Membership continued to decline in 1881. In January 1882, Mr. Thomas Ritchie, a prominent businessman, offered to donate $100 towards the purchase of two billiard tables, on condition that membership could be brought up to 200.[19] Canvassers were hard at work, and a week later the

Intelligencer reported that over 100 names had been secured; in addition, the gymnasium had been reopened.[20] The membership drive must have been successful, because billiard and pool tables were added during the year.[21]

Public lectures were one way of raising money. No doubt the most famous lecturer engaged by the Mechanics' Institute was Oscar Wilde, who was touring North America in 1882. For his lecture at the City Hall on May 23, 1882, he took as his subject "The Practical Application of the Principles of the Aesthetic Theory to Exterior and Interior House Decoration, and to Dress and Personal Ornaments; The Value of Art in Education and the Relation of Art to Morals."[22] A long and somewhat tongue-in-cheek report in the *Daily Intelligencer* dwelt as much on Mr. Wilde's dress, appearance and mannerisms as on the text of his speech and stated that "the audience was appreciative and very sympathetic, being chiefly composed of ladies." At the conclusion of this article, the reporter remarked that

> It was with some difficulty that he [Wilde] made his way through the throng of female admirers who would fain have delayed him. He was driven back to the Dafoe House, where he divested himself of his "good clothes", and was soon dissecting the elements of beauty which are found in chops and Bass' ale.[23]

In May 1883, the directors were pleased to report that the Institute was now solvent, free of debt, and fully equipped.[24] The three lectures given during the year had been well attended, and the billiard and pool tables were being well used and were becoming a source of revenue. Two hundred and fifty books had been added, bringing the collection to over 1,400 volumes, and a new, classified catalogue[25] had been printed for the use of members. The directors hoped that, with increased membership revenue, the Institute would soon be able to add new books as soon as they were published.

In the annual report of May 1884, an encouraging decline was noted in the proportion of novels circulated, compared with other works:

> The Directors are glad to notice this significant evidence of a growing taste for the study of standard works replete with instruction stimulating to the mind and having a refining influence on the life. It is gratifying to know that the efforts of the Institute in endeavoring to bring first-class books in all branches of knowledge within the reach of those who could not otherwise benefit by them are being more and more appreciated.[26]

During the year 1886-87, there was a large expenditure for alterations, owing to increased accommodation required for the library, which now numbered over 2,200 volumes. An enterprising citizen had proposed erecting a building suitable for the accommodation of the Institute.[27] However, no such building was built, and the library continued to occupy rented premises until 1908.

The Institute's interest in lectures and classes was changing by this time. The May 1888 annual report was the last one to mention lectures. That year, only one poorly attended lecture had been given; it netted the Institute $1.50.[28] During the year 1888-89, evening classes were held in connection with the Ontario Business College, and they were most successful, with 33 pupils.[29] The beginning of this partnership showed that the Mechanics' Institute was moving away from trying to give classes on its own and towards leaving formal adult education to other educational institutions.

The May 1890 annual report, with statistics for 1889-90, boasted that "Belleville Mechanics' Institute is now second to none east of Toronto, and there are only two in Western Ontario, which are classed above that of Belleville."[30] The Institute's financial situation at the beginning of this decade was secure enough that, in 1892, directors voted to reduce the annual membership fee from $3.00 to $2.00.[31] However, difficult times lay ahead. In the April 15, 1893, *Intelligencer*, an editorial and a long letter from Thomas Ritchie expressed concern that the establishment of a Young Men's Christian Association in Belleville would conflict with support for the Mechanics' Institute.[32] Both organizations had similar purposes (provision of reading rooms and recreational activities), and both were directed at the same clientele (young working men who needed a place for wholesome activity and intellectual and moral improvement). A YMCA was established soon afterward, but it was not necessarily the reason for the financial difficulties of the library during the next few years.

At the annual meeting in May 1895, the name "Mechanics' Institute" was dropped and "Public Library" adopted instead, in accordance with the Ontario Act Respecting Public Libraries, which came into force on May 1, 1895.[33] By now, the library had a ladies' auxiliary, and, at this meeting, the ladies were thanked "for their efficient aid during the year." Fund-raising was a major activity for the auxiliary. In October 1895, they put on a spectacular and well-attended entertainment entitled "Cosmorama" which raised over $500 for the library. Held in the Regimental Drill Hall, it included such popular attractions of the times as tableaux, an Italian band, minstrels, a fine art exhibit, booths representing different countries, high tea, and music by Riggs' Orchestra.[34]

Thomas Ritchie, president of the Public Library Board of Directors, thanked the Ladies' Auxiliary for their successful "Cosmorama" in a letter to the editor of the *Intelligencer*[35] and then went on to express his concept of a public library as "a necessary adjunct to our educational system." Schools and colleges, he said, "train the mind and furnish the groundwork," but acquisition of knowledge must be a life-long pursuit. The old idea of an Institute that provided formal classes for the practical education of young working men had been abandoned; the public library was now seen as a resource for life-long self-education for all people.

By the autumn of 1896, the library was in danger of having to close, in spite of its success and growth during the previous two decades. Membership had fallen again, the Ontario legislative grant to libraries had been greatly reduced,[36] and the city was still unwilling to provide municipal funding for a free public library. The directors decided at their September meeting that they would have to close on January 1.[37] By coincidence, within a week of their decision, one of the directors, W.N. Ponton, received a letter from Gilbert Parker which gave them some cause for hope.

Parker, then resident in Britain and a member of the British Parliament, was by this time well known as a novelist on both sides of the Atlantic. But he never forgot his Belleville roots, and in his letter to Ponton he said he would be presenting $100 worth of books to the library annually. In addition, if a free library were to be established, he would make a more substantial contribution.[38] Ponton urged the people of Belleville to follow Parker's public-spirited example. If they could not donate books or money, they could at least secure new members. At a meeting on September 30, the directors decided that if 100 new members could be added by November 1, a further attempt would be made to carry on.[39]

The library struggled on towards the new century, and did not close. At the annual meeting in January 1900, Gilbert Parker was praised for his promise of a yearly donation to the library as long as he lived. The report reiterated the fact that "Mr. Parker's idea was that it should eventually become a public library. He wished the city to assume it, and he would contribute generously towards purchasing a site and putting up a suitable building."[40]

The annual meeting held on January 14, 1901, was probably one of the longest and most heated in the library's history.[41] The fund-raising activities of the ladies had provided so much support that one member proposed a slate of nine ladies to be the new board of directors. A number present spoke in favour of the ladies having the management "for the time being," although a more cautious member amended the motion to say that the directors should be composed of five ladies and four gentlemen.

An argument then arose because someone said "that the ladies intended to have a Yankee brought here as librarian." One of the women who had been nominated replied that they were considering having a trained librarian engaged for a brief period "so as to give useful instructions to whatever permanent librarian might be chosen." Opponents objected to "importing a foreigner to run the institution," and a motion was put forth that no one be employed as Librarian unless he or she was a permanent resident of Belleville, "this being a Belleville institution, and there being many citizens competent to perform the duties of the office."

Nothing having been accomplished at the first meeting, another public meeting was held after a week's adjournment to elect the Board of Directors.[42] The ladies who had been nominated had unanimously decided to withdraw because they felt that the opposition they had encountered implied a lack of confidence in their ability. Harmony was restored, however, and nine men were elected as directors. The newspaper account says nothing more about the choice of a librarian, but there was to be no librarian with professional training, apparently, until Angus Mowat came in 1928.

Belleville Free Public Library

In 1903, the dream of a municipally funded free library became a reality. At the first meeting of the Civic Committees of the new city council in January 1903, a deputation representing the Public Library Association presented a petition signed by many ratepayers to the Executive Committee asking the council to grant $800 to establish a free library. After some discussion, the Executive Committee passed a motion to grant this amount, "provided the library be kept open as a free institution for the year 1903; ... And that the present Library Board guarantee to leave the library free of debt at the end of the year, and provided that the City Solicitor considers we have the power to grant the money."[43]

The annual report for 1903 showed that membership in 1903 had increased by 507 to 1,467; either the $2.00 fee had been too high for some people, or else its becoming a free library created renewed interest in the library, prompting more people to join. Also, with the city grant now making up the largest part of its income, the library was able to add over 500 new books, the greatest increase in any year. There was therefore more to read.[44]

Although 1904 was "the most prosperous year in the existence of the library," according to the annual report,[45] the directors had been able to spend only $156.00 on books, and so were only eligible to receive an Ontario government grant of $150.65. They hoped that in 1905 they would be able to spend enough on books to earn the full provincial grant of $200; this was a dollar-for-dollar grant which would thus enable them to add $400 worth of books to the collection. Accordingly, a deputation from the Public Library Board went to the meeting of the Civic Committees of City Council on January 20, 1905, to ask that their grant be increased to $1,000, the additional funds to be used entirely for purchasing new books. City Council raised the library grant to $1,000 beginning in 1905.[46]

Corby Public Library

In 1905, the Library Board apparently made enquiries about the conditions under which a Carnegie Library could be established.[47] However, it was Harry Corby, a former member of Parliament and the owner of Corby Distilleries, who became the library's most generous benefactor. In November 1905 he offered to present the city with a new library building at a cost of $10,000 if the city would provide a site, the only condition being that City Council agree to maintain it.[48]

Mr. Corby explained that he and his wife had been wanting to give substantial assistance to some Belleville institution and decided to select one that was open to all and conferred benefits on all. They had noticed that the Belleville Public Library not only was doing good work but also was becoming more and more a public necessity, yet it was hampered by insufficient accommodation and unattractive surroundings. Therefore, they decided to donate $10,000 for the erection of a suitable building. A Toronto architect, F.H. Herbert, had offered to furnish plans and specifications for the library.[49]

At their meeting on November 27, 1905, City Council gratefully accepted Mr. Corby's offer, despite the reservations of some people who thought it would cost the city a large amount to maintain such a library. The mayor, however, felt it would not cost any more for maintenance than the present building, and they would be saving the $400 annual rent they now paid.[50]

At the inaugural meeting of City Council in January 1906, a committee was appointed to secure a proper site for the new public library building,[51] and, at the March 19 council meeting, this committee was authorized to purchase the piece of property they had selected on Campbell Street, for $700.[52]

The new building was never constructed. Instead, Mr. Corby bought the Merchants' Bank building at the corner of Pinnacle and Campbell Streets for $6,000. F.H. Herbert was retained as the architect for the alterations to the bank building. When questioned about the site which had been selected for a new building, the mayor explained that the City had not actually purchased it. "The arrangements for its purchase were all made, but the deal fell through."[53] A newspaper report in September 1907 promised readers that the new library would be "ornate and complete." Total cost to Mr. Corby would be $22,000 when renovations were completed.[54]

The main topic of discussion at the inaugural meeting of City Council in January 1908 was acceptance of Mr. Corby's gift of the library building. As matters stood, Council could only legislate for the current year the funds necessary for the library's maintenance. Both the mayor and Mr. Corby wanted a by-law passed which would provide, for all time, for funds for proper library maintenance. Some councillors were hesitant about accepting Mr. Corby's gift before such a by-law was passed, because they would be committing themselves to its maintenance. However, it was finally decided that City Council would officially take over the library on January 20, 1908, and that citizens would be invited to attend the opening ceremonies at the library.[55]

The *Daily Intelligencer* of January 21, 1908, reported at great length on the festivities when the Corby Public Library was handed over to the City. The reporter described in detail the four floors of the building, from the basement furnace room to the librarian's apartment on the top storey, but devoted most of his description to the main floor, with its mosaic floor, marble pillars, fireplace, carved oak desk and staircase, and magnificent stained glass window depicting William Shakespeare.[56] Three reading rooms on the second floor, including one for children, provided seating for 125 people.[57]

All chairs were occupied, many people were standing, and a large number were unable to get in by 8:00 p.m. on January 20, when the guests of honour arrived. In addition to the Corbys and the architect, F.H. Herbert, they included former prime minister Sir Mackenzie Bowell, who had been a founding member of the Mechanics' Institute, and Thomas Ritchie, also a founder and its first president, in 1876. Speeches reflecting on the 30-year history of the library were given by Harry Corby, Thomas Ritchie, Mackenzie Bowell, and others, and the gathering ended with congratulations and hearty cheers for Mr. and Mrs. Corby.

The annual report of January 1908 said that 1907 had been the most successful year in the history of the library. The library now had 2,640 members and a collection of 7,281 volumes.[58] The prospects for the library's future were brighter than ever, with growing public interest, secure financial support from the municipality, and a magnificent new building. The Belleville Public Library was firmly set on the course of its twentieth-century development.

Notes

Unfortunately, few primary sources relating to the early history of the Belleville Public Library are still in existence — the earliest available minute books of the Boards of Directors begin in 1916. For much of the historical data I have had to rely on newspaper accounts of annual meetings and other events.

[1] "The purpose of Mechanic's Institutes in Upper Canada and Ontario, 1831-1895" [10-page off-print of a paper, author and source unknown] (Belleville Public Library files), p. 2.

[2]S.P. May, "Brief Historical Sketch of Public Libraries in Ontario, from the Superintendent of Libraries, for the Hon. Minister of Education, up to 20th March, 1905," Ontario Archives RG 2, Series D-7, Box 18, File: Libraries—Public, p. 1.

[3]William Hutton correspondence, Hastings County Historical Society Archives, File no. 3359, p. 218.

[4]*Hastings Chronicle*, October 7, 1857, p. 3, and *Weekly Intelligencer*, October 16, 1857, p. 3.

[5]"Lecture Delivered at the Opening of the Reading Room of the Belleville Mechanics Institute, by Benjamin Beddome: the Pleasures and Advantages of Mental Cultivation," *Weekly Intelligencer*, November 20, 1857, p. 1.

[6]"Mechanics Institute," *Hastings Chronicle*, December 14, 1859, p. 2.

[7]May, 3.

[8]N. Burwash, "A Public Library for Belleville" [letter, dated May 7, 1863], *Hastings Chronicle*, May 13, 1863, p. 2.

[9]"Mechanics' Institute," *Weekly Intelligencer*, October 27, 1876, p. 3.

[10]"The Public Meeting," *Daily Ontario*, November 29, 1876, p. 3.

[11]May, 4-7 and 13, explains the provincial grants available at this time to Mechanics' Institutes. He shows Belleville as having received a total of $2,000 from the Ontario government from 1877 to 1881; Belleville was thus getting the maximum grant of $400 per year. This continued until a change in 1885 in the distribution of government grants greatly reduced the amount available.

[12]"Belleville Mechanics' Institute," *Daily Intelligencer*, December 9, 1876, p. 2.

[13]"Belleville Mechanics' Institute," *Weekly Intelligencer*, January 11, 1877, p. 3.

[14]"Mechanics' Institute," *Daily Intelligencer*, January 16, 1878, p. 3.

[15]Ibid. However, according to the statistics for 1877 published in the *Ontario Sessional Papers*, v. 11, pt. 2, no. 3, 1879: 204-205, Belleville was actually fourth in terms of net income, with $1382.69. Ahead of Belleville were Hamilton ($8159.07) and Toronto ($6131.18), but Port Hope, in third place, was only 61 cents ahead of Belleville, with a net income of $1383.30. However, in terms of membership, Belleville, with 241 members, was sixth, behind Hamilton (1006), Toronto (1004), London (376), Woodstock (297), and Peterborough (251). These statistics do not list "equipment," but Belleville ranked 40th for volumes in the library, 6th for volumes issued, 31st for expenditure for books, 4th for expenditure for classes, and 16th for expenditure for reading rooms.

[16]"Belleville Mechanics' Institute: Annual Meeting," *Daily Intelligencer*, May 12, 1880, p. 3.

[17]"Evening Classes" [advertisement], *Daily Intelligencer*, October 16, 1879, p. 2. The advertisement listed English branches, mechanical drawing, phonography, French, and German.

[18]"Mechanics' Institute," *Daily Intelligencer*, May 11, 1881, p. 3.

[19]"City and Vicinity" column, *Daily Intelligencer*, January 12, 1882, p. 3.

[20]"City and Vicinity" column, *Daily Intelligencer*, January 19, 1882, p. 3.

[21]*Daily Intelligencer*, May 22, 1883, p. 1.

[22]Advertisement, *Daily Intelligencer*, May 17-22, 1882.

[23]"Oscar Wilde: His Lecture on 'Decorative Art'," *Daily Intelligencer*, May 25, 1882, p. 2.

[24]"Mechanics' Institute: Synopsis of the Year's Doings," *Daily Intelligencer*, May 22, 1883, p. 1.

[25]Belleville Mechanics' Institute and Library Association, *Alphabetical and Classified Catalogue of Books in the Library* (Belleville: Printed at the *Daily Intelligencer* Office, 1883), Archives of Ontario, MU 2019, Mechanics' Institutes—Various. This is a 52-page booklet, about 3" x 5", listing the books in seven broad subject areas: History, pp. 3-10; Art, Science, Philosophy, Natural History and Mechanics, pp. 11-17; Travels, pp. 18-22; Biography, pp. 23-25; General Literature, pp. 26-35; Poetry, p. 36; Fiction, pp. 37-51. The catalogue listed books in each subject by author and by significant words in the title, being, in effect, a KWIC index to the collection. For example, Item 375 appears three times:

Leagues, 20000 Under the Sea . . Jules Verne

Sea, 20000 Leagues Under the . . . Jules Verne

Verne's 20000 Leagues Under the Sea

[26]"Mechanics' Institute: The Annual Meeting," *Daily Intelligencer*, May 14, 1884, p. 3.

[27]"Mechanics Institute: Annual Meeting," *Daily Intelligencer*, May 3, 1887, p. 3.

[28]"Belleville Mechanics' Institute: The Annual Meeting," *Daily Intelligencer*, May 9, 1888, p. 3.

[29]Composition and grammar, bookkeeping, arithmetic, and writing were taught in 1888-89, shorthand was added the following year, and typewriting in 1891-92. (*Ontario Sessional Papers*, v. 23, pt. 2, no. 4, 1891, p. 294; v. 24, pt. 2, no. 11, 1892, p. 234; and v. 25, pt. 1, no. 3, 1893, p. 233.)

[30]"Mechanics' Institute: Annual Meeting," *Daily Ontario*, May 8, 1890, p. 4. Again, statistics printed in the *Ontario Sessional Papers*, v. 23, pt. 2, no. 4, 1891, reveal that the newspaper was slightly inaccurate. In terms of total receipts, Belleville, fourth, with $1311.18, was "second to *one* east of Toronto" (Brockville, with $1984.00), and behind London ($2364.25) and Chapleau ($1318.95). Belleville was 13th out of 193 Institutes for number of members. Though Belleville was 23rd in number of volumes in the library, it was 4th in number of volumes circulated. However, by then, Toronto, Hamilton, and seven other Institutes had become free public libraries, and they appeared in a separate table in this report. Most of these nine free libraries were ahead of Belleville in all respects.

[31]"Annual Meeting," *Daily Intelligencer*, May 11, 1892, p. 4.

[32]Editorial, and "The Mechanics Institute and Christian Association" [letter], *Daily Intelligencer*, April 15, 1893, p. 2.

[33]"Belleville Public Library: Annual Meeting and Appointment of New Directors," *Daily Ontario*, May 15, 1895, p. 4. S.P. May's report, *Ontario Sessional Papers*, v. 29, pt. 1, no. 1, Appendix L, p. 280, says that under this "Act respecting Public Libraries" the name "Mechanics' Institute" was changed to "Public Library" and that, by this act, directors of any Mechanics' Institute could transfer the

property of a Mechanics' Institute to the municipal corporation on condition that the public library be free. However, in Belleville there was still no support from municipal public funds, except for the annual $200 grant from the City, and a membership fee of $2.00 was still required.

34Advertisement, *Daily Ontario*, October 23, 1895, p. 1. Reports in the *Daily Ontario*, October 23, p. 5, and October 25, p. 4, provide an entertaining description of the variety of amusements at the Cosmorama.

35"The Public Library" [letter], *Daily Intelligencer*, November 2, 1895, p. 3.

36There was a reduction in the provincial grant as early as 1884-85, when it was reduced from $400 to $300, and to $250 in the following year, according to statistics for receipts shown in the *Ontario Sessional Papers*, v. 11, 1879, to v. 41, 1908, and quoted in the statistical charts in Appendix II at the end of this paper. By the year ending April 1896, the provincial grant had fallen to $241.

37Editorial, *Daily Intelligencer*, September 14, 1896, p. 2. Unfortunately, no report could be found of the Directors' meeting held, presumably, during the week of September 8-12.

38"Gilbert Parker and the Public Library" [letter from W.N. Ponton], *Daily Intelligencer*, September 19, 1896, p. 2.

39"The Public Library" [letter, signed Thos. Ritchie], *Daily Intelligencer*, October 1, 1896.

40"Mechanics' Institute [sic]: Annual Meeting and Election of Officers Last Evening," *Daily Intelligencer*, January 24, 1900, p. 4.

41"Canada for Canadians," *Daily Intelligencer*, January 15, 1901, p. 3.

42"The Angel of Peace," *Daily Intelligencer*, January 22, 1901, p. 3.

43"Civic Committees Met Last Night: Aldermen Decided to Grant the Prayer of the Public Library Petition," *Daily Intelligencer*, January 24, 1903, p. 7.

44"Annual Meeting of the Public Library," *Daily Intelligencer*, January 12, 1904, p. 7. This report shows major sources of income in 1904 as a grant from the City, $800; a grant from the Ontario government, $175; and the donation from Sir Gilbert Parker, $100.

45"Annual Meeting of the Public Library," *Daily Intelligencer*, January 10, 1905, p. 7.

46"Civic Committees Hold First Meeting: Public Library Asks for Larger Grant, and City Fathers Decide to Give It," *Daily Intelligencer*, January 21, 1905, p. 7.

47"Public Library Notes" [report of March 24 meeting of Board of Directors], *Daily Intelligencer*, March 27, 1905, p. 7.

48"Mr. H. Corby Will Present City with New Public Library," *Daily Intelligencer*, November 17, 1905, p. 7.

49Plans of Corby Free Public Library to be erected and presented to the City of Belleville by H. Corby, Esqre. [blueprints], F.H. Herbert, Architect, Toronto. Scale : 4 feet = 1 inch. 6 sheets. Herbert's blueprints are preserved in the Canadiana Room of the Belleville Public Library.

50"Mr. H. Corby's Offer Gratefully Accepted by the City Council," *Daily Intelligencer*, November 28, 1905, p. 7.

51*Daily Intelligencer*, January 8, 1906, p. 7.

52*Daily Intelligencer*, March 20, 1905, p. 7. This amount, along with the regular annual grant of $1,000 to the library, was included in the City estimates passed by council on April 3, 1906. See "Council Passed the Estimates," *Daily Intelligencer*, April 4, 1906, p. 3.

[53]"Mr. Corby Buys the Old Bank Building," *Daily Intelligencer*, July 28, 1906, p. 5.

[54]"New Library Will be Ornate and Complete," *Daily Intelligencer*, September 28, 1907, p. 7.

[55]"Inaugural Meeting of City Council ... Corby Library to be Taken Over Next Monday," *Daily Intelligencer*, January 13, 1908, p. 7.

[56]"Corby Public Library Was Handed Over to the City Last Night by the Donor," *Daily Intelligencer*, January 21, 1908, p. 3.

[57]*Ontario Sessional Papers*, v. 41, pt. 5, no. 12, 1909, pp. 163-169, includes a description of the new library, with photographs of the exterior and the interior ground floor, as well as the floor plans of all four floors.

[58]"Annual Meeting of Public Library Held Yesterday Afternoon: Reports Showed Excellent State of Affairs," *Daily Intelligencer*, January 14, 1908, p. 2.

Additional Sources

Association of Mechanics' Institutes of Ontario. *Letterbook, 1880-1884*. Archives of Ontario, MU 2017.

Davison, Thomas. "Mechanics' Institutes and the Best Means of Improving Them." *Canadian Monthly* 10 (September 1876): 220-23.

Eadie, James A. "The Napanee Mechanics' Institute: the Nineteenth Century Mechanics' Institute Movement in Microcosm." *Ontario History* 68, no. 4 (December 1976): 209-21.

Lewis, Richard. "Mechanics' Institutes and the Best Means of Improving Them." *Canadian Monthly* 10 (September 1876): 223-38.

Ontario. Department of the Commissioner of Agriculture and Arts. "Report of the Commissioner of Agriculture and Arts for the Province of Ontario." *Ontario Sessional Papers* 11 (1879) to 12, (1880).

Ontario. Education Department. "Report of the Minister of Education." *Ontario Sessional Papers* 14 (1882) to 41 (1908).

Ontario. Department of Education. *Special Report of the Minister of Education on Mechanics' Institutes*. Toronto: C. Blackett Robinson, 1881. (Text by S.P. May, Superintendent of Educational Museum and Library).

"Seventeenth Annual Report of Mechanics Institutes, 15 Aug., 1885." Archives of Ontario, MU 2387, Reynolds (James) Papers, 1882-1908.

Appendix I

Annual meetings of the Boards of Directors of the Mechanics' Institute and the Public Library were usually reported in great detail in the newspapers, with text and statistics of annual reports included. Newspaper sources were available for the following annual reports (* indicates a fairly long report which included statistics):

*	1877.	*Daily Intelligencer*, January 16, 1878, p. 3.
*	1877/78	*Daily Intelligencer*, May 18, 1878, p. 2
*	1878/79	*Daily Intelligencer*, May 14, 1879, p. 3
*	1879/80	*Daily Intelligencer*, May 12, 1880, p. 3
*	1880/81	*Daily Intelligencer*, May 11, 1881, p. 3
	1881/82	*Daily Intelligencer*, May 17, 1882, p. 3
*	1882/83	*Daily Intelligencer*, May 22, 1883, p. 1
*	1883/84	*Daily Intelligencer*, May 14, 1884, p. 3
*	1885/86	*Weekly Intelligencer*, May 6, 1886, p. 8
*	1886/87	*Daily Intelligencer*, May 3, 1887, p. 3
*	1887/88	*Daily Intelligencer*, May 9, 1888, p. 3
	1888/89	*Daily Intelligencer*, May 15, 1889, p. 3
*	1889/90	*Daily Ontario*, May 8,1890, p. 4
	1890/91	*Daily Intelligencer*, May 7, 1891, p. 3
	1891/92	*Daily Intelligencer*, May 11, 1892, p. 4
	1894/95	*Daily Ontario*, May 15, 1895, p. 4
	1897/98	*Daily Intelligencer*, May 10, 1898, p. 1
	1899	*Daily Intelligencer*, January 24, 1900, p. 4
	1900	*Daily Intelligencer*, January 15, 1901, p. 3, and January 22, 1901, p. 3
*	1903	*Daily Intelligencer*, January 12, 1904, p. 7
*	1904	*Daily Intelligencer*, January 10, 1905, p. 7
*	1905	*Daily Intelligencer*, January 9, 1906, p. 7
*	1906	*Daily Intelligencer*, January 29, 1907, p. 3
*	1907	*Daily Intelligencer*, January 14, 1908, p. 2

Appendix II: Statistics, 1851-1908

Statistics for year ending:	No. of members	No. of volumes in library	Circulation	No. of classes /pupils	No. of lectures given	Total receipts	Provincial govt. grant	Municipal grant	Population of Belleville [c]	President of Board	Librarian
							(Included in Total Receipts)	(Included in Total Receipts)			
1851 [a]											—
1852-1857 : (presumably Belleville continued to receive $200 each year.) [a]											—
Nov. 1857	100 (approx.)						$200	0	4,569		William Tilley
1858							$200	0			—
1861							None given	0	6,277		—
1871									7,305		—
Jan. 1878 [b]	241	913	5,930	4 / 55	7	$1382.69	$400	0		Thomas Ritchie	David C. Ferguson
Apr. 1878		906	2,505	6	—	$657.60	$400			Thomas Ritchie	David C. Ferguson
			(Jan-Apr)				(Jan-Apr)				
Apr. 1879	247	923	5,724			$1171.48	$400			Thomas Ritchie	David C. Ferguson
Apr. 1880	505	1,053	8,418	3 / 52		$1796.79	$400	$150		Rev. M.W. Maclean	—
Apr. 1881	352	1,008	6,379	2 / 14	1	$2535.80	$400		9,516	Rev. M.W. Maclean	—
Apr. 1882	216	1,184	1,953	2 / 24		$1380.23	$400	$200		Rev. M.W. Maclean	
Apr. 1883	164	1,428	2,505		3	$2239.29	$400	$200		Rev. M.W. Maclean	Joseph Maiden
Apr. 1884	173	1,587	3,164	0		$1718.63	$400	$200		Rev. M.W. Maclean	—
Apr. 1885	160	1,818	3,638	0		$1696.88	$300	$200		Rev. M.W. Maclean	—
Apr. 1886	186	2,042	3,638	0		$1329.43	$250	$100		J. Lyons Biggar	—
Apr. 1887	243	2,285	7,113			$1461.35	$250	$200		J. Lyons Biggar	Mr. Roblin
Apr. 1888	317	2,485	8,669	4 / 34 [d]	1	$1319.82	$387	0		W.N. Ponton	Alex Walker (temp. replacement for Mr. Roblin)

[a] Information for the years 1851-1858 is from May, S.P. "Brief historical sketch of public libraries in Ontario ..."

[b] Statistics for 1878-1907 have been compiled from newspaper reports, and from reports on Mechanics' Institutes and libraries, in the Ontario Sessional Papers, v. 11 (1879) to v. 41 (1980). Blank spaces indicate no information available. In cases of discrepancy, figures in the Sessional Papers were taken as more accurate.

[c] Population figures are from the Census of Canada, 1851 to 1901.

[d] Beginning this year, classes were held in connection with Ontario Business College.

Appendix II: Statistics, 1851-1908 (cont.)

Statistics for year ending:	No. of members	No. of volumes in library	Circulation	No. of classes /pupils	No. of lectures given	Total receipts	Included in Total Receipts — provincial govt. grant	Included in Total Receipts — municipal grant	Population of Belleville [c]	President of Board	Librarian
Apr. 1889	301	2,860	7,880	4 / 33	—	$1607.17	$333.00	$200.00	—	C. Bogart	
Apr. 1890	242	3,118	8,655	6 / 22	—	$1311.18	$330.00	0		William Tennant	Miss Brodie
Apr. 1891	245	3,382	9,656	5 / 36	—	$1288.54	$316.00	$200.00	9,914	William Tennant	—
Apr. 1892	167	3,645	9,108	6 / 20	—	$1240.73	$332.00	$300.00		William Tennant	—
Apr. 1893	140	3,540	5,431	6 / 36	—	$1661.12	$286.00	0		William Tennant	—
Apr. 1894	211	4,325	9,596	3 / 16	—	$3,444.16	—	—		William Tennant	—
Apr. 1895	181	3,298	8,234	3 / 8	—	$2,266.13				—	—
Apr. 1896	189	3,348	8,920	0 [e]	—	$2,067.95	$241.20	$100.00		—	—
Apr. 1897	216	3,569	8,794	0	—	$1,409.54				—	—
Apr. 1898	200	3,536	2,800 [f]	0	—	$1,903.99				—	—
Dec. 1899	144	4,159	6,396 (8 months)	0	—	$1,416.11 (8 months)				—	—
Dec. 1900	151	4,164	7,340	0	—	$2,312.09				Thomas Rotchie	
Dec. 1901	134	4,484	7,314	0	—	$1,169.17	$100.00	$100.00	9,117	Rev. M.W. Maclean	—
Dec. 1902	986	4,960	17,726	—	—	$1,151.15	$200.00	$200.00		—	—
Dec. 1903	1,463	5,440	25,569	—	—	$1,493.28	$175.00	$800.00		J.T. Luton	Alex R. Walker
Dec. 1904	1,803	5,634	34,467	—	—	$1,291.61	$150.65	$800.00		J.J.B. Flint	Alex R. Walker
Dec. 1905	1,970	6,185	33,797	—	—	$1,545.30	$214.59	$1,000.00		J.J.B. Flint	Alex R. Walker
Dec. 1906	2,366	6,714	35,262	—	—	$1,575.93	$250.00	$1,000.00		John Williams	Alex R. Walker
Dec. 1907	2,639	7,342	33,202 [g]	—	—	$1,698.16	$250.00	$1,000.00		John Williams	Alex R. Walker

e When Mechanics' Institutes became Public Libraries by the "Act respecting Public Libraries," May 1895, almost all libraries, including Belleville, discontinued their classes. Belleville was among the 32 Mechanics' Institutes offering classes in the year ending April 1895. The next year, only 6 libraries had classes, and the number declined rapidly. Statistics for 1902 and after do not show classes.

f This figure is probably a misprint, but is the number given in the *Ontario Sessional Papers*, v. 31, pt. 1, no. 2, 1899, Table A, p. 131.

g All books were called in on Dec. 7, 1907, to be moved to the new building.

171

Les Bibliothèques publiques à Montréal au début du XXe siècle : essai d'histoire socio-culturelle

Marcel Lajeunesse

Résumé

Il y eut, aux États-Unis et au Canada, à la fin du 19ᵉ siècle et au début du 20ᵉ siècle, un essor considérable des bibliothèques publiques qu'on a appelé « Public Library Movement ». La ville de Montréal, grande ville nord-américaine, a été confrontée à ce problème de l'institutionnalisation de la lecture publique. Dans ce texte, nous voulons rendre compte des événements et du début relativement à la création d'une bibliothèque municipale. En 1900, Montréal n'avait pas de véritable bibliothèque publique « municipale », et la population francophone de l'est de Montréal n'était pas desservie. L'établissement de la bibliothèque municipale de Montréal qui se fit de 1901 à 1917 donna lieu à des débats virulents relativement à la lecture publique, à la censure, à l'Index, au contrôle des idées. Ce débat sur la bibliothèque publique à Montréal, au début du 20ᵉ siècle éclaire tout le problème du développement des bibliothèques publiques au Québec dans les décennies qui suivirent. Le Québec reste à l'écart du courant continental du « Public Library Movement ».

Abstract

At the end of the nineteenth century and the beginning of the twentieth century in the United States and Canada there was a considerable thrust for public libraries known as the "Public Library Movement." Montreal, a major North American urban centre, was confronted with the problem of the institutionalization of public access to reading. In this article, we trace the events that led to the creation of the "municipal" library in Montreal. In 1900 Montreal had no municipal library as such, and the francophone population in the eastern part of the city had no access to this kind of facility. The creation of the Montreal Public Library, a process that spanned the period 1901 to 1917, provoked heated debates concerning public access to reading, censorship, the "Index," and the control of ideas. The debate over the Montreal Public Library at the very beginning of this century sheds light on the development of the public library system in Quebec in the decades that followed. Quebec remains outside the continental trend known as the "Public Library Movement."

―――――▶◆◀―――――

S'il est une époque où les bibliothèques publiques ont été l'objet d'un débat important dans la vie publique montréalaise, c'est vraiment au début du présent siècle. Le propos de cette étude est de débroussailler et d'analyser les nombreuses polémiques relatives à ces bibliothèques, car il n'est pas indifférent de les lier à la vie d'une métropole en formation : « It is of course plain to all that libraries are among the things that are products of human effort, so if some larger configuration of meaning is to be found in their history, it is better to relate them to the whole stream of social evolution than to separate them as it were from human strivings ».[1]

L'usage de la presse (*La Presse* et *Le Devoir*), source essentielle, permet de voir les problèmes de lecture publique à la lumière de la vie politique municipale. Dans la première décennie du XXe siècle, *La Presse*[2] est une puissance dans la vie municipale montréalaise.

> Le journal de Berthiaume ne s'oppose pas seulement à la prolongation du contrat des tramways et à la prolongation de contrat de la Montreal Light, Heat and Power pour la fourniture du gaz. D'une manière générale, il demande, avec la nationalisation du port de Montréal, la municipalisation des services publics. Cette tendance socialiste, implantée par Helbronner, permet à *La Presse* d'affecter un dévouement unique et absolu à l'intérêt général. Le mouvement correspond encore à celui qu'Adam Beck propage en Ontario.[3]

Par son intérêt à la vie de la communauté, ce quotidien est intéressé à l'établissement d'une bibliothèque publique à Montréal.[4] Bien que plus préoccupé par les grands problèmes nationaux et internationaux, *Le Devoir*, fondé par Henri Bourassa en 1910, s'intéresse aussi à la vie culturelle de la collectivité québécoise.

Au début du XXe siècle, Montréal est une métropole en pleine progression. La ville s'étend de tous côtés,[5] la population passe de 268 000 habitants en 1901, dont 61 pour cent des francophones, à 470 480 en 1911, et à 618 000 en 1921, dont 63 pour cent des francophones. Montréal est la place financière du Canada ; de plus, les communications (chemins de fer, port) y sont capitales. Le *Lovell's Directory* pouvait écrire orgueilleusement de Montréal en 1914 : « the largest city in Canada; the largest in the British colonies; the ninth in North America; the second largest port on the continent ».[6]

Cette ville dont le dynamisme porte l'empreinte des entrepreneurs anglo-saxons se francise par le prolétariat francophone qui arrive de la campagne et aussi par l'annexion de banlieues. Les travailleurs canadiens-français deviennent vraiment conscients de leur force avec l'élection du cigarier populiste Médéric Martin, en 1914.[7] Ils mettent fin à l'alternance qui avait prévalu jusqu'à ce moment entre un maire de langue anglaise et un maire de langue française.

En 1909, l'Association des Citoyens de Montréal composée d'hommes d'affaires et de professionnels demande une enquête sur l'administration municipale et une réforme définitive :

> La réforme consisterait à doubler les échevins d'un « Bureau de contrôle », également élu par le peuple, mais surveillant les édiles et limitant leur puissance. Les échevins garderaient le pouvoir légis-latif, et les quatre commissaires, membres du Bureau au profit du budget municipal. Le Comité des citoyens compte bien faire élire ses candidats au bureau de contrôle.[8]

En avril 1909, le premier ministre Gouin charge le juge Lawrence John Cannon, de Québec, de faire enquête sur l'administration municipale. En septembre, la population accepte, par référendum, l'établissement d'un bureau de contrôle. Ayant entendu 914 témoignages et reçu 548 documents, le juge Cannon dépose son rapport en décembre 1909 : le mal, c'est le patronage, et le patronage naît du système d'élection par quartier et du grand pouvoir des comités (police, incendie, etc.) à l'hôtel de ville qui adjugent ou font adjuger les contrats.

Le juge Cannon constate que 25 pour cent d'un budget annuel de 24 000 000 $ environ est dépensé en détournements, pots-de-vin, abus de toutes sortes, que le népotisme est généralisé. L'affairisme qu'on constate à ce moment lors de la constitution des grands cartels se trouve transposé, appliqué à un niveau différent à l'administration de la collectivité locale.

L'offre d'Andrew Carnegie

En 1880, l'Institut canadien offre à la ville de Montréal la collection de plus de 10 000 volumes qu'elle possède pour l'établissement d'une biblio-thèque publique. Prudent, le conseil municipal refuse, le 4 juillet 1881, ce don. En 1892-93, les autorités municipales font l'acquisition du château de Ramezay pour y établir une bibliothèque publique. En 1900, l'administration municipale collige des renseignements sur les diverses bibliothèques de la ville pour évaluer le besoin d'une autre bibliothèque, publique celle-là.

Le 6 mars 1901, le maire Raymond Préfontaine, ambitieux, soucieux d'une administration marquée de grandes réalisations, le contraire d'un maire soliveau, sollicite d'Andrew Carnegie une aide pécuniaire pour l'établissement d'une bibliothèque publique à Montréal, à l'instar de beaucoup de villes américaines et canadiennes. Dès le début d'avril, le maire faisait campagne pour l'acceptation de la somme de 150 000 $ qui ne sera offerte par Carnegie qu'en juillet 1901.[9] Le maire donnait la ville d'Ottawa en exemple et était en relation avec plusieurs villes canadiennes et américaines sur le mode suivi pour la fondation et l'administration de leurs bibliothèques publiques. L'échevin-homme d'affaires Hormisdas Laporte affirmait que si la ville était incapable de fournir annuellement 15 000 $, « elle ne méritait pas son titre de métropole du Canada ».[10]

En octobre 1901, Préfontaine projette d'affecter une partie de la somme offerte à la constitution des collections :

> The City will donate a piece of land ... of an approximate value about $30,000.[...]
> The City will engage itself to expend annually $15,000 on the maintenance and extension of the library. [...]
> The sum of, say, $50,000 out of the $150,000 donated by you to be expended in purchasing books to form the nucleus of the said public library ....[11]

Le secrétaire de Carnegie lui rappelle que la somme ne s'applique qu'à l'édifice, et que la ville doit s'engager à verser annuellement 15 000 $ pour les livres et l'entretien.[12] Le 26 mai 1902, le Conseil municipal, sous recommandation de la Commission des finances, accepte l'offre de Carnegie, selon les conditions établies par le donateur, et la ville était assurée que, « when the City has acquired a site satisfactory to the Community, funds for the building will be provided as work proceeds ».[13]

Le journaliste Tardivel annonçait, en juin 1902, que « nous sommes menacés d'une bibliothèque Carnegie ».[14] Il y voit « un foyer d'infection ».[15] *La Presse* fait écho au sermon du père Hamon à l'Église Saint-Pierre, qui voit dans les projets de bibliothèque publique et d'hôpital municipal « le cri de « Le cléricalisme, voilà l'ennemi ».

> Dans l'un et dans l'autre cas, un cri de révolte insensé s'est fait entendre : « pas de prêtre ».

> Un hôpital sans Dieu ; une bibliothèque où le prêtre ne soit pas admis à traiter des questions de morale, voilà l'idéal qu'une partie de la population a en vue [...]. C'est ainsi qu'à propos du projet de fondation d'une bibliothèque destinée à l'usage de la population aux trois quarts canadienne-française, et catholique, de notre ville, on

manifeste déjà l'intention d'exclure du bureau de censure tout ministre de notre religion.[16]

On sentait à ce moment que les choses seraient longues et difficiles. Comme l'affirmait *La Presse*, aux États-Unis, les travaux seraient déjà commencés, mais au Canada, « il y a les susceptibilités, les principes religieux, « l'index » à ménager et à défendre ».[17]

Le Conseil de ville eut, en octobre 1902, une longue séance sur le principe du comité de censure, sous la présidence du maire James Cochrane, un entrepreneur, « le grand asphalteur de nos rues »,[18] qui avait succédé à Préfontaine en février 1902. Il rejette ce principe après avoir entendu surtout l'échevin Laporte affirmer « que s'il fallait faire représenter dans le comité de censure toutes les religions et toutes les nationalités, il faudrait un comité fort nombreux ».[19] Le Conseil propose l'établissement d'un comité spécial de la bibliothèque qui aura sous contrôle le fonctionnement de la bibliothèque.

La question de la censure était au cœur du problème. Tardivel écrivait qu'« une bibliothèque ne peut être neutre, car il y a de bons ou de mauvais livres »[20] ; il déplorait que *La Presse* et *La Patrie* aient appuyé le projet de bibliothèque Carnegie et il affirmait : « La franc-maçonnerie triomphe encore une fois à Montréal ».[21] Dès le 14 octobre 1902, l'échevin Laporte reconnaissait « la nécessité de faire des concessions pour ne pas faire manquer complètement le projet ».[22]

L'échevin Louis-A. Lapointe qui a visité la bibliothèque de la ville de Détroit se demande pourquoi Montréal n'en ferait pas autant avec l'argent « que met à notre disposition un grand américain ».[23] Le 3 novembre 1902, après des imbroglios de procédure, le Conseil votait le règlement municipal n° 291 qui incluait les articles suivants :

> Le Conseil de Ville votera tous les ans, sur le revenu ordinaire de la Cité une somme de pas moins de $15,000 pour entretenir ladite bibliothèque ainsi que pour acheter et tenir en bon ordre des livres, recueils, revues, tableaux, statues, peintures et autres objets d'art. [...]

> Le Conseil nommera une Commission spéciale d'échevins, composée de pas plus de neuf membres pour construire ledit édifice et pour l'administrer ainsi que la bibliothèque qui y sera installée.[24]

En tout cas, l'administration municipale manifestait son intérêt en faisant faire par un fonctionnaire, le greffier L.-O. David, une étude sur l'organisation des bibliothèques publiques aux États-Unis.[25]

Le principe de l'établissement d'une bibliothèque admis, la question de la construction se pose. On admettait que cette bibliothèque devait être centrale, être à proximité des tramways, en même temps que dans un endroit calme ; et être construite dans un endroit qui n'occasionne pas des coûts exagérés.

Le premier site proposé fut celui du marché Saint-Laurent, ce qui a provoqué une réaction fort vive des bouchers.[26] Entretemps le comité de la bibliothèque fut établi, et l'échevin Hormisdas Laporte en devient le président ; ceci faisait dire à *La Presse* « que la question de la bibliothèque publique a fait encore un pas ».[27]

Après l'opposition des bouchers, le nouveau site choisi, le carré Viger, souleva celui des propriétaires cossus habitant près de ce parc. De plus, on reprochait au nouvel emplacement de se trouver trop loin de la partie nord de la ville.[28] L'aliénation d'une partie du carré Viger était problématique[29] ; enfin, le Conseil législatif, se rendant aux pressions des habitants de ce square, fit insérer, dans un amendement à la charte de la ville, une clause à l'effet « que la ville ne pourrait ériger une telle construction sur tout parc ou jardin public ».[30]

En fait, le projet de bibliothèque publique battait de l'aile depuis le début de 1903 ; l'échevin Chaussé demanda l'abrogation de la résolution d'acceptation de l'offre de Carnegie le 29 janvier, et la renouvela par la suite au moins une fois par mois. De profondes divergences étaient perceptibles parmi les échevins : il y avait ceux qui ne voulaient pas du tout de bibliothèque, dirigés par Édouard Chaussé et Henry A. Ekers, président de la Canadian Breweries Limited ; il y avait ceux qui en voulaient à tout prix, notamment Louis Payette, l'entrepreneur qui a construit notamment la gare Viger, le château Frontenac et le collège Saint-Laurent, et l'échevin Dr Elphège-Gaspard Dagenais ; il y avait enfin ceux qui n'en voulaient pas dans certains quartiers, comme par exemple, l'important commerçant et sociologue Herbert Brown Ames.[31]

Il est important de connaître les principaux arguments de l'opposant Chaussé :

> La Ville de Montréal n'a pas besoin d'une bibliothèque comme on en trouve dans les grandes villes d'Europe. Nous n'avons pas ici cette classe d'hommes plongés dans les études scientifiques, et pour qui les bibliothèques sont des cabinets de travail.
>
> Et combien d'autres ne fréquentent les bibliothèques publiques que pour se repaître de lectures dangereuses et immorales.
>
> D'ailleurs, n'avons-nous pas déjà plusieurs autres bibliothèques à Montréal, surtout pour ceux qui veulent se livrer à des études spéciales. Elles offrent de plus l'avantage de prêter des livres aux abonnés.[32]

Avez-vous bien considéré quelle source de malentendus et de disputes continuelles sur une bibliothèque publique pour une population mixte comme la nôtre ? Elle donnera lieu à des difficultés nombreuses et délicates pour ce qui est de l'achat des livres, de la censure, etc. Les protestants voudront avoir leurs livres et les catholiques les leurs.
Et voyez les dépenses énormes que nous occasionnera annuellement une institution de ce genre. [...]
Une bibliothèque, c'est une chose de luxe, et, certes, nous avons bien trop de besoins d'absolue nécessité pour y penser.[33]

À la séance du 4 mai 1903, une majorité d'échevins se prononça contre le projet de bibliothèque. Le président de la commission de la bibliothèque, l'échevin Laporte, qui vota avec la majorité, constate « que le clergé paraît moins favorable et même y est opposé ».[34] L'échevin Chaussé qui préférait voir cet argent consacré à la police, aux rues et trottoirs, déclarait que la classe ouvrière elle-même est opposée à l'érection d'une bibliothèque publique et qu'à tout considérer, 75 pour cent de la population n'en veut pas dans les circonstances actuelles. Le vote pris le 4 mai 1903 fut contesté ; les avocats de la ville émirent l'opinion que cette non-validité provenait d'une majorité des échevins présents au lieu d'une majorité de l'ensemble des membres du Conseil municipal.

Quoi qu'il en soit, l'offre de Carnegie ne fut pas spécifiquement refusée, mais le projet de construction était devenu irréalisable. Le règlement 291 relatif à la bibliothèque municipale (1902) ne sera abrogé que le 27 novembre 1905 et remplacé par le règlement 347 en fonction de la bibliothèque industrielle.[35]

Le compromis d'une bibliothèque industrielle

La Chambre de commerce demandait, dès février 1903, une section séparée pour les « sciences pratiques, industrielles et commerciales » de façon que celles-ci ne fussent pas négligées dans la bibliothèque municipale et faisait de cette section une priorité, les bibliothèques générales étant nombreuses à Montréal.

Le 6 mai 1903, la Chambre de commerce, à l'instigation de F.X. Perrault, « l'âme de la Chambre de Commerce du district de Montréal, le promoteur du Monument National »,[36] pria la Ville de Montréal de s'intéresser à l'établissement d'une bibliothèque scientifique et industrielle sous la direction de la Société Saint-Jean-Baptiste. L'échevin Laporte accepte d'en être le parrain au Conseil de ville : « le projet de M. Perreault me sourit ; j'ai toujours prétendu que nous avions besoin des livres de référence plus que des livres de fictions [*sic*] ; ce projet ne peut avoir d'ennemis, il rencontre le vœu de l'immense majorité ».[37]

La Commission de la bibliothèque, sous la présidence de l'échevin Laporte, recommandait le 16 juin 1903 l'acceptation de l'offre de la Société Saint-Jean-Baptiste d'ouvrir, dès le 1ᵉʳ septembre 1903, une bibliothèque technique au Monument National. Cette bibliothèque devrait être accessible tous les jours, y compris le dimanche, de 9 heures à 22 heures.

La commission demandait au Conseil municipal d'autoriser la somme de 600 $ pour l'ameublement de la bibliothèque, 1000 $ pour l'achat de livres et 700 $ pour payer cinq mois de loyer, le salaire du bibliothécaire et les abonnements à des revues scientifiques.[38] La commission crut bon de consulter les directeurs des bibliothèques publiques de Boston et de New York pour l'achat des livres techniques les plus utiles et les plus modernes.[39]

Le 11 juillet, la commission demandait un crédit supplémentaire de 600 $ pour la décoration de la salle de lecture car « il ne faut pas, dit l'échevin Dagenais, qu'une bibliothèque ait l'aspect d'une prison. Pour que le public la patronne suffisamment, il faut que le lecteur y trouve le repos sinon le luxe ».[40] Elle recommandait aussi l'engagement du bibliothécaire ; des cinq candidats, dont deux hommes, la commission décida de « nommer d'abord une femme, puis plus tard lorsque les besoins de services l'exigeront, on nommera un homme ».[41] Éva Circé fut nommée bibliothécaire au salaire de 33,32 $ par mois.

La commission approuva l'achat de 1500 volumes d'une valeur de 4000 $. Cette collection de base comprenait des encyclopédies Larousse et Britannica, des volumes français et anglais en architecture, minéralogie, métallurgie, électricité, construction et travaux publics, photographie, gouvernement municipal, sociologie, chimie, physique et géométrie, zoologie et économie politique. Cette collection était aux trois quarts française.[42]

L'échec de la bibliothèque Carnegie n'a pas désarmé complètement le clergé. Rendant visite, à l'Hôtel de ville, au nouveau maire, Hormisdas Laporte, l'archevêque de Montréal, Mᵍʳ Bruchési, aborda la question des mauvais livres et de la littérature pernicieuse répandus parmi la population. Il suggéra « la fondation d'un département civique d'inspection ad hoc, composé de littérateurs consciencieux et honnêtes ».[43]

Quant à la bibliothèque industrielle, par sa modestie, elle attirait les sarcasmes de quelques échevins. *La Presse* s'inquiétait de ce persiflage : « Il ne faut jamais désarmer vis-à-vis les gens qui présentent en plaisantant une idée dangereuse : de plaisanteries en plaisanteries ils arriveraient à leur but si on ne mettait pas le public en garde contre leurs agissements ».[44] Des milliers de travailleurs, affirmait *La Presse*, connaissaient le chemin de cette bibliothèque.

La bibliothèque industrielle élargit, avec les années, son champ d'intérêt. Le 20 juin 1906, l'Association symphonique d'Amateurs demandait la création, à la bibliothèque, d'une section consacrée aux études sur l'art musical.[45] En 1907, la bibliothèque industrielle possédait 4000 volumes,[46] dont un certain nombre à caractère historique, littéraire et artistique. Ce retour à une bibliothèque générale causa une réaction fort vive de Mgr Bruchési à l'adresse des membres de la commission de la bibliothèque :

> Lors de l'établissement de la bibliothèque civique à Monument national, il y a quelques années, il avait été entendu, si je ne me trompe, qu'on y mettrait que des ouvrages techniques, pouvant être utiles à la classe laborieuse en particulier.
>
> Depuis on y a ajouté les livres qui ne me semblent pas être conformes à ce but que l'on avait indiqué tout d'abord. Et j'apprends que l'on veut encore y installer des ouvrages qui n'ont aucun caractère technique et qui de plus seraient dangereux pour la foi et la morale. Je sais que dans la liste de ces livres, il y en a qui sont absolument condamnables et condamnés.
>
> C'est là une grave question à laquelle je ne puis pas me désintéresser. Je crois remplir un devoir de ma charge pastorale en veillant à ce que dans une bibliothèque ouverte à tout le monde il n'y ait pas de livres qui soient dommageables aux âmes confiées à ma charge.
>
> Aussi, je viens en toute confiance, vous prier de vouloir bien me dire ce que vous avez l'intention de faire relativement au choix des ouvrages à mettre dans la bibliothèque civique.[47]

La Presse réagit avec prudence à cette lettre qui fut lue à la commission municipale de la bibliothèque le 7 mars 1907. Ce journal « applaudit hautement... l'acte de vigilance et de bonne direction que vient de poser l'archevêque de Montréal », et ajoutait ne pas savoir « sur qui retombe la responsabilité du choix des listes d'ouvrages dont il est question ».[48]

L'échevin Joseph-Charles-Émile Lévy posa au contentieux de la ville des questions, notamment sur la signification à donner à la dénomination « bibliothèque *technique* », et sur la possibilité pour une bibliothèque purement technique de comprendre des œuvres littéraires.[49] Le contentieux ne trouva pas de définition précise de « bibliothèque technique », et il se référa plutôt aux débats de 1903 pour conclure qu'ils excluaient tout ouvrage littéraire. Le président de la commission de la bibliothèque, l'échevin Labrecque, fut d'avis que « le bureau légal exclut trop facilement de la bibliothèque les livres de pure littérature qui, après tout, constituent la technologie de la littérature, un art comme les autres ».[50]

À cette même séance du 24 avril 1907, l'avocat Gonzalve Desaulniers vint appuyer la requête de l'École littéraire de Montréal d'affecter une somme de 75 000 $ à la construction d'une véritable bibliothèque publique. Le président de l'École littéraire, Jean Charbonneau, avait demandé à la

Commission l'élargissement des cadres étroits de la bibliothèque et il avait noté que la Bibliothèque du Monument National n'était pas digne de Montréal et qu'elle ne s'élevait pas au niveau des autres bibliothèques de la ville.[51] La Commission de la bibliothèque reçut très bien cette demande.

En fait, la bibliothèque technique était un palliatif insatisfaisant. On revenait au point de départ, l'établissement d'une véritable bibliothèque publique. L'échevin Honoré Mercier proposa, en juillet 1908, ce projet, ajoutant qu'il ne souhaitait pas que les autorités religieuses aient le contrôle de la bibliothèque.[52]

L'opinion discute le projet. On se demandait « quelle espèce de bibliothèque veut-on créer ? Là est bien la question, là surtout ».[53] On attaquait la bibliothèque Carnegie d'Ottawa : « Qu'avions-nous besoin de ce jardin littéraire où ne fleurissent que des fleurs infectes […]. À part l'ornement qu'elle donne à la rue Metcalfe, elle ne vaut rien ».[54] *La Presse* constatait la difficulté d'entente sur l'établissement d'une bibliothèque publique :

> Il est certain que l'on n'arrivera jamais à une opinion commune sur la formation d'une bibliothèque municipale. Notre société se compose de catholiques et de protestants, d'Anglais et de Français, de croyants et de libre-penseurs, de fervents et d'indifférents, de gens studieux et d'esprits frivoles, de lecteurs mêlés où les uns trouvent déplacé et immoral ce que les autres jugent tout simplement récréatif et instructif. Quel est le critérium qui devra former la conscience publique ?[55]

Elle constatait aussi que la question était chargée d'émotivité et elle faisait référence à l'Institut canadien, car « l'ancienne bibliothèque de l'Institut Canadien n'était, pourtant, pas considérable ; cependant, quel malaise, quel bouleversement n'a-t-elle pas produit dans notre état social! »[56] Pendant ce temps, le nouveau bibliothécaire, Frédéric Villeneuve, nommé le 21 octobre 1909,[57] réclamait un deuxième assistant, un budget accru et plus d'espace pour ses collections.[58]

L'achat de la collection Gagnon

En novembre 1909, le principal de l'École Normale Jacques-Cartier de Montréal, et grand bibliophile, l'abbé Nazaire Dubois, obtint une option d'achat sur la collection de Canadiana, rassemblée par Philéas Gagnon, l'archiviste du Palais de Justice de Québec. Ce contrat a créé « une profonde sensation » dans le monde intellectuel de Québec. *La Presse* publia des entrevues avec les érudits Thomas Chapais, Eugène Rouillard, Narcisse-Eutrope Dionne, Pierre-Georges Roy et Cyrille Tessier ; ils s'accordaient pour affirmer que « c'est la plus vaste collection d'ouvrages canadiens …

surtout pour ce qui se rapporte aux événements d'avant 1850 »[59] ou pour l'évaluer à plus de 30 000 $.

Aussitôt un groupe d'échevins désira que la ville entrât en lice comme acquéreur de cette collection et « que Montréal ne laisse pas échapper cette occasion d'agrandir sa bibliothèque technique »[60] ; pour l'échevin Joseph Lespérance, « ce sera le moyen d'avoir bientôt une bibliothèque municipal [*sic*] digne de Montréal ».[61] Le notaire Victor Morin faisait appel au civisme de ses concitoyens : « L'occasion qui s'offre de doter Montréal d'une bibliothèque aussi précieuse que celle de Philéas Gagnon est unique ; pour aucune considération, il ne faudrait la laisser échapper ».[62]

L'option d'achat du principal Dubois prenait fin en mars 1910. Celui-ci l'offrit à l'Université Laval de Montréal et à la Ville de Montréal. Un groupe de Boston était à prélever un demi-million de dollars pour ériger une bibliothèque à la mémoire de l'historien Francis Parkman ; il convoitait cette collection pour la future bibliothèque bostonienne.[63]

En décembre 1909, l'abbé Dubois, toujours à l'affût de Canadiana, achetait à Québec la collection Neilson, au prix de 8000 $ pour son école normale montréalaise.[64] Dubois tenait à trouver un acheteur montréalais ; les Sulpiciens semblaient intéressés pour leur bibliothèque paroissiale, de même que la Société des Antiquaires pour le château de Ramezay. L'Université Laval de Montréal déclina la première, faute d'argent.

Le 12 janvier 1910, le principal de l'École Normale Jacques-Cartier incitait la Commission des finances d'appuyer l'achat de cette collection unique pour 31 000 $. Il poursuivait :

> ... En 1908, lors de la fermeture des cours de cette université (Laval de Montréal), Mᵍʳ l'Archevêque a dit que certains parlent d'« éteignoirs » qui s'opposent à la création d'une bibliothèque à Montréal ; et que, comme il n'ignorait pas à qui s'adresse cette épithète, il a ajouté qu'il appuierait très volontiers un projet de bibliothèque municipale, pourvu qu'on ne donnât pas à n'importe qui, n'importe quel livre. Quant à la collection dont il est question, non seulement elle ne contient que des livres d'une scrupuleuse moralité mais elle est d'une abondance, d'une richesse de documentation qu'on ne retrouverait nulle part ailleurs, et l'on sait que nos quelques bibliothèques publiques sont entièrement dépourvues de documents historiques.[65]

En somme, la sécurité par l'histoire.

Après l'avis d'achat de la collection Gagnon accordé par la Commission des finances, la question alla au Conseil municipal où le maire Louis Payette désirait la vider le plus rapidement possible. Le représentant du quartier

Saint-André, Joseph Ward, avait de fortes réticences à propos de cet achat dont la valeur était, selon lui, surestimée par l'opinion publique[66] ; de plus, la ville ne saurait où le loger.

Après un court débat, le Conseil accepte le 21 janvier 1910, l'avis de la Commission des finances d'acheter la collection Gagnon pour 31 000 $, par deux virements de fonds pris sur l'administration générale et les taxes à percevoir. Le vote fut de 26 à 10. Un seul échevin de langue française, Doris Couture, s'opposa à cet achat, et il fut appuyé en cela par les neuf échevins de langue anglaise ; les deux arguments apportés pour ce refus furent l'absence de bibliothèque et les besoins d'amélioration matérielle de la ville.[67]

La collection de plus de 10 000 pièces arriva à Montréal le 15 février 1910 ; l'inventaire fut effectué par le bibliothécaire Villeneuve à la bibliothèque de Sainte-Cunégonde.[68] Villeneuve qui avait perçu que cette collection « serait le noyau d'une bibliothèque de référence magnifique », reçut, le 23 juillet 1910, l'autorisation de composer le deuxième volume du catalogue, *Essai de bibliographie canadienne*, qui parut en 1913. N'ayant pas de local, la Ville de Montréal signa un contrat de dépôt des 64 caisses de la collection dans les voûtes de la firme Royal Trust.[69]

La bibliothèque Saint-Sulpice

Les Sulpiciens furent des promoteurs des « bons livres » au Québec dès la décennie 1840.[70] De la bibliothèque de l'Œuvre des Bons livres à celle du Cabinet de lecture paroissial de Montréal, puis à celle du Cercle Ville-Marie, il y a une succession d'une même œuvre. En 1909, l'élégant Cabinet de lecture, en face du Séminaire Saint-Sulpice, dû aux esquisses de monsieur Étienne-Michel Faillon, est vendu et démoli pour faire place à une maison d'affaires.

Les journaux montréalais du 2 mars 1910 annonçaient la décision des messieurs de Saint-Sulpice de construire une « bibliothèque publique, large ouverte à tous les chercheurs, à tous ceux qui veulent s'instruire ou se récréer, et qui ne coûtera rien, ni à la ville ni au gouvernement ».[71] Cette bibliothèque de 200 000 volumes serait construite rue Saint-Denis sur un terrain qui appartenait déjà aux Sulpiciens, et l'on priait « les hommes d'études, les chercheurs, les spécialistes, de bien vouloir leur communiquer des indications et des suggestions, leur dire les livres qu'ils désireraient particulièrement voir acheter, dans tel ou tel ordre d'idées ».[72] Les 40 000 volumes du Cercle Ville-Marie y formeraient le noyau de la collection de cette bibliothèque.

Cette construction fut annoncée avec la discrétion habituelle[73] de l'ordre fondé par monsieur Olier. Il nous semble que la vente du Cabinet de lecture et le désir de procurer un nouvel édifice à la bibliothèque paroissiale soient une première raison. De plus, même si le projet de bibliothèque publique n'aboutissait pas, il conservait de nombreux supporteurs et demeurait présent dans la vie de la métropole canadienne. Une requête de plus de 1600 signatures ne fut-elle pas présentée au Conseil municipal, en février 1910, demandant la construction d'une bibliothèque publique ?[74] Une bibliothèque publique, établie et dirigée par les Sulpiciens, devait rencontrer l'entière approbation de la hiérarchie catholique et écarter ses craintes de voir naître une bibliothèque municipale neutre. Enfin, dans les circonstances, cette libéralité des anciens seigneurs de Montréal devait renforcer la présence des Sulpiciens dans l'espace montréalais. En tout cas, l'opinion applaudit à cette annonce.

Celui qui devint le conservateur, Aegidius Fauteux, « un enfant de Saint-Sulpice », put écrire quelques années plus tard : « Son établissement n'est sans doute pas l'œuvre la plus importante de Saint-Sulpice, mais j'oserais dire que de tous les bienfaits de Saint-Sulpice depuis son existence, il n'en est peut-être pas qui ait été accueilli aussi favorablement par l'opinion et qui, à ce titre, ait mieux servi le prestige sulpicien ».[75]

Un concours était ouvert du 1er avril au 1er juin 1911 « à tous les architectes canadiens-catholiques de la province de Québec »[76] pour un édifice d'environ 150 000 $.[77] Les plans de Payette furent acceptés et reproduits. On y voyait une bibliothèque de deux étages, avec une salle de conférences de 923 sièges au sous-sol, et au 1er étage, une salle de lecture, quatorze cabinets spéciaux, une salle de périodiques et un magasin de livres.[78] La construction de la bibliothèque fut plus lente que prévue : on l'inaugura le 12 septembre 1915 en présence d'une assistance distinguée et par une surenchère d'éloquence académique. On rappela qu'elle fut construite et pourvue « sans qu'il en coûte un sou au public, et qu'elle sera entretenue de même jusqu'à la fin des temps ou, du moins, de la Compagnie fondée par M. Olier ».[79]

Pour remplir les rayons, la direction de la bibliothèque avait, dès le début de 1913, offert asile aux précieuses collections de l'Université Laval de Montréal, telles la collection Baby, la collection Chapleau,[80] la bibliothèque de littérature française fondée par le professeur Louis Arnould.[81] Sans fusionner les deux collections, « Le Séminaire serait heureux d'offrir à l'Université, pour ces diverses collections d'intérêt général, l'hospitalité la plus large dans sa nouvelle bibliothèque publique ».[82]

L'Université Laval donna un accord de principe deux mois plus tard. Le principal Dubois, de l'École normale Jacques-Cartier, offrit, pour l'Université Laval, à la bibliothèque sulpicienne, la collection du juge Sicotte qui comprenait plus de 7000 volumes.[83] Le conservateur Fauteux consacra l'année 1914 à parcourir les bibliothèques et les librairies américaines et françaises, et rapporta de France environ 60 000 volumes.[84] La bibliothèque Saint-Sulpice possédait donc en propre, à l'ouverture en 1915, incluant la partie utile de la collection du Cabinet de lecture, près de 100 000 volumes.

La bibliothèque Saint-Sulpice se voulait plus qu'une simple collection de volumes, si précieux fussent-ils ; elle se voulait un « foyer d'études » par un cercle littéraire, et des conférences sur les arts, les sciences, la littérature et l'histoire, qui en étaient le complément. La première conférence fut donnée par Aegidius Fauteux, le 26 octobre 1915 sur le « Règlement d'une bibliothèque catholique ».

Le Conservateur de la bibliothèque séparait les volumes en trois catégories : les livres prohibés, les livres dangereux et les livres inoffensifs. Il se demandait d'abord : « Pourquoi trouverait-on étrange que, bibliothèque catholique, nous suivions les prescriptions de l'Église ? C'est le contraire qui serait singulier. Il n'y a d'ailleurs rien de plus sage que la législation de l'Index ».[85] Les livres dangereux posaient un problème autrement plus complexe :

> Si, des livres nettement prohibés, nous passons aux livres qui ne sont que relativement dangereux, la ligne de conduite à suivre n'est plus aussi simple. Tout dépend de l'idée plus ou moins haute que se font les bibliothécaires de leur responsabilité morale. Les bibliothèques, on le sait, partagent avec la langue d'Esope la rare distinction d'être, à la fois ce qu'il y a de meilleur et ce qu'il y a de pire. Il n'y a rien de meilleur pour édifier et il n'y a rien de pire pour détruire. Et qui sait si, en somme, elles ne détruisent pas plus qu'elles n'édifient.[86]

Admettant que « ce sont les romans qui constituent le principal danger d'une bibliothèque »,[87] le conservateur était, lui aussi, tenté par la sécurité morale que procure une collection d'ouvrages historiques, tentation à laquelle il succombera en peu d'années. Quelques années plus tard, à la demande des autorités de l'Université de Montréal, discutant l'association de la Bibliothèque Saint-Sulpice à l'université naissante, Fauteux alléguait aux autorités de Saint-Sulpice que « cette modification aurait pour avantage de vous libérer de l'inutile roman et d'alléger d'autant votre responsabilité morale ».[88]

Une deuxième bibliothèque publique à Montréal : la Bibliothèque civique

L'achat de la riche collection Gagnon avait rendu faux le caractère technique et industriel que les édiles montréalais avaient donné à la bibliothèque municipale de leur ville. Dans un éditorial, *La Presse* du 29 octobre 1910, après avoir constaté qu'en Europe et aux États-Unis « une ville de quelque importance qui n'a pas sa bibliothèque publique ou municipale est considérée comme un centre rétrograde », constatait la situation à Montréal et souhaitait une action du conseil municipal :

Nous avons bien un noyau de bibliothèque municipale à Montréal, mais peut-on en être fier ? Les bons livres qu'elle renferme sont en petit nombre, malheureusement, et, chose non moins regrettable, la ville n'a pas de local où elle puisse être chez elle et étendre les rayons de sa bibliothèque. N'est-il pas souverainement ridicule, par exemple, de voir les précieux livres, bouquins et documents, si utiles à consulter, de la collection Gagnon, enfouis, dans des caisses, sous les combles de l'édifice du « Royal Trust ». Combien de temps y demeureront-ils ? Il semblerait que cette situation doive s'éterniser. En attendant, les chercheurs envahissent les bibliothèques privées où l'on est assez complaisant pour les recevoir. [...] Va-t-on, enfin, sortir de la torpeur du passé ? Va-t-on comprendre, une bonne fois, qu'une bibliothèque publique, aussi complète que possible, dans un local vaste, bien situé, bien éclairé, aménagé spécialement pour y recevoir un grand nombre de lecteurs à la fois, est absolument nécessaire dans une ville de l'importance de Montréal. Jusqu'ici, tout ou presque tout a été laissé à l'initiative privée ; cette façon de comprendre l'administration de la chose publique paraît s'être trop généralisée ici. Il est grand temps que cela cesse.[89]

Par ailleurs, le local du Monument National était devenu trop petit pour la bibliothèque de la ville. Le bibliothécaire, Frédéric Villeneuve, réclamait un nouveau local ; il propose de louer une partie de l'édifice Blumenthal, alors en construction au coin des rues Sainte-Catherine et Bleury.[90] L'École technique de Montréal offrit alors gratuitement un local, comprenant trois salles, pour y loger la collection municipale.

Le rapport de Villeneuve ne fut pas élogieux : les salles n'étaient pas assez vastes, les lecteurs se recrutaient assez peu dans ce quartier, et la bibliothèque accentuerait dans cet établissement son caractère technique. Pourtant, le bail fut signé le 1er mai 1911, pour cinq ans et la bibliothèque municipale s'installait rue Sherbrooke ouest.[91]

Le notaire Victor Morin, élu échevin, dans une équipe réformiste, aux élections du 1er février 1910, avait inscrit, dans son programme particulier, la fondation d'une bibliothèque municipale.[92] Devenu échevin, il relançait le projet de bibliothèque publique. Le 21 août 1911, il proposait au Conseil l'acquisition de l'édifice de l'Université Laval de Montréal, devenu trop petit pour les besoins universitaires, en échange d'un terrain au Parc Mont-Royal.[93]

À partir de 1911, l'échevin Morin se consacrait totalement à son projet de bibliothèque, assuré d'y réussir, et convaincu « que Mgr Bruchési ne sera pas opposé au projet, pourvu qu'il ait des garanties sérieuses concernant la moralité et l'orthodoxie des livres ».[94] En septembre 1911, un nouveau comité de la bibliothèque, composé de cinq échevins et présidé par Victor Morin, était formé à l'hôtel-de-ville et se mettait résolument à l'œuvre.[95] Les autorités de l'Université Laval refusèrent de se départir de leur édifice construit en 1893, bien que la Société Saint-Jean-Baptiste, par sa commission des intérêts scolaires, eût poussé la conclusion d'un accord entre la ville et l'Université.

À l'instar des années 1902 et 1903, le projet de bibliothèque publique se compliquait de points de vue divergents. Serait-ce une bibliothèque centrale ou plusieurs petites bibliothèques dispersées à travers la ville ?

> On a souvent parlé d'établir, au lieu d'une seule et vaste biblio-
> thèque, plusieurs petites disséminées un peu dans tous les quartiers
> de la ville. Je ne crois pas qu'un projet soit de nature à exclure
> l'autre. Dans les banlieues, on demande surtout de la lecture légère :
> romans, contes, nouvelles. Rien n'empêcherait l'administration
> municipale de créer de petites bibliothèques, par exemple dans les
> hôtels-de-ville   des   anciennes   municipalités,   aujourd'hui
> annexées.[96]

L'échevin Louis-A. Lapointe s'opposait au projet, en raison des querelles de terrain et des dissensions de race et de religion qui en résulteraient. D'aucuns suggéraient de s'adresser de nouveau au philanthrope Carnegie. Le notaire Morin était prêt à des compromis pour l'établissement d'une bibliothèque : il prévoyait, dans le règlement qu'il fit adopter par le conseil le 1er avril 1912, un bureau de censure. L'archevêque Bruchési n'avait-il pas fait connaître ses réserves au projet :

> Mgr l'Archevêque approuve le projet de l'échevin Morin en ce qui
> regarde la bibliothèque civique, mais il y met des conditions : c'est
> le choix des livres qu'il faut surveiller. Beaucoup d'ouvrages sont à
> l'Index ; un grand nombre d'autres ne sont pas très bons et notre
> peuple y trouverait la ruine de ses principes et de sa foi, sans compter
> la perte de ses mœurs et de sa conscience.[97]

Dans le règlement municipal, le comité de la bibliothèque avait défini le caractère de la bibliothèque, en affirmant « que cette bibliothèque, tout en étant une bibliothèque d'étude et de référence, servira de bibliothèque centrale pour l'approvisionnement des bibliothèques locales qui pourront être établies plus tard dans les diverses parties de la ville ».[98] Le comité des échevins proposait d'affecter un demi-million de dollars à la construction de cette bibliothèque centrale.[99] L'échevin O'Connell, appuyé par l'échevin Clément, recommandait d'affecter 700 000 $ à plusieurs petites bibliothèques.[100]

Les échevins de langue anglaise, supportés par le quotidien *The Gazette*, s'opposèrent au terrain le plus souvent cité, le parc Mance, alléguant que l'on priverait Montréal d'un terrain de jeu et d'un parc.[101] Dans un éditorial, *La Presse* nota que l'argument des anglophones était spécieux, en rappelant que la ville de Westmount avait bien sa bibliothèque dans un parc.[102] Il y avait bien anguille sous roche. Les échevins anglophones ne voulaient pas de bibliothèque municipale nulle part ; pour eux, les bibliothèques du Fraser Institute et du Mechanics' Institute étaient suffisantes à leurs besoins. Pour leur part, les échevins francophones souhaitaient construire la bibliothèque projetée au parc Lafontaine.[103]

Le maire Arsène Lavallée, premier magistrat depuis février 1912, favorisait la rue Sherbrooke, entre les rues Beaudry et Montcalm. Les échevins anglophones trouvaient que ce site était trop à l'est. Les édiles francophones répliquaient que leurs collègues anglophones ne voulaient pas de bibliothèque et qu'ils appuyaient plutôt la construction d'un nouvel édifice pour le Mechanics' Institute.[104]

Face à ces oppositions, l'échevin Victor Morin « jure qu'il mènera le projet à bonne fin coûte que coûte ».[105] Morin proposa l'érection d'une bibliothèque publique dans l'est, et l'établissement, dans l'ouest, d'une bibliothèque semi-publique, érigée et entretenue par une institution, mais subventionnée, chaque année, par la ville.[106] Somme toute, Morin cherchait un compromis avec les anglophones par le biais du projet du Mechanics' Institute.

Le 13 janvier 1913, les formalités essentielles étaient remplies : les autorités municipales (Bureau de contrôle) décidaient d'affecter 500 000 $ à la construction d'un édifice que l'on voulait digne de Montréal.[107] *La Presse*, soucieuse de faire avancer le projet et voulant accommoder tout le monde, favorisait, à l'instar de *La Patrie*, un emplacement au coin des rues Sherbrooke et Saint-Laurent.[108] On avançait aussi, en plus du parc Mance déjà mentionné, le carré Saint-Louis.

Le projet s'embourbait dans une querelle de terrains ; des dizaines de terrains étaient proposés. Morin, dégoûté de toutes ces tergiversations, fit appel à la législature provinciale comme seule solution dans les circonstances.[109] Enfin, en juin 1914, on décida de construire, rue Sherbrooke, en face du parc LaFontaine ; ce terrain, qui appartenait déjà à la ville, était le seul capable de rallier les administrateurs municipaux de la métropole. Aucun des parcs de la ville n'était entamé.[110]

Ensuite, les événements se précipitèrent. En mai 1914, l'architecte Eugène Payette fit valoir l'expérience qu'il avait acquis en construisant la bibliothèque Saint-Sulpice et les études qu'il avait réalisées en architecture des bibliothèques. Il était choisi le 17 juillet pour dessiner les plans du futur édifice que le Bureau de Contrôle approuvait le 9 octobre.[111] La Municipale aurait 109 pieds sur 115, avec une annexe de 109 pieds sur 45, alors que Saint-Sulpice en avait 108 pieds sur 144, c'est-à-dire 12 pour cent de plus pour la Municipale.[112] Les travaux de fondations particulièrement importants pour ce terrain accidenté et sablonneux débutèrent à la fin octobre 1914. Le contrat de construction de l'édifice, « un véritable monument », était octroyé le 16 avril 1915 à la John Quinian and Co., selon les plans et devis de Payette, au prix de 445 000 $.[113] La Ville qui tenait au marbre et au granit, ajouta une rallonge de 16 000 $ pour que les fûts monolithes de la façade soient en granit de Stanstead.

Le 20 novembre 1915, le lieutenant-gouverneur Leblanc posait la pierre angulaire du « nouveau Temple des livres ». Le maire, Médéric Martin, était heureux de l'endroit où serait érigée la bibliothèque, parce que celle-ci « embellira l'aspect de cette partie de notre ville, qui a peut-être été trop négligée dans le passé. Enfin, cette bibliothèque sera plus à la portée de ceux qui font partie de la grande masse des travailleurs ».[114] L'évêque auxiliaire, Mgr Georges Gauthier affirma : « Je voudrais qu'il y eût ici une bibliothèque technique de premier ordre ».[115] Le premier ministre du Québec, Sir Lomer Gouin, constatant le grand désir de lecture chez la population, concluait : « Parce qu'il y a peu de bibliothèques publiques dans la province de Québec, il ne faut pas conclure et il ne faut pas laisser dire que sa population ne lit point ou ne lisait point. »[116]

En dépit de la guerre qui rendait les ouvriers rares et les matériaux coûteux, l'édifice de la Bibliothèque était livré à la ville le 17 mai 1917. Une semaine plus tard, le 13 mai, le vainqueur de la Marne, le général Joffre, dirigeant une mission française en Amérique, inaugurait, au cours d'une cérémonie d'une rare brièveté (10 minutes) — qui faillit d'ailleurs être rayée du programme — la nouvelle bibliothèque publique de Montréal.[117] Ce n'est que le 4 septembre 1917 que « le palais des livres de la ville » est ouvert à la population.

Après avoir signalé que « l'ouverture d'une bibliothèque devrait être un signe de réjouissance pour tous les citoyens, surtout pour la classe ouvrière », la plupart des orateurs à l'inauguration officielle de la bibliothèque enchaînèrent en affirmant « qu'il est beaucoup plus avantageux d'acheter des collections privées ou aux encans que de parcourir les libraires »[118] ; le commissaire Thomas Côté, du Bureau de Contrôle de la ville, ajoute « que, dans quelques années, la ville dotera l'ouest d'un nouveau temple des livres ».[119]

Le remarquable bibliothécaire Frédéric Villeneuve étant décédé en avril 1915,[120] Hector Garneau fut nommé, le 19 janvier 1916, bibliothécaire en chef de la Cité, à cause de « fortes aptitudes littéraires et d'une intellectualité spéciale ».[121] Il avait à développer une institution chèrement acquise.

Conclusion

Nous avons voulu rendre compte du débat montréalais sur les biblio-thèques publiques au début du XXe siècle, pour en dégager les traits principaux et faire voir les mentalités, les attitudes face à la bibliothèque publique.[122] Nous constatons l'incompréhension du concept de biblio-thèque publique, c'est-à-dire une institution publique, supportée par l'État, non religieuse, libre, ouverte à tout citoyen dans un but d'information, d'éducation, de culture ou de loisir ; nous y constatons la distance face à ce concept développé dans le reste de l'Amérique du Nord, dans le « Public Library Movement », au cours de la seconde moitié du 19e siècle.

Le long et pénible débat rend compte plus de rivalités d'échevins, de disputes de terrains, de pressions ecclésiastiques, de préoccupations adminis-tratives pressantes que d'un débat élevé sur l'éducation populaire. Que d'atermoiements et que d'intérêts! Un « manque d'esprit public », selon *La Presse*.[123] Et pourtant, que de civisme et d'obstination chez l'échevin Victor Morin, le véritable instigateur de la création de la bibliothèque municipale de Montréal.

Nous croyons que l'idée d'une bibliothèque publique, annoncée par les Sulpiciens en 1910, avait pour objectif, parmi d'autres évidemment, d'empêcher la fondation d'une bibliothèque publique laïque et neutre « en la rendant inutile ».[124] Cette opinion circulait dans la décennie 1910 :

> Quoi que fasse la Ville de Montréal, ce n'est pas la Bibliothèque municipale, mais celle de Saint-Sulpice qui comptera aux yeux, non seulement de notre public éclairé, mais des savants des autres provinces canadiennes, de l'Europe et des États-Unis. [...]

> À mon sens, tout ce que gagnerait Saint-Sulpice en se déchargeant de sa bibliothèque sur l'Université de Montréal, serait de donner quelque corps à cette opinion qui a eu cours quelque temps et d'après laquelle la bibliothèque de la rue Saint-Denis aurait été bâtie uniquement pour faire échouer le projet d'une bibliothèque muni-cipale.[125]

Ce que les administrateurs désiraient par-dessus tout, c'était la construc-tion d'un monument digne de la métropole canadienne qu'était Montréal : « un palais de livres en marbre ».[126] La Ville de Montréal a été gâtée, de ce côté, avec la construction en moins d'une décennie des deux bibliothèques dans le style Beaux-Arts :

> ... Il y a bien les deux bibliothèques d'Eugène Payette : la biblio-thèque municipale et la bibliothèque Saint-Sulpice, aujourd'hui

Bibliothèque nationale. La première, avec ses puissantes colonnes corinthiennes monolithiques en granit, présente sur la rue Sherbrooke une monumentale façade romaine ; la seconde, qui se rapproche d'assez près de l'hôtel particulier parisien, est délicieuse, est raffinée ; son plan est un reflet de l'École française.[127]

Dans tout ce débat sur l'établissement d'une bibliothèque municipale, et principalement sur la localisation et l'organisation de celle-ci, quel rôle accordait-on au bibliothécaire de la ville ? Il n'y a que *La Presse*, dans un éditorial, en juin 1914, pour s'en préoccuper en demandant : « M. Villeneuve est-il consulté ? »[128]

Inutile de dire que les préoccupations des administrateurs municipaux étaient autres. Pendant que l'on ne lésinait pas sur la construction de la bibliothèque, le maire Médéric Martin remarqua que le bibliothécaire Garneau « voyage trop sur les tramways et qu'il écrit trop de lettres » et il obtint du Conseil la réduction de moitié de son compte de dépenses en timbres de poste et en billets de tramways.[129]

Notes

[1]Carl M. White, « The International Destiny of Literate Society and Librarianship », in *Bases of Modern Librarianship; A Study of Library Theory and Practise in Britain, Canada, Denmark, The Federal Republic of Germany and the United States*, ed. Carl M. White (New York: Macmillan, 1964), 1.

[2]Pierre Godin écrit dans *L'information-opium. Une histoire politique de La Presse* (Montréal: Éditions Parti-pris, 1972), 46, que, de 1900 à 1914 « La Presse se fait aussi la championne des réformes sociales. Dans les débats qui ont cours alors au sujet des écoles du soir, de la création de sociétés pour venir en aide à l'enfance et de la reconnaissance du syndicalisme, elle appuie les revendications populaires ».

[3]Robert Rumilly, *Histoire de Montréal* (Montréal: Fides, 1972), III: 347.

[4]Dans le numéro spécial à l'occasion de son 25ᵉ anniversaire, publié le 3 septembre 1910, *La Presse* reconnaissait cet intérêt : « Que n'a pas fait *La Presse* pour l'avancement des sciences et des arts [...] avec ses campagnes soutenues en faveur des bibliothèques publiques, campagnes d'où est sortie du moins la bibliothèque civique ».

[5]Parmi les annexions réalisées par Montréal dans les deux premières décennies du XXᵉ siècle, citons : Saint-Henri et Sainte-Cunégonde (1905), Villeray et une partie de la paroisse Saint-Laurent (1907), Rosemont, Sault-au-Récollet, Notre-Dame-des-Neiges (1908), village Delorimier et ville de Saint-Louis, de même qu'une parcelle d'Outremont (1909), le village d'Ahuntsic, la ville de Bordeaux, la ville de Notre-Dame-de-Grâce, Ville Émard, Ville Saint-Paul, Longue-Pointe et le village de Tétreaultville (1910), Cartierville (1916), et Maisonneuve (1918).

[6]Cité par Kathleen Jenkins, *Montréal Island City of the St. Lawrence* (New York: Doubleday, 1966), 447.

[7]John Irwin Cooper, *Montréal, A Brief History* (Montréal: McGill-Queen's University Press, 1969), 125.

[8]Rumilly, 402.

[9]Lettre de James Bertram au maire Préfontaine, 23 juillet 1901, Archives municipales de Montréal, Bibliothèque publique, Contribution Carnegie. Pour complément d'informations sur l'action d'Andrew Carnegie et son secrétaire Bertram pour les bibliothèques publiques américaines, voir l'étude de Georges Bobinski, *Carnegie Libraries; Their History and Impact on American Public Library Development* (Chicago: American Library Association, 1969). 257p.

[10]*La Presse*, 7 avril 1901, p. 2.

[11]Lettre du maire Préfontaine à Andrew Carnegie, Skibo Castle, Ardgay, Scotland, 8 octobre 1901, Archives municipales de Montréal.

[12]Lettre de James Bertram au maire Préfontaine, 27 novembre 1901, Archives municipales de Montréal.

[13]Lettre de James Bertram à L.-O. David, Greffier de la Cité, 9 juin 1902, Archives municipales de Montréal.

[14]*La Vérité*, 21 juin 1902. Voir la discussion de ce sujet par Tardivel dans *Jules-Paul Tardivel, la France et les États-Unis, 1851-1905* par Pierre Savard (Québec: Presses de l'Université Laval, 1967), 382-84.

[15]Ibid.

[16]« La bibliothèque sans prêtre et l'hôpital sans Dieu », *La Presse*, 30 juin 1902, p.1.

[17]« Quels seront les censeurs de la bibliothèque civique ? », *La Presse*, 30 juin 1902, p. 1. Pour sa part, le journal *Les Débats* du 4 mai 1902 écrivait : « Qu'on ait le courage de dire qu'à Montréal, dans l'état actuel de nos divisions religieuses, une bibliothèque vraiment publique est une utopie […]. Si M. Carnegie veut contribuer à instruire les Montréalais, il ne pourrait pas mieux donner son appui financier qu'à l'Institut Fraser. […] Cette bibliothèque est indistinctement fréquentée par des Anglais et des Canadiens. Elle est parfaitement dirigée, sans aucun parti pris, s'alimentant chaque année d'ouvrages de valeur, français ou anglais. »

[18]Rumilly, 313. Pour des notes biographiques sur maires et échevins de Montréal, voir J.-Charles Lamothe, *Histoire de la Corporation de la Cité de Montréal depuis ses origines jusqu'à nos jours* (Montréal, 1903). 848p.

[19]« La bibliothèque publique de la Ville de Montréal », *La Presse*, 9 octobre 1902, p. 3.

[20]*La Vérité*, 18 octobre 1902.

[21]Ibid., 15 novembre 1902.

[22]« Aurons-nous une bibliothèque publique ? », *La Presse*, 15 octobre 1902, p. 8.

[23]« La question difficile », *La Presse*, 24 octobre 1902, p. 2.

[24]Archives municipales de Montréal, Bibliothèque publique, Contribution Carnegie.

[25]Archives municipales de Montréal. Bibliothèque publique. Établissement projeté à Montréal. Il semble que le greffier de la ville, L.-O David en soit l'auteur.

[26]Voir « La Marché Saint-Laurent et la bibliothèque publique », *La Presse*, 20 novembre 1902, p. 1, et « La bibliothèque et la police », *La Presse*, le 27 janvier 1903.

[27]« Le Comité d'Administration de la Bibliothèque choisie », *La Presse*, 25 novembre 1902, p. 7.

[28]« Le site de la bibliothèque », *La Presse*, 30 janvier 1903, p. 10.

[29]« La Bibliothèque publique », *La Presse*, 10 février 1903, p. 8.

[30]« La Bibliothèque civique reçoit son coup de mort », *La Presse*, 2 mai 1903, p. 21.

[31]Ibid.

[32]On fait référence ici au Cabinet de Lecture, aux bibliothèques de McGill et de Laval, au Fraser Institute, à la bibliothèque du Gésu, à la bibliothèque du Barreau, à celle de l'École normale Jacques-Cartier.

[33]« La bibliothèque civique », *La Presse*, 30 avril 1903, p. 2.

[34]« Le coup de mort de la bibliothèque Carnegie », *La Presse*, 5 mai 1903, p. 1. *La Presse* du 18 novembre 1902 avait interviewé un curé canadien-français de l'État de New York, le père Blanchard, lequel avait affirmé : « Le don de Carnegie est très beau, mais je préfèrerais plutôt le voir refuser que de voir la bibliothèque sous le contrôle d'hommes dont l'absence de sens moral a tué toutes les idées religieuses. Cette question est une question vitale pour la race canadienne-française. Si nous voulons garder nos ouailles, nous devrions voir à ce qu'on ne leur mette pas la tentation sous les yeux. »

[35]Archives municipales de Montréal, Bibliothèque publique, Établissement projeté à Montréal ; « Montréal aura sa bibliothèque technique », *La Presse*, 17 juin 1903, p. 8.

[36]« Et la Chambre de Commerce », *La Presse*, 7 mai 1903.

[37]Ibid.

[38]Archives municipales de Montréal, Bibliothèque publique, Établissement projeté à Montréal ; « Montréal aura sa bibliothèque technique », *La Presse*, 17 juin 1903, p. 8.

[39]« Nos futures bibliothèques », *La Presse*, 8 juillet 1903, p. 2.

[40]« La Bibliothèque industrielle », *La Presse*, 12 juillet 1903, p. 5.

[41]Ibid.

[42]« La Bibliothèque technique », *La Presse*, 29 octobre 1903, p. 7.

[43]« Mgr Bruchési à l'Hôtel-de-Ville », *La Presse*, 25 février 1904, p. 1.

[44]« La Bibliothèque civique », *La Presse*, 27 juin 1906, p. 4.

[45]Archives municipales de Montréal, Bibliothèque publique, Établissement projeté à Montréal.

[46]Juliette Chabot, *Montréal et le rayonnement des bibliothèques publiques* (Montréal: Fides, 1963), 32.

[47]Lettre de Mgr P.-N. Bruchési aux président et membres du comité de la bibliothèque civique, 18 février 1907, citée par Chabot, *Montréal et le rayonnement...*, p. 33 ; Antonio Drolet, dans son volume *Les bibliothèques canadiennes 1604-1960* (Montréal: Cercle du livre de France, 1965) fait référence à cette lettre à la page 177. Mgr Bruchési mentionnait, en post-scriptum, notamment les œuvres de Voltaire, Rousseau, Balzac et Georges Sand comme n'ayant pas leur raison d'être dans une bibliothèque civique.

[48] « La bibliothèque technique et les mauvais livres », *La Presse*, 8 mars 1907, p. 4. Sans pouvoir le prouver, nous croyons qu'il y a une relation entre ces faits qui ont donné à la bibliothécaire Éva Circé une réputation de « radicalisme » et sa destitution par le Conseil de Ville le 9 juin 1909.

[49] « Bibliothèque municipale », *La Presse*, 18 avril 1907, p. 10.

[50] « Bibliothèque municipale », *La Presse*, 25 avril 1907, p. 13.

[51] Lettre citée par Léo-Paul Desrosiers, « La municipale de Montréal », *Le Devoir*, 17 juin 1944.

[52] « Bibliothèque », *La Presse*, 25 juillet 1908, p. 3. Le journal ultramontain *La Croix* fit campagne en juillet 1908 contre le projet de bibliothèque publique qui refaisait surface. Dans son édition du 16 juillet, on présentait ainsi le directeur du Fraser Institute Pierre B. de Crèvecœur qui avait défendu, dans *Le Canada*, 4 juillet 1908, sa bibliothèque : « un pauvre petit Français, échoué sur les rives du Saint-Laurent, plein de lui-même, c'est-à-dire plein d'ignorance et de préjugés anti-catholiques ».

[53] Ibid.

[54] « La Bibliothèque Carnegie », *La Presse*, 15 avril 1908, p. 4.

[55] « À propos de bibliothèque », *La Presse*, 13 novembre 1908, p. 4.

[56] Ibid.

[57] Archives municipales de Montréal, Bibliothèque publique, Bibliothécaires successifs.

[58] « Les besoins de la bibliothèque », *La Presse*, 2 décembre 1909, p. 8.

[59] « Cette rare collection de livres canadiens », *La Presse*, 16 novembre 1909, p. 1.

[60] « La bibliothèque Gagnon », *La Presse*, 17 novembre 1909, p. 16.

[61] Ibid.

[62] « Précieuse collection », *La Presse*, 20 novembre 1909, p. 32.

[63] « Cette rare collection de M. Philéas Gagnon », *La Presse*, 26 novembre 1909, p. 1.

[64] « La collection Neilson s'en vient à Montréal », *La Presse*, 10 décembre 1910, p. 1. Cette collection d'imprimés d'avant 1820 et de manuscrits, édifiée par John Neilson, était vue comme le complément de la collection Gagnon.

[65] « Cette précieuse bibliothèque Gagnon », *Le Devoir*, 13 janvier 1910. Le juge Lafontaine, promoteur de l'achat de cette collection, affirmait au Conseil de ville : « Il n'y a là aucune discussion politique ou religieuse, c'est une œuvre patriotique… ». Voir « La ville achètera la collection Gagnon », *Le Canada*, 13 janvier 1910, p. 10.

[66] « Encore la bibliothèque Gagnon », *La Presse*, 18 janvier 1910, p. 4.

[67] « La bibliothèque Gagnon achetée par la ville », *La Presse*, 22 janvier 1910, p. 24 ; « La bibliothèque Gagnon », *Le Devoir*, 22 janvier 1910 ; et « Le Conseil décide d'acheter la collection Gagnon », *Le Canada*, 22 janvier 1910, p. 14.

[68] « L'inventaire est commencé », *La Presse*, 16 février 1910, p. 14. Le Conseil municipal de Sainte-Cunégonde avait fondé une bibliothèque publique en septembre 1905 et E.Z. Massicotte y était nommé bibliothécaire. Sainte-Cunégonde étant annexée à Montréal, sa bibliothèque, 12 000 volumes, devenait propriété montréalaise à l'été 1906. Cette institution dynamique fut ouverte au public de 1905 à 1918. Voir à ce sujet Desrosiers, « La municipale de Montréal », *Le Devoir*, 17 juin 1944.

[69]*La Presse*, 22 mars 1910, p. 1. Il en coûta 20 $ par mois à la ville pour la location des voûtes de la Royal Trust.

[70]Voir Marcel Lajeunesse, « Les cabinets de lecture à Paris et à Montréal au XIXe siècle », *Recherches sociographiques* XVI, no. 2 (mai-août 1975): 244-47, et Olivier Maurault, *Marges d'histoire : Saint-Sulpice* (Montréal: Librairie d'Action canadienne-française, 1930), 3: 55-104 ; Marcel Lajeunesse, *Les Sulpiciens et la vie culturelle à Montréal au XIXe siècle* (Montréal: Fides, 1982). 278p.

[71]« La création d'une bibliothèque publique par les MM. de Saint-Sulpice est chose décidée », *Le Devoir*, 2 mars 1910. *La Presse* du 2 mars 1910 l'annonçait sous le titre « Un vœu populaire qui se réalise ».

[72]*Le Devoir*, 2 mars 1910.

[73]« C'est une maxime de Saint-Sulpice de faire le bien sans faire de bruit », Archives du Séminaire Saint-Sulpice de Montréal, Lettre d'Aegidius Fauteux à M. Wilfrid Hébert, procureur du Séminaire, 8 septembre 1920.

[74]« À l'hôtel-de-ville », *Le Devoir*, 28 février 1910.

[75]Archives du Collège de Montréal. Lettre d'Aegidius Fauteux à M. Neveu, supérieur du Collège, 26 novembre 1920.

[76]« Montréal aura enfin une bibliothèque publique », *Le Devoir*, 29 mars 1910.

[77]« Le concours de la bibliothèque », *Le Devoir*, 29 juillet 1911. Pour plus de détails, voir Jean-René Lassonde, *La Bibliothèque Saint-Sulpice* (Montréal: Bibliothèque nationale du Québec, 1987), 51-113.

[78]« La Bibliothèque du Cercle Ville-Marie », *La Presse*, 9 décembre 1911, p. 1.

[79]« Brillante inauguration », *Le Devoir*, 13 septembre 1915.

[80]« La bibliothèque Chapleau à l'Université Laval », *La Presse*, 7 juillet 1909, p. 4 ; il s'agit, en fait, de la collection de 4000 volumes de Sir Adolphe Chapleau, léguée par Lady Chapleau à l'Université.

[81]Cette bibliothèque générale d'études littéraires et historiques fut fondée en 1906 par le titulaire de la chaire de littérature française créée et dotée par les Sulpiciens. Elle comprenait des périodiques et des ouvrages de littérature, de critique et d'histoire. Un an après sa fondation, elle comptait 2000 volumes. Voir « Notre bibliothèque canadienne-française », *La Presse*, 21 février 1906, p. 4.

[82]Archives du Séminaire Saint-Sulpice de Montréal. Lettre de M. Wilfrid Hébert, p.s.s., procureur du Séminaire, à Mgr Dauth, vice-recteur, 11 janvier 1913.

[83]« Collection Sicotte », *La Presse*, 13 février 1913, p. 9.

[84]Chabot, 53.

[85]Elie-J. Auclair, « Chronique des revues », *La Revue canadienne*, nouvelle série, XVI (juillet-décembre 1915): 551. Par ailleurs, Fauteux obtient de Rome que l'Index ne s'applique pas à la Bibliothèque Saint-Sulpice : voir Lassonde, p. 201-4.

[86]Auclair, 552.

[87]Ibid., 553.

[88]Archives du Séminaire Saint-Sulpice de Montréal, Lettre d'Aegidius Fauteux à monsieur Wilfrid Hébert, procureur du Séminaire, 8 septembre 1920.

[89]« Les bibliothèques », *La Presse*, 29 octobre 1910, p. 20.

[90]Au Monument National, le local avait 900 pi.ca., loué à 0,70 $ le pi.ca. Cet édifice Blumenthal mettait à la disposition de la bibliothèque 6000 pi.ca. à 0,75 $

le pi.ca. pour un bail de cinq ans à raison de 4500 $ par an. Voir *La Presse*, 17 janvier 1911, p. 4.

[91]Voir à ce sujet *La Presse*, 31 janvier 1911, p. 5, *Le Devoir*, 17 juin 1944 à l'article de Léo-Paul Desrosiers, « La Municipale de Montréal », et Archives municipales de Montréal, Bibliothèque publique, Établissement à Montréal.

[92]Rumilly, 411.

[93]*Le Devoir*, 22 août 1911.

[94]Ibid., 26 septembre 1911.

[95]Renée Morin, *Un bourgeois d'une époque révolue : Victor Morin, notaire, 1865-1960* (Montréal: Éditions du jour, 1967), 112.

[96]*Le Devoir*, 3 novembre 1911.

[97]*La Presse*, 11 octobre 1911, citée par Morin, *Un bourgeois d'une époque révolue...*, p. 114-15.

[98]Léo-Paul Desrosiers, « La Municipale de Montréal » (suite), *Le Devoir*, 23 juin 1944.

[99]« Bibliothèque de $500,000 », *La Presse*, 6 avril 1912, p. 40.

[100]« Répandre le goût de la lecture », *La Presse*, 27 juin 1912, p. 22.

[101]« La bibliothèque publique », *La Presse*, 2 juillet 1912, p. 4.

[102]« La Bibliothèque municipale », *La Presse*, 23 novembre 1912, p. 18. Sur les origines de la Westmount Public Library, voir Elizabeth Hanson, « Architecture and Public Librarianship in the Early Twentieth Century : The Westmount Public Library, 1899-1939 », *Libraries & Culture* 23 (1988): 172-203.

[103]« Une bataille en règle à propos de la bibliothèque », *La Presse*, 5 décembre 1912, p. 11.

[104]« Les opinions sur la bibliothèque », *La Presse*, 28 décembre 1912, p. 9.

[105]« Un contribuable anglo-saxon veut envoyer « au diable » la bibliothèque », *La Presse*, 4 janvier 1913, p. 9.

[106]« On va tenter de provoquer un compromis », *La Presse*, 22 février 1913, p. 11. Cette bibliothèque d'association aurait été le Fraser Institute. En 1910, le Fraser possédait 58 767 volumes et recevait 349 usagers par jour en moyenne. Edward C. Moodey, *The Fraser-Hickson Library : An Informal History* (London: Clive Bingley, 1977), 90.

[107]Léo-Paul Desrosiers, « La Municipale de Montréal » (suite), *Le Devoir*, 23 juin 1944.

[108]« Les bibliothèques publiques », *La Presse*, 7 juin 1913, p. 1 et 4.

[109]« L'intervention de la législature et la bibliothèque », *La Presse*, 22 décembre 1913, p. 11.

[110]« Chaque parc de la ville de Montréal demeurera intact », *La Presse*, 23 décembre 1913, p. 1.

[111]Léo-Paul Desrosiers, « La Municipale de Montréal », *Le Devoir*, 23 juin 1944.

[112]Daniel Reicher, « Lignes de forces dans l'architecture contemporaine des bibliothèques québécoises », in *Livre, bibliothèque et culture québécoise ; Mélanges offerts à Edmond Desrochers*, Georges-A. Chartrand, éd. (Montréal: ASTED, 1976), 471.

[113]*La Presse*, 16 avril 1915, p. 9 et 12.

[114]*Le Devoir*, 22 novembre 1915.

[115]Ibid.

[116]Ibid.

[117]*La Presse*, 13 mai 1917, p. 2, et 14 mai 1917.

[118]*Le Devoir*, 4 septembre 1917. Le Conseil de Ville avait voté, le 25 mars 1916, une somme de 25 000 $ pour l'achat des livres pour la bibliothèque en construction.

[119]Ibid.

[120]Frédéric Villeneuve, bibliothécaire à partir du 21 octobre 1909 jusqu'à sa mort le 23 avril 1915, à l'âge de 48 ans. Voir *La Presse*, 24 avril 1915, p. 12 et 27.

[121]*La Presse*, 20 janvier 1916, p. 4. Hector Garneau sera conservateur de la bibliothèque municipale jusqu'au 31 mai 1930. Voir Archives municipales de Montréal, Bibliothèque municipale de Montréal, Bibliothécaires successifs.

[122]Sur les mentalités face à la bibliothèque publique au Québec, voir l'essai d'André Castonguay, « La bibliothèque publique et les Québécois », *Documentation et bibliothèques* XX, no. 4 (décembre 1973): 149-52.

[123]« Le manque d'esprit public », *La Presse*, 15 octobre 1913, p. 10.

[124]Rumilly, 457.

[125]Archives du Séminaire Saint-Sulpice de Montréal, Lettre d'Aegidius Fauteux à M. Wilfrid Hébert, procureur du Séminaire, 8 septembre 1920.

[126]« Un palais de livres en marbre », *La Presse*, 3 mars 1915, p. 1.

[127]Jean-Claude Marsan, *Montréal en évolution. Histoire du développement de l'architecture et de l'environnement montréalais* (Montréal: Fides, 1974), 227. Pour Olivier Maurault, directeur de la bibliothèque Saint-Sulpice à ses débuts, la façade de cette bibliothèque a quelque ressemblance avec celle de l'Hôtel Carnavalet de Paris. Voir Olivier Maurault, *Marges d'histoire : Saint-Sulpice*, III: 101.

[128]« Et le bibliothécaire ? », *La Presse*, 12 juin 1914, p. 10.

[129]« Notre bibliothécaire », *La Presse*, 12 octobre 1917, p. 7.

4 Diverse Perspectives

"Ruins, Ruins Everywhere!"
Canadian Libraries in Flames

Claire England

Abstract

A brief history of fire and its aftermath in Canadian libraries, surveyed by type, from early times to the late twentieth century. Initially, collections were often lost to a pioneer environment and the endemic fires prevalent in newly founded cities down to the early twentieth century. Canadian libraries have always incurred fire damage from accidental cause, but they have also suffered fire in war, rebellion and suspected political arson. Ottawa's parliamentary library has figured in six fires over its first 150 years. Nowadays, in more fire-resistant settings, collections are still irretrievably damaged by arson and accident. Fires as great disasters are often tied to the wealth and reputation of the library, but Canada, relative to its age and wealth as a nation, has suffered its equal magnitude of diminished collections. Any record of damage makes more visible the past and always potential loss caused by that impartial predator, fire!

Résumé

Cet article relate, des origines jusqu'à nos jours, l'histoire des feux dans les bibliothèques canadiennes et leurs conséquences. Les conditions de vie précaires de nos ancêtres et les feux endémiques qui ravagèrent les villes jusqu'au début du vingtième siècle détruisirent un grand nombre de collections. Les bibliothèques canadiennes ont subi des feux de nature accidentelle, mais elles ont également été victimes de la guerre, de la rébellion et même de trahison politique. La bibliothèque du Parlement à Ottawa par exemple, a brûlé six fois dans les premiers 150 ans de son histoire. Aujourd'hui, dans un milieu beaucoup plus résistant au feu, les collections sont encore endommagées par des incendies criminels et des accidents. On crie au désastre surtout quand une bibliothèque riche et renommée est victime d'un incendie. Mais si l'on tient compte de son âge et de sa richesse, le Canada a eu sa juste part de catastrophes. Chaque nouveau sinistre ramène des souvenirs anciens et suscite la crainte de ce dangereux prédateur qu'est le feu!

"THE GRAND OLD LIBRARY UTTERLY GONE! ... A PREY TO THE DEVOURING ELEMENT!"

Nineteenth-century newspaper headlines were emotive in their reaction to fires. They had cause, since fires were frequent and destructive. Great fires live in memory, although the Toronto headline repeated here may not remind librarians of a specific Canadian incident. Librarians probably think first of fabled burnings in far-off times, the conflagrations of World War II, or the well-publicized fires of more recent decades, like the Los Angeles Public Library (1986) or the Leningrad Library of the Soviet Academy of Sciences (1988). Canadian library fires seem to have a diminished importance in the context of great libraries and great collections, but that conclusion may underestimate the case for Canadian libraries.

Entering the 1980s, Guy Sylvestre, who was then the National Librarian, remarked of the libraries in the United States and Great Britain that their problem was division of wealth, whereas in Canada the problem was sharing a common poverty — "Canada is still, as it has always been, a book poor country."[1] In face of this poverty, it can be asserted that major collection losses in large library fires are serious. This paper enumerates, in an anecdotal and largely chronological manner, the history of fire damage to Canadian libraries with the emphasis on collections.[2] Libraries are surveyed by type (legislative, university and public libraries) within three time periods (Pre-Confederation: Before 1867; Confederation's First Century: 1867-1967, and After the Centennial: 1968-1992).

Pre-Confederation: Before 1867

Early library history in Canada is about collections owned by individuals or by institutions such as legislative bodies, religious orders, trading and military posts, public subscription libraries, and Mechanics' Institutes. Many of the very early libraries survive in memory as historical references, as booklists and as catalogues, or survive in part in various collections.

The Collège de Québec

The Collège de Québec was founded in 1632 by the Jesuits; the College's wooden buildings burned in 1640. Early in the eighteenth century, the Jesuits built a more imposing structure, and attempts to reconstruct the catalogue of their now long dispersed library are based on records from this period. Although 685 books are known, many more must have been in the library.

In 1759, the College became the barracks of the British army, and the library was pillaged and its holdings lost or variously distributed, with some remnants saved in other libraries. In early Canada, then, the first books came into a harsh environment, and, in a largely unrecorded toll, items have been lost to fire or other damage and disposal down the years.

The War of 1812 and the Burning of Newark and York

Fire is a weapon of war, and there are two records of library fire loss during the War of 1812-14 in Upper Canada. At this time, both Upper and Lower Canada had collections attached to their respective legislatures, and there were some "public" libraries in the major towns.

The first public subscription library in Ontario was founded in 1800 in the village of Newark (Niagara-on-the-Lake) near the U.S. border. It was "a most valuable public library well-supported" having 827 volumes in 1812.[3] The library remained open during the war, suffering "the vicissitudes of the years 1812, 1813, 1814, ... fire and sword alternately doing their cruel work," with the trustees of the time wondering at "how this library was preserved, for preserved in part it at least was." The town was occupied and then burned by the Americans in 1813. "That many [books] were destroyed or lost is certain."

In 1816, the library had 900 books, but went into a decline and closed in 1820. At the final meeting of trustees, it was recorded that "the Niagara library has been greatly wasted, first, by being plundered by the army of the United States, and has since been greatly neglected." The librarian, Andrew Heron, who was also the town printer and bookseller, took over the existing bookstock, and he made some continued provision for lending books. There are booklists from the years 1800 to 1820 which testify to the titles bought and show the collection interest of subscription libraries at the time. Many titles would be familiar today as typical nineteenth-century material; the library survived the fire but it might have had a longer history had the burning of Newark not happened.

Later, York (Toronto), capital of Upper Canada, was also burned by the Americans, and its legislative library was not as fortunate as the subscription library in Newark. York's first parliament was built of wood, and its library housed items donated by Lieutenant-Governor John Graves Simcoe. Accounts of loss vary. In 1813, government and military buildings were burned; "the provincial papers were found out, but ordered to be protected, so that nothing was destroyed, excepting the books, papers and records and furniture of the Upper and Lower Houses of the Assembly."[4] Another account is more sweeping, stating that the parliament buildings "were destroyed by the Americans on the taking of the town in 1813 when the library and all the [parliamentary] paper and records ... were consumed, and at the same time, ... the church was robbed and the town library totally pillaged."

Two prominent citizens of York, Dr. Powell and Bishop Strachan, shortly thereafter reported that the American naval commander Chauncey had "expressed much regret at the destruction of our public library, April 27th, informing us that he had made strict search through his fleet for the books; many of them had been found which he would send back by the first flag of truce."[5] Some books, one source says two boxes of them, were returned and eventually became part of the collection at the Metropolitan Toronto Reference Library.[6]

The Legislative Libraries

The burning of York's parliament buildings by the Americans was the first in a series of major fires affecting legislative libraries. After the War of 1812, the Legislature of Upper Canada, in 1816, voted £800 to replace the library's war loss. New quarters were ready in 1823, only to burn in December of 1824. On that occasion, journals and other papers were destroyed in a fire "caused by a defect in flues, a fruitful cause of accidents to parliament houses in Canada!"[7] When the next parliament building was formally opened in 1833, the books, now numbering about 30,000 volumes, were in the spacious accommodation of a library in one wing and reading room in another.

In 1841, this collection in Upper Canada combined with the larger collection in Lower Canada when the two assemblies united in the Province of Canada. A few years later, books originally from Upper Canada's Legislative Council were added, and the merged collections became the basis for the present Library of Parliament. The government of the Province of Canada, accompanied by its library, moved between Kingston, Montreal, Toronto, and Quebec City. The system became impractical, for it was soon found that "public documents of great value and two constantly increasing libraries cannot be moved about, packed and unpacked without injury."[8]

The legislative libraries contained a breadth of materials. Patrons donated to the libraries, and the librarians collected a variety of historical, political and other items useful to governance generally. Maps and newspapers were typically acquired, and collecting cast a wide net as demonstrated in the 1842 purchase, for £1000, of two sets of *Birds in America* from Audubon himself. One set was for the Legislative Council and one for the Legislative Assembly. A librarian's report of 1843 notes the purchase of "valuable and scarce works relating to the history of Canada and America" and also remarks that "the splendid and valuable work on American ornithology by the celebrated naturalist Audubon has been received and proper stands and cases made for its use and preservation."[9]

In April 1849, citizens angry at the Rebellion Losses Bill burned the parliament buildings in Montreal. Only 200 of the 25,000 volumes in the library's collection were saved. Among the items lost were the "splendid and valuable" Audubon books[10] and the 8,000 Council volumes sent to augment the combined assembly libraries. Among the items saved were the series of Upper Canada *Journals* from 1825 to the Union and the portraits of Queen

Victoria. James Curran, an employee, rescued many items and was hailed as the last person in service of the House to leave his post on that occasion. He was publicly commended and given a £10 gratuity. Donations from libraries and individuals restarted the library's collection, and the librarians once more rebuilt the stock by purchase and solicitation of books and maps. These solicitations often included visits to and correspondence with librarians and dealers in London and Paris.

After some four years, the collection had regrown to 17,000 volumes and had been transferred to Quebec City. There, the parliament buildings burned in February 1854. Because of other major fires in the city at that time, a commission investigated but discovered nothing which suggested arson. Histories vary on the damage to bookstock. One reports that more than half of the 17,000 volumes was destroyed, and another that more than half was saved.[11] The librarian (and also physician), Dr. William Winder, who had lost personal effects in the fires of 1849 and 1854, asked the government for personal compensation. The government did receive £5,700 in insurance monies, and rebuilding began with sources in London and Paris once more approached for gifts and purchases. Not surprisingly, the legislative librarians were becoming more vocal about fire prevention as necessary to any future building plans.

In 1865, Ottawa became the country's capital designate, and the parliamentary library settled in its present fixed location. At this time, the soon-to-be first dominion parliamentary librarian, Alpheus Todd, had rebuilt the collection to some 55,000 volumes.

Government buildings with records of various sorts and legislative libraries had been established early in the life of the country, and so were much afflicted with loss from fire. The country's growth meant that university and public libraries ultimately replaced legislative libraries as the types of library more often in flames. Concurrent with the growing country, the fires and other disasters that most librarians readily recall as tragic for the Library of Parliament and for other libraries lay ahead in the century after Confederation.

Confederation's First Century: 1867-1967
The nineteenth through early twentieth century was the era of the great city fires, when timber construction was common and fire-fighting inadequate. The number of books destroyed in these fires is impossible to know, particularly in eastern Canada, where urban settlements had the longest history and where numerous fires occurred.

Saint John (New Brunswick) burned several times in city fires. In the Great Fire of February 1849, comparisons were made with the Great Fire of London. No identifiable library figures in a list of buildings burned, but five bookbinders and seven bookstores were destroyed. Of a later and equally sweeping fire in June 1877, it was remarked that "no city of the same size as St John could claim finer or more unique collections ... not many of these remain ... much that was irreplaceable was destroyed. Books in the fields of British poetry, biography, science, theology, history, belles-lettres, drama, pamphlets covering all sorts of controversial topics and the history of the locality ... all were gone."[12]

Legislative Libraries

At Confederation, the Province of Canada became Ontario and Quebec. Federal compensation helped these provinces to acquire their independent libraries. At the turn of the century, Ontario's library was housed in the then almost new parliament buildings. In 1909, tinsmiths repairing the gutters of the main building left two charcoal braziers unattended under the roof rafters. The wooden attics with heavy cross timbers caught fire.

Ten thousand volumes were removed from the burning library and piled on the lawn outside; these were all the books saved from a collection of over 100,000 volumes, excluding manuscripts. A newspaper account reported the "broken-hearted librarian" as saying that "three hundred thousand dollars will not begin to cover the total loss in books .... In addition we have lost twenty thousand State and historic documents which cannot be duplicated in America ... to say nothing of a multitude of records which cannot be replaced going up in flames or being water-soaked ... births, deaths, marriages, election records, work of committees."[13]

The legislative librarians, with their knowledge of past fires, were more than ever convinced that any future construction needed fireproofing. They also wanted electric light, marble floors and a central core of metal stacks closed to the public.

In Ottawa, the country's new federal Parliament Buildings were an architectural triumph, with the polygon Gothic library at the rear an ornament planned to house 200,000 volumes. A fancy dress ball marked the 1876 opening of the library, then with a collection numbering 83,883 volumes.

The Houses of Parliament were fireproofed. Stone and concrete went into the foundation; the first floors and the towers had large water tanks. Still, in 1897, there was a fire in the West Block that affected not the library, but the archives. There was no loss of archival documents, but there was water damage to bindings and to some catalogues.

The disastrous fire of February 3, 1916, belied all assumptions of fireproofing. In that fire, the Library of Parliament was the only part spared in the Centre Block. It was saved partly by a wind blowing away from the library, but primarily by the library's position at the rear of the main building. Library staff had time to shut iron fire doors, closing off a stone hallway between the library and the main building.

However, water dousing the fire penetrated the library and settled on the floor to a depth of two inches. The floor, of Canadian wood inlays, warped badly; stacks of bound newspapers stored on or near the floor were water-logged, and almost all of the volumes suffered water damage. Many other volumes stored in the destroyed block were lost. Lost too were items in the Commons Reading Room — a room separated from the library proper. Here current newspapers and 20,000 volumes were lost, including rare bibles and valuable documents dating back to the French régime.

The fire actually started in the Reading Room; a member of parliament browsing through a newspaper at the time later testified, "I felt an unpleasant heat from behind and turned ... it looked so simple — no flame." He summoned a policeman outside the Speaker's quarters to attend to the "little blaze."[14] Within minutes it was impossible to enter the room; flames, fed by newspapers and the varnished and oil-saturated woodwork, were out of control. Within the hour, the building was blazing and, within twenty-four hours, destroyed.

Public interest demanded that a royal commission be called to determine the cause of the fire, and the commission, in a preliminary report, confirmed the suspicion of incendiarism. Rumour suggested a disgruntled employee. As Canada was at war, rumour also favoured German sympathizers and mentioned American terrorists — a New England newspaper had carried an earlier letter warning of a fire at the Parliament Buildings. In the two weeks just before the fire, extra guards had been employed and only the main entrance was in use. Buried secrets were surmised when a final commission report was not forthcoming and conclusions, if any, on the cause of the fire were never made public.[15]

By the early 1950s, the Librarian considered the Library of Parliament seriously congested; the collection of "over 550,000 volumes ... some rare and valuable ... are still in a building too small to hold the 83,000 volumes owned by the Library when it was built ... the fire hazard is grave."[16] When a fire came in 1952, it actually started in the dome, but caused extensive damage to the collection and the building. As in the 1916 fire, rare and unusual items were lost, and stored Canadian copyright deposit items were destroyed.[17]

Although the fire was contained within the library and controlled, its aftermath was costly. Describing the collection salvage work, Robert Hamilton, then the Assistant Librarian, credited the Keeper of the Collections at the Library of Congress with the "invaluable advice" that was a major factor in the salvage operation. "It is rather staggering to conjecture on the probable results to our books (and our sanity) had not this advice been forthcoming."[18]

Restoration took four years and nearly $3,000,000. The main reading room with its white pine panelling and carvings and its original statue of Queen Victoria looks as it did before the fire, but collections cannot be so effectively restored. The string of fires affecting the parliamentary collection began in 1813 at York and continued in 1842, 1849, 1854, 1916 and 1952. Thus, the federal parliamentary library has been in flames six times in 150 years, and that unenviable record invited a comment that the "history of the Library of Parliament is a sad story of loss of books by fire."[19]

University Libraries

Picking up the story of fires in university libraries and returning to the nineteenth century, one collection to suffer a major fire was that of the University of Toronto. On the evening of February 14, 1890, Toronto society was prepared for a St. Valentine's gala at its university. Kerosene lamps were brought into the library's hall. A spill, and the guests arrived to a fire in progress. The resulting damage, again with varying figures for buildings and collections, was put at half a million dollars.

The library, with its carved oak alcoves and its architecture modelled after the older university libraries of Europe, was in the gutted wing of the college building. Fewer than 100 volumes were saved from the 33,000 or so that were the library's "prized contents." Complete sets of periodicals were lost, estimated at some 200 titles, plus scientific and technical works and rare and valuable items.

The University Librarian said the collection was worth at least $100,000; the University President amended that value to $150,000. The actual insured value was $50,000. Of the collection's intrinsic value, the Librarian reported it as "second only to the parliamentary library in Ottawa and contained 'no rubbish' [but some] some very rare items and some very complete collections, for instance that in chemistry .... nothing in North America nearly equal to what had been lost in archaeology and epigraphy."[20]

However, of the volumes lost many were "antiquated classical texts and theological treatises" shortly replaced by a library of "over 50,000 books chosen for the most part with a view to their usefulness in a 'modern university' ... there had been, of course, losses which it was difficult or impossible to replace. A magnificent edition of Audubon's birds, now virtually unobtainable, and a valuable collection of works on Greek and Latin epigraphy."[21]

Volumes on loan at the time were saved. On the basis of his borrowings, David Keys, a lecturer (later professor) in English, claimed to be the library's greatest benefactor after the fire. He was described as "the most gregarious, as well as the most absent-minded of academics," and he happened to have 700 volumes belonging to the library at his home. According to an authoritative source, this oft-circulated anecdote is very exaggerated.[22]

Since "neither the building nor its contents, including the library, were adequately insured ... the catastrophe bade fair to cripple the university at a critical stage in its history." The librarian who wrote this comment considered that the fledgling university library, aided by legislative and many other donations, acquired a new, larger and more serviceable library. Hence, the fire was "a blessing in disguise."[23] The University constructed its first building designed as a separate library, and its collection was quickly replaced and enlarged. In a little over a year, the library had nearly 31,000 volumes and fully 5,000 pamphlets, and, by the fall of 1892, the collection was well over 41,000 volumes.

A wide and distinguished roster of donors gave to the university and library.[24] Committees were established in England and Germany to manage donations. The list of benefactors is impressive — Queen Victoria, the Prince of Wales (later Edward VII), the Prince of Monaco, the Kings of Saxony and Württemberg, and Kaiser Wilhelm II, who ordered that some 500 volumes of duplicates from major German libraries be donated. The Duke of Devonshire sent books formerly in the libraries of Edward Gibbon, Edmund Burke, and Henry Cavendish. Robert Browning gave books from his parents' library. The list goes on through individuals and numerous institutions and countries. At least 16 individual universities of note from Columbia, Cambridge and Oxford to Melbourne, Calcutta and Copenhagen contributed.

Public Libraries

The outcome of great city fires and individual fires was not often as sanguine for public libraries, and it was not rosy for a public library that suffered a similar fate in the same closing decade of the nineteenth century. In St. John's, Newfoundland, the great fire of July 1892 destroyed the Athenaeum, which, with its library of some 2,500 books, 60 newspapers, and lecture programs, was bringing knowledge and culture to the local population. Although the Athenaeum re-opened after the fire, it did not regain its former state and closed in 1898.

As a new century began, the eighteenth annual report of the Toronto Public Library (1901), noted that "the Central Library building is neither fire, water nor burglar proof, and action ought to be taken without delay to induce the City Council to provide funds for the erection of a proper fireproof building in a convenient location of the city." (A Carnegie building was still in the future then.)

Luckily the library escaped damage in the great Toronto fire of 1904. The library's annual report for that year notes that the only damage sustained by the library was indirect — an edition of the book catalogue at the printers was burned. However, there was a set of proofs from which the catalogue was reconstructed. The library also had to renegotiate some expenses, because the fire destroyed all the city's binding firms.

Sault Ste Marie, a much smaller Ontario city, suffered in its own version of the sweeping city fire. The public library, a Carnegie building, opened in 1904 and, three years later in March of 1907, burned. The building was under-insured because the City presumably thought that a library situated next door to the town's fire station was adequately protected from fire. However, the adjacent buildings of town hall, library and fire hall were all destroyed in that fire. The Carnegie Corporation again gave a grant, but with an admonition to the town council for its "penny-wise" attitude and with a requirement of assurance that the new library building be insured to its value.[25]

By mid-century, the country had grown well past the era of city fires, but, at any time, major fires could occur as individual events. In 1953, the librarian of a small public library in Lacombe, Alberta, became aware of "a peculiar crackling" noise and, looking out a window, "was amazed to see grass burning ... and embers falling on the steps." Taking her purse and coat, she "grabbed the library money and cash box" and left the library. She felt a "terrific heat" behind her, and "flames came pouring through the inside wall."[26]

After the Centennial: 1968-1992

Generations after the first examples of library fires, there are still many instances of libraries badly hit by fire and, in modern times, of libraries also hit with heavy water or other damage that results from effective fire-fighting. Table 1 itemizes some of the fires.

Universities

In 1977, there was a second major fire at the University of Toronto. The engineering building with its library burned in the early morning hours. Although the building was old, it was well-built and the fire risk considered minimal. About 70 per cent of the library's 80,000-volume collection was saved by the efforts of a salvage team and was eventually moved into a new library. Losses were minimal and, aside from older mining journals of historic interest, not too injurious for this collection.

When it came time to rebuild, repairs and replacement of books were estimated at about $700,000, with the building replacement estimated at between $3,000,000 and $5,000,000. When the library re-opened in 1982,

TABLE 1

Fires in Libraries Since 1950, with Cause*

Year	Prov.	Library	Cause
1952	Ont.	Library of Parliament, Ottawa	electrical
1953	Alta.	Lacombe Public Library	
1956	N.B.	Moncton Hospital Library	smoking
1957	N.S.	Pictou County Regional Library, New Glasgow	
1959	Ont.	Village of Lanark Library	spread of lumberyard fire
	N.S.	Cape Breton Regional Library, Sydney	building repair
1960	Que.	Hull Bibliothèque Municipale	adjoining building
1962	Que.	Institite of Experimental Medicine & Surgery, Université de Montréal	unofficially from building work
1963	Ont.	Collingwood Public Library and Huron Institute Museum (1901 Carnegie building)	arson
1964	Que.	Outremont Bibliothèque	
1968	Ont.	Etobicoke Public Library (Toronto)	
	Que.	Saint-Jean Bibliothèque Municipale	
1976	Que.	Montreal Book Depository	arson
1977	B.C.	Delta Pioneer (Public) Library	arson
	Ont.	Engineering Library, University of Toronto	
1980	Ont.	Perth Public Library	started in caretaker's area
	Que.	Bibliothèque nationale du Québec, Longueuil	
1982	Que.	Concordia University Archives	
1984	Ont.	Cobalt Public Library	
1985	N.S.	Weldon Law Library, Dalhousie University	lightning
1986	Ont.	Carleton Place Public Library	arson
1989	B.C.	Greater Victoria Public Library, Nellie McClung Branch	

* This list does not fully represent university fires and does not represent any major fires in schools which may have had a library on the premises.

the cost had risen to $13,000,000, with the expanded library occupying a small portion of the rebuilt facility.[27]

A 1982 fire at Concordia University resulted in soot and smoke damage to the university's archives, but water and debris caused the most serious collection problem. The building was cordoned off by the fire department for three days after the fire was doused.

At the time of this January fire, the organization of archives and records at Concordia was "on hold" and the work of the archivists was primarily acquisition. There was about 2,000 feet of material in some 1,500 cardboard storage boxes without much description.

The cold winter weather maintained the water-swollen boxes in a frozen state and slowed deterioration from mould but, as the archivist correctly surmised, recovery would be expensive, slow and potentially incomplete. University yearbooks were beyond salvage when coated paper started to dry and pages stuck together; university calendars from early years were irretrievably soggy, and other dried items were badly "cockled." There were photographs in a similar condition. Coloured folders and bindings ran into other materials, so that working with some of the aftermath reminded the archivist of dealing with "rotten strawberries."[28]

Another significant fire occurred at the Dalhousie University Weldon Law Library in 1985.[29] In the very early morning hours, lightning damaged electrical circuits and caused smouldering in the roof of the five-storey building. With the morning start-up of ventilation and electrical systems, the fire took hold and spread quickly. Unfortunately, the library occupied the two top floors; a main section was destroyed, including a technical services area, circulation records, and the public card catalogue.

Collection losses included irreplaceable art and 60,000 volumes of federal and provincial Canadian documents, British documents, U.S. statutes and law cases. The most serious losses were to the primary materials and case reports. About 90,000 books, among them 3,000 rare volumes dating back to the 1600s, were retrieved from the unburnt but water-soaked fourth floor.

Most of the rare books were removed and were salvageable, although some books were in areas containing up to six inches of water. Another 20,000 volumes, stored in the university's main library, were safe. Aside from off-site material, an estimated 56 per cent of the collection was saved, either intact or salvaged. The library, serving the oldest university common-law school in the Commonwealth, began its recovery and instituted its regular service shortly after the fire.

Public Libraries

As with any type of institution, fires in public libraries are now largely individual incidents attributable to accident or arson. In 1963, a teenager broke into the public library in Collingwood, Ontario, in the night and stole $10 from the cash drawer. He set fire to the drawer's contents, and the library had to be demolished after the fire. Collection loss is not well documented, but there was an architectural loss. The library had been a small brick Carnegie building from 1901 with the typical classical rotunda favoured by Carnegie planners.

Another modern library, built to a prize-winning design, was severely damaged by arson in 1977. Two teenage boys put a gunpowder and gasoline device in the book return of the Delta Pioneer Library in British Columbia. This $200,000 "fire bombing" was done in daytime but not at a time when the library was open to patrons. The library's interior with an additional $75,000 worth of stock was destroyed, including 12,000 books, 14,000 paperbacks, 3,000 periodicals, and audiovisual items. Although irreplaceable volumes on the history of the area were lost, some very old books and portraits of local pioneers under glass were among the few items saved.[30]

Four juveniles caused a $1,000,000 fire in 1986 when they started a fire that destroyed about 16,000 volumes and damaged more of the 40,000-volume book collection at Carleton Place near Ottawa, Ontario. Fiction was the hardest hit, but recovery was aided by community support.[31]

A collection estimated at $2,000,000 and a building at $1,000,000 were lost in a 1989 fire, which spread rapidly through the Nellie McClung branch in Saanich, British Columbia. About 45,000 books burned, but the librarian tried to be positive about the experience, remarking that "after all, we'll end up with new books and a brand new branch that is probably going to be better than the old building."[32]

The Impact of Library Fires

The individual fires characteristic of the late twentieth century are still dramatic and harmful events. Newspaper headlines like "Small Town Shows It Cares" (about its burned library) or "Library in Flames" are somewhat less emotionally charged than headlines of earlier times as they report fires or advertise recovery from a fire. There is recovery, of course, and often a rejuvenation of various sorts after a library fire. Past reports and librarians with current experience of fires speak of the benefits of fire, such as library-disaster education, public good will, administrative attention and, if insurance or other monies are adequate, new construction and collection replacement.

New construction usually means an improvement in housing the library, and collection replacement may be adequate to a library's service. At the time of a fire, community volunteers help in salvage activities and people typically donate books and money. Not all the donated items are directly useful, but all are gratefully received as a token of interest; it is often possible for public libraries to sell items in fund-raising endeavours. After a while,

213

the community interest subsides and some less agreeable side-effects surface, such as working in a series of temporary quarters or dealing with the insurance and replacement issues.

Recovery of collections is variable. Some losses are incalculable; replacement of items is not always possible. Obviously the loss of rare, unique and valuable items is a cultural loss and may represent a steep financial loss as well. Items without a market value but with a substantial cultural value may also be lost, and may not be replaceable. Some examples from fires mentioned here are the statistical records collected by various levels of government, the historical materials relating to an institution, and the varied collection of local and ephemeral items relating to a particular place.

In fact, many items which are not easily replaced are among the very ones vulnerable to fire loss and, in modern times, to the water damage resulting from fire-fighting. Libraries have materials that allow fire to take hold and, after dousing, to smoulder; burning libraries require vast amounts of water (or other fire-fighting agents) to subdue the fire and, for safety and investigation purposes, are generally declared "off-limits" by a Fire Marshall for long periods after a fire. The amount of water used and the time lapse before salvage work can start significantly decrease chances for recovery.

Since 1980, fires are considered "major" in fire statistics if the financial loss is over $500,000, but fires in libraries do not have to reach that level for substantial and permanent damage to occur in collections. Perhaps librarians are not inclined to view Canada as book-poor, but as visibly rich enough in its library collections and services. That may be true for most library functions, but it is also true that our library inheritance would be the more enriched were it whole.

Notes

[1]"The Library Scene Today," *The Future of the National Library of Canada* (Ottawa: National Library of Canada, 1979), 2.
[2]There is also the aspect of architectural and human loss. Fortunately, there is no comment on loss of life directly attributable to a library fire. Seven people did lose their lives in the 1916 fire at the Parliament Buildings in Ottawa.
[3]A history of this and parts of the original record book are in Janet Carnochan's paper, "Niagara Library, 1800-1820," read to the Canadian Institute, January 6, 1894. Quotations are from this paper.
[4]John Ross Robertson, *Robertson's Landmarks of Toronto*, vol. 1 (Toronto: J. Ross Robertson, 1894), 189, 352.
[5]Ibid., 189-91.
[6]Florence B. Murray, "Toronto Public Library and the War of 1812," CLA/ACB *Bulletin* 11 (December 1954): 102.
[7]Robertson, 354.

[8]Ola A. Cudney, *A Chronological History of the Legislative Library of Ontario*, CLA Occasional Paper no. 78 (Ottawa: Canadian Library Association, 1969), 2. This history also records at least one major incident of water damage when 7,000 books were in transit on the St. Lawrence.

[9]Ibid., 8-9.

[10]Binks (p. 35-36), mentions the original purchase of Audubon books, and their replacement set, bought in 1857 for $1,100 from Audubon's brother. The replacement set had some plates with Audubon's own pencilled comments, such as "too blue" or "not light enough here." A four-volume first edition of *Birds of America* realized $1,540,000 (US) at a Sotheby's London auction in February 1984.

[11]A. Fauteux in his *Les bibliothèques canadiennes: étude historique*, Extrait de la *Revue canadienne* (Montreal: Arbour et Dupont, 1916), 32, reports a three-quarters loss; Binks (p. 14) reports a more exact figure, and Cudney (p. 12) cites *Legislative Journals* in stating a loss of less than half. It appears that the saved books became part of the Quebec Seminary and that there was a total collection replacement, done by Alpheus Todd.

[12]D.R. Jack, "The Bestowal of Private Libraries," *Acadiensis* 7 (1947): 307-13, as quoted by E. Harrop in "Some Early Canadian Libraries" (MS(LS) paper, School of Library Science, Western Reserve University, 1950), 40.

[13]*The Globe*, Sept. 2, 1909. Some report of the fire and subsequent library planning is in Cudney, p. 27.

[14]Quotations and some history taken from the National Film Board's *Stones of History: Canada's Houses of Parliament: A Photographic Essay* (Ottawa: Queen's Printer, 1967), unpaged.

[15]Ibid., "an investigation into the fire was begun but its results proved inconclusive" [p. 8]. *Canadian Heritage* (December 1979): 17-18 refers to the rumours and Royal Commission, chaired by R.A. Pringle and Judge D.B. MacTavish.

[16]Royal Commission on National Development in the Arts, Letters and Sciences, *Report* (Ottawa: King's Printer, 1951), 101. (Vincent Massey, Chair).

[17]Information on destroyed Canadian material deposited at various periods at the Library of Parliament, the Copyright Office and the British Library is given in Patricia Pearce's *Canada: the Missing Years: The Lost Images of Our Heritage, 1895-1924* (Don Mills, Ont.: Stoddart, 1985), 7-20. See also P. O'Neill and J. Ettlinger, "Copyright Canada 1895-1924," *Canadian Library Journal* 40 (June 1983): 143-45.

[18]Robert M. Hamilton, "The Library of Parliament Fire," CLA/ACB *Bulletin* 9 (November 1952): 77.

[19]Kenneth Binks, *Library of Parliament Canada* (n.p.: KCB Publications, 1979), 36.

[20]Robert H. Blackburn, *Evolution of the Heart; A History of the University of Toronto Library up to 1981* (Toronto: University of Toronto Library, 1989), 59. Chapters 9 to 11 concern the 1890 fire.

[21]Quotations in this paragraph from William Stewart Wallace's *History of the University of Toronto* (Toronto: University of Toronto, 1927), 145.

[22]The anecdote, and quoted material, is repeated in *Old 'Varsity in Ashes: The Great Fire of 1890 and its Aftermath* (Toronto: University of Toronto, 1978), an unpaged pamphlet, but discounted by Blackburn, p. 60.

[23]Wallace, 145-46.

[24]*The Benefactors of the University of Toronto: After the Great Fire of 14 February, 1890.* (Published for the University of Toronto by the Williamson Book Co., 1892). 58 p. (Facsimile ed., 1973).

[25]M. Beckman, S. Langmead, and J. Black, *The Best Gift: A Record of the Carnegie Libraries in Ontario* (Toronto: Dundurn Press, 1984), 36.

[26]Newspaper clippings and information from the Lacombe Public Library.

[27]J. Knelman, "Sandford Fleming — Five Years After the Fire," *University of Toronto Bulletin* (June 7, 1982): 5.

[28]In conversation with the archivist, Nancy Marelli, who also describes the fire in "Fire and Flood at Concordia University Archives, January, 1982," *Archivaria* 17 (Winter 1983-84): 266-74.

[29]Fred W. Matthews discusses the fire and recovery operations in "Dalhousie Fire," *Canadian Library Journal* 43 (August 1986): 221-25. Brief news articles closer to the time of the fire are in *Feliciter* (October 1985 and November 1985); the *Globe & Mail* (November 10, 1985); and *Quill & Quire* (December 1985).

[30]Information on the fire was supplied, as a clipping file, by the Fraser Valley Regional Library headquarters.

[31]*Feliciter* (November 1986 and April 1987).

[32]*Feliciter* (February 1990): 1, 20.

In Support of an "Information System": The Case of the Library of the Natural History Society of Montreal[1]

Bertrum H. MacDonald

Abstract

During the nineteenth century, when scientific work was undergoing a transformation, the libraries of scientific societies performed an important role. These libraries were integral to the dissemination of scientific information among individuals and associations. One such library, which represents the history of scientific documentation in the nineteenth century in microcosm, was the one established and maintained by the Natural History Society of Montreal. Throughout the history of the Natural History Society from 1827 to 1925, the collections of the library grew, particularly after 1860, when exchange arrangements were set up for its journal, *The Canadian Naturalist and Geologist*. These exchanges ensured that patrons of the library were provided with current, relevant scientific information, and as a result scientific work in Montreal was promoted. Nonetheless, the prospects of the library were tied to the varying financial health of the Natural History Society itself, and when the Society was disbanded in 1925 the library collections were merged into the larger holdings of McGill University.

Résumé

Au cours du dix-neuvième siècle, la recherche scientifique se transforma et les bibliothèques des sociétés scientifiques jouèrent un rôle très important. Ces bibliothèques participèrent grandement à la diffusion de l'information scientifique autant chez les individus que dans les associations. La *Natural History Society of Montreal* a créé et maintenu une bibliothèque, qui représente bien, en microcosme, l'histoire de la documentation scientifique au dix-neuvième siècle. Tout au cours de l'histoire de la *Natural History Society of Montreal*, de 1827 à 1925, les collections de la bibliothèque s'accrurent, particulièrement après 1860 alors qu'elle établit des échanges avec son journal *The Canadian Naturalist and Geologist*. Ces échanges permirent aux usagers de la bibliothèque d'avoir accès à l'information scientifique à jour et pertinente, et par conséquence de promouvoir le travail scientifique à Montréal. Toutefois, les projets de la bibliothèques étaient étroitement liés à la santé financière de la *Natural History Society of Montreal* et quand la société fut dissoute ne 1925, les collections de la bibliothèque furent intégrées à celles de l'Université McGill.

━━━━━▶❤◀━━━━━

"The Age of Science" is how one scholar has characterized the nineteenth century, and during that century scientific work around the world underwent considerable transformation.[2] In his Pulitzer-prize-winning study, *The Launching of Modern American Science, 1846-1876*, Robert V. Bruce outlined the extent of the evolution:

> In science as in other matters, the nineteenth century was a time for organizing. Until then, the scientific pursuit had for the most part been a small-scale, spare-time indulgence of individual curiosity. But science and technology had lately begun getting together to offer mankind a new range of possibilities for ease or adventure, pleasure or gain, increase or extinction. With such vistas opening, men began pursuing science more urgently, and the farther they pursued it, the more it ramified. The proliferation of its branches meant that individual scientists had to become more specialized. The growing complexity of science demanded formal scientific education and full-time professional work, not casual, intermittent attention of self-taught amateurs. The spread of scientific investigation in so many directions called for the recruiting of scientists, the systematizing of communication among them, and the reliable evaluation of their work. And all this required money, even beyond the rising cost of more elaborate materials and apparatus.[3]

Not surprisingly, as Bruce went on to note, scientific work flourished best in urban settings where scientists "welcomed the electricity generated by the rubbing together of minds."[4] It was in the cities that learned societies, including scientific associations, were established, and these organizations not only afforded members the opportunity to share news and ideas with one another but also, almost without exception, organized and equipped a library so that members could have access to the rapidly growing volume of literature that was published in the decades after 1850. Associations with their libraries served as focal points for the communication of information.

In an analysis of eighteenth- and nineteenth-century associations, A. Hunter Dupree stated that a learned society could be thought of as "an information system."[5] Among the components of such systems are those libraries founded by numerous scientific societies. Much like the scientific work that they supported, libraries, too, underwent transformation during the century. It is from the middle of the last century that we hear Francis Fulford lamenting to an audience of the Natural History Society of Montreal that:

> in the whole of Canada, with the exception of perhaps the Library of the Houses of Parliament, now just in the course of formation, there is not one Library, public or private that deserves notice, as supplying the wants of Literature or Science, or to which reference can be made, in case of need, with any reasonable hope of finding, required information on any particular subject.[6]

Fulford placed his rather critical comments in the context of the expansion of libraries in the United States, where, he noted, Americans could boast of "50 Libraries containing upwards of 15,000 volumes each; and six of them with over 60,000." Some of these, he added, included that of Harvard College, Boston, largest of all, with 112,000 volumes, having been in existence for a long period; and most afforded "immense advantages to students in every department."[7]

While Fulford's complaint raises a number of questions about the history of Canadian libraries, in this paper I will pay particular regard to the unfolding of science in the country, especially in Montreal. As the largest urban centre in Victorian Canada, Montreal had a number of the advantages that Bruce suggested were requisite for scientific development. It was the publishing centre of British North America, the location for academic scientific research at McGill University, the headquarters for a major government-sponsored research agency (the Geological Survey), and a city with financial capital that could be called upon to underwrite scientific work. The Natural History Society of Montreal, located in this conducive environment, was one of the more prominent of such societies in Canada during the Victorian period.[8]

Since Fulford addressed his complaint to members of this society, we might ask what role the library of the Natural History Society played within the "information system" of its parent organization. How important was this library in fostering communication of scientific information? By presenting the story of this Canadian science library we shall see that in a number of ways it represents the history of scientific documentation in microcosm in the nineteenth century. During the second half of the century the library of this society, even with limited resources, reflected the patterns of distribution of scientific literature witnessed in the international information configuration.

The Natural History Society of Montreal

The Natural History Society of Montreal was one of the leading (if not the foremost) scientific associations in Canada in the last century. Established in 1827 and incorporated in 1833, it functioned for almost a century until it was disbanded in 1925.[9] Although its history was marked by periods of slow growth, from the mid-1850s until the end of the century the society played a significant role in the development of science in Montreal, the province of Quebec and, indeed, in Canada as a whole, for it was during this period that some of Canada's more prominent scientists were its active members.[10] For over 50 years, beginning in 1857, the society's journal, *The Canadian Naturalist and Geologist* (and its title variants), published some of the more important Canadian scientific research.[11] As a vehicle of exchange, copies of this periodical found their way around the world, thereby giving publicity to the society and to Canada.

As a measure of its success, the society was able to convince the American Association for the Advancement of Science (AAAS) to come to Montreal in 1857 to meet for the first time outside the United States, and 25 years later, in 1882, the society was once again the host for the AAAS. Two years following this latter meeting, the British Association for the Advancement of Science travelled to Montreal to hold its annual meeting for the first time outside the British Isles. In addition, the society co-sponsored other international congresses in Montreal, e.g., the American Institute of Mining Engineers in 1879 and the American Society of Civil Engineers, in 1881. With its lectures and outings, its museum and library, the society maintained an active presence in the city of Montreal. Furthermore, on a number of occasions the society acted as a lobby for action by the colonial or provincial legislatures.[12]

The Library of the Natural History Society of Montreal

Throughout the nineteenth century a growing number of institutional libraries devoted to scientific literature were founded in North America and Europe. This trend has not been well documented in the historical literature and least of all for Canada, even though a few such libraries were organized here in the nineteenth century.[13] In contrast to the eighteenth and early nineteenth centuries, institutional libraries became more important in Canada during the mid- to late nineteenth century. Except for an analysis of the personal collection of the French-Canadian naturalist Léon Provencher, completed by Raymond Duchesne, most of these libraries have not yet received the attention of historians.[14]

The history of the library of the Natural History Society of Montreal is not glamorous. Yet in the operation of the society the library played an important function. From the foundation of the society in 1827 the library was considered a necessary component. The Constitution and Bye-laws of 1828 list a librarian as one of the officers of the society, and these governing documents also set out the administrative structure for the library, including the rules under which it was to operate. For example, the Library Committee, to which was delegated the responsibility of administering the library, could not purchase any book over the value of $12 without seeking the concurrence of the society as a whole. The purpose of the library collection was encapsulated in the following statement: "No book shall be purchased for the Library, unless it shall treat of some scientific subject, or of some branch of Natural History." However, not to be limited by this declaration, the policy went on to say that "donations of books on any subject may be received."[15] In the Act of Incorporation of 1833 and in the revised Constitution and Bye-Laws of 50 years later in 1886, these statements remained unchanged except for the limit on the cost of a book above which the society had to approve the purchase.[16]

Prior to the society's second decade in the 1840s, when the first and only printed catalogue of the library was published, the surviving records for the early years of both the library and the society are not extensive.[17] A number of activities can be documented, however. For example, the £200 grant the society received in 1829 from the Lower Canada legislature was used for the organization of both a library and a museum. Three years later, in 1832, the society did not meet, nor were there any library acquisitions, because of the cholera epidemic in the city.[18]

Since a catalogue from 1846 is the only printed document that by itself deals exclusively with the library, it is useful at this point to digress briefly and note the sources from which the history of the library can be constructed. Prior to 1857, the annual reports of the society are the most important records but, beginning with publication of the Proceedings of the Society (issued in the *Canadian Naturalist* starting with volume 2 in 1857), these latter records become the leading source. Both the annual reports and the proceedings recorded the activities of the librarian and the Library Committee and often listed the acquisitions of the library. In addition to the published accounts, other information about the library can be found in the few surviving manuscript records of the society, columns in newspapers of the day, other contemporary published reports, and histories of other institutions.

A review of the 1846 catalogue reveals that by that date the library had acquired about 870 volumes plus about a dozen maps.[19] After almost 20 years of accumulation, the composition of the collection (using the classification of the catalogue itself) consisted of the subjects set out in Table 1.

The catalogue of this collection of 870 volumes reveals a number of features of the library and its management. First, like many other catalogues

---

TABLE 1

Composition of the Mid-1840s Library

Subject	No. of volumes
Botany	49
Chemistry	46
Geology and mineralogy	55
Natural history in general	206
Philosophy & general science	86
Voyages, travels, etc.	34
Biography and history	36
Periodicals, reports of scientific societies, etc.	252
Miscellaneous	106
Total	870

---

of the period, full bibliographic details, which are now desirable for precise identification of the books, are sometimes lacking. Titles, such as *Journal of a Naturalist*, *Taxidermy*, and *Zoonomia*, are listed without authors. But, in general, most of the entries in the catalogue provide sufficient information for proper identification. A second characteristic of this catalogue is the fact that the classification scheme was not consistently applied. A number of "miscellaneous" titles, such as *Report on the Geology of Michigan* (1838) could have been assigned to the category "Geology and mineralogy," and *List of Animals of the London Zoological Society, 1830* could have been more accurately listed under "Natural History in General." This classification inconsistency, however, was not an unusual feature of contemporary catalogues. Roger Meloche, who analyzed three published catalogues of the Bibliothèque de l'Institut canadien de Montréal from the same period, observed that "le classement systématique des livres ne constituait pas la préoccupation majeure des bibliothécaires."[20]

Another conclusion we can draw about this library is that over 80 per cent of the volumes in the collection dealt directly or indirectly with the stated mandate of the library, i.e., publications that "treat of some scientific subject or some branch of Natural History." As well, even at this early date, periodicals claimed a significant position in the collection. Finally, we can note that the library contained works by prominent scientists of the period as well as earlier authors read for reference: the English botanist, Sir William Hooker (1785-1865); the Swedish taxonomist, Carl Linnaeus (1707-1778);

the American geologist, James Hall (1811-1898); the English chemist, Sir Humphrey Davy (1778-1829); the American chemist, Benjamin Silliman (1779-1864), who was editor of the *American Journal of Science*; the French chemist, Antoine L. Lavoisier (1743-1749); the Scottish geologist, Charles Lyell (1787-1875); the American ornithologist, John James Audubon (1785-1851); the French naturalist, the Comte de Buffon (1707-1788); and the English zoologist, Sir Richard Owen (1804-1892), among others.

Beginning with the mid-1850s, more extensive surviving records allow us to assess the place of the library in the overall management of the society and at the same time permit the creation of a catalogue of a sizeable portion of the library collection. The preparation of the catalogue is a large task, however, for is it necessary not only to attempt to identify some inadequately described items[21] but also to match the catalogue entries with records of holdings at McGill University, for it is believed that all of the volumes of the library of the Natural History Society were integrated into the McGill collections when the society disbanded in 1925.[22]

The financial affairs of the Natural History Society were never very secure, although, to its credit, the society was able to erect a building to house its museum, lecture rooms, and library. In annual report after annual report, the council of the society lamented the society's inadequate financial state and frequently compared itself with the Canadian Institute in Toronto, which was allegedly more successful in obtaining government assistance. The library, of course, bore some of the brunt of the financial situation. In 1853, for example, the council noted that it was to be "deplored, that this utter want of funds has for some years past precluded the purchase of a number of works highly requisite for the Library."[23]

For the two decades following the council's 1853 report, the standing of the library in relation to overall affairs of the society was marked by advances and alternating downswings. In those same years recurring themes can be found in the official records. First we may note that repeated statements about the inadequacy of the collection were voiced, such as this assertion of the Library Committee in 1858:

> There is no department of the Society's collection in which the Council feel so little satisfaction as that of the Library. Its progress has not at all kept pace with the advancement of knowledge. While it contains some ancient volumes of much value, and several modern works of scientific note, it is still extremely defective in books of recent publication, without which it is scarcely entitled to the name of a Scientific Library. The Council hope that means may ere long be found to supply this manifest defect, and to make ... [the] Library worthy of its name.[24]

Dissatisfaction with both the museum and library arose because of concern for the welfare of the society itself. That same 1858 report went on to state that "... it is now felt that if the Society is to take that place which the rapid progress of modern science demands, large additions *must* be made to its museum and library."[25]

The position of the society and of scientific endeavours in Canada as a whole were highlighted by J.W. Dawson in his annual address as president of the Natural History Society in 1869. He remarked that although considerable progress had been made, Canada, in marked comparison to the United States and England, had not yet established a single science school. Dawson's concern reflected the level of interest (which he believed required raising) of Canadians in science education. The Natural History Society, of course, served to advance the profile of science education in Montreal; yet Dawson recognized that support for the society and ultimately the effect of that patronage on the progress of the library required further enhancement.[26] Dawson was well qualified to speak on these matters, as he was one of Canada's outstanding scientists in the nineteenth century and also principal of McGill University.

Even though there had been a number of good years in those middle decades (as will be noted below), the early 1870s continued to show seemingly little progress in the development of the library. In 1870, the acting president, Alexander A. De Sola, claimed pride in displaying the museum to Prince Arthur during his visit to Montreal, but considered the library an embarrassment, "displaying evidence of apathy and neglect."[27]

Those middle decades of the nineteenth century were not all apathy and neglect, however. The collection did grow and it was used, and this constitutes a second theme of the period. Of the several methods the society employed to increase the size of the collection, the most common was through donations. The number of volumes donated each year fluctuated widely, however. In 1853, for example, only five volumes were received from local citizens.[28] Yet in other years the number of donations was considerably higher and sometimes outstripped the number of contributions to the museum, a more popular recipient of gifts.[29] On other occasions, the Library Committee recommended that as an inducement for donations life membership in the society be granted to anyone who contributed volumes worth at least $50.[30]

Acquisitions by the library were, as finances permitted, made by purchase. While there is no doubt that books were bought by the society from the beginning years, the first time that actual purchases appear in the surviving records is in the list of acquisitions in 1858. Three years later the financial statement of the society shows a major expenditure on the library, representing about 25 per cent of the society's annual budget for that year.

In this year as well over 75 monographs were donated to the collection.[31] By 1861 the financial affairs of the society had improved, and this improvement allowed for additional purchases of publications. Increased membership complemented the financial well-being of the Society: members numbered about 300 during the early years of the 1860s.

The most significant method of acquisition for the library, however, was through exchange. The society profited from its new publishing venture, the *Canadian Naturalist and Geologist*, which it used to advantage for reciprocal donation with other Canadian and international organizations. The initial account of such transactions was reported in 1859, two years after undertaking the publication of the journal, and over the next several decades the exchanges took on ever-increasing significance. In 1861 the colonial government allocated a grant of $1,000 to the society; this grant was used, in part, to establish a better system of exchanges with the *Canadian Naturalist*. The grant also provided the means to hire an assistant secretary and curator, who was expected, among other duties, to "take measures for the increase of the [museum] collection and the library."[32]

By 1865, when J.F. Whiteaves was Curator and Librarian, the number of exchanges had grown considerably. Most of Whiteaves' attention was devoted to the museum (he was a palaeontologist with the Geological Survey of Canada), but he also undertook an extensive review of the exchange programme. His report uncovered a number of the problems that the programme generated.[33] He noted, for example, that some publications were received on an irregular basis and that ongoing attention to the programme was needed to ensure that missing issues were obtained. Two years later the council reported on another continuing problem with the exchange programme, namely the growing number of reports and issues of journals that needed to be bound. Strapped for funds, the society often found that periodical issues were left unbound, and the council of the day claimed this situation had rendered them "almost useless for reference."[34] Binding costs were an ongoing concern, yet in some years the society was actually able to handle the inflow and place many volumes in the library. In 1882, for example, close to 200 bound volumes of periodicals and pamphlets were added to the collection.

While many efforts were undertaken to augment the collection, members of the society often had a cavalier attitude to returning borrowed volumes, and this forms a third theme for the decades right after mid-century. In 1854, the librarian, Dr. William Wright, reported that the library contained 1,500 volumes, but one tenth were missing. When his efforts to obtain the missing volumes failed, he suggested that advertisements in the local newspapers might lead to more success.[35] Five years later, when the society had moved to a new building and the Library Committee had had an opportunity to inspect the collection, missing numbers of the periodicals were noted. Besides recommending that issues of periodicals and pamphlets be properly bound for better preservation, the committee chided members for their "habit of taking books from the library, and retaining them in their possession for months, if not years, and, as a consequence, many works of great value" had been lost.[36]

The problem of missing volumes was often coupled with inadequate accommodation for the collection, and here is another theme echoed in a number of reports of librarians or library committees. The council of the society voiced this opinion in 1855 when it drew attention to the inferior quarters, which gave "little inducement for members either to give to, or consult, the library." In the same year Dr. Wright stated similar sentiments when he wrote that "many valuable books have ... to be temporarily stowed away in obscurity."[37] Until the end of the decade, when the society moved into a new building, the accommodation for the library remained inadequate. But even in the new building, where space was no longer a problem, missing volumes still were. To remedy this administrative headache, the Library Committee in 1861 recommended that all the books be locked in cases, a proper catalogue be prepared, and the Cabinet keeper or librarian be instructed to let no book out of the library unless it had been properly recorded in the register. At the end of the century, when the collection had grown considerably, the subject of inadequate space reappeared in annual reports.

A final theme from the reports of mid-century and succeeding decades centres on attempted cooperative ventures with other organizations. Throughout the life of the society, several bids for collaboration were undertaken. The first occurred in 1840-41 when an amalgamation of three institutions was contemplated — merging the Natural History Society, the Montreal Mechanics' Institute, and the Montreal Mercantile Library into a Montreal Institute of Literature, Science, and the Arts. The combined libraries of the three institutions would have formed a notable scientific library for the period. The government of the Province of Canada indicated that it would provide this new major institute with an annual grant, but the idea died after the parliamentary riots and the removal of the government from Montreal.[38]

Twenty years later a second call for collaboration was made, this time among other Montreal institutions (McGill University, the Board of Arts and Manufactures, the Geological Survey of Canada, and the Natural History Society) so that purchases of books for one institution would, as far as possible, "supplement the deficiencies of others."[39] Whether anything came of this recommendation is not known. But it is likely that cooperative activity of this nature did occur. Leading members of the Natural History

Society were also key individuals in the other organizations. J.W. Dawson, as noted above, was the principal of McGill University and was instrumental in building the library holdings at McGill. As another example, William E. Logan was the director of the Geological Survey, where his personal library formed the core of the Survey's library holdings.

Thirty-five years following the first failed effort at amalgamation with other institutions, a third partnership was considered. In 1875 the society believed that it had, at long last, the means of resolving some of its financial insecurity. But it was a short-lived dream. Hugh Fraser, a wealthy Montrealer, had on his death donated his fortune for the establishment, in the words of the will, "of a free public library, museum and gallery, to be open to all honest and respectable persons whomsoever of every race in life without distinction."[40] After protracted legal wrangling with members of Fraser's family, the executors of the estate were finally free in the 1870s to carry out his wishes.

A fusion between the Natural History Society and the Fraser Institute (as it was called), in which the Institute would accept complete responsibility for the provision of a building, was proposed. While the Natural History Society would retain its separate identity, it was expected to provide the museum and library and was to be guaranteed free access to both. The Natural History Society could then devote its funds to the improvement of both the library and the museum. Negotiations with the executors of the Fraser estate proceeded, and a memorandum of agreement was drawn up and accepted by the society in early 1876.[41] But this is as far as the records of the Natural History Society take us. The annual reports do not explain why the plan failed.

At least on the surface of the idea, the Natural History Society would have gained the most from the proposed merger. In exchange for free accommodation, it was to contribute its museum and library plus any remaining funds following sale of its building (less liabilities, which at the time amounted to about $7,000). Initially, the executors of the Fraser estate looked favourably on the proposal. However, the negotiations failed when the price that McGill University asked for the proposed site of the new institution was more than the executors were prepared to pay. At this point the negotiations broke down, and both institutions went off in separate directions. To the misfortune of the Natural History Society, an opportunity to shake off the financial burden of maintaining a large building was lost.

The memorandum outlining the proposed merger contains interesting information not only on the physical dimensions of the building which the Natural History Society occupied[42] but also on the stock of the library. The extent of the library collection as reported by the Library Committee is outlined in Table 2.[43]

TABLE 2

Library Holdings in 1875

Subject	No. of Volumes
Botany	96
Chemistry	37
Geology and mineralogy	64
Natural History in general	280
Philosophy and general science	91
Voyages & travel, etc.	50
Biography and history	44
Periodicals, reports of scientific societies, etc.	556
Miscellaneous	115
Total	1,333

If a comparison is made with the printed catalogue of 30 years earlier, the slow growth of the library is evident.[44] Only about 460 volumes had been added, amounting to an annual rate of accumulation of about 16 volumes. The more important feature to note, however, is the large increase in the number of periodicals, a growth of about 120 per cent, or more than double the figure from the mid-1840s. This increase emphasizes the dominant role this form of literature had come to play in scientific communication. Drawing attention to this increase does not downplay the fact that books were not frequently purchased for the library. But the growing number of periodicals that were published in the nineteenth century, illustrated by the sizeable increase of journals in this library, points to the importance of this form of literature in the exchange of scientific information. All other categories of publications in the library had grown at a much slower rate, and one group, chemistry, actually decreased!

A more rapid addition to the category of geology and mineralogy might have been expected, since much of the activity of the society was concerned with these topics. However, the library of the Geological Survey of Canada was located in Montreal at this time and, when necessary, members most likely took advantage of the close proximity of this collection. Furthermore, the records of donations to the society's library indicate that members with geological interests were not generous contributors of books, probably because there were those other nearby libraries with strong geological holdings. As a final comment about this 1875 inventory, it is instructive to note that most of the books dealt directly or indirectly with the sciences, showing that the library was still adhering to its declared mandate.

During the last two decades of the century, the library received renewed attention. The society itself attracted considerable international notice with meetings of American and British societies in Montreal. In 1883-84, for example, more than 3,000 visitors to the museum were recorded.[45] In the late 1880s librarians who saw the need for upgrading the collection were appointed and they were, at the same time, willing to spend considerable time doing this. Charles Robb was engaged in 1886 to prepare a classified catalogue of the holdings of the library. The collection now contained close to 3,000 volumes and it was noted that the Smithsonian Institution, which had taken on the role of distributing scientific documents, had forwarded numerous publications. In the decade following 1875 the library more than doubled its holdings and even disposed of duplicates.[46] By 1890 the continued regard of the librarian to the arrangement and accessibility of the collection led to the comment that "the library has received more attention than other years and special thanks are due to the honorary librarian, who has attended regularly every week arranging the books and the catalogue."[47]

The better arrangement and maintenance of the collection, the value of the exchanges received annually, a few judicious purchases of reference books that were in demand, plus the fact that there was a librarian more familiar with the collection who could assist the members in more efficient use of the collection than previously — all these improvements led to reports of increased use of the library at the end of the century.[48]

Additions to the library, largely from exchanges, continued to accumulate into the new century so that by 1904 the library quarters were again cramped, recalling a theme noted earlier. The shelves were reported to be overloaded and "in many cases 'two-deep' so that access to the volumes" was difficult.[49] But there was no relief in sight. Five years later the report was the same: "many inquiries are made, reference is sought, and a great deal of labour is involved in supplying the information owing to the Library being inaccessible."[50] The life of the Natural History Society, however, was drawing to an end. Much of the activity of the society wound down during World War I. The museum and library were put into storage; although attempts were made to resuscitate the organization following the war, the efforts failed. When there seemed no value in maintaining the society, largely because natural history had been surpassed by more specialized sciences pursued at McGill University and elsewhere, the society was disbanded in 1925.

Discussion

The ups and downs in the well-being of the library of the Natural History Society of Montreal during the Victorian period allow us to note those features that also characterized the history of other similar organizations. First, the library of the society grew slowly and mostly from donations rather than purchases. A reliance on gifts was not uncommon among many other contemporary Canadian libraries. Nora Robins, for example, traced the history of the Montreal Mechanics' Institute between 1828 and 1870 and noted that from the outset the library was "dependent on donations."[51] From the same period an annual report for McGill University in 1891 records that most of the 1,601 books added to the collection in the previous year had come as gifts.[52] The Mechanics' Institute and McGill University were both Montreal institutions, yet similar observations could be made about libraries in many other locations in North America and Europe.

The financial state of the Natural History Society in large measure dictated the nature of support that the library received. As the society grappled with balancing its books, the library received a lower priority than other matters, such as the expansion of the museum. The popular museum provided greater leverage for soliciting financial support for the society and, as a result, the library was often relegated to a lower status. Yet the library was important for the development of the museum, because specimens could not be properly identified without consulting the journals and reference books that only a library could supply. The library, therefore, often received well-intentioned lip-service support from the officers of the society even when they could not follow through with financial assistance. Robins found a similar situation at the Mechanics' Institute.[53]

Second, to state that the library depended largely on donations, while true, does not give satisfactory attention to the journals and reports that were received in exchange for the *Canadian Naturalist*. Without these acquisitions the library would have been very deficient and would not have been able to support the research activities of members of the society, principally those conducted with specimens in the museum. Executive officers were fully aware of this situation and endeavoured to maintain an extensive exchange programme with other associations and institutions in Canada and abroad. At its peak, the mailing list for exchanges numbered well over 100, and on numerous occasions the librarian or Library Committee sought to fill gaps in periodical holdings, usually by requesting that the organization that published the periodical(s) supply the missing items *gratis*.[54]

Sarah Gibson has suggested that the high priority many scientific societies placed on communicating the results of their research can be described as a "messianic attitude."[55] The Natural History Society of Montreal fits Gibson's description, for executive members realized that exchanges brought prestige to the society, afforded "a wider range of material for comment and selection" in the *Canadian Naturalist*, and tended "materially to the increase of the library."[56]

In 1876, in a major report on American public libraries commissioned by the Bureau of Education of the U.S. Department of the Interior, Theodore Gill of the Smithsonian Institution remarked that:

> among the most important and really indispensable works of refer-
> ence for the scientific investigator, and indeed for any student who
> desires to become familiar with the progress of science in its several
> branches, are the annual volumes in which are recorded the various
> contributions to the literature during the successive years.[57]

Periodical holdings formed a major portion of the library of the Natural History Society of Montreal, demonstrating that the library contained the important literature needed to support ongoing scientific research. By acquiring these periodicals, the library was fulfilling its supporting role in the information system of the Natural History Society and was following a pattern adopted by many scientific institutions around the world.[58]

A third observation concerning the library relates to the various means by which the society attempted to overcome the problem that financial con-straints imposed. Among the methods chosen (the proposed merger with the Fraser Institute, proposed cooperative acquisitions programmes with other Montreal libraries, inducements for donations, requests for external funding usually from the colonial or provincial legislature, etc.), most met with little success. Government support for specialized libraries, for example, went to other institutions, such as the Geological Survey of Canada and the Central Experimental Farm of the Department of Agriculture.

In a study of scientific libraries in London, England, J.B. Tooley suggested that there were three phases in the development of scientific libraries. The first phase was marked by scientific collections mostly in the hands of individuals. The second was characterized by the foundation of association libraries collecting in specialized areas, and the third phase occurred when governments committed themselves to the development of research and departmental libraries.[59] The libraries of the Natural History Society of Montreal, the Geological Survey of Canada, and the Central Experimental Farm seem to follow this pattern as well. The library of the society had no major benefactors and never got beyond the limitation of relying almost solely on donations and exchanges. Yet despite these constraints, the library gave its readers access to some of the more important scientific journals of the day and, when the library received sufficient atten-tion from a librarian, use of the collection increased and the library more effectively fulfilled its mandate.

Besides these observations, there is much about the operation of the library of the Natural History Society that remains obscure. In particular, information about who used the collection or how actively is not readily apparent, since circulation data are unavailable. It is known, albeit rather tangentially, that the books circulated, since several reports comment on missing or stolen volumes and the need for tighter control of access. Further, some measure of use was recorded in a number of the annual reports when the librarian noted that the collection was more actively used than previously. Some clues concerning the use of the library can also be obtained from comments made about librarians whose knowledge of the collection was commended. Other evidence touching on use is found in statements about the difficulty of responding to inquiries when the collection was cramped for space and volumes were in storage. And another indication about use can be found in the reading patterns of members as determined from citations in research reports published in the *Canadian Naturalist and Geologist*.[60]

But none of this is concrete evidence. The records do not state whether only members had access to the library or whether it was open to wider use. For example, did students at McGill University have access to the collection? There is some evidence to suggest that students did in fact use the society's library. Robert Bell, for example, was a student at McGill University during the late 1850s and graduated in 1861. During his student days he also worked part-time for the Geological Survey (later in the century he gained considerable recognition in international scientific circles for his work with the Survey) and was a participant in the activities of the Natural History Society. His diary from this period indicates that he had ready access to the library collections of all three institutions.[61] It is unlikely that he was alone in this regard. Other more senior members of the society, among whom were J.W. Dawson, A.A. De Sola, William E. Logan, J.F. Whiteaves, Thomas Sterry Hunt, and Elkanah Billings, also had connections with each of these organizations.

The records of the Natural History Society are to a large extent silent about the relationship its library had with other libraries or science collections in the city. But it seems probable that its place was not insignificant, at least in the decades leading up to the twentieth century, before natural history as a broad sweeping subject lost ground to the specialized sciences that grew out of this field. Take the situation at McGill University, for example. In 1855, when J.W. Dawson was appointed principal, the library at the university was willingly acknowledged to be exceedingly inadequate. The Chancellor wrote to Dawson prior to his appointment that with "respect to a Library & Museum I have not much to say that is encouraging; the Library of the University is too small to deserve the name."[62] By the end of the century, however, the library at McGill had been transformed. The new Redpath Library was opened in 1893 and, as Peter McNally has shown, during the early decades of the twentieth century under the principalship of Sir William Peterson the university endowments grew at a pace far above the cost of living and wholesale price indexes.[63] The impact of these accumulating funds was seen in the growth of library holdings. But these developments occurred at the time when the demise of the Natural History Society was inevitable. Earlier, when the society was a stronger organization, its library did supplement the holdings at McGill. With respect to the library of the Geological Survey, the collections of the Natural History Society acted as a buffer against the loss of the former library when the Survey moved from Montreal to Ottawa in 1881. By 1895, the Survey library contained more than 14,000 volumes.[64] In the period following the move to Ottawa, Morris Zaslow claimed that its programme of acquisition of books and periodicals made the Survey library "one of the great scientific libraries of the continent."[65]

While there may be remaining questions about the patrons of the library, it can be said emphatically that those who did use it were not seeking "light" literature, simply because the collection did not hold such.[66] The evidence suggests that, for Mechanics' Institutes, works of fiction circulated more frequently than the remainder of their library holdings.[67] But for the library of the Natural History Society this could not have been the case, because, as President J.W. Dawson noted in 1873, the library could not by its very nature "become a popular or general library, but ... mainly one for scientific reference and consultation."[68] The re-created catalogue of the library confirms Dawson's comment.

We might now ask how far we have progressed in our search for an answer to the question about the role of the library within that information system, the Natural History Society of Montreal. At this point we are able to account for the holdings of this science library and how they were acquired. Although we know less of the patterns of use than we would like, the evidence demonstrates that the library promoted the communication of scientific information principally by obtaining copies of the leading scientific reports and periodicals published around the world and making them available to members. This was a vital role and it permitted patrons of the library to have access to current scientific literature in a timely manner. In an age of continuing discovery, scientists in Montreal needed timely access to published reports of other researchers, and within its means the library of the Natural History Society facilitated this transaction. The study of reading habits of members of the society, noted earlier, bears this out.

Was Francis Fulford correct in his assessment of libraries in mid-nineteenth-century Canada? The answer has to be both yes and no. If comparison is made solely with some of the libraries in the United States and Europe, then there were few Canadian libraries of similar size. Yet Fulford's indictment needs qualification. To state that there were no Canadian libraries capable of answering any reference questions leads one to question how any of the scientific or other scholarly work in the country was conducted and ignores the fact that science libraries, as illustrated by this study of the Natural History Society library, contained important, relevant literature. While the library of the Natural History Society was by no means the best possible, it was not entirely inadequate, either.

Notes

[1] Earlier versions of this paper were presented to the Library History Interest Group of the Canadian Library Association and to the Fourth Kingston Conference of the Canadian Science and Technology Historical Association. I wish to acknowledge the helpful comments of the editor of this volume, Peter F. McNally, and those of the anonymous reviewer provided by the Canadian Library Association.

[2] David Knight, *The Age of Science. The Scientific World-View in the Nineteenth Century* (Oxford: Basil Blackwell, 1986).

[3] Robert V. Bruce, *The Launching of Modern American Science, 1846-1876* (New York: Alfred A. Knopf, 1987), 3-4.

[4] Ibid., 31.

[5] A. Hunter Dupree, "The National Pattern of American Learned Societies, 1768-1863," in *The Pursuit of Knowledge in the Early American Republic. American Scientific and Learned Societies from Colonial Times to the Civil War,* ed. Alexandra Oleson and Sanborn C. Brown (Baltimore: Johns Hopkins University Press, 1976), 21.

[6] Francis Fulford, *Five Occasional Lectures, Delivered in Montreal* (Montreal: Printed and published by John Lovell, 1859), 103. This quotation is taken from "Lecture V. On the State and Prospects of Science and Literature in Montreal. Delivered in the Lecture Room of the Montreal Natural History Society, as the Concluding Lecture of the Winter Course, on Tuesday, April 5, 1859."

[7] Ibid.

[8] The Natural History Society of Montreal was created prior to the formation of the country of Canada and flourished until well after 1867. Here "Canada" is taken to mean the territory circumscribed by current national boundaries.

[9] Yvan Lamonde gives 1825 as the date for the beginning of the Natural History Society of Montreal and 1827 as the date of incorporation. These dates are incorrect, however, since the reports and publications of the society give 1827 and 1833, respectively. See Yvan Lamonde, *Les bibliothèques de collectives à Montréal (17e-19e siècle)* (Montreal: Bibliothèque nationale du Québec, 1979), 41. Henry T. Bovey in *A Lecture on the Progress of Science in Canada* (Montreal: [Montreal Herald?], 1886?) gives the founding date as 1832. But this date, too, must be incorrect. Stanley B. Frost provides the correct founding date of 18th

May 1827. See Stanley Brice Frost, "Science Education in the Nineteenth Century. The Natural History Society of Montreal, 1827-1925," *McGill Journal of Education* 17 (1982): 32.

[10]For further information on this theme, see Hervé Gagnon, "The Natural History Society of Montreal's Museum and the Socio-Economic Significance of Museums in 19th-Century Canada," *Scientia Canadensis* 18, no. 2 (1994): 103-35.

[11]Elkanah Billings published the first volume of the *Canadian Naturalist and Geologist* single-handedly but with the second and subsequent volumes the Natural History Society of Montreal took over responsibility for its publication and editorial matters fell to a committee appointed by the society.

[12]The Natural History Society in the early 1840s was an effective lobby for the establishment of the Geological Survey of Canada. On another occasion the society petitioned the legislature for protection of smaller birds, in 1862. See *Annual Report of the Natural History Society of Montreal for the Year Ending May, 1862, with the Amending Act Recently Passed; Also, a List of the Officers, Life, Corresponding, Honorary, and Ordinary Members of the Society* (Montreal: Printed by John Lovell, 1862), 12.

[13]Ellen B. Wells has provided an overview of scientific libraries in her paper, "Scientists' Libraries: a Handlist of Printed Sources," *Annals of Science* 40 (1983): 319f. Canadian libraries are for the most part ignored. But the Geological Survey of Canada had a library at least from mid-century. See Morris Zaslow, *Reading the Rocks. The Story of the Geological Survey of Canada 1842-1972* (Toronto and Ottawa: Macmillan Company of Canada in association with the Department of Energy, Mines and Resources and Information Canada, 1975), 65. While the library of Canada Agriculture traces its history from a formal launching in 1910, books and periodicals had been acquired a number of decades earlier. (See, for example, Minister of Agriculture, *Experimental Farms. Reports ... for 1890* (Ottawa: Queen's Printer, 1891), 50, and *Canada Agriculture Library. The First Sixty Years*, Historical Series no. 7 (Ottawa: Information Canada, 1971)). A history and analysis of both of these Canadian libraries is found in my dissertation, "'Public Knowledge': The Dissemination of Scientific Literature in Victorian Canada as Illustrated from the Geological and Agricultural Sciences" (PhD thesis, University of Western Ontario, 1990).

[14]Raymond Duchesne, "La Bibliothèque scientifique de l'Abbé Léon Provencher," *Revue d'histoire de l'Amérique française* 34 (1981): 535-56. Léon Provencher was one of the few outstanding French-Canadian scientists of the nineteenth century. He founded and edited the periodical, *Le naturaliste canadien*. A study of the personal libraries of six other Canadian scientists is found in my dissertation, "'Public Knowledge': The Dissemination of Scientific Literature in Victorian Canada," cited in the previous note.

[15]*Constitution and Bye-laws of the Natural History Society of Montreal with Directions for Preserving and Forwarding Objects of Natural History* (Montreal: Printed at the Montreal Gazette Office, 1828), 10.

[16]See *Act of Incorporation and Bye-laws of the Natural History Society of Montreal. (Incorporated by Act of the Provincial Parliament, 2 Will. IV. Cap. 65)* (Montreal: A.H. Armour & Co., 1833), 22; and *Constitution and Bye-Laws of the Natural History Society of Montreal, with the Amending Act, 20th Vict., Ch. 118* (Montreal: Mitchell & Wilson, Printers, 1886), 17.

[17]Not long after its formation, some of the initial records of the Natural History Society were lost. In an address in 1852, Major R. Lachlan noted that a committee of the society had conducted a search for the early documents of the society and reported that "many of the records of the Society appear to have gone astray." See R. Lachlan, *A Retrospective Glance at the Progressive State of the Natural History Society of Montreal, with a View to Ascertaining How Far It Has Advanced the Important Objects Contemplated by Its Founders: Being a Lecture Delivered Before the Natural History Society, on the 31st March, 1852, and Published by Desire of the Society* (Montreal: Printed by J.C. Becket, 1852), 18. Stanley Brice Frost also implicitly recognized the gap in the records of the society since he refers mostly to the period up to the early 1830s and the period after the early 1850s. See Frost, "Science Education in the Nineteenth Century," cited earlier.

[18]From notes in the "Register Book, of Donations, to the Natural History Society; From Its Foundation, in 1827;- Compiled from the Society's Records, in 1853 - by Alex[ander] Geo. Lachlan." Manuscript record book, Blacker-Wood Library, McGill University, M//8M76re, 5, 18.

[19]*Catalogue of the Library and Museum of the Natural History Society of Montreal* (Montreal: Printed by Lovell & Gibson, 1846). In Table 1 the number of volumes has been determined from the designation of the catalogue itself. This means, for example, that entries described as pamphlets are included in the total as volumes.

[20]Roger Meloche, "Inventaire des catalogues de 1852, 1857 et 1870 de la bibliothèque de l'Institut canadien de Montréal," *Documentation et bibliothèques* 27 (1981): 24.

[21]For example, the identity of "Seven Papers on Mathematical Subjects" and "Pamphlets on Scientific Subjects" will probably remain a mystery.

[22]Personal communication with Eleanor MacLean, librarian of the Blacker-Wood Library, McGill University. In fact, I have identified numerous volumes with a Natural History Society bookplate in the McGill collections. The reconstructed catalogue, while well advanced, is not yet completed.

[23]*Twenty-fifth Annual Report of the Natural History Society of Montreal, Delivered by the Late Council and Read at the Meeting of the Society, 30th May, 1853* (Montreal: Printed at the Sun Office, by Moore, Owler & Stevenson, 1853), 5.

[24]"Annual Report of the Natural History Society," *Canadian Naturalist and Geologist* 3 (1858): 232.

[25]*Annual Report of the Council of the Natural History Society of Montreal, For the Year Ending May 18th, 1858* (S.l.: s.n., 1858?), 3. Emphasis in original.

[26]"Natural History Society, Monthly Meetings," *Canadian Naturalist*, new series, 4 (1869): 66-69.

[27]*Proceedings at the Annual Meeting of the Natural History Society of Montreal, For the Year Ending May 1870; With a List of the Officers, Life, Ordinary, Honorary and Corresponding Members and Associates of the Society* (Montreal: Printed at the Gazette Steam Printing House, 1870), 10. De Sola, rabbi to Montreal's Sephardic Jewish congregation, Shearith Israel (1847-82), also taught oriental languages at McGill University and played a leading part in the scientific activities in the city. See Carman Miller, "De Sola, Alexander Abraham" in *The Canadian Encyclopedia*, 2d ed. (Edmonton: Hurtig Publishers, 1988), and Stanley Brice Frost, *McGill University for the Advancement of Learning. Vol. 1. 1801-1895* (Montreal: McGill-Queen's University Press, 1980), 118.

[28]Reported in a manuscript register of donations now held in the Blacker-Wood Library, McGill University. The 1828 constitution of the Natural History Society stipulated that a register of donations was to be kept, but it seems that such a record was not begun until 1853.

[29]*Twenty-seventh Annual Report of the Natural History Society of Montreal, Delivered by the Late Council and Read at the Meeting of the Society, 18th May, 1855* (Montreal: Printed by H. & G.M. Rose, 1855), 4, [9].

[30]*Annual Report of the Natural History Society of Montreal for the Year Ending May, 1861; With a List of the Officers, Life Members, and Ordinary Members of the Society* (Montreal: Printed by John Lovell, 1861), 11.

[31]*Annual Report of the Natural History Society of Montreal for the Year Ending May, 1862; With the Amending Act Recently Passed: Also, a List of the Officers, Life, Corresponding, Honorary, and Ordinary Members of the Society* (Montreal: Printed by John Lovell, 1862). The financial statement shows an expenditure of $252.30 on the library.

[32]*Annual Report of the Natural History Society of Montreal for the Year Ending May, 1861: With a List of the Officers, Life Members, and Ordinary Members of the Society* (Montreal: Printed by John Lovell, 1861), 11.

[33]J.F. Whiteaves, "Report of the Scientific Curator and Sub-Librarian for the Session 1864-65," *Proceedings at the Annual Meeting of the Natural History Society of Montreal, for the Year Ending May, 1865: With a List of the Officers, Life, Ordinary, Honorary, and Corresponding Members of the Society* (Montreal: Printed by John Lovell, 1865), 10-21.

[34]"Report of the Council to the Annual Meeting of the Natural History Society, May 18, 1867," *Canadian Naturalist and Geologist* 3 (1866-68): 398.

[35]William Wright, "Librarian and Cabinet-Keeper's Report. 1853-4" in *Twenty-sixth Annual Report of the Natural History Society of Montreal, Delivered by the Late Council, and Read at the Meeting of the Society, 18th May, 1854* (Montreal: Printed by Wilson & Nolan, 1854), 7-8.

[36]"Report of the Library Committee," *Canadian Naturalist and Geologist* 5 (1860): 237.

[37]*Twenty-seventh Annual Report*, 4, [9].

[38]See Frost, "Science Education in the Nineteenth Century," 36-37. See also Patrick Keane, "Priorities and Resources in Adult Education: The Montreal Mechanics' Institute (1828-1843)," *McGill Journal of Education* 23 (Spring 1988): 182.

[39]"Report of the Natural History Society," *Canadian Naturalist and Geologist* 5 (1860): 235.

[40]Quoted in Edgar C. Moodey, *The Fraser-Hickson Library: An Informal History* (London: Clive Bingley, 1977), 37.

[41]Records of the discussion about the merger with the Fraser Institute are found in a number of the proceedings of the Natural History Society but principally in *Proceedings at the Annual Meeting of the Natural History Society of Montreal, For the Year Ending May 18th, 1875, With a List of the Officers, Resident Members, and Associates of the Society* (Montreal: Mitchell & Wilson, Printers, 1875), 12-13. A copy of the memorandum is found in "Natural History Society. Proceedings for the Session 1875-6," *Canadian Naturalist* 8 (1875-78): 173-74.

[42]The museum of the Natural History Society was 87 x 42 feet with a gallery entirely around the room, two sides 5 feet, 8 inches wide; one side 17 feet, 4 inches, and one 16 feet, 8 inches wide. The lecture room was 42 x 43 feet with folding doors that connected the library of 28 x 16 feet. See *Canadian Naturalist* 8 (1875-78): 174.

[43]"Report of the Library Committee," *Canadian Naturalist* 8 (1875-78): 453.

[44]Although, as noted earlier, Dr. Wright had reported that there were 1,500 volumes in the library in 1854, the 1875 account of 1,300 volumes must be considered more accurate.

[45]"Report of Council, May 26th, 1884," *Canadian Record of Science* 1 (1884-85): 126.

[46]"Annual Report of the Library Committee," *Canadian Record of Science* 2 (1886-87): 189-92. The duplicates uncovered while Robb was reclassifying the collection were sold, realizing $88.68. The list of duplicates was printed on a single sheet and dated 22 April 1889. The date, however, seems to be an error and should be 1886.

[47]"Proceedings of the Society," *Canadian Record of Science* 4 (1890-91): 190.

[48]For the purchase of reference materials, see "Report of the Library Committee," *Canadian Record of Science* 5 (1892-93): 200-1. For the remarks about librarians, see, for example, the comment made on the death of F.B. Caulfield, librarian for some time, who, it was said, " ... always took great interest in examining new books as they were added, was so well acquainted with the contents of the cases, that his knowledge and advice were at all times of great assistance." *Canadian Record of Science* 5 (1892-93): 201.

[49]"Library Report," *Canadian Record of Science* 9 (1903-4): 257.

[50]"Report of the Natural History Society of Montreal, 1909-10," *Canadian Record of Science* 9 (1915): 449.

[51]Nora Robins, "The Montreal Mechanics' Institute: 1828-1870," *Canadian Library Journal* 36 (1981): 375.

[52]*Annual Report of the Governors, Principal and Fellows of McGill University, Montreal for the Year 1891* (Montreal: [s.n.], 1891).

[53]Robins, "The Montreal Mechanics' Institute," 377.

[54]In 1865, for example, J.F. Whiteaves conducted a survey of the exchanges and found that the receipt of some was erratic. See *Proceedings at the Annual Meeting of the Natural History Society of Montreal, For the Year Ending May, 1865: With a List of the Officers, Life, Ordinary, Honorary, and Corresponding Members of the Society* (Montreal: Printed by John Lovell, 1865), 13-21.

[55]Sarah Gibson, "Scientific Societies and Exchange: A Facet of the History of Scientific Communication," *Journal of Library History* 17 (1982): 152.

[56]*Annual Report of the Natural History Society of Montreal for the Year Ending May, 1861*, 9.

[57]Theodore Gill, "Scientific Libraries in the United States," in *Public Libraries in the United States of America, Their History, Condition, and Management. Special Report* (Washington: Government Printing Office, 1876; reprint, University of Illinois Graduate School of Library Science, Monograph Series, number 4), 188.

[58]See A.J. Meadows, "Access to the Results of Scientific Research: Developments in Victorian Britain," in *Development of Science Publishing in Europe*, ed. A.J. Meadows (New York: Elsevier North-Holland, Inc., 1980), 43-62.

[59]See J.B. Tooley, "London Scientific Libraries in the Nineteenth Century, I: The Springs of Action," *Library History* 2 (1970-72): 139-51, and "London Scientific Libraries in the 19th Century, II: Government Intervention," *Library History* 3 (1973-75): 129-39.

[60]See Bertrum H. MacDonald, "Nineteenth-Century Canadian Scientists Read the World's Scientific Literature: A Case Study of Authors in the *Canadian Naturalist and Geologist*." Paper presented to the Fifth Kingston Conference of the Canadian Science and Technology Historical Association, Ottawa, October 1987. Available from the author.

[61]See his diary for 1857, 1858, 1859 and 1861. Robert Bell Papers, National Archives of Canada.

[62]Letter dated Montreal, 20th August 1855, from Mr. Justice Day to Dawson. Copy of letter in the James Dawson papers, McGill University Archives.

[63]Peter F. McNally, "The *McGill University Magazine*, 1901-1906; An Evaluation and a Bio-Bibliographical Analysis" (M.A. research paper, McGill University, 1976), 16-17.

[64]James Bain, "The Libraries of Canada," *The Library* 7 (1895): 242.

[65]Morris Zaslow, *Reading the Rocks*, 143.

[66]Richard Jarrell has suggested that the function of the libraries of such societies as the Natural History Society was to provide "light" literature more so than scientific works. See Richard A. Jarrell, "The Social Functions of the Scientific Society in Nineteenth-Century Canada," in *Critical Issues in the History of Canadian Science, Technology and Medicine*, ed. Richard A. Jarrell and Arnold E. Roos (Thornhill, Ont.: HSTC Publications, 1983), 31-44.

[67]Louis-Georges Harvey and Mark Olsen have made a similar observation based on the circulation records of the library of the Institut canadien de Montréal, namely, that fiction was the most widely circulated category of the library holdings. Louis-Georges Harvey and Mark Olsen, "A Quantitative Study of Book Circulation: The Library of the Institut-Canadien de Montréal," *Historical Methods* 18 (1985): 97-103. A more recent study illustrates this case further. See Louis-Georges Harvey, "Books and Culture in French Canada: The Library of the Institut-Canadien de Montréal, 1852-1880," *Primary Sources & Original Works* 1 (1991): 153-74.

[68]J.W. Dawson, "Address of the President," *Canadian Naturalist & Quarterly Journal of Science*, new series, 7 (1875): 106. The address was given at the annual meeting on May 19, 1873.

Bringing Librarianship to Rural Canada in the 1930s: Demonstrations by Carnegie Corporation of New York

Maxine K. Rochester

Abstract

Two demonstrations of rural library services were established and operated in Canada in the 1930s by the Carnegie Corporation of New York. One demonstration service was the Fraser Valley Regional Library in the lower Fraser Valley in the province of British Columbia on the west coast of Canada; the other was Prince Edward Island Libraries in the province of Prince Edward Island on the east coast. Funding through local taxes was taken over by the communities at the conclusion of both demonstrations. The reasons for the success of these aid projects are explored in the second part of the paper. The services showed the enormous book hunger in rural areas, and the administrative arrangements of a regional or province-wide library service that could deliver adequate services. The reading interests of adults are examined as well as the fears of cultural imperialism because of the American content of the collections and the contribution the libraries made to adult education.

Résumé

Deux expériences de bibliothèques rurales furent tentées au Canada au cours des années 1930 par la *Carnegie Corporation* de New-York. Un premier service fut installé à la *Fraser Valley Regional Library* dans la vallée de la rivière Fraser en Colombie-Britannique sur la côte ouest du Canada et un deuxième dans les *Prince Edward Island Libraries* dans la province de l'Île-du-Prince-Édouard, sur la côte est. A la suite de ces expériences, les deux collectivités prirent en mains le financement de leurs bibliothèques. La seconde partie de l'article examine les raisons du succès de ses projets d'aide. Ces expériences démontrèrent que le monde rural avait un appétit vorace pour la lecture et qu'il était possible de faire les arrangements administratifs

Reprinted from *Libraries & Culture*, Vol. 30, No. 4, Fall 1995 nécessaires pour qu'une bibliothèque régionale ou provinciale puisse offrir des services adéquats. L'article se penche sur l'intérêt des adultes pour la lecture, sur la menace d'impérialisme culturel que représente le contenu américain des collections et sur l'importance des bibliothèques dans l'éducation des adultes.

Two demonstrations of rural public library service were carried out in Canada in the 1930s; one was in the lower Fraser River Valley in the province of British Columbia on the west coast and the other in the province of Prince Edward Island on the east coast. Both provinces were predominantly English speaking. In the lower Fraser River Valley fifteen separate local governing areas joined together to provide a cooperative regional library service; in Prince Edward Island the unit was the province, and a province-wide public library service was set up. Both demonstrations were funded by grants from the Carnegie Corporation of New York as part of its library development program for the British dominions.

Rural library services had begun in Canada with traveling libraries operated by some provincial library agencies and by McGill University in Montreal, but they did not provide an adequate service. In the 1920s the model of rural library services based on the county government unit came from the United Kingdom and from the states of California and New Jersey in the United States. Most of the Canadian counties were too small to provide adequate services, so the idea of regional and cooperative services as pioneered in the Fraser Valley and of a province-wide service as demonstrated in Prince Edward Island in the 1930s acted as a catalyst for development in Canada and the United States and in other countries in the late 1930s and the 1940s.[1]

Carnegie Corporation Library Program

The Carnegie Corporation of New York (CCNY) was set up in 1911 with an endowment of $125 million by the American philanthropist Andrew Carnegie, who had made his money in steel. The aim of the corporation was to "promote the advancement and diffusion of knowledge and understanding among the people of the United States."[2] The trust was to continue the philanthropic work of Carnegie in the United States, the United Kingdom, and the British dominions and colonies. A fund of $10 million was set aside for the British dominions (Canada, South Africa, Australia, and New Zealand) and colonies, administered alongside the CCNY funds from New York. In 1913 a separate fund was set up for the United Kingdom, with headquarters there. This foundation funding was enormous, approximately $1.5 billion in today's figures.

The CCNY has been involved over the last eighty years in a variety of knowledge-related and cultural enterprises, and has had an influence, usually indirect, on the formulation of public policy.[3] Corporation activities from 1911 were concerned with the creation, organization, and dissemination of knowledge; from the late nineteenth century, knowledge was becoming important for economic activity and for formation and implementation of public policy.[4]

The philanthropic gifts of Andrew Carnegie had favored libraries from the beginning; Carnegie provided public library buildings in the United States, United Kingdom, and the British dominions from the late nineteenth century. After the formation of the CCNY, grants shifted to the provision of library education, books for college libraries, demonstration library services, and support of library associations. A 1961 summing up of Carnegie funding in the library area shows that in the period from 1911 to 1961 a total of over $68 million had been spent in library programs, nearly $6 million of this going to the British Commonwealth. Over half of this $6 million funded public library buildings, the main activity in Andrew Carnegie's day, and nearly $3 million had supported library programs from the 1920s to 1961.[5]

Keppel's Presidency: 1923-1941

Andrew Carnegie served as president of the corporation from 1911 until his death in 1919. In 1923 Frederick Paul Keppel became president as a paid chief executive, a position he retained until 1941; during this period he dominated the corporation's activity, which mainly concerned cultural philanthropy. Keppel (1875-1943) had had a career in publishing, university leadership, and the federal civil service. Grants, usually modest, went to programs in the areas of adult education, museums and libraries, and art and music. In her recent assessment of the CCNY, Ellen Condliffe Lagemann wrote that decision making about grants during Keppel's presidency was "directed more by hunch, coincidence, opportunity, friendship, and a wish to help than by clear, specific, consistently applied 'scientific' goals or principles."[6]

To carry out its aims, the CCNY did not give grants to schools, but to alternative agencies of education, namely libraries and adult education programs, and to art museums. The trustees of the corporation, through Keppel, designed programs to popularize access to culture without "debasement." Reflecting the attitudes of the trustees, this culture was "high" in the Western European tradition.[7]

British Dominions and Colonies Fund

The programs supported by the British Dominions and Colonies Fund in Canada, South Africa, New Zealand, and Australia during the time of

Keppel's presidency followed the pattern of those within the United States, with an emphasis on cultural diplomacy. Grants went to adult education, libraries, support of library associations and education for librarianship, and also to book collections for college and university libraries. To prepare the local personnel to carry out these programs, there were grants for study and travel in the United States and Europe. For Carnegie Corporation programs in the dominions, local advisory committees were set up to oversee projects and advise the corporation on small grants, including suitable recipients of travel and study grants.

Between 1912 and 1927 almost all the grants from the British Dominions and Colonies Fund were allocated to Canada. The area was geographically accessible and known to the CCNY. Grants went to several Canadian universities, with the Atlantic provinces receiving the most attention. Then, in the period 1927 to 1942, the program was extended to Africa, Australia, and New Zealand, and then the West Indies and other colonial areas.

There were several large grants for library projects in the dominions of Canada, South Africa, New Zealand, and Australia, and the Caribbean colonies. Canada received American $931,978 in the period 1911 to 1961,[8] the largest amount for any of the British dominions. Two grants were for rural library demonstrations: the British Columbia Public Library Commission received $119,000 in the period 1929-1936 for demonstration and development of library services, and $95,000 was allocated for the Prince Edward Island demonstration of library service in the period 1933-1935.

Canada in the 1930s

There was a population of about ten and a half million Canadians in the 1930s. The impact of the economic Depression was severe; in the period 1929 to 1933 the Gross National Product declined by 42 percent; by 1933, 30 percent of the labor force was unemployed.[9] Yet the federal government had no policies for economic recovery. The movement of people from the land to urban areas ceased.

Officially, the 1931 census gave figures for the literate population ten years and older as 96 percent,[10] but in reality more than 4 percent were probably functionally illiterate. Schools were managed by local school boards, under direction from provincial education departments, and most Canadians attended school until age fourteen. Single-teacher schools existed in the rural areas.

Many daily newspapers were published, although numbers of copies printed declined during the Depression. Canadians read mainly imported books; the major British and American publishers had set up branch offices in Canada to supply the English-speaking population, and cheap editions

244

from American publishers flooded the market. With Canadian publishers able to operate only inside Canada, Canadian publishing slumped during the Depression.[11] The Canadian Radio Broadcasting Commission was set up in mid 1933, and films were also imported and very popular.

Nearly 80 percent of the Canadian people had no access to library service at the beginning of the 1930s. Because education was a provincial responsibility, the idea of planning for library services in Canada as a whole had been concluded to be impossible by the authors of the document *Libraries in Canada: A Study of Library Conditions and Needs* (Toronto: Ryerson Press, and Chicago: American Library Association, 1933). This report of a survey that had been carried out in 1930 by three Canadian librarians had been financed by the CCNY.* The surveyors suggested the larger library unit on the model of county libraries in the United Kingdom as the solution to the problem of providing rural public library services in sparsely populated Canada. The Fraser Valley scheme was already showing how local governing and taxing authorities could group together to provide library service. The report also suggested Prince Edward Island on the east coast as a good site for a province-wide demonstration of library service. The surveyors wanted provincial governments to formulate policies for providing public library services to all citizens, whether they lived in urban or rural areas. They also wanted the dominion government to set up a national library for Canada.

British Columbia

British Columbia (BC) had a population of about 700,000, mostly of British descent, in 1931. Public libraries in British Columbia were supervised by a three-member Public Library Commission. Members served in a voluntary capacity and were appointed by the provincial government. They administered small provincial library grants, which provided some traveling boxes of books, and sent out books by mail on request to rural people from headquarters in the provincial capital, Victoria. There were public libraries in the cities. Under the chairmanship of Norman F. Black, a teacher, the commission had gathered information on library needs in the province in the hope of improving the situation, and a grant from the CCNY had enabled Clarence B. Lester, secretary of the Free Library Commission of Wisconsin, to act as advisor for the survey. The report, *British Columbia Library Service 1927-1928*, was published in 1929.[12] Impressed by the survey report, the CCNY donated $100,000 to support the activities of the com-

* Also known at the Ridington Report, after the chair of the Commission of Enquiry, John M. Ridington (Librarian of the University of British Columbia Library). The other two members of the commission were Mary J.L. Black (Librarian of the Fort William Public Library) and George H. Locke (Librarian of the Toronto Public Library).

mission, which then chose a regional library demonstration as the best method of improving rural library services. The lower Fraser River Valley was chosen as a suitable area of eighty miles long and ten miles wide, with a population of 44,000. The mild climate and plentiful rain supported mixed farming such as dairies and fruit orchards on the valley floor and a lumber industry in the foothills of the mountains.

Fraser Valley Regional Library (FVRL)

One of the aims of the 1930-1934 demonstration of a regional library service in the lower Fraser River Valley was for local citizens to be so impressed by the value to their community of such a service that they would continue to fund it from local taxes after the demonstration was finished. Helen Gordon Stewart, who had been librarian of the Victoria Public Library in British Columbia and a foundation member* of the BC Public Library Commission, and who had just completed a doctoral program in sociology at Columbia University in New York, assumed leadership of the library in February 1930. She had to persuade fifteen separate local political units to agree to join to provide the regional library service. The first step was to hold public meetings in the small political units in the valley, arousing public interest and explaining how the library would operate. Most of the population had no library service experience. At the public meetings, those present voted on accepting the library demonstration; not surprisingly this offer of a free community service was always accepted.[13] Next, a local management committee was set up.

Stewart established an office at New Westminster (near Vancouver in the western end of the valley), selected staff, including two permanent and one temporary professional librarians, selected and acquired the first book-stock, which was cataloged and organized for use, and acquired a truck which was converted into a bookvan. The library commenced operation in August 1930. The distribution center for the library was set up at Chilliwack, the largest town, and from there the bookvan operated around the valley. Local communities provided the accommodation and basic furnishings for the branches in the larger settlements. By the end of 1930, there were seven branches, two sub-branches, six deposit stations, three school deposit stations, and fifty bookvan stops. At Chilliwack there was a professional library staff member but branches and sub-branches had local staff, their salaries paid by demonstration funds. The service to schools was not vigorously promoted at first; the schools already received provincial aid funds, and the chief effort went to service to adults. They would be the people voting for local tax support to continue the library.[14]

---

*i.e., founding member

The local residents welcomed the library services. A year after operating, 13,278 residents were registered borrowers — 30 percent of the population. Stewart wrote to the president of the CCNY:

> They come to the branches from miles around, and nothing the weather can do seems to keep them from the book van when it makes its fortnightly rounds. They splash along muddy roads in gum boots and slickers, often for one mile, two miles, or more, and when they arrive stand in the open with the wind catching them in the small of the back and the rain cascading down the points of their noses and exclaim "Wasn't it a red-letter day for us when this bus started!"[15]

By the end of November 1931, twenty months after the FVRL demonstration began, there were 16,494 volumes in the library collection, 12,063 adult and 4,431 juvenile books. Ten newspapers, seventy-six magazines, and eighteen learned-society journals were received.

In the first sixteen months 230,000 books were circulated. The book-van followed seven routes every two weeks, covering 1,250 miles monthly. A year later there were ninety-two points for library service, circulating 248,313 volumes. By August 1933, 38 percent of the population was registered as borrowers, which didn't include children served through the schools.[16] At the end of the demonstration there were 19,000 registered borrowers, 120 distribution points, and 24,000 volumes in the library collection. The library service was overwhelmed by the phenomenal response in the early years. Funds ran short in 1932 for the closing years of the demonstration, and the provincial government did not give any assistance, as was expected, because of the financial situation. The CCNY made some extra money available for the demonstration to continue to 1936. It was found that at least 50 cents per capita was needed to fund the library service.

The stock of library materials was rotated regularly. Every few weeks part of the collection in the branches and deposit stations was changed when the bookvan called. Also there was a request service with five hundred to seven hundred interbranch requests for particular titles or subject materials supplied every week. Books not held were considered for ordering or were borrowed from other libraries in British Columbia. Also subject lists of books were prepared, and posters and displays were set up in branches.

In August 1931 a meeting was held of representatives of all the local committees, and a central committee of one representative from each government unit in the library service was formed to advise the director and the Public Library Commission of British Columbia on policy for the library. Looking to the future of the service, lobbying started at the end of 1932 for amendments to the Public Library Act of British Columbia to allow regional library services to be set up. A citizens' petition was sent from the valley to the provincial government, and the amendment was passed in 1933. Then lobbying started for a vote to raise local taxes to support the continuation of the library service. At the municipal elections of January 1934, despite the Depression, twenty out of twenty-four districts voted to support the library with local taxes. In June 1934 these twenty districts continued the Fraser Valley Union Library.

The demonstration was also a success in that two more regional libraries were set up in British Columbia. Wide publicity was given at many meetings, in the form of papers and photographs at conferences, and articles and photographs in professional journals, magazines and newspapers. A film was also made (*The Fraser Valley Public Library*, 16mm. [BC Public Library Commission, c1931-1934]), and news of the demonstration regional library spread throughout Canada, the United States and farther. It was a pioneer in joining separate local government authorities to cooperatively provide a rural library service.

Prince Edward Island

Prince Edward Island (PEI) is the smallest province of Canada, both in size and population. An island 120 miles long and about 20 miles wide, it lies in the Gulf of St. Lawrence, sheltered from the Atlantic Ocean. The island was first settled in 1719 by the French and later ceded by France to Great Britain. In 1931 there was a population of 88,000, of which 14,000 were of French descent, and the rest of English, Scottish, and Irish descent. The capital, Charlottetown, had a population of 12,000, and there was only one other town with a population over 1,000. The industries were agriculture, with mixed farming and fishing. The province was poor, but most farmers owned their own farms.[17]

Prince Edward Island Libraries

The report of the Canadian Library Commission, *Libraries in Canada*, had picked the province of Prince Edward Island as an ideal site for a demonstration of public library service for the east coast of Canada. In September 1932 the Carnegie Corporation had Gerhard Lomer, the librarian of McGill University, visit the island to give a second opinion, and his report recommended a three-year demonstration of a provincial public library service. In 1933 the CCNY made available a grant of $95,000 for such a demonstration. Selected as director of the demonstration was Nora Bateson, a staff member of McGill University Library School, who had also worked for a short time in the Fraser Valley demonstration. An MA graduate of Manchester University, she went to Canada from England in 1922 at the age of twenty-six.

On 1 June 1933 the headquarters for Prince Edward Island Libraries were set up in Charlottetown. A qualified assistant librarian was appointed, books ordered, and the first four branches established in three months. As in the Fraser Valley demonstration, a meeting of citizens was called in each centre and the library demonstration explained. Bateson could carry three hundred books in bookshelves fitted into the back of her modified car, so she could show people what materials would be supplied. People on Prince Edward Island had had little access to books,[18] and there was no qualified librarian on the island. As in Fraser Valley, local committees were set up, with local centres supplying suitable accommodation along with heating, lighting, and equipment; the custodians and the collections were paid for through the central library. In 1933 McGill University Library School ran a four-week summer school in Charlottetown to prepare staff for the Prince Edward Island libraries.

By 1935 twenty-two branches had been established, with a collection of one thousand to twelve hundred books and ten current journals in each. One-third were children's books, and half of the adult books were non-fiction; some were in French. Because of the long snowy winters and the poor roads, a bookvan could not be used to distribute books. Every summer the collections in each branch were completely changed. Books in the Prince Edward Island Libraries were available to readers anywhere. To make users aware of what was available, subject lists were issued on topics such as agriculture, ships and the sea, biography, economics, war, and peace. There were about 150-200 books supplied in response to requests each week. New books could be requested, and if the title met the collection-building criteria and money was available, the book was bought and made available in a few weeks. A member of the staff later explained, "We made the collection a viable, sort of living thing."[19] Requested books that could not be made available from the collection were borrowed on interlibrary loan, mainly from McGill University Library.[20]

The teachers in the rural schools could borrow collections, one book per pupil, for two months at a time from the branches, but only 50 percent had done so by 1935. Books were also distributed to remote areas through the Women's Institutes. The institutes aimed "to promote an appreciation of rural living, and to develop informed citizens through the study of national and international issues (particularly those affecting women and children)."[21] In the 1935-1936 winter, sixty-seven boxes, each containing thirty carefully selected titles, were sent out from headquarters, and this method of book distribution proved a success. The library also helped with books and pamphlets for adult education study groups.

By the end of the demonstration there were 41,000 volumes in the collection. The number of registered borrowers out of the population of 88,000 was 23,517 — 37 percent. There were also children in the rural schools and the people using the Women's Institute collections. The annual circulation was 261,029 items in 1935. Nora Bateson noted that in winter several people read each book circulated, so that actual potential readership might be tripled. She also said that the idea of the library as a source of information was growing.[22]

A library act setting up a provincial library commission comprising the lieutenant-governor and the premier of the province and five other persons was secured by Bateson. She enlisted support from both the Protestant and Roman Catholic clergy to ensure support for the continuation of the service.[23] The director herself provided good publicity for the service by talking at meetings, getting articles in the newspapers, and providing exhibits. She also publicized the service in the other Atlantic provinces.

With a new government in the provincial elections of 1935, which came in with an austerity policy, the library service was threatened. The library act was repealed. The twenty-two local library committees organized a petition to the government, and the Women's Institutes, the churches, and teachers lobbied their local members. The government grant was $24,238 for each of the two next years, half of the amount requested, but enough to ensure the survival of the library until the political and economic situation changed.

Adult Reading Interests

In both library demonstrations, investigations of adult reading interests for rural areas were carried out. These expanded on the scientific research work on adult reading that was being carried out in the 1920s and 1930s mainly in the United States, but also in the United Kingdom, Germany, and Switzerland. The results were of interest to adult educators, librarians, and publishers.

During the Fraser Valley Regional Library demonstration, Stewart aimed to carry out social research that would assist in establishing other rural library services. One area to be examined was reading needs and interests, and she planned projects in three areas: individual reading interests and habits, community reading needs, and the relation of individual community reading needs to a library service. She noted in a letter to the CCNY in 1932 that they already had results in some areas that had been incorporated into the program.[24] Stewart had taken courses with E.L. Thorndike, an educational psychologist at Teachers College, Columbia University, who had published *Adult Learning* (Macmillan, 1928) and shown that adults continue to learn throughout their lives. Her application for the FVRL position stated also that she had attended a summer session at the Graduate Library School at the University of Chicago in 1928.[25]

There Douglas Waples was carrying out research on individual reading interests.[26] On the way to take up the position in British Columbia, Stewart met with Waples in Chicago.

One of the methods that Stewart used to study reading interests, namely the numbers of books borrowed in various subject categories, was the most popular method used in libraries in the United States in the 1920s. Statistics were kept of book borrowings according to the broad subject categories used in the Dewey Decimal Classification scheme, by category of fiction or nonfiction, and adult or juvenile.[27] These circulation figures were kept for each branch. The reading studies were carried out alongside attempts to analyze the community and thus match books to readers, and encourage wider use of the library. Readers' library cards in the FVRL circulation system noted all books borrowed. Monthly statistics were kept for the circulation of fiction and nonfiction books from each section of the FVRL. The subject interests for nonfiction reading were monitored by keeping statistics for the ten subject divisions of the Dewey Decimal Classification scheme, with the 900 subject division further subdivided into travel, biography, and history. Stewart stated that the response to the demonstration library service was so overwhelming that there was no time to write up the research findings; instead the results were used immediately for building the collection and distributing it among the service points.

The final report on the FVRL, submitted by Stewart in February 1936, included statistics on circulation for each service point by subject for the demonstration period 1930 to 1934.[28] By September 1934 adult membership comprised 21,061 and juvenile membership 4,559, making a grand total of 25,620 members, or about 60 percent of the population of 44,000. Total circulation for the four-year period totaled 914,593 — 714,040 adult and 227,553 juvenile loans.

The majority of the books borrowed were fiction. Adult fiction totaled 539,263 loans, about 75 percent; nonfiction comprised 174,777, making total adult loans of 714,040. County libraries in the United Kingdom found that about 30 percent of loans were nonfiction.[29] The circulation figures for the breakdown by major Dewey Decimal Classification scheme divisions for the first four years of the demonstration are shown in Table 1. We can see that the 900 subdivision, comprising travel, biography, and history, was overwhelmingly the most popular. Of the categories used, travel material was the most popular, followed by the 600 classification division, the applied sciences, followed by the 700 classification, comprising the arts. Stewart said the FVRL staff had been astonished by the variety of books that were wanted. "Our modest definition of 'varied' fell so far short of the real thing that we have hardly yet got it stretched to its proper proportions."[30] It had been assumed in the early 1920s in the United Kingdom that rural readers would have unsophisticated reading tastes, but experience there with the county library services showed that rural readers were as discriminating and had tastes as varied as urban readers.[31] Stewart found this also to be true in the FVRL.

TABLE 1

Circulation Statistics for Fraser Valley Regional Library, 1 September 1930 to 3 September 1934, for Adult Nonfiction Materials

Dewey Decimal Classification Scheme subdivisions	Total adult circulation
000 Generalities	19
100 Philosophy	6,529
200 Religion	6,526
300 Social Sciences	11,622
400 Language	625
500 Pure Sciences	10,834
600 Technology (Applied Sciences)	26,309
700 The Arts	24,249
800 Literature	21,705
900 General Geography and History	
travel	26,763
biography	21,916
history	17,680
Total nonfiction	174,777

Source: Adapted from Appendix A, Circulation Record, Carnegie Demonstration of B.C. September 1, 1930 - September 3, 1934, p. 4.

The same record-keeping system for circulation statistics and readers' cards as had been used in the Fraser Valley was used in the Prince Edward Island Libraries. Since Nora Bateson had worked in the Fraser Valley library, she would have been aware of Stewart's research. The analysis of these records for the first five years of operation of the PEI Libraries was carried out by Nora Bateson's successor, H.B. Chandler, together with J.T. Croteau, professor of economics and sociology jointly at St. Dunstan's University and Prince of Wales College (which later merged to form the University of Prince Edward Island, in Charlottetown).[32] The study sought to answer such questions as: Who has read the books? What have these people read? What groups of people have profited most from the library? Has there been any change in reading habits during the five-year period?[33] As in the Fraser Valley scheme circulation records were kept and the individual reader's card showed the author and title of each book read and the dates for its borrowing and return. This was combined with information obtained from the local small branch librarians, who knew their readers well, as to reader's sex, age, education, occupation, and place of residence. It was a landmark study of rural reading interests. With concern about confidentiality of records and personal privacy, such a study would be impossible today.

The study examined the reading interests of twenty-five thousand people who had borrowed over one million books during the five years from 1933 to 1938. The re-registration of readers at the end of the first five years of the library made it possible to analyze the reading records. The data was collected at library headquarters then sent off to the Dominion Bureau of Statistics in Ottawa, where it was transferred to tabulating cards and counted. The same system of Hollerith punched cards had been used to analyze the replies to questionnaires for the study of reading interests carried out for the Woodside Branch of the Queens Borough Public Library in New York.[34]

There were few other sources of books other than the library available to the people of Prince Edward Island. There were no rental libraries and few booksellers. Chandler and Croteau thought only a few hundred books each year were purchased through book clubs or directly from publishers. Thus, the library supplied the majority of books read on Prince Edward Island.

Chandler and Croteau also studied the availability of other sources of reading matter in PEI. They gathered information on magazines and newspapers. The newsagent business handling most of the periodical sales within Prince Edward Island gave them access to their records for 1937 and 1938. Also the major periodical publishers were contacted and gave information about their subscription statistics for Prince Edward Island. Most of the nineteen thousand families in Prince Edward Island took a newspaper, despite the competition from radio, with eleven thousand radio sets in the province.[35]

There were over one million issues of periodicals sold annually in PEI, and in addition to those there were religious periodicals. Five farm magazines accounted for over 500,000 copies sold annually, followed in numbers by popular magazines. A tariff agreement between the United States and Canada meant that from 1936 all magazines came into Canada duty free, resulting in cheap so-called "pulp" fiction magazines from the States flooding in. The authors concluded that in 1938 the per capita magazine circulation on Prince Edward Island for those over five years of age was about fifteen per year.[36]

There were two picture theatres in Prince Edward Island, in larger towns, and traveling picture-show men, but in the Depression attendance was relatively low.[37]

The book circulation for the library in 1938 was 252,000 books — 168,000 to adults and 84,000 to children. For the adult books 125,000 (73 percent) were fiction. For the FVRL the percentage was 75 in the years 1930 to 1934. The library stock consisted of 49,006 volumes, of which 34,666 were adult books, and 14,340 juvenile. Of the adult books, 19,699 were nonfiction and 14,967 fiction. The per capita book circulation for Prince Edward Island Libraries was just over three books per year, and ten per year per registered reader. This was comparable to the circulation for the Fraser Valley Regional Library.[38] The library had made about 10,000 loans of pamphlets during 1938; they were on topics such as agriculture, fisheries, home economics, and the cooperative movement.

From the book circulation analysis for 1934 to 1938 for 1,187,000 books, Chandler and Croteau found a marked annual seasonal variation, with few books read during the summer months when farming and fishing activities were busiest. Over the five-year period there was a slight relative increase in the reading of adult nonfiction books, which may have been the result of adult education study groups. There was also a trend for a relative increase in the number of children's books borrowed.[39]

While male readers formed 46 percent of registered borrowers, they borrowed 56 percent of the nonfiction books, so they showed a preference for nonfiction books. The favorite subjects were science and history. Readers with a greater amount of education read more nonfiction books, and older readers borrowed more nonfiction.[40] Most of the fiction borrowing was from the lighter classes of fiction, such as adventure and mystery stories.

By the end of 1938 there were 24,428 registered readers, 46 percent being males, and most registrants were in the 25 to 34 and 35 to 44 year age groups. The average education level of Prince Edward Island readers was lower high school level. When occupation of registrants was examined, it was found that the greatest number were in the student and housewife groups. When compared to their percentage in the total Prince Edward Island population, the highest proportion of an occupational group holding library cards was the professional group, with more than four out of five being members. They were followed by the occupational groups of trade and transportation and student groups.[41]

The authors also analyzed place of residence with borrowing records, and found that "the effective range of service seems to extend five or six miles from a library."[42] Almost 89 percent of borrowers lived within five or six miles, and 60 percent lived within one mile of a library service point. This effect of distance from the service point was more marked for younger and older borrowers.

Thus we see that the circulation figures for the nonfiction section of the collections in both demonstrations were closely monitored; there was an assumption among librarians at that time that nonfiction was more valuable in assessing the potential value of library collections to the community. Also there was categorization of the types of fiction in the collection that assessed its quality and potential impact on readers. Selection of materials for the collection was not based on what most library readers demanded. "The place of the library in society is not that of a competitor of the newstand and its pulp-filled shelves; it has a definitive educative function to perform."[43] Fiction materials had an educative value, according to a qualitative classification used by librarians. Thus the highest category contained the "classics, first-rate modern books selected on the basis of style and theme, and translations of the works of European writers." The lowest category included "mystery stories, adventure stories, westerns, and ... light romance."[44] Librarians' attitudes indicated this by the fact that light fiction titles were not available on request from other branches in Prince Edward Island.[45] Readability levels too were associated with this classification, with the lowest category of fiction generally being the easiest to read. This was important for the Canadian rural population, with most people leaving school after only a year or two of high school. Bateson thought that the people with little formal education were the most interested in the library, so the book collection included books which were popular and easy to read.[46]

Library Collections and Cultural Imperialism

As with other aid programs from abroad, there was concern about American cultural imperialism with the CCNY grants. Concern about Canadian-American attitudes, and whether Canadian library collections contained too much American material led to the Carnegie Corporation appointing H.L. Stewart of Dalhousie University in Halifax, Nova Scotia, to investigate the matter. In response to his enquiries, Nora Bateson replied that approximately one-third of the books in the PEI Libraries were published in the United States, and therefore gave an American viewpoint. Most of the applied science books were published in the United States. Up to 50 percent of the fiction books were published in the United States, with about an equal percentage from Great Britain. However many British books were reissued by American publishers.[47] Thus British books such as those by James Hilton, *Good-Bye Mr. Chips* and *Lost Horizon*, bestsellers in the United States in 1934 and 1935, were reissued by American publishers.

Bateson noted there was a great demand in PEI for the American bestseller for the years 1933 and 1934, Hervey Allen's *Anthony Adverse*, an historical novel set in the Napoleonic era, published by Farrar and Rinehart. Sinclair Lewis's books, in which he satirized conventional middle America, were popular as well. In general, people read American or British fiction, without caring about its origin. Also popular with readers were American-published books such as Walter Pitkin's *Life Begins at Forty* (Whitlesey House), which topped the American nonfiction bestseller list in 1933, Paul de Kruif's popular scientific biographies, *Microbe Hunters* (NY: Harcourt, Brace, 1926) and *Hunger Fighters* (NY: Harcourt, Brace, 1928), and books on the New Deal. Most of the magazines in the library collection were British, but popular American titles were *National Geographic, Popular Mechanics, Good Housekeeping,* and *Current History.*

The collections of books and magazines in both demonstration libraries seem to have been a mixture of American and British publications, with Canadian material whenever it was available. Despite the fact that English-speaking Canadians in general favored British rather than American books, Bateson noted that books were selected for the library service for their subject matter and suitability for the readers rather than on the grounds of place of publication. Bateson said: "There is always in Canada the danger of neglecting British publications because most library lists and aids come from the American Library Association. Because of this I have taken particular pains to use English sources when I could."[48]

Bramwell Chandler, who worked with Bateson and became her successor when she left after the demonstration was completed, reports that it did not matter for selection purposes where the material was published, as long as it fitted the needs of the library users.[49] Ruth Goodall, who worked as a librarian in the Chilliwack branch of the Fraser Valley Regional Library, reports the same situation. She also notes that Canadian materials were popular.[50]

Both Goodall and Chandler report there were sometimes fusses on moral grounds about the inclusion of materials in the library collections and selection decisions had to be defended. Chandler reports there were also questions asked on religious grounds in PEI; there was distrust between the Roman Catholic and Protestant groups in the community.

The collection building and reference guides for the FVRL can be gathered from the list of material sent from Stewart's office at New Westminster to the headquarters of the Fraser Valley Union Library on the completion of the demonstration. It included copies of the Wilson Co. publications, Catalog Series for various subject areas, the American Library Association's *Catalog* of 1926, Ernest A. Baker's *Guide to the Best Fiction* 1932 edition, W.F. Gray's *Books that Count*, Mahoney and Whitney's *Realms of Gold*, I. Mudge's *Guide to Reference Books*, Jonathan Nield's *Guide to the Best Historical Novels and Tales*, and the seven annual volumes of the *Book Review Digest 1928-1934.* The only Canadian selection guide noted was *Books for Boys and Girls* 1927 of the Toronto Public Library.[51]

The collection building and reference guides in the PEI library[52] were also the standard American ones: American Library Association publications such as Mudge's *Guide to Reference Books*, 5th ed. 1929; the ALA *Catalog* 1926 and *Supplement, 1926-1931*; guides published by the H.W. Wilson Co.; *Children's Catalog*, 4th ed. 1930 and supplements; *Standard Catalog for High School Libraries*, 2nd ed. 1932 plus supplements; and also *Public Libraries* 1934; and an indexing service, *Readers' Guide to Periodical Literature.* A Publishers' Weekly publication, *Publishers Trade List Annual* gave access to the current American publishing output. There was also the British standard catalogue *Reference Catalogue of Current Literature*, published by J. Whitaker & Sons in London. Published every three to four years, it listed all books in print and on sale in the British Isles. To assist in selecting children's books, Bateson used the same Canadian source as Stewart, *Books for Boys and Girls*.

There were plenty of book review media available. The major Canadian newspapers carried book pages, from the United Kingdom weeklies like *The Times Literary Supplement* and from the United States the *New York Times* books supplement were readily available. There were also broadcasts of book reviews by Canadian academics on radio.[53]

There was a demand in both demonstration libraries for materials in languages other than English. The French-language books in the PEI collection were well used, but Bateson noted they needed to be increased, since the number in the collection was not proportional to the number of French speakers in the population. When possible, French books published in Quebec had been bought for the collection.[54]

Stewart would have liked to include materials in foreign languages to meet the needs of her FVRL users. As well as those from French speakers, she noted requests from Swedes, Norwegians, Danes, Germans, Finns, Czechs, Japanese, Russians, and Poles within the first year of operation. She saw the need for a cooperative endeavour among BC libraries to supply an adequate stock of material in foreign languages and suggested points for consideration for such a scheme to the BC Public Library Commission, but nothing seems to have come of it.[55]

Adult Education

Both demonstration libraries played an active role in adult education activities. Adult education ideas in Canada came from three sources: Great Britain, the United States, and Denmark. The universities had begun adult education extension departments on British or American models, and the Scandinavian influence brought study clubs and discussion groups, along the lines of folk high schools and agricultural programs for young farmers in Denmark.[56] Study materials were also supplied by pamphlets on specific topics.

257

In the FVRL Stewart always had the adult education function of the library service in mind, but meant to provide such programs only when basic services were available. However, from the beginning there was a great demand from groups in the community. She noted that "Frankly, I never intended to plunge into it so precipitately." By the beginning of 1931 the library was supplying materials for a University of British Columbia Extension group and discussing with the university cooperation for summer schools. The FVRL was supplying materials for debating groups and study groups associated with farmers cooperatives, was planning to help choral and theatre groups, and was helping some women's institutes. Response was so great that Stewart spent funds set aside for future years to buy materials.[57] In the report for 1932-1933, Stewart noted that there were twenty-three reading and study clubs that the library helped in organizing programs and providing books and magazines for courses.[58]

From the beginning, the PEI Libraries supplied materials for group study clubs, small groups of people who met with a local group leader once a week for a period of six to eight weeks and read and discussed a small shared collection of books on a particular topic loaned by the library. An enthusiastic leader got various members to read a part of or a whole book and give reports to the group, followed by discussion. Nora Bateson recommended to the study group leaders the article "Projects for Group Study" from the *Wilson Bulletin* January 1934.[59] In 1933-1934, thirty-seven groups met during the winter; by 1936 there were ninety-three study clubs. Popular topics in the winter of 1933-1934 were modern biography, world social and economic conditions, disarmament, Russia today, modern science, Canadian literature, and polar exploration.[60]

Bateson sent out some popular and simply written books, together with one or two more advanced ones, to study groups for a month or longer. For example, a group studying Soviet Russia with W.A. Paterson, a United Church of Canada minister at Cavendish, PEI, was recommended to start with Maurice Hindus, *Humanity Uprooted* (NY: J. Cape and H. Smith, 1929), which Bateson thought gave a "very fair and unbiased analysis," and the following titles: Emile Dillon, *Russia Today and Yesterday* (London and Toronto: J.M. Dent, 1929), Maurice Hindus, *Broken Earth* (N.Y.: International Publishers, 1926), and Julian Huxley, *Scientist among the Soviets* (London: Chatto and Windus, 1932). Huxley was recommended for more advanced readers.[61]

Paterson reported on 16 January 1934 that the group was keen so Bateson sent three more books: E.T. Brown, *This Russian Business* (London: G. Allen and Unwin, 1933), George Sherwood Eddy, *The Challenge of Russia* (N.Y. : Farrar and Rinehart, 1931), and Ernst Glaeser, *The Land without Unemployment — Three Years of the Five-Year Plan* (London: M. Lawrence

Ltd, 1932). The Brown book was recommended for more advanced readers.[62]

In the 1930s, capitalist economics were being questioned, and young people and intellectuals were interested in Marxism. Books on Russia were among the American best sellers.[63] The number of books about Russia by American authors reached a peak of twenty-four titles in 1931, the period of the Depression in the United States and the Five-Year Plan of 1928-1933 in Russia.[64]

Conclusions

The Fraser Valley Regional Library showed the possibility of joining together a variety of taxing and governing authorities to provide library service; it was claimed to be a world first. Some rural library services for large areas had already been developed in the United Kingdom and the United States, but only in single large government and taxing units, such as counties. The Prince Edward Island Libraries showed the possibility of a province-wide library service.

As well as continuing the demonstration libraries, new regional libraries were set up on Vancouver Island and in the Okanagan Valley in British Columbia; a new provincial library in the Atlantic province of Nova Scotia was established with CCNY seed money immediately after the two original demonstrations were completed. Stewart later went on to head a CCNY demonstration library service in the Caribbean, and Bateson headed the provincial library in Nova Scotia. The demonstrations had shown that there was an enormous book hunger in the rural areas, and that once a library service sufficiently financed and of an adequate population base was developed on a trial basis, the citizens were willing to pay for such a service through their taxes. The demonstrations dispelled any assumptions about reading interests of rural people being less sophisticated than people living in cities.

It was a suitable time for the development of public libraries in Canada. There was an interest in educational matters, and because of the Depression and political changes in Europe, it was a time of questioning and search for reasons. It was also because of the Depression, a time for cheap forms of education and entertainment, that people turned to public libraries for reading materials. The circulation statistics for public libraries in the United States increased to their highest point in 1933 and then declined again. This decline in circulation after 1933 was attributed to the decline in acquisition of new books because of budget cuts during the Depression.[65] This was not a problem for the demonstration libraries with their Carnegie funds.

The happy conjunction of responsive local communities who wanted educational, informational, and recreational materials from public libraries, the availability of grants for the demonstrations from the CCNY, together with the abilities of Stewart and Bateson as directors and support from local community leaders, led to successful outcomes for the two aid projects. The two demonstrations show us what can be achieved by the injection of funds together with careful selection of library collections and of sites, good planning, and able administrators. Demonstrations can lead to adoption of responsibilities for funding library services by the local communities, and also to adoption of such services by other communities once they can see the services operating. This all took place despite a time of severe economic constraint; rural public library services had become an essential community service.

Notes

[1]Lisa de Gruyter, "The History and Development of Rural Public Libraries," *Library Trends* 28 (Spring 1980): 513-23.

[2]Florence Anderson, "Carnegie Corporation of New York" in *Encyclopedia of Library and Information Science* (New York: Dekker 1968-1992).

[3]Ellen Condliffe Lagemann, *The Politics of Knowledge: The Carnegie Corporation, Philanthropy, and Public Policy* (Middletown, Conn.: Wesleyan University Press, 1989), 3.

[4]Ibid., 4.

[5]Florence Anderson, *Carnegie Corporation Library Program* (New York: Carnegie Corporation of New York, 1963), 25.

[6]Lagemann, 7

[7]Ibid., 90-97.

[8]Anderson, *Carnegie Corporation Library Program*, 25

[9]James Struthers, "Great Depression" in *The Canadian Encyclopedia*, 2d ed. (Edmonton: Hurtig Publishers, 1988; Detroit: Gale Research, 1988).

[10]Canada, Dominion Bureau of Statistics, *Canada Year Book 1934-1935* (Ottawa: King's Printer, 1935), 159.

[11]James Marsh, "Book publishing, English-language" in *The Canadian Encyclopedia*.

[12]British Columbia, Public Library Commission, *British Columbia Library Service, 1927-1928* (Victoria, B.C.: King's Printer, 1929).

[13]Geoffrey Rex Des Brisay, "A Historical Survey of the Fraser Valley Regional Library, Abbotsford, British Columbia" (master's thesis, University of Washington, 1956).

[14]C.B. Lester, "Report to the Carnegie Corporation: Fraser Valley Demonstra-tion of a District Library System in British Columbia." November 1932. CCNY Archives; File for British Columbia Library Commission 1930-1946.

[15]H.G. Stewart to F.P. Keppel, 5 February 1931, British Columbia Library Commission.

[16]"Carnegie Demonstration of British Columbia. Progress Report, August 31, 1933," British Columbia Library Commission.

[17]Canada, Dominion Bureau of Statistics, *Canada Year Book 1934-1935*, 296.

[18]Nora Bateson, "Prince Edward Island's Demonstration," *Ontario Library Review* 18 (August 1934): 111-12; Violet L. Coughlin, *Larger Units of Public Library Service in Canada, with Particular Reference to the Provinces of Prince Edward Island, Nova Scotia and New Brunswick* (Metuchen, N.J.: Scarecrow Press, 1968).

[19]Bramwell Chandler, P.E.I. Librarian 1936, interview by David Crowley, Popular Communications History Project, McGill University, 8 August 1985. (Transcript, p. 2) Prince Edward Island Public Archives and Records Office.

[20]Nora Bateson, *The Carnegie Library Demonstration in Prince Edward Island, Canada, 1933-1936* (Charlottetown, P.E.I.: Prince Edward Island Libraries, 1936).

[21]Jean E. Dryden, "Federated Women's Institutes of Canada" in *Canadian Encyclopedia.*

[22]Bateson, *The Carnegie Library Demonstration*, 32-33.

[23]Milton J. Ferguson to F.P. Keppel, CCNY, 19 September 1934. CCNY Archives, File for Prince Edward Island Libraries. Ferguson was chief librarian of Brooklyn Public Library and a CCNY library adviser. He visited Prince Edward Island in September 1934 for the CCNY.

[24]H.G. Stewart to F.P. Keppel, 6 May 1932. CCNY Archives, File for British Columbia Public Library Commission 1930-1946.

[25]H.G. Stewart's application for director's position, 24 October 1929. Provincial Archives and Records Office of British Columbia, Library Services Branch, GR 1387, Box 2, File 4, H.N. Lidster, personal correspondence.

[26]Stephen Karetzky, *Reading Research and Librarianship: A History and Analysis* (Westport, Conn.: Greenwood Press, 1982), 93-94.

[27]Ibid., 4.

[28]Appendix A, Circulation Record, Carnegie Demonstration of B.C. 1 September 1930 - 3 September 1934. Provincial Archives of British Columbia Library Services Branch, GR 1387, Box 1, File 11. [This appendix appears to have become detached from Carnegie Demonstration of British Columbia, Summary Report, February 29th, 1936, Helen G. Stewart, Box 2, File 17.]

[29]Thomas Kelly, *A History of Public Libraries in Great Britain, 1845-1975*, 2d ed. (London: Library Association, 1977), 223.

[30]H.G. Stewart to F.P. Keppel, CCNY, 5 February 1931. CCNY Archives, File for British Columbia Public Library Commission.

[31]Kelly, 286.

[32]H.B. Chandler and J.T. Croteau, *A Regional Library and Its Readers: A Study of Five Years of Rural Reading* (New York: American Association for Adult Education, 1940).

[33]Ibid., 2

[34]*Woodside Does Read! A Survey of the Reading Interests and Habits of a Local Community*, conducted for the Queens Borough Public Library by Grace O. Kelley (New York: Queens Borough Public Library, 1935), 20.

[35]Chandler and Croteau, 21.

[36]Ibid., 23.

[37]Ibid., 25.

[38]Canada, Dominion Bureau of Statistics, *Survey of Libraries in Canada* (Ottawa: DBS, 1938), 17.

[39]Chandler and Croteau, 30-31.

[40]Ibid., chap. 7.

[41]Ibid., chap. 6.

[42]Ibid., 108.

[43]Ibid., 56.

[44]Nora Bateson to Ruth Menzies, FVRL, 3 July 1935. Public Archives and Records Office of Prince Edward Island, File RG 10, Provincial Library Administration Files 1933-1964, M-PEI.

[45]Nora Bateson to Peter A. Nearing, 23 January 1936, Library Administration Files.

[46]Nora Bateson to H.L. Stewart, 12 November 1934, Library Administration Files.

[47]Ibid.

[48]Ibid.

[49]Bramwell Chandler, interview with author, 29 August 1989, Cavendish, P.E.I. Tape recording.

[50]Ruth Goodall (nee Menzies), interview with author, 14 September 1989, Chilliwack, B.C. Tape recording.

[51]Books referred to in the first clause of page two of the Agreement for the Transfer of the assets of the Fraser Valley Public Library under the Carnegie Demonstration, Provincial Archives and Records Office of British Columbia, GR 1387, Box 3, H.N. Lidster Files, File 2, Carnegie Demonstration Reports.

[52]"Reference Books Bought." Public Archives and Records Office of Prince Edward Island, File RG 10, Provincial Library Administration Files 1933-1964, Prince Edward Island Libraries.

[53]Frederick Niven, "A Word from Canada," *Library Review* (Scotland) 37 (Spring 1936): 211-14.

[54]Bateson, 22.

[55]Helen G. Stewart to Herbert Killam, 28 March 1931. Provincial Archives and Records Office of British Columbia, Library Services Branch, GR 1387, Box 1, File Carnegie Demonstration correspondence 1931.

[56]Alexander Fraser Laidlaw, *The Campus and the Community: The Global Impact of the Antigonish Movement* (Montreal: Harvest House, 1961), 19.

[57]H.G. Stewart to F.P. Keppel, CCNY 5 February 1931, Carnegie Demonstration correspondence 1931.

[58]"Carnegie Demonstration of British Columbia. Progress Report, August 31, 1933."

[59]Nora Bateson to Everett Cahill, 14 March 1934. Public Archives and Records Office of Prince Edward Island, File RG 10, Provincial Library, Administration Files 1933-1964, Study Clubs. The section Projects for Group Work of an article by Lois C. Schuette, "Dividends from Leisure Hours," *Wilson Bulletin* 8 (January 1934): 267-73, is probably what was referred to.

[60]Nora Bateson to Angus Bernard, 15 March 1934, Administration Files 1933-1964.

[61]Nora Bateson to W.A. Paterson, 13 December 1933, Administration Files 1933-1964.

[62]Nora Bateson to W.A. Paterson, 18 January 1934.

[63]James D. Hart, *The Popular Book: A History of America's Literary Taste* (New York: Oxford University Press, 1950; reprint, Westport, Conn.: Greenwood Press, 1976), 249-50.

[64]Peter G. Filene, *Americans and the Soviet Experiment, 1917-1933* (Cambridge, Mass.: Harvard University Press, 1967), Appendix A. Number of Books on Russia by American Authors and Outstanding Soviet American Events, 1917-1933, 287.

[65]Douglas Waples, *People and Print: Social Aspects of Reading in the Depression* (Chicago: University of Chicago Press, 1938), 97, 105.

From: "Bringing Librarianship to Rural Canada in the 1930s: Demonstrations by Carnegie Corporation of New York" by Maxine K. Rochester in *Libraries & Culture* vol 30: 4 pp 366-390 By permission of the author and the University of Texas Press.

A Neglected Milestone:
Charles F. McCombs' Report
on Canadian Libraries, 1941

Charles R. Acland and William J. Buxton[1]

Abstract

Accounts of Canadian library history commonly identify two major surveys as having particular importance: the Ridington Report of 1933 and the Massey-Lévesque Royal Commission Report of 1951. More or less midway between these reports a third — largely unnoticed — major survey was undertaken. It was conducted for the Humanities Division of the Rockefeller Foundation by Charles Flowers McCombs of the New York Public Library. McCombs visited some 70 libraries and archives in Canada between June and October 1941, and he submitted his report in December of that year. Focusing on research collections, McCombs' survey included information about the nature and extent of holdings, the state of library facilities, leading figures in the library community, the use of microphotography, and the prospects for a national library. The article examines the background, themes and recommendations of the report; it concludes with an assessment of its significance for our understanding of Canadian library history.

Résumé

L'histoire des bibliothèques canadiennes souligne généralement deux études particulièrement importantes : le rapport Ridington en 1933 et le rapport de la Commission royale d'enquête Massey-Lévesque de 1951. Pourtant entre ces deux rapports, il y en eut un autre tout aussi important et qui passa pratiquement inaperçu. Cette enquête fut dirigée par Charles Flowers McCombs de la bibliothèque de New-York pour le compte de la *Humanities Division* de la Fondation Rockefeller. McCombs visita près de 70 bibliothèques et centres d'archives canadiens entre juin et octobre 1941 et soumit son rapport en décembre de la même année. Orienté surtout sur les collections de recherche, l'enquête de McCombs contient des renseignements sur la nature et l'importance des collections, l'état des lieux, les personnalités importantes dans le milieu, l'usage de la microphotographie et même des projets de bibliothèque nationale. L'article étudie le contexte, les thèmes et les recommandations du rapport et en conclusion, il souligne l'importance de ce rapport pour la compréhension de l'histoire des bibliothèques canadiennes.

It has largely been taken for granted that the contours of recent Canadian library history have been shaped by the publication of two major surveys. The first was *Libraries in Canada: A Study of Conditions and Needs,* which appeared in 1933.[2] Sponsored by the American Library Association with funds from the Carnegie Corporation, it was prepared by librarians Mary J.L. Black, George H. Locke, and John Ridington, the chair of the committee whose name has become associated with the report. The second was the Massey-Lévesque Royal Commission Report of 1951, which included a section on the state of Canadian libraries.[3] More or less midway between these two reports, a third major survey of Canadian libraries, whose appearance has largely gone unnoticed, was undertaken. It was conducted for the Humanities Division of the Rockefeller Foundation by Charles Flowers McCombs, superintendent of the reading room of the New York Public Library.[4]

McCombs made four separate trips to Canada between June and October 1941, and he spent about eight weeks in the country all told. Focusing primarily on research collections, he surveyed more than 70 libraries and archives. In addition to conducting personal interviews, McCombs read through a number of memos and university presidents' annual statements. His report was submitted in December 1941. It included information concerning the condition of library buildings, their funding, the prices of books, key librarians and central figures in Canadian library development, the state of the collections, and the prospects for microphotography. He described public libraries, public archives, and university and government libraries, with particular attention given to research materials.

It may seem odd that the Rockefeller Foundation would have sponsored a survey of this kind. Unlike the Carnegie Corporation, whose support for education and librarianship is longstanding, the Rockefeller philanthropies are better known for their contributions in other areas, such as medical research and public health. This lack of recognition is undoubtedly rooted in the general reluctance of Rockefeller philanthropy to call attention to itself as a donor. But it is also linked to its tendency to choose its areas of support on the basis of their relevance to its guiding principles, particularly that of "improving the welfare of mankind throughout the world."

The growing support of Rockefeller philanthropy for librarianship — of which the McCombs report was a part — was not based on an interest in the well-being of libraries *per se*. Support was given for certain aspects of librarianship because it was believed that reforms in specific areas represented progress towards Rockefeller's philanthropic goals. Consistent with its support for building the foundations of the social sciences in the 1920s, Rockefeller philanthropy was interested in libraries as repositories of knowledge and culture that could provide the basis for intelligent and well-informed human action.[5] In contrast to Carnegie philanthropy, it had little interest either in building public libraries or in developing collections for the general reader. It put its efforts into helping to consolidate stocks of knowledge that could be drawn upon by academic researchers, policy elites, and decision-makers. This support involved making collections more accessible through better cataloguing, increasing the amount of material available through microphotography, improving cooperation among research collections, and training personnel to become more effective research library administrators.

The Rockefeller Foundation's sponsorship of the McCombs report was consistent with these concerns. It was prompted by a request to the Humanities Division by Canadian librarians for assistance in the development of a body that could represent their interests. The response of John Marshall, associate director of the Humanities Division, was to propose a comprehensive survey of the situation of research libraries in Canada. To this end, the search began for a consultant to undertake the study. The standard practice was to select a Canadian-born academic who had relocated to the United States. For instance, Nova Scotia-educated Anne Bezanson was chosen to do a study of the social sciences,[6] and former University of Toronto historian J.B. Brebner was commissioned to write a report on graduate studies.[7] It was rare, however, for the foundation to appoint an individual with little Canadian background.

Marshall sought the advice of both K.D. Metcalf, Harvard College librarian, and H.M. Lydenberg, director of the New York Public Library — originally hoping that the latter would agree to take on the task. Both recommended Charles F. McCombs as the ideal person for the assignment. McCombs had no previous contact with the Rockefeller Foundation. He had been superintendent of the reading room at the New York Public Library since 1921 and prior to that had worked at the Library of Congress and at Ohio State University. McCombs, then, had broad experience in public, university, and national libraries and was well versed in the new technology of microphotography. Nevertheless, his experience with Canada had been limited to the preparation of an exhibit at the New York Public Library in 1935 to commemorate the 400th anniversary of Jacques Cartier's landing at the mouth of the St. Lawrence River. Like John Marshall, he was a both a francophile and fluent in French. Indeed, he had lectured at the American

Library School in Paris in 1926. Perhaps most importantly, Lydenberg was willing to release him "to undertake the study provided his salary during his absence can be cared for."[8]

A grant-in-aid for $2,700 to the New York Public Library was passed in late May 1941. It was to cover the nine months it was estimated it would take McCombs to complete his study. The first six months were expected to involve travel and research, during which time McCombs would visit libraries throughout Canada; the final three months would involve the completion of the report.

Topics for study were to include "effect of the war, library activities as an index of cultural growth both within and without the universities, the possibilities of national microfilm service, and the development of studies of American-Canadian tradition and relations."[9] Though he was primarily preparing this report for the Humanities Division, McCombs was to be open to the suggestions and interests of other divisions of the Rockefeller Foundation. Finally, though McCombs was not to conceal his sponsor, it was made clear that he was acting as an official of the New York Public Library.

In a letter to Lydenberg, Marshall spelled out the intentions of the survey. By focusing upon the larger libraries, the final report would help the Humanities Division "get a better acquaintance with the general cultural life of Canada in so far as libraries are indicative of that." Marshall used Lydenberg's own description, and he referred to libraries as the "laboratories" of the people in the humanities and "as such provide a certain index of their work." He additionally wanted attention paid to "indications of growth in the study of Canadian tradition, and more particularly of Canadian-American tradition." A related interest was "the possibilities of better national organization, particularly as they relate to the possibilities of better international exchange." To this end, an evaluation of the development of work in microphotography was important.[10]

McCombs' Assessment

McCombs did not pull any punches in composing his report. He recorded his impressions of chronic underfunding, cramped and inappropriate buildings, debilitating book taxes and tariffs, and low salaries for librarians. His assessments of particular institutions were often harsh. Concerning Montreal's public libraries, he wrote, "[t]here is no city in the United States or Canada that is doing less."[11] The library at the University of Saskatchewan was characterized as "hopelessly crowded — both as to shelving for books and seats for readers. It is not well organized and does not appear to be very efficiently run. The reason is not far to seek. The university has never had an experienced, full-time librarian."[12]

268

With a degree of disbelief, McCombs noted that Canadian university and college expenditures on books and periodicals for 1939 was $184,108, while Columbia University alone spent $144,818.[13] This, of course, was not for lack of interest on the part of Canadian librarians. McCombs, however, had favourable impressions of several individuals whom he met, including Arthur Maheux, Elizabeth Dafoe, W. Kaye Lamb, and C.R. Sanderson.

The single most pressing concern, McCombs felt, was the lack of national coordination of activity. Many, if not all, the librarians he encountered confirmed this opinion. For too long, efforts to organize libraries nationally had come to nothing. And the formation of some national association — one that would connect the existing provincial library associations — was necessary to the coherent articulation and representation of library interests in Canada.

The relative isolation of communities was a major stumbling block to Canadian library development. McCombs wrote, "[b]y far the greater part of Canada's research materials are concentrated in the relatively small triangle formed by Toronto, Ottawa, and Montreal. Halifax is more than twenty-four hours by train from Montreal; Edmonton over forty-eight hours from Toronto, and twenty-four hours from Vancouver. Distance, the cost of travel, and the relative poverty of Canadian libraries and universities have effectively prevented any but regional or provincial meetings of Canadian librarians for consultation and discussion of common problems."[14]

McCombs pointed to the importance of regional libraries, particularly in the West and in the Maritimes — like the Prince Edward Island Libraries — as well as the travelling library.[15] Here, the work of Nora Bateson, director of the Nova Scotia Regional Libraries Commission, was singled out. But he maintained that a system of national organization would facilitate contact and standardize procedures. This was crucial, for it would help to arrest what McCombs called "a sectionalism that is almost separatism."[16]

It is not surprising, then, that McCombs was extremely supportive of the Canadian efforts to establish a national library. This had been discussed since 1883, and efforts had been sparked again by the British Columbia Library Association's submission to the Royal Commission on Dominion-Provincial Relations (Rowell-Sirois) in 1938, entitled "A National Library for Canada."[17] Indeed, the fact that the Commission did not respond favourably to the recommendation further marked the need for a better voice for library concerns. The requests for help that resulted in the initiation of McCombs' survey soon followed. McCombs felt that the submission to the Rowell-Sirois Commission was important enough to include in his report.[18]

As McCombs argued, "[i]ndividual institutions of course have their immediate and pressing problems — inadequate appropriations, low salaries, rising costs of books, crowded buildings — but I still maintain, that, apart from aid given to particular libraries, nothing would be of greater benefit to Canadian libraries as a whole than the creation of some sort of central library."[19] Toward the end of the report, McCombs made very specific recommendations with respect to the formation of a national library, and how it should be run separately, but in tandem with, the Library of Parliament.[20]

Recommendations for Action

McCombs was rather modest about his report, claiming that his "conclusions are based on impressions."[21] He also felt that "[t]o judge Canadian libraries and their accomplishment solely by American standards, or from insufficient data, would be unjust."[22] McCombs found that the very act of preparing his report, the process of travelling to meet a variety of librarians and facilities, was itself a valuable enterprise. He wrote, "it was clear that my visits served a very useful purpose in affording librarians cut off from frequent professional contacts, an opportunity to talk shop, to discuss problems with a disinterested outsider who was there to learn, and not to criticize or instruct."[23]

The continuation of this process would be of immeasurable worth, particularly as a means to begin to construct ties between disparate libraries. For this reason, McCombs recommended that a "travelling fellowship" be awarded to the Canadian Library Council (CLC), an advisory board within the American Library Association. This funding would allow a prominent librarian to travel for a number of months, meeting informally and making contacts with all the libraries, either in a particular region or in the entire country.

The other general recommendation was in the area of training. Though the chief librarians were mostly men, the low salaries of other positions meant that "not many young men of ability are interested in preparing themselves for a career in which opportunities are so limited."[24] McCombs felt that scholarship development was essential to improve the qualifications of the librarian. It is unclear whether or not McCombs meant to imply, as he definitely does, that improving the status of librarianship meant attracting more men and fewer women to the occupation. But he certainly felt that the "volunteer" librarian would not help the development of the humanities. In his bid for professionalism and research expertise, he suggested, in particular, travel grants to selected individuals for "a period of study and observation in well organized American libraries."[25]

McCombs laid out more explicit recommendations, which were intended to be seen by the Humanities Division only, in the cover letter to the submission of his report. On December 1, 1941, he wrote to Marshall, "[h]ere at last is my report on Canadian libraries" which he hoped "will be helpful to the Foundation in considering any programme of aid for the benefit of Canadian research or for the promotion of cultural interests."[26] He provided a list of the most likely areas of potential support, including aid in establishing a national library, the development of microphotography, aid to the purchase of American books and periodicals, the production of summary guides to manuscript collections, and the production of indices of Canadian books and periodicals. But the most important area, one requiring immediate attention, according to McCombs, was the Canadian Library Council.

Significance of the McCombs Report

Arguably, the production of the McCombs report contributed to the chain of events that culminated in the formation of the Canadian Library Association (CLA) in 1946.[27] This body had metamorphosed out of the Canadian Library Council, whose founding in the fall of 1941 was made possible by Rockefeller Foundation support.[28]

That McCombs' report led to tangible support by the Rockefeller Foundation for Canadian librarianship was evident in a grant-in-aid approved in April 1942, "appropriated to the American Library Association for use of the Canadian Library Council in establishing microphotographic and general advisory services for Canadian libraries."[29] The grant was for a total of $17,500 over a three-year period. The majority of the funds (approximately $15,000) would go towards the purchase of microphotographic equipment and the copying of Canadian newspapers that had appeared before 1870, since "Canada now has no facilities for the use of microphotography as a means of exchange between libraries nationally or internationally."[30] The remainder of the grant would be spent by the CLC on a field visitor, who would "maintain contacts among Canadian libraries and with library activities in the United States."[31] At the time, this was seen as the beginning of a long-term financial commitment to the CLC, with the more distant goals of a national association and a national library always in mind.

While the plans for microphotography and a field visitor fell far short of their goals,[32] the establishment of a national library was a leading priority of the Canadian Library Association. Its first official submission to the Government of Canada was made in December 1946 and was discussed further with the Secretary of State on January 25, 1947. A number of other influential societies, including the Royal Society of Canada, the Canadian Historical Association, the Canadian Political Science Association, and the Social Science Research Council of Canada, also signed the brief. It would still take the Massey-Lévesque Royal Commission, and another few years, before the opening of the National Library of Canada on January 1, 1953.

Aside from the grant-in-aid to the CLC, McCombs' recommendations were reflected in subsequent Rockefeller Foundation support for a number of smaller initiatives related to the advancement of librarianship in Canada.[33]

There is some evidence, then, that the McCombs report was a catalyst in both the formation of a national library organization and the establishment of a national library. But, overall, the significance of the report is difficult to assess, for it is not evident that more than a handful of people read what McCombs had written. The implications of the document are to be found not in the report itself, but in the visits and discussions upon which it was based.

The very fact that Canadian librarians became the object of careful attention through McCombs' "mapping" of their interests, concerns and situations undoubtedly gave them a sense of community and common discourse that had previously been lacking.[34] His visit may very well have served as an impetus for Canadian librarians to overcome their isolation and to seek common cause. One can safely say, however, that the McCombs report fully deserves to join the ranks of the Ridington and Massey-Lévesque surveys as one of the major milestones in the history of Canadian libraries.

Notes

[1]The names of the authors appear in alphabetical order; both shared equally in the writing of this paper. William J. Buxton wishes to acknowledge the assistance of grants from the Social Sciences and Humanities Research Council of Canada and from the Rockefeller Archive Center for the preparation of his contribution to the manuscript. Material from the Archives of the New York Public Library (Astor, Lenox and Tilden Foundations) and from the Rockefeller Archive Center is published with permission.

[2]John Ridington, Mary J.L. Black, and George H. Locke, *Libraries in Canada: A Study of Conditions and Needs* (Chicago: American Library Association, 1933).

[3]Canada, Royal Commission on National Development in the Arts, Letters and Sciences, *Report* (Ottawa, 1951).

[4]Charles F. McCombs, Report on Canadian Libraries, 1941. RF. RG 1.1. Series 427. Box 26. Folder 258. Rockefeller Archive Center. The report (hereafter referred to as McCombs) will be published as an appendix to *American Philanthropy and Canadian Libraries: The Politics of Knowledge and Information* by William J. Buxton and Charles R. Acland (in press).

[5]Such concerns were evident in the gift of $490,000 from John D. Rockefeller, Jr., to the Library of Congress from 1927 to 1935. This support allowed the Library to undertake an extensive microfilming programme known simply as "Project A" through which it acquired over 3,000,000 document images (William Saffady, *Micrographics* (Littleton, Colo.: Libraries Unlimited, 1978), 14).

[6]Anne Bezanson, "Report on Social Sciences in Canada," RF. RG 2-1941. Series 427. Box 222. Folder 1548. Rockefeller Archive Center.

[7]J. Bartlet Brebner, *Scholarship for Canada: The Function of Graduate Studies* (Ottawa: Canadian Social Science Research Council, 1945).

[8]Grant-in-aid to Charles F. McCombs for Canadian libraries study, May 23, 1941, RF, RG 1.1, Series 427, Folder 256, Rockefeller Archive Center.

[9]Ibid.

[10]Marshall to Lydenberg, May 26, 1941, New York Public Library Archives, RG 6, Central Administration, Director's Office General Correspondence, 1934-1954, Box 54, Rockefeller Folder.

[11]McCombs, 65.

[12]McCombs, 15.

[13]McCombs, 38.

[14]McCombs, 4.

[15]McCombs, 65-66.

[16]McCombs, 3.

[17]For a more complete history, see F. Dolores Donnelly, *The National Library of Canada: A Historical Analysis of the Forces which Contributed to its Establishment and to the Identification of its Role and Responsibilities* (Ottawa: Canadian Library Association, 1973). See also Peter McNally, "Canada," in *Encyclopedia of Library History*, ed. W.A. Wiegand (New York: Garland, 1994), 101-4; and Peter McNally, "National Library of Canada. Ottawa," in *Encyclopedia of Library History*, ed. W.A. Wiegand (New York: Garland, 1994), 453-54.

[18]McCombs, 77-78.

[19]McCombs, 51.

[20]McCombs, 74.

[21]McCombs, 1.

[22]McCombs, 1

[23]McCombs, 79.

[24]McCombs, 81.

[25]McCombs, 81.

[26]McCombs to Marshall, December 1, 1941. RF. RG 1.1. Series 427, Box 26, Folder 257, Rockefeller Archive Center.

[27]F.F. Waldon of the Hamilton Public Library was the president and Elizabeth H. Morton served as executive secretary.

[28]The Humanities Division of the Rockefeller Foundation provided $900 to the American Library Association "to aid in the establishment of a Canadian library council." (Grant-in-aid, Canadian Library Council, October 9, 1941, RF, RG 1.1, Series 427, Box 26, Folder 251, Rockefeller Archive Center.) This covered travel expenses of council members incurred at the first meeting, which took place October 28-29, 1941, in Ottawa.

[29]Grant-in-aid, American Library Association - Canadian Library Council, May 1, 1942, RF, RG 1.1, Series 427, Box 26, Folder 252, Rockefeller Archive Center.

[30]Ibid.

[31]Ibid.

[32]The aftermath and implications of the McCombs report are discussed in more detail in William J. Buxton and Charles A. Acland, *American Philanthropy and Canadian Libraries*, cited above.

[33]For instance, in January 1945, Raymond Tanghe, the new librarian of the Université de Montréal, received a three-month grant-in-aid of $1,000 to observe "methods of library organization and administration and of book purchase in the United States." The plan was that the first month of his work would be with McCombs at the New York Public Library. (Grant-in-aid, University of Montreal, 23 January, 1945, RF, RG 1.1, Series 427, Box 26, Folder 252, Rockefeller Archive Center.)

[34]As Sanderson commented shortly after McCombs' visits, "the visits which Mr. McCombs made emphasized in all our minds the valuable results of such outside contacts." (Sanderson to Marshall, February 18, 1942, RF, 427R, Rockefeller Archive Center.)

Learning to Love the Computer:
Canadian Librarians and
New Technology, 1945-1965

Basil Stuart-Stubbs

Abstract

By 1965 a number of Canadian libraries were using computers for purposes of automation and information retrieval. Although the main developments involving computers and libraries took place in the United States, several Canadian librarians who were initially observers of these developments became active participants and the pioneers of the era of computers in Canadian libraries.

Résumé

En 1965, un certain nombre de bibliothèques canadiennes utilisaient déjà des ordinateurs à des fins d'automatisation ou de recherche d'information. Les principaux développements de l'informatique dans les bibliothèques eurent lieu aux États-Unis. Mais plusieurs bibliothécaires canadiens, qui observaient le phénomène, sont devenus des participants actifs et furent les pionniers de l'ère de l'informatique dans les bibliothèques canadiennes.

It's now a time-worn cliché to say that we live in the "computer age." It is difficult to think of a field that has not been significantly affected by the advent of this machine, from art to zoology, but few areas have been so significantly affected as that of information. Under the rubric of "information" must be included not just libraries as accumulators and dispensers of information, but all the creators and purveyors of recorded ideas, feelings and facts.

A question will arise in the mind of anyone contemplating the relationship between computers and libraries: just how did librarians learn to love the computer?

At the end of World War II computers were massive experimental contraptions, and their existence was not then a subject of common knowledge. Two decades later, their use in libraries, while still not yet commonplace, was spreading, and it was recognized generally that these machines were going to change the ways libraries did business. So this love affair must have been consummated in roughly a 20-year period, between 1945 and 1965.

This paper explores three questions. First, how was the technology of the computer transferred from the laboratory to the library? Given that the computer was designed primarily for purposes of scientific calculation, how was it adapted to the needs of librarians?

Second, by whom? Since few librarians were equipped by training or experience to deal with electronic technology, who was responsible for this transfer?

Third, how were Canadians involved in this process? The first computers were designed and constructed in the United States, and the first experimental applications to information handling took place there. How did Canadians become acquainted with these developments, and what did they do about them? Applications of the computer in Canadian libraries can be studied only in the context of events in the United States; technology does not respect national boundaries.

In the time period under consideration, who was interested in machines as they related to information? It is possible to identify two groups of individuals who approached machines, each with different objectives. One group can be termed "documentalists" and the other group "mechanists." There was some overlap between the two groups and eventually, somewhat after 1965, they tended to merge.

That there was a group called documentalists there was no doubt, because they defined themselves by that name and were attached to institutions that practised documentation and to national and international organizations that promoted the interests and dealt with the concerns of documentalists. What were their concerns, and how did these differ from the concerns of librarians?

In January 1950 the journal *American Documentation* commenced publication under the editorship of Vernon Tate, the librarian of the Massachusetts Institute of Technology. In his first editorial Tate stated that the journal was adopting the definition of documentation used by the International Federation of Documentation, and stated that it "... refers to the creation, transmission, collection, classification and use of 'documents'; documents may be broadly defined as recorded knowledge in any format."[1] He then listed some formats: voice script, directly recorded sound, photo-composing machines, magnesium plates, xerography, microfilm, microprint, microcards, facsimile processes, punched card machines, digital computers, electronic brains, rapid selectors and integrators.

Probably very few librarians in 1950 would have perceived all of this as falling under the ambit of librarianship, whereas today they would.

American Documentation was the journal of the American Documentation Institute, an organization that had been in existence since 1938. Leafing through issues of this journal and others in the same field published in the same time period, one sees that documentalists were concerned mainly with four kinds of problems.

First, problems of information retrieval. There was growing concern among scientists, partly arising out the experiences of the Second World War and partly out of the burgeoning literature, that conventional schemes for handling that information were inadequate. This was the subject of a major conference held in London in 1948 under the auspices of the Royal Society.[2]

Second, problems of classification and subject description. There was dissatisfaction with conventional classification schemes and lists of subject headings and a desire to develop more refined systems and to index documents in greater depth.

Third, problems of information storage. The increasing number of printed documents pointed to problems in information storage, already being experienced in many smaller technical libraries. Scientists being scientists, they could not resist projecting growth into the future and predicting that one day all the scientific journals in existence would weigh more than the Earth. So documentalists had a keen interest in methods of shrinking information, of which there were then two: miniaturization by print, as in microprint and microcard, and miniaturization by film, as in microfilm in a variety of formats. In both instances an optical device was needed for the purpose of reading, and there was a constant quest for equipment that would copy documents efficiently and display and reproduce them legibly.

Fourth, problems of information handling. Machinery to assist in dealing with numbers and statistics had been around since the turn of the century. As the story goes, in 1890 Dr. John Shaw Billings, director of the U.S. Surgeon General's Library, provided a Census Bureau employee, Herman Hollerith, with the idea that led to the creation of the first punched card and its allied equipment. Six years later Hollerith founded the company that was to become International Business Machines Incorporated, so the claim can be made that one can give credit to a librarian for indirectly founding IBM.

Punched cards in all their variations were popular with documentalists, and the literature of the 1950s abounds with descriptions of their use in various information-handling applications. Much attention was given to the development of coding systems to be used in association with improved thesauri of subjects and classification schemes. Cards and punched tape (developed later) were used to drive a variety of sorting and printing machines so as to produce accession lists, bibliographies and indexes.

Among librarians there were few documentalists but considerably more mechanists, a term derived from the subject heading in *Library Literature*, where one can find the relevant literature. That subject heading is "Library Mechanization."

Mechanists focused on problems of repetitive and routine work, of which there was an abundance in libraries, and their hope was that machines could perform this work more efficiently and accurately. These burdensome tasks could be found mainly in three areas of the library. First among these was the lending department where, as usage increased, more and more cards had to be sorted and filed by hand. On the other side of the counter, which in the days of closed library stacks was as far as many patrons ever got, users were expected to fill out call slips, and in one system in common use these two were filed, one under call number, the other under due date. Charging and discharging of borrowed items was carried out manually.

The catalogue card, it must be acknowledged, was a great invention, and card catalogues had and have many virtues: being large, they could be accessed by many people simultaneously; and if one could keep up with accessions, ideally they could be completely current. But making cards presented a major problem. All kinds of devices were tried, from addressograph plates to tape-driven typewriters called flexowriters. Years in the future one of the first uses of the computer was to generate catalogue cards, which, as has often been observed, was like using a pile driver to crack a walnut.

A third source of burdensome clerical work was created by periodicals. Even in the days when journals were not so numerous, checking in journals and claiming missing issues was a chore that most people wanted to avoid. In common use was Kardex equipment, banks of narrow drawers containing individual cards on which issues were recorded as they arrived. This arrangement also meant that the current record of unbound periodical holdings was kept in one location, and patrons had to inquire constantly about the availability of individual issues. Where branch libraries existed, duplicate manual records were often maintained, at considerable cost. Technology, the mechanists hoped, would eliminate or at least assist in the reduction of the amount of mind-numbing work and improve access to information about current holdings.

Librarians were not slow in using new machines: witness their early adoption of the typewriter and of various kinds of photocopying devices. If documentalists were interested in possible applications of punched cards and allied sorting machinery, so were library mechanists. But the equipment available to them, as they frequently complained, was not designed for library applications but for some other sector large enough to constitute a profitable market for manufacturers. Librarians therefore found themselves adapting equipment which had been designed primarily for Big Science, Big Government or Big Business. Sometimes this equipment could be successfully adapted to the needs of libraries, sometimes it could not, or could be used only with difficulty and partial success.

A simple example was the common and relatively inexpensive duplicating machine known as the mimeograph, now rendered obsolete by contemporary high-speed, low-cost photocopy machines. The mimeograph used a kind of flexible membrane backed up by a piece of paper; by typing on this membrane one produced a kind of template, which was then mounted on a drum. Ink was loaded onto an absorbent panel on the surface of the drum and was squeezed through the template onto paper, which was fed through the machine. The mimeograph was designed to print letter and legal size paper documents.

Libraries used the mimeograph to produce catalogue cards, but only with considerable effort and messiness. Attempts were made to produce a card at a time by masking off a 3 inch by 5 inch area on the drum, and other attempts were made to print cards six at a time. Since 3 by 5 into 8 1/2 by 11 doesn't go, this involved subsequent chopping and hole-punching. One manufacturer came out with a miniature mimeograph for cards, but it didn't work all that well. And this experience was not unusual for most so-called business machines.

Such was the state of affairs with respect to technology at the beginning of the 1950s. An account of the next 15 years would be long and complex, and worthy of a book, and can be dealt with here only in outline. The story remains to be told about all the events and all the people that contributed to the building of the foundation on which information technology rests today. Moreover, there is not just one story, but many stories, all taking place simultaneously.

First, there is the story of the computer itself, which developed rapidly throughout this period. Experimental prototypes built for specific clients were succeeded by versions manufactured in considerable numbers for public consumption, that is, for anyone who could afford to buy one. Second, there is the story of computer applications in the information sector. Third, there is the story of the people who were responsible for these pioneering applications. Fourth, there is the story of the institutions and organizations involved in these pioneering applications, in other words, the institutions and organizations that served as the vehicles for the work of creative people.

While four separate strands that together account for the early history of computers and libraries can be identified, of the four the most important, or at least the most interesting, is the story of the people. Ultimately, people are responsible for everything. Computers were created by people.

They do only what people tell them to do, except in science fiction. Institutions and organizations also don't do anything; people in them do things. Thus in this paper a few important figures have been identified as ones who made some significant contribution as innovators, creators, inventors, thinkers or educators. But they are only a selection.

The inventors of the computer did not set out to create a machine for handling information as we now define it, but to create a machine simply to compute better and faster than anything then in existence. Surely that is what IBM had in mind when its engineers collaborated with Howard Aiken of Harvard University to produce the Harvard Mark I. It has even been suggested that IBM thought that their involvement was nothing more than good public relations.[3]

The Harvard Mark I, also called the Automatic Sequence Controlled Calculator, like many of the machines of this era, was a monster: it was 51 feet long and 8 feet high, with two more 6-foot panels extending from the back. An electro-mechanical as opposed to electronic machine, it contained over 750,000 parts. It went into operation in January 1943 and was succeeded by the Mark II in 1947, the Mark III in 1949 and the Mark IV in 1952.

Not long after the Mark I was turned on, in March 1943, the U.S. Army negotiated with the Moore School of Electrical Engineering at the University of Pennsylvania for the construction of a computer, which commenced operation in the spring of 1945 under the name of ENIAC, which stands for Electronic Numerical Integrator and Calculator. It was the first electronic calculator, and it was better than as well as bigger than the Harvard Mark I: 100 feet long, 8 feet high, and 3 feet wide, and it weighed 30 tons.

Two of the individuals responsible for the creation of ENIAC, J. Presley Eckert and John Mauchly, left the University of Pennsylvania to establish the Electronic Control Company, which, under contract to the U.S. Bureau of Census, produced in 1952 a machine called UNIVAC, Universal Automatic Computer. Public awareness of the existence of the computer increased when the UNIVAC was used to predict the outcome of the U.S. presidential election. At 8:30 p.m. it predicted an unexpected landslide victory by Eisenhower over Stevenson. However, the sponsoring Columbia Broadcasting System (CBS) did not trust the results, so they were not aired until more results were in from the polls. The computer was right, the pundits wrong.

This cursory examination of the early history of computers will suffice to make the point that these huge and, in today's terms, cumbersome machines were initially thought of as super-calculators and not much more. In 1951 IBM decided that it would attempt to design a machine that would attract potential customers who shared the same kinds of needs for calculation, and this led to the production of the IBM701, the first commercially available programmable computer. In December 1952 IBM set up a working model in its New York office. By 1955 they had succeeded in installing 19 of these machines; of these, only 3 ended up in major corporations, and the rest went to customers in the U.S. military and government. By 1955 IBM had completed work on another computer, the IBM702, a machine designed not just for scientific calculation but for the manipulation of character-based, variable-length records. Half of the decade of the 1950s elapsed before a computer that had the potential for use in libraries appeared, and it was an expensive and scarce commodity.

Computers could be found in Canada too: the University of Toronto acquired a computer from Ferranti, a Manchester electronics manufacturer, in September 1952, and other universities across the country installed them as soon as they could afford them. The simple fact of the presence of computers at universities accounts in part for the later fact that early library applications of computers were initiated in university libraries, and that was true in Canada as well as in the United Sates and the United Kingdom. But the commercial development of computing machinery in this period was taking place beyond the borders of Canada. It is also important to remember that there were more players in the computer game than IBM, though IBM was a dominant presence in the market and its products tended to set the standard against which the machines of competitors were measured.

In these first years of the development of computers, only a few people were speculating about their possible application to library automation or information retrieval. Serious consideration of their potential came later in the decade, as computers and programming languages became better adapted to managing large files of alpha-numeric data.

What did documentalists and library mechanists think about computers in the mid-1950s? The answer appears to be "not much."

The attention of both documentalists and mechanists was fastened on the punched card in all shapes and sizes — punched in the middle, punched on the edges, sorted both manually and by machines large and small. Punched cards were used by documentalists to create what we would now call databases for purposes of information storage and retrieval. Library mechanists for their part were using them to charge out books and to create serials lists and book catalogues. Journals such as *Special Libraries* and *American Documentation* were replete with articles about individual applications, and entire books were devoted to the subject.[4]

If anything, there were misconceptions about computers, and a genuine fear of them and their implications among some librarians. In popular literature they were referred to as "thinking machines" and "electronic brains," and they were presumed to have the potential of depriving humans of volition and the control of events. In 1955 we find James E. Myers of the Burroughs Corporation saying to the Special Libraries Association convention in Detroit:

> The electronic digital computer field has done much, in my opinion, to contribute to the furor over automation. I do not believe there has ever been a field in which quite so many amateur publicists and practitioners plunged in with so resounding a splash — unless maybe it was in witchcraft and the psychology of sex.[5]

The essence of the speech from which this quote was taken is that computers do hold out the promise of taking over much of the routine work in organizations. But the tenor of the speech suggests that Mr. Myers, representing a computer manufacturer, was talking to an audience that needed to be reassured and convinced.

Even five years later, articles contained in the November 1960 issue of *Special Libraries* were aimed at acquainting librarians with the elements of computer operations. Here's a quotation from Herbert White, who appears to have been the editor for the issue:

> Periodicals have carried a large number of articles about information retrieval by librarians and non librarians (mostly the latter) on how information approaches must be modernized. Valid as many of these discussions are, they have caused a certain amount of resentment among many librarians, who feel that the field is being invaded by specialists with little appreciation for us, our concepts or the values we hold dear.[6]

Who were these invaders? Well, they were the sort of people who belonged to the American Documentation Institute (ADI), not the American Library Association (ALA). They were predominantly scholars and scientists, not librarians. The American Documentation Institute had been founded in 1938, and its membership was made up of representatives nominated by 66 learned and scientific societies, federal government departments, and a few library associations. Of the 66 members in 1951, only 7 are identifiable as librarians, but, of these, 4 played an important role in the future of computers and libraries.

Fred Kilgour, the medical librarian of Yale, represented the History of Science Society; later he founded the Ohio College Library Center, which became OCLC.[7] Mortimer Taube, representing the Special Libraries

Association, established the first information consulting firm, in 1952; his work on indexing theory served as a basis for contemporary computer searching strategies.[8] Frank Bradway Rogers, representing the U.S. Surgeon General, possessed rare qualifications: he was both a medical doctor and librarian and, as the director of the National Library of Medicine, was responsible for the development of MEDLARS, the first major online information retrieval system.[9] Ralph Shaw represented the U.S. Department of Agriculture. He was its librarian and, since he features prominently later in this tale, he deserves a longer introduction. For the sake of the historical record his name must be associated with that of Vannevar Bush.

For a person who wasn't a librarian, Vannevar Bush must have been in his day one of the most frequently cited authors in library literature. In the summer of 1945, readers of the *Atlantic Monthly* found a futuristic article by this distinguished professor from the Massachusetts Institute of Technology and president of the Carnegie Institution, bearing the title "As We May Think." In his article Bush describes the information problem as it was then encountered by scientists and suggests how technological devices then being designed might help to overcome this problem:

> Consider a future device for individual use, which is a sort of mechanized private file and library. It needs a name, and to coin one at random, "memex" will do. A memex is a device in which an individual stores all his books, records and communications, and which is mechanized so that it may be consulted with exceeding speed and flexibility .... It consists of a desk .... On the top are slanting translucent screens, on which material can be projected for convenient reading. There is a keyboard, and sets of buttons and levers .... In one end is the stored material ....[10]

As familiar as this description sounds, Bush was not visualizing a future microcomputer, but was instead thinking about a kind of microfilm reader, one in which the highly miniaturized images would be accompanied, frame by frame, by a coded index which could be read by light scanners as the film proceeded at high speed through a transport mechanism. And this was the machine he set out to build, calling it the Rapid Selector.

This device found an enthusiastic advocate in Ralph Shaw, who had a well-deserved reputation as an imaginative adapter of current technology to library operations, having experimented with punched card equipment and photography in his earlier assignments at the Engineering Societies Library and the Gary Public Library.[11] Shaw continued to promote the use of the Rapid Selector throughout the decade, in speech after speech and article

after article. Shaw's library became a Mecca for anyone interested in applying machines to knowledge. But there was a problem: the equipment was
not reliable. At least two Canadian librarians found that the Rapid Selector
was broken when they visited the Department of Agriculture Library to see
it. As Joseph Becker and Robert M. Hayes were to point out later, the purely mechanical problems of the Rapid Selector should not be allowed to
obscure the fact that the objectives and operating principles of the machine
were sound.[12]

If the American Documentation Institute was one organization that
served as a vehicle for communication and cooperation among pioneers in
library automation and information retrieval, it was not alone. It is possible
to categorize the types of organizations to which such people were drawn
and in which they participated during the years before 1965.

First, there were the manufacturers of computers. Many long-time
manufacturers of business machines ventured into computer production,
with varying degrees of success. But IBM ascended to a dominant position
in the market-place, and part of their success must be attributed to the
work of their research division. There, in the 1940s and 1950s worked an
important innovator in information retrieval, Hans Pieter Luhn, a German
engineer.[13] In 1940 he developed for IBM a punched card system for
recording and sorting chemical compounds, and he invented a machine to
scan the cards. In the 1950s he devised a method for what he called
"auto-abstracting," extracting essential text from a document. He invented
Key-Word-in-Context indexing, the "KWIC" index, and he invented the
technique we know by its initials SDI, the Selective Dissemination of
Information. Eugene Garfield, who founded the Institute for Scientific
Information in 1961 and who created citation indexes, is much in Luhn's
debt.[14]

Situated where he was, Luhn was in a position to experiment with
whatever new products IBM was developing, and many of his written
contributions appeared in the company's own publications. The impact of
his work on the functioning of libraries was profound, yet it is probable that
most librarians had never heard of Hans Luhn during his lifetime, which
ended in 1964, only a year after he had edited the papers presented at the
26th meeting of the American Documentation Institute. The title of this
publication is "Automation and Scientific Communication," and it has the
distinction of being the first publication to be produced by computerized
typesetting.[15]

Later, as librarians began to experiment with computer applications,
they turned routinely to the manufacturers for assistance. We will never
know the names of the many technical staff members who helped librarians
to bend the computer to their will, but they were important in forging the

link. Second, complementary to the computer manufacturers were the consulting firms, some small, one-person organizations, some large and employing specialists in information technology. Consultants, many of whom lacked training and experience in librarianship, were often in the forefront of innovations in computer applications generally, and they brought to libraries expertise gained in other sectors.

The following individuals stand out in the historical record: Lawrence Buckland of Inforonics, who in 1964 wrote the study that served as a prelude to the development of the MARC format[16]; Gilbert King of Itek Corporation, formerly director of research at IBM, who prepared the 1963 feasibility study on the automation of the Library of Congress[17]; Joseph Becker and Robert M. Hayes of Advanced Information Systems, Inc. who, in addition to their involvement in many key projects, wrote the first practical textbook on information storage and retrieval, published in 1963.[18]

Third, there were the foundations, agencies and government departments that provided the funding — and in some cases the impetus — for initiating projects in library automation and retrieval. Foremost among these was the Council on Library Resources, founded in September 1956 with a grant from the Ford Foundation "for the purpose of aiding in the solutions of the problems of libraries generally, and of research libraries in particular." In the period 1945-1965 the activities of the Council were directed by the brilliant and energetic Verner Clapp.

Clapp had spent all of his working life in the Library of Congress and had risen to the position of Chief Assistant Librarian when he was invited to become the first president of the Council on Library Resources. In his new role Clapp was a catalyst for many developments in library automation and information retrieval. It has never been easy for libraries or librarians to find money with which to conduct research, and the Council on Library Resources proved to be an important resource for those who wished to experiment with technology. Among those that received grants were libraries large and small, corporations, universities and individuals. Where Clapp thought something needed to be done, he would contract a consultant to do it.[19]

Fourth, there were the minority of library schools and faculty that elected to be at the forefront of intellectual and experimental development in the field of computers and information and began to train a generation of librarians who could deal with the new technology in an institutional setting. At that time, even up to and into the 1970s, there was an acute shortage of personnel familiar with systems. In these early years of automation, librarians working with computers were largely self-taught.

Among the pioneering schools were the University of Illinois, which commenced a series of clinics on library applications of data processing beginning in 1963, and Drexel University and the University of Chicago, which started offering courses in information retrieval early in the 1960s. In 1963 the University of Chicago set a precedent by appointing as the director of its library school a scientist rather than a librarian, Don Swanson. But in advance of all of these was Western Reserve University in Cleveland, Ohio, under the directorship of the creative thinker and writer Jesse Shera; there he established in the spring of 1955 the Center for Documentation and Communication. Its first director and associate director were James W. Perry and Allen Kent, respectively, both recruited from the Battelle Memorial Institute.[20]

Fifth, there were the libraries that decided to take the plunge into a new era and, at considerable risk and expense, implemented pioneering systems, some of which evolved into systems still in use today. At the national level in the U.S. one thinks of the work of Frank Bradway Rogers, already mentioned, in automating *Index Medicus* and establishing MEDLARS early in the 1960s. The Library of Congress (LC), in the view of some, was slow off the mark (no pun intended) but, spurred on by the Buckland and King reports, the urging of the Council on Library Resources and the library community, the Library of Congress established the MARC Office under the direction of Henriette Avram, who served as LC's creative intellect and spokesperson in the area of computer technology until her retirement in 1992.

At the local level, several universities started to introduce computer-based systems early in the 1960s: these were essentially "mechanist" systems dealing with circulation, serials control, and cataloguing. It is important to remember that these ventures took place at a time when there were virtually no ground rules, precedents or standards. These were not always major universities. Indeed, a review of the proceedings of the Association of Research Libraries (ARL) reveals that its agenda reflected little interest in computers, and it was not until July 1963 that ARL established an automation committee. However, there were important developments taking place at Yale University under Fred Kilgour; at Washington University in St. Louis under Estelle Brodman and Irwin Pizer[21]; and at new universities, such as Florida Atlantic under Ed Heiliger and the University of California at San Diego under Melvin Voigt.

Why did some universities experiment when others did not? Although it would take more investigation to prove it, it appears that the pioneering systems were developed at those universities where the director was sympathetic to if not keenly interested in the prospects offered by computerization; where there were staff members who either shared this enthusiasm or conveyed it to the university librarian; where the university administration was receptive to experimentation with computers and willing to risk money on it; where there was a computer, of course; and where those responsible for the computer were interested in collaborating with the library in the development of software, because obviously there were no off-the-shelf packages in those days.

Sixth among the agencies that served individuals in ushering in the age of computerized information were the associations, which through their publications and meetings supported the continuing education of librarians. Most librarians were struggling to come to terms with something they didn't fully understand and, given that most of them had undergraduate and graduate degrees in the humanities, perhaps were not well equipped to understand. It is significant that the majority of the individuals identified as pioneers so far in this paper possessed a background in the sciences. Garfield, Kilgour, Kent, Perry and Voigt all had degrees in chemistry. Hayes and Avram were mathematicians. Buckland was a mechanical engineer, Becker's first degree was in aeronautics, Pizer was a biologist. It was through reading and through attending conferences that librarians who were neophytes became familiar with the work of such individuals.

The way in which meetings contributed to the dissemination of information during this period could be the subject of another study. In his excellent article in volume 6 of *Library and Information Science Research*, Alvin Schrader lists 21 meetings pertinent to information science that took place between 1948 and 1965.[22] Add to that the other meetings dealing with library automation, and yet other meetings where information science and library automation formed a part of the agenda, and one can see the importance of these events as a means of transmission of information.

Yet librarians working in this new, exciting and exotic realm had no place to go, no home of their own, in terms of an organization. Only the largest university libraries were members of the Association of Research Libraries, and in any case only the directors attended those meetings. There was no section in the American Library Association for those interested in the computer. So a "non-organization" was established by Howard Dillon of Ohio State University, a kind of club, to which he gave the name the Committee on Library Automation (COLA). At its largest, COLA had no more than 40 members, and that would have comprised the entire library automation establishment in the U.S., by which I mean the people who were actually doing something and not merely talking about it. The committee used to meet during the American Library Association and the American Documentation Institute conferences, but full attendance could never be expected. After the American Library Association got around to forming the Information Science and Automation Division, in 1967, COLA faded away.

Seventh, and finally, expositions served as another means by which a relationship between libraries and computers was established. Exhibits mounted by computer manufacturers were a regular feature of the displays at major conferences, which were visited by thousands of librarians. But there were other expositions that introduced not just librarians but the general public to the notion of a connection between computers and information, most notably two major displays called Library 21 and Library/USA.

To suggest to the public just where libraries might be headed in the age of the computer, the American Library Association, cooperating with equipment manufacturers and supported by the Council on Library Resources, conceived of the idea of an exhibit at the Seattle World's Fair. It is probably more accurate to say that Joseph Becker conceived of the idea and sold the Council and ALA on it. An advisory committee was established, including such individuals as Ralph Shaw, a long-time proponent of library mechanization, and Robert M. Hayes, who became responsible for training the staff for the exhibit. The display was opened to the public on April 21, 1962, and closed on October 21 of the same year. The reference, of course, was to the 21st century.[23]

Library 21 occupied 9,000 square feet. Its centrepiece was a UNIVAC computer in which was stored information drawn from biographical directories, gazetteers and books of quotations. That is, it contained a database of limited size and of a specific type; therefore, it could answer only some kinds of questions, within the broad areas of international relations, current affairs in the U.S., history, the arts, space science, and mental health. This computer proved to be a crowd pleaser, but it didn't satisfy many librarians, who were quick to observe that they could provide information just as quickly and probably better from a current encyclopedia. But these were on hand too: a quick reference collection was included in the exhibit, as were a children's collection and displays of microfilm readers, closed-circuit television and sundry other toys of the time. To staff the exhibit, ALA recruited librarians from all the states and one each from Mexico, the Federal Republic of Germany, and Canada. They were rotated on a monthly basis and were trained at the University of Washington library school by Hayes.

While this event was in progress, Hayes was invited to talk to a meeting of the Pacific Northwest Library Association, which met in August 1962 on the campus of the University of British Columbia. There he delivered a paper with the title "The Meaning of Automation to the Library Profession." This speech was probably the first exposure many Canadian librarians had had to this subject, and Hayes' remarks met with some expressions of concern from the audience. Hayes is recorded as having responded to these comments by saying that "... if librarians feel that automation is an 'invasion' of the profession perhaps there is something lacking in its image."[24] It is fair to say that at this time there was indeed concern among librarians that the computer would somehow dehumanize library service and would soak up and divert money simply because computers had more appeal to administrators than conventional library services. It was certainly the case that many administrators looked upon automation with the hope not so much that it might improve service but that it would lower the costs of library operations.

The American Library Association considered Library 21 so successful that before the exhibit closed ALA was already planning to mount something bigger and better at the forthcoming New York World's Fair. This event was held in two consecutive years, in the period from April to September, 1964 and 1965. The display (entitled Library/USA), this time sponsored by ALA, the Special Libraries Association and the American Documentation Institute, also featured a UNIVAC, but a later model, the 490 Real-Time System. It was loaded with short essays in each of 76 subject areas — again, a limited database, but bigger. In Joe Becker's words,

> The use of the computer system at Library/USA demonstrates to the public how machine storage and retrieval of information may in time supplement conventional library reference service.... ALA's Library/USA is the first public demonstration of a real-time computer, with random access memory, performing non-numerical work in a library context and the first professional demonstration of how information may be communicated over future library and information networks.[25]

Hundreds of thousands of people visited these exhibits, and undoubtedly these exhibits had the effect of connecting in the public mind the library and the computer. Most librarians were somewhat less dazzled. In Toronto in 1965, Don Swanson had this to say: "My general comment on this kind of exhibit is that perhaps it fires the imagination, but sheds very little light on the real problems of answering reference questions."[26]

Up to this point I have omitted any reference to Canadians and to activities in Canada because, as I stated at the outset, Canadian participation in these developments can be understood only against the background of developments in the United States. As is often the case in developments relating to technology, Canadians lack the resources to participate on a grand scale. Was this true in the case of library automation and information retrieval?

It was even more true in the 1950s than it is today that Canadian librarians looked to the south for leadership: if things were going to happen, it was thought, surely they would happen first in the United States. Generally speaking, this attitude was valid, so Canadian librarians were regular consumers of library literature from the U.S., and less so from the U.K. or elsewhere. It was probably the case, in the first decade of the existence of the Canadian Library Association (CLA), that almost as many or perhaps more Canadians belonged to the American Library Association as belonged to their own national association. Since Canadian librarians could and did belong to library organizations such as ALA and the Special Libraries Association, which had their headquarters in the U.S., these individuals had the same opportunity as their American counterparts to find out about library developments reported in the literature. Furthermore, Canadians could and did attend conferences of these associations. Canadians were thus able to hear about developments in automation and information retrieval insofar as these topics were included in the conference programs. And there were the conference displays, where one could find demonstrations and literature pertaining to the products of manufacturers such as IBM.

However, there was a problem. The mainline library associations, whether national, like ALA, or regional, like the Pacific Northwest Library Association, were not where the action was in these early years. A considerable gulf existed between librarians, whether in the mechanist camp or not, and documentalists. Serious experimentation involving computers and information retrieval was taking place in the ranks of the membership of the American Documentation Institute. Until 1952 membership in the ADI was on the basis of organizational affiliation; 66 organizations with a supposed interest in documentation were members and therefore 66 was the number of its members. When the constitution and by-laws were changed to open up membership to anyone who wished to pay a fee, membership grew.

The membership list for 1961 was published in the October issue of *American Documentation* for that year. Of the 879 members only 5 were Canadians, and of those 5, 3 were librarians: the librarian of the Defence Research Board, the librarian of Canadian National Railways in Montreal, and a librarian in the Serials Division at Université Laval. Of course, one could subscribe to the journal, but, of 2,905 subscribers, just 54 had addresses in Canada. Even as late as 1965, when ADI convened a symposium on education for information science, no Canadians were invited. Suffice it to say that in the 1950s and early 1960s interest in the work of the documentalists appears to have been slight within the Canadian library community.

If Canadians were not to be found at meetings of the American Documentation Institute, there were also other important meetings which they did not attend, and these were the early invitational meetings organized by the Library of Congress, the Council on Library Resources, and other agencies in the U.S. For example, no Canadians were present at the Conference on Libraries and Automation convened at the Airlie Foundation at Warrenton, Virginia, in May 1963, sponsored by the Library of Congress, the Council on Library Resources, and the National Science Foundation. The proceedings of this important meeting became a virtual textbook for anyone interested in library automation at that time.[27]

On this side of the border our own literature during the 1950s does not reflect great interest in library automation and information retrieval, or even much awareness of what was happening during this period. Only mild curiosity about these topics is reflected in that decade's issues of the *Canadian Library Journal, Feliciter*, the *A.C.B.L.F. Bulletin*, or *Ontario Libraries*. If one were among the limited number of Canadians attempting to stay abreast of developments in the U.S. in the area of library technology during the 1950s and early 1960s, one had to take the initiative oneself, seek out the literature, read it, pay visits to people, and attempt to crash the gate.

What evidence do we have of Canadian interest? In 1955 the Canadian Library Association distributed a questionnaire to its members on the topic "Promoting Library Service." Responses to the questionnaire are quoted selectively in the first issues of *Feliciter*, starting in January 1956. A few individuals thought that library mechanization had a role to play in promoting library service, and mentioned it. Here are some direct quotations:

Mrs. J.W. Falkner, Toronto Public Library Board: "The desirability of the use of library machines seems obvious. In our library we explored the I.B.M. method which has by far the most advantages of mechanical charging but it also has some drawbacks."[28]

Bernard Ower, Dominion Bureau of Statistics: "The more machines and mechanisms to handle routine work the better."[29]

Mary Donaldson, Saskatchewan Provincial Library: "Simplification of work processes and the use of library machines are important. Could we have a display and a real discussion of some of the machines?"[30]

Louise Lefebvre, Pulp & Paper Research Institute, Montreal: "Very much interested in the use of machines, if they can take care of tedious, lengthy mechanical work, of which it seems that there are unlimited amounts."[31]

Feliciter also reported in March 1956 that CLA's Research Section was holding a meeting on March 2nd to discuss documentation in relation to the training of librarians: "The discussion is to be purely informal round-table. Both Miss Bassam and Miss Ross are attending as well as Ottawa members. This discussion is preparatory to Niagara Falls and will consider the Niagara Falls agenda."[32] At that meeting the Research Section referred the matter of documentation in relation to the training of librarians to the Library Education Committee, then chaired by Samuel Rothstein.

In 1957 the Canadian Library Association annual conference was held in Victoria. At one point, the conference broke up into discussion groups, one of which, under the chairmanship of Morton Coburn of the Edmonton Public Library, grappled with the question, "How do we promote books and libraries in an age of automation?" A good deal of time was spent attempting to define automation, but it was concluded that whatever it was, it "would and does create a use of library resources .... The group bemoaned the lack of personnel capable of dealing with automation." It was becoming apparent that something was happening, and no one was sure how to come to terms with it.[33]

In the fall of 1957 CLA had an important announcement to make: in response to the request from the Research Committee, the Library Education Committee had proposed a special seminar on documentation, and one was being organized for January 21-22, 1958, to be held at McGill University under the sponsorship of its library school, CLA, and a score of other associations and corporations. The steering committee consisted of Douglas Lochhead, librarian of Dalhousie University; Vernon Ross and Virginia Murray, the director of the McGill school and its professor of cataloguing, respectively; three librarians from the National Research Council (NRC) Library, Jack Brown, Edna Hunt and Robert Kennedy; Lachlan MacRae of the Defence Research Board; and Harry Campbell of the Toronto Public Library. They had landed a big fish: the seminar was to be directed by none other than Ralph Shaw, the guru of scientific management in libraries and the foremost expert on the application of machines to information retrieval and library routines, thus both a documentalist and a mechanist.

As a warm-up to this event, *Feliciter* reprinted a number of articles by Shaw, one by Herbert Coblans, the head of the Scientific Information Service, European Organization for Nuclear Research, in Geneva, and one by Barbara Kyle from Social Sciences Documentation in London. There had been nothing quite like these articles in Canadian library literature before this time. However, readers were in for a disappointment, or for confirmation of their suspicions, depending on what their perspective on automation happened to be. Here are some passages from Shaw's "Machines and the Bibliographical Problems of the Twentieth Century":

... it appears exceedingly improbable that machines will replace bibliographers or even catalogers .... the more recently developed machines indicate, that if enough human wisdom is applied, they may possibly, in time — a long time — present means by which the ideas available in recorded form may economically be brought to bear when and as needed."[34]

Shaw spoke disparagingly of "... those who admit inability to bring these titles into the record but hopefully look toward the machine — to be built by someone else, always — which will solve all of these problems with a minimum of effort or discomfort on their part. And it is this group which has led us into the folds of gadgetry."[35] A final quote: "If and when we master the problem of handling information by completely electronic means (assuming that the end is worth what it will cost to do so) the fastest of the present day devices — either built or building — will be obsolete."[36]

If that didn't establish Shaw as a conservative, the next reprint from a successor to the previous paper, appearing in *Feliciter* just before the main event, did. From Shaw's "Management, Machines and the Bibliographic Problems of the Twentieth Century": "Machines now available or in sight can not answer a quick reference question either as fast or as economically as will consultation of standard reference works such as dictionaries, encyclopaedias or almanacs ...."[37] To be fair to Shaw, the first part of his statement was true: machines then available could not answer quick reference questions, but they would be able to much sooner than he thought.

Meanwhile, the Executive Secretary of the Canadian Library Association, Elizabeth Homer Morton, was concerned. By the end of December, only 20 paying registrants had materialized. But things must have turned around rapidly, for she was able to write to Shaw early in January that there would be at least 120 people present. When the day of the event arrived, there were over 200 people in attendance.

The proceedings of this event constitute one of the most important and interesting documents in the recent history of Canadian librarianship. It consists of a transcript of Shaw's remarks, the statements made by panelists, and questions and responses from the audience, so one gains an insight into what librarians, and especially the leading librarians in Canada in that day, had on their minds. Did they expect Shaw to promote the principles and methods of the documentalists, or to come out strongly in favour of machine applications? If so, they were in for a shock. Shaw virtually assaulted the work of the documentalists, and he didn't hold out much hope that machinery was going to improve the functioning of libraries. Here is a taste of Shaw's message:

Documentation deals with documents — you know, government stuff in soft covers, mostly done on quick copying machines. Frankly, if you have to make a career out of the fact that something doesn't have hard covers on it and comes in small packages, you can have it.

This documentation is a field in which we have a lot of words, and it is very hard to dig out the substance.

… I have examined probably as many as 75 or 90 installations using punched cards for information searching, and I have yet to see the first one that we couldn't beat by hand in terms of speed and cost.[38]

At the end of two days, listeners who were so inclined could have walked away from the meeting with the feeling that documentation and machinery was something they could safely ignore, though from time to time Shaw did concede that there were some basic applications of machinery that were cost-effective. A closing panel of Canadian librarians revealed that, like it or not, machine techniques were being successfully employed at a number of special and government libraries. However, Shaw's overall message must have got through powerfully, for he was a compelling speaker, and his message was this: you're doing fine, librarians, so don't get swept away with promises made to you by those who promote the use of machines, including the manufacturers.

Later that year, in November 1958, a follow-up conference to the Royal Society conference of 1948 was held in Washington. Fourteen Canadians attended the International Conference on Scientific Information, among them Jack Brown of the National Research Council, who reported to *Feliciter* that "… mathematicians, linguistic experts and computer designers had a field day."[39] Regardless of Shaw's views, the world was moving on.

It would not be the last time, however, that McGill University or the Canadian Library Association invited an expert from the United States to speak to Canadian librarians. On December 8, 1958, McGill offered anyone who could pay the fee of one dollar an opportunity to hear Dr. Mortimer Taube on the "Implications of Documentation for Librarians." In June 1965 the Canadian Library Association invited Don Swanson of the University of Chicago to speak at its conference in Toronto. His talk, and the discussion that followed, may be found in CLA Occasional Paper no. 61. Curiously, he sounds a bit like Shaw:

… the application or function is yet to be conceived which cannot be performed by conventional techniques as well as by mechanical techniques.

... I contend that the decision whether to use computing machines ... is entirely one of economics.[40]

This was sound advice but if everyone had cleaved to that dictum, experimentation would have come to a halt. Another quote:

There are some, myself included, who have described computer consoles, that is, keyboards and displays attached to large computer centres. We have imagined the user striking keys on the console and receiving information on the display .... It would be far too expensive to put a keyboard and a cathode ray tube display device in the home and at the desk of every conceivable library user.[41]

Among the questioners was the librarian at Dalhousie University, John Wilkinson, who wanted to know what the role of librarians would be in a fully automated library. Swanson's reply has been proven correct in the intervening years: "The loftiest role of the librarian is that of planning future library information services... in other words, planning jobs for machines to do.... the profession will stand to be upgraded by the introduction of automation because it forces this distinction [between professional and clerical work]."[42]

It would be difficult even after the passage of just 30 years to draw up a list of all the practical applications in Canadian libraries of technology to information retrieval or routine work. To do so would require an examination of files of annual reports of individual libraries or access to their archives. Canadian librarians did not tend to advertise in print their use of machines such as flexowriters and punched card sorters, technology that predated the computer. Only a few applications were described in the literature. In 1954 Edgar Robinson went into print with a description of the Vancouver Public Library photocharging system; he said it didn't work very well.[43] In the proceedings of the McGill Documentation Seminar are references to what some librarians were doing, and, in particular, Rodolphe Lavergne of Canadair provided a survey of activities in Montreal special libraries.

For the period 1960-1965 about the only single source of information is CLA's Occasional Paper no. 48, published in June 1965, and incorporating some of the papers delivered at a joint meeting of the Research Section and the Canadian Association of College and University Libraries at the Halifax conference of 1964. The preface frankly states, "This collection does not describe all the library mechanization projects in Canada at the present time. Indeed, even the slightly deaf ear of the overworked librarian can hear rumours of many more."[44] The impression one gains from examining the available evidence is that Canadian librarians, though not included (with one very notable exception) in the mainstream of developments in the U.S. before 1965, were as quick as anyone in the world to make practical use of new techniques and equipment as they became available. The few early ventures described below are notable because they were early, innovative and successful for their time, a time when there were no standards, no existing software, no equipment capable of dealing with massive files or printing in upper and lower case, and no agreement on coding for machine-readable bibliographical files.

At the National Research Council Library, Jack Brown, Peter Wolters and their colleagues had been keeping a watching brief of the work of documentalists since the 1950s. Late in the decade they decided to attempt to create a listing of serials using punched card equipment, one of the main objectives being to achieve the ability to update the listing with less effort and cost. The first list was printed (in capitals only) in 1963, and the experience acquired during this enterprise served as the basis for the preparation of the second edition of the *Union List of Scientific Serials in Canadian Libraries*, which was the first national union list to be produced on a computer. Jack Brown was also familiar with the work of Hans Pieter Luhn at IBM, and in 1966 Brown implemented an SDI system for NRC scientists similar to the one described by Luhn in his landmark work of 1959, *Selective Dissemination of New Scientific Information with the Aid of Electronic Processing Equipment*.[45] This system grew into CAN/SDI, which was the first national service of its kind in the world. Brown was the first Canadian to deliver a paper at the University of Illinois Clinic on Library Applications of Data Processing, at the second of those meetings, held in 1964.[46]

Second, Université Laval must be recognized as the institution which, in the first years of the 1960s, was involved in a greater variety of applications than any other library in the country. In 1962, acting on the recommendations of a report written by Edwin Williams of Harvard University and Paul-Emile Filion,[47] Université Laval established a centre for documentation and placed it in the charge of Guy Forget. In short order Forget created an authority file of subject headings with cross references, in French. He developed the first successfully operating serials check-in system in Canada at a time when the only systems one ever heard about were in the United States. The system generated annual and weekly lists, subject lists, lists by location, and a list of subscriptions by date of renewal. To cap it off, Laval was also engaged in massive indexing projects: the *Index Analytique*, which indexed 60 French-language periodicals published in Quebec; an index to the newspaper *Le Devoir*; and a listing of 20,000 theses presented to universities in France. These projects were accomplished with programs written at Laval, some of which contained features unavailable elsewhere at that time.[48]

Third, but by no means least, the University of Toronto embarked on a project of staggering dimensions in 1963 when it became responsible for the Ontario New Universities Library Project (ONULP), the objective of which was to create from scratch catalogued collections for five new universities, Brock University, the University of Guelph, Trent University, and Scarborough campus and Erindale College at the University of Toronto. Robert Blackburn, the university librarian, had always kept abreast of developments in the technology of librarianship, and he was receptive to a plan put forward by the head of the Cataloguing Division, Ritvars Bregzis. His proposal was to use only machine-readable records and to create book catalogues with a computer.[49]

At this time there were few other libraries and individuals experimenting with this approach to cataloguing: one such experiment was at the Yale Medical Library, conducted by Fred Kilgour, of OCLC fame; the other was at Florida Atlantic University. This was in 1963 and the King Report on the Library of Congress was just being written. Few people in Canada if any had a clearer notion than did Bregzis of just what the implications of the computer would be for future systems of bibliographic control. But visionary though he was, he probably did not know that he was laying the foundation for UTLAS, any more than Fred Kilgour knew that he was starting up a global enterprise when he moved to Columbus, Ohio, to help a group of colleges solve their cataloguing problems collectively.

In 1964 Bregzis published in *College & Research Libraries* an article that deserves the overworked adjective of seminal.[50] It is called "Some Prerequisites to Cooperative Cataloging" and it is only four pages long. It contains no references or footnotes, for the reason that it is a work of complete originality. According to Robert Blackburn,[51] Verner Clapp was able to use this article to persuade the Library of Congress to get on with the task of devising a standard format for recording bibliographical records (it appeared before the Buckland report and was more succinct). Almost two years later, in February 1966, when the Library of Congress was ready to mount its MARC pilot project, the University of Toronto was one of 16 libraries, and the only Canadian library, to be invited to participate. And no wonder: one year before, in February 1965, the ONULP Project produced its first book catalogues.

By the mid-1960s applications of the computer to library needs, some successful, some unsuccessful, were to be found at institutions scattered across North America. In March 1966 the first conference on computers in Canadian libraries was convened at Université Laval; representatives of every Canadian library known to be developing or to have developed computer-based systems attended. In addition to the implementations at the National Research Council, Université Laval and the University of Toronto, delegates heard descriptions of an acquisitions system at Simon Fraser University; serials listing systems at the University of Waterloo, Dalhousie University, the University of British Columbia and Simon Fraser University (but only at Laval did the system automatically update and revise holdings); and a circulation system at the University of British Columbia. Other universities represented at the meeting had various systems in the planning stage.[52]

The horse was out of the gate, as the saying goes. Librarians had learned to love the computer and, though the relationship has had its uncertain moments, it is solid today. The intervening years have witnessed, among other developments, the provision of bibliographical records in machine-readable form by national libraries; the transfer of catalogue cards from paper to computer-output microfiche to the computer screen itself; the invention of denser and more compact forms of storage; increasingly sophisticated software for information handling; the growth of networks and bibliographic utilities; and the advent of more powerful yet smaller and less expensive computers.

A quarter century beyond the end of the experimental period described in this paper, the situation imagined by Vannevar Bush and portrayed at the Seattle and New York world's fairs has become a reality. The microcomputer, far more powerful than the huge machines of the 1940s and 1950s, is now in the hands of a new species of library patron known as the end user, who sits comfortably at home dialling up catalogues, bibliographical and full-text databases, images both static and moving, taking it all for granted.

Notes

[1]Vernon Tate, "Editorial," *American Documentation* 1 (1950): 3-5.

[2]Royal Society, "Reports and Papers Submitted," in *Royal Society Scientific Information Conference, 21 June - 2 July, 1948, in London* (London: Royal Society, 1948).

[3]Michael R. Williams, *A History of Computing Technology* (Englewood Cliffs, N.J.: Prentice-Hall, 1985).

[4]R.S. Casey, J.W. Perry, Allen Kent, and M.M. Berry, eds., *Punched Cards*, 2d ed. (New York: Reinhold, 1958).

[5]James E. Myers, "Automation: What It Is, What It Is Not," *Special Libraries* 46 (September 1955): 308-13.

[6]Hebert S. White, "Applications of Machines to Library Techniques," *Special Libraries* 51 (November 1960): 492.

[7]David Kaser, "Kilgour, Frederick G. (1914-   )," in *ALA World Encyclopedia of Library and Information Services*, ed. Robert Wedgeworth, 2d ed. (Chicago: American Library Association, 1986), 420.

[8]Herbert S. White, "Taube, Mortimer (1910-1965)," in *ALA World Enclyclopedia of Library and Information Services*, ed. Robert Wedgeworth, 2d ed. (Chicago: American Library Association, 1986), 797-800.

[9]Estelle Brodman, "Rogers, Frank Bradway (1914-   )," in *ALA World Encyclopedia of Library and Information Services*, ed. Robert Wedgeworth, 2d ed. (Chicago: American Library Association, 1986), 710-711.

[10]Vannevar Bush, "As We May Think," *Atlantic Monthly* 76 (August 1945): 101-8.

[11]Mary V. Gaver, "Shaw, Ralph (1907-1972)," in *ALA Word Encyclopedia of Library and Information Services*, ed. Robert Wedgeworth, 2d ed. (Chicago: American Library Association, 1986), 760-62.

[12]Joseph Becker and Robert M. Hayes, *Information Storage and Retrieval; Tools, Elements, Theories* (New York: John Wiley, 1963).

[13]John F. Harvey, "Hans Pieter Luhn (1896-1964)," in *Dictionary of American Library Biography*, ed. Bohdan S. Wynar (Littleton, Colo.: Libraries Unlimited, 1978), 324-26.

[14]Belver Griffith, "Garfield, Eugene (1925-   )," in *ALA World Encyclopedia of Library and Information Services*, ed. Robert Wedgeworth, 2d ed. (Chicago: American Library Association, 1986), 298-99.

[15]"Automation and Scientific Communication; Short Papers," in *American Documentation Institute Annual Meeting in Chicago*, ed. Hans Pieter Luhn (Chicago: American Documentation Institute, 1963).

[16]Lawrence F. Buckland, *The Recording of Library Congress Bibliographical Data in Machine Readable Form: A Report Prepared for the Council on Library Resources* (Washington: Council on Library Resources, 1965).

[17]Gilbert King, *Automation and the Library of Congress* (Washington: Library of Congress, 1963).

[18]Becker and Hayes.

[19]Foster E. Mohrhardt, "Verner Warren Clapp (1901-1972)," in *Dictionary of American Library Biography*, ed. Bohdan S. Wynar (Littleton, Colo.: Libraries Unlimited, 1978), 77-81.

[20]Howard W. Winger, "Jesse Hauk Shera (1903-1982)," in *Supplement to the Dictionary of American Library Biography*, ed. Wayne A. Wiegand (Englewood, Colo.: Libraries Unlimited, 1990), 119-23.

[21]Irwin Pizer, "Looking Backward, 1984-1959," *Medical Library Association Bulletin* 72 (October 1984): 335-48.

[22]Alvin Schrader, "In Search of a Name: Information Science and its Conceptual Antecedents," *Library and Information Science Research* 6 (July 1984): 227-71.

[23]American Library Association, *The Library and Information Networks of the Future* (Chicago: American Library Association, 1963).

[24]Robert M. Hayes, "The Meaning of Automation to the Library Profession," *PNLA Quarterly* 27 (October 1962): 7-34.

[25]Joseph Becker, "Demonstrating Remote Retrieval by Computer at Library/USA," *A.L.A. Bulletin* 58 (October 1964): 822-24.

[26]Don Swanson, *Library Service with or without Automation*, Occasional Paper no. 61 (Ottawa: Canadian Library Association, 1965).

[27]Library of Congress, National Science Foundation, and Council on Library Resources, "Libraries and Automation," in *Conference on Libraries and Automation at the Airlie Foundation, Warrenton, Virginia,* ed. Barbara Evans Markuson (Washington: Library of Congress, 1963), 268.

[28]"Promoting Library Service," *Feliciter* 1, no. 1 (January 1956): 8.

[29]Ibid.

[30]"Promoting Library Service," *Feliciter* 1, no. 2 (March 1956): 17.

[31]Ibid.

[32]Ibid.

[33]"Workshop on Promoting Books and Libraries in an Age of Automation," *Feliciter* 2 (July 1957): 3.

[34]Ralph Shaw, "Machines and the Bibliographic Problem of the Twentieth Century," in *Bibliography in an Age of Science,* ed. Louis N. Ridenour (Urbana, Ill.: University of Illinois Press, 1951), 37-71.

[35]Ibid.

[36]Ibid.

[37]Ralph R. Shaw, "Management, Machines and the Bibliographic Problems of the Twentieth Century," in *Bibliographic Organization,* ed. Jesse Shera and Margaret Egan (Chicago: University of Chicago Press, 1951).

[38]Canadian Library Association, "Proceedings of the Documentation Seminar 'New Methods and Techniques for the Communication of Knowledge'," in *Documentation Seminar at McGill University* (Ottawa, Ont.: Canadian Library Association, 1958), 76.

[39]Jack E. Brown, "International Conference on Scientific Information," *Feliciter* 4 (5 January 1959): 31-33.

[40]Swanson.

[41]Ibid.

[42]Ibid.

[43]Edgar S. Robinson, "The Technique of Photocharging," *Canadian Library Association Bulletin* 10 (February 1954): 165-68.

[44]Canadian Library Association, *Library Automation Projects; a Collection of Papers by Canadian Librarians,* Occasional Paper no. 48 (Ottawa: Canadian Library Association, 1965).

[45]Hans P. Luhn, *Selective Dissemination of New Scientific Information with the Aid of Electronic Processing Equipment* (Yorkton Heights, N.Y.: IBM Advanced Systems Development Division, 1959).

[46]Jack E. Brown, "Applications of Data Processing at the Canadian National Research Council Library," in *University of Illinois Graduate School of Library Science 1964 Clinic on Library Applications of Data Processing in Champaign, Illinois* (Urbana, Ill.: Illinois Union Bookstore, 1964), 105-11.

[47]Edwin E. Williams and Paul-Emile Filion, *Rapport d'une enquête sur la bibliothèque de l'Université Laval* (Québec: Université Laval, 1962).

[48]Guy Forget, "The University Library and Information Center: a New Dimension," in *University of Illinois Graduate School of Library Science 1968 Clinic on Library Applications of Data Processing in Urbana, Illinois,* ed. Dewey E. Carroll (Urbana, Ill.: University of Illinois Graduate School of Library Science, 1968), 1-10.

[49]Ritvars Bregzis, "The ONULP Bibliographic Control System: An Evaluation," in *University of Illinois Graduate School of Library Science 1965 Clinic on Library Applications of Data Processing in Champaign, Illinois* (Urbana, Ill.: Illinois Union Bookstore, 1964), 112-40; and "The Ontario New Universities Library Project — An Automated Bibliographic Data Control System," *College & Research Libraries* 26 (November 1965): 495-508.

[50]Ritvars Bregzis, "Some Prerequisites to Cooperative Cataloging," *College & Research Libraries* 25 (November 1964): 497-500.

[51]Robert H. Blackburn, *Evolution of the Heart; a History of the University of Toronto Library up to 1981* (Toronto: University of Toronto Library, 1989).

[52]Canadian Association of College and University Libraries, "Report," in *Conference on Computers in Canadian Libraries, Université Laval,* ed. Basil Stuart-Stubbs (Vancouver, B.C.: University of British Columbia Library, 1966), 13.

5 Biography

John Ross Robertson and the
Toronto Public Library, 1885-1929

Darrel R. Reid

Abstract

One of the strongest interests of John Ross Robertson, philanthropist and publisher of the *Toronto Evening Telegram*, was the collection of pictorial Canadiana. From as early as 1885 he began to see the Toronto Public Library as a worthy beneficiary of his collecting efforts. As the volume of these donations, grew, however, the library board began to realize the cost of Robertson's munificence: he expected them to build a worthy repository for his collection. This, despite the steadily growing size of the John Ross Robertson Collection, the political manoeuvring of Robertson, and the repeated pleas of successive chief librarians, did not occur until the collection had reached such a size that its existence threatened to undermine completely the library's service to the public.

Résumé

John Ross Robertson, philanthrope et éditeur du *Toronto Evening Telegram* s'intéressait tout particulièrement aux illustrations Canadiana. Dès 1885, il décida que la Bibliothèque publique de Toronto deviendrait l'heureuse bénéficiaire de ses collections. Avec la croissance de ses généreux dons, les administrateurs de la bibliothèque commencèrent à comprendre le coût réel des largesses de Robertson. Il voulait faire construire un sanctuaire pour sa collection. Pourtant, en dépit de la croissance constante de la collection de John Ross Robertson, de ses manoeuvres politiques et des suppliques successives des bibliothécaires en chef, son désir ne se concrétisa que lorsque la croissance de la collection mit en péril les services publics de la bibliothèque.

John Ross Robertson, Philanthropist

Any endeavour to which John Ross Robertson (1841-1918) chose to dedicate his energetic support, it seems, was destined to flourish — even if the fiery Toronto newspaperman had to drag it towards success himself.

Robertson was a hard-driving entrepreneur who had learned what hard work, money and motivation could accomplish, and he had very little inclination to suffer fools who got in the way. Upon his death, his paper, the *Toronto Evening Telegram*, paid him a high compliment: "No man, woman or child ever got the worst of it with J. Ross Robertson trying to give that man, woman or child the best of it."[1]

In the late nineteenth century Robertson had guided his paper to success in the Toronto market by espousing a fiercely independent political line at a time when that was unheard of and by showering loving editorials and features upon the Toronto area. He had achieved his reputation and wealth by speaking his mind forcefully and letting the chips fall where they may. And there was no shortage of chips. Thus Robertson, a Tory by conviction, managed first to alienate, then infuriate, a succession of Canadian Conservative and Liberal prime ministers through his determined stands against the monopolistic power of the Hudson's Bay Company in the West, French rights, and government sponsorship of the railways. His readers, however, loved him.

Robertson took all his other interests — and he had many — as seriously as he did his work. Chief among these were philanthropic endeavours, specifically his involvement with Toronto's Hospital for Sick Children. In light of his generous care for that institution, he has been characterized, rightly, as the one "who shaped its course more than any other man."[2] His generosity, however, had a price: in return for his benevolence he insisted upon — and usually received — complete freedom to run things in the same dictatorial manner in which he ran his paper. The long-time chairman of the board and president of the Hospital for Sick Children played no favourites, treating successive board members, medical staff, and administrators alike as unceremoniously as he did his own employees. As he did with the *Telegram*, he would allow no one to interfere with his efficient running of the place.

John Ross Robertson was a man of contradictions: he could be generous and when he was convinced of a need his generosity seemingly knew no bounds. Yet, as a hard-driving entrepreneur, he got his way too often to be remembered simply as a genial old philanthropist. He derived great pleasure from giving money away, yet proved equally able to quibble over pennies when it suited his purpose.

One of Robertson's main personal interests, even passions, was Canadian history and the collection of material that documented and illustrated the early days of the country. He attracted much public attention through a series of articles on local history which he regularly ran in the *Telegram*; these eventually grew into a six-volume series, *Robertson's Landmarks of Canada*, which provided a detailed pictorial record of the histories of Toronto and Upper Canada from 1792 to 1914.

The materials he collected for the series formed the nucleus of the John Ross Robertson Historical Collection of the Toronto Public Library. And through his development of this collection, two of Robertson's greatest interests — his philanthropy and his love of Canadian history — converged. Between 1885 and 1918, accordingly, the Toronto Public Library became the focus of Robertson's attention.

Robertson, His Collection, and the Toronto Public Library

Robertson had long shown an interest in the Toronto Public Library, seeing it as a logical and desirable resting place for any historical materials with which he might wish to part. Following his first recorded gift of some early Upper Canadian newspapers in 1885,[3] he became a regular patron of the library. Indeed, by 1896 his patronage was significant enough to merit the attention of the library board, which expressed its "special thanks… to J. Ross Robertson, Esq. for his interesting and valuable donation of manuscript letters and documents relating to and forming a portion of the early part of this Province."[4] Robertson's gifts continued unabated into the first decade of the twentieth century; a list of his donations to the Toronto Public Library from 1904 to 1912 records 21 bound and 122 unbound items.[5] In addition, Robertson allowed materials from his private collection to be publicly displayed at the library.[6]

These were not merely random offerings by the newspaperman, however, for John Ross Robertson had a plan. According to a 1910 letter from Robertson to the board, these donations were the result of conversations between him and James Bain, chief librarian at Toronto from 1883 to 1908, almost since the latter's assumption of that post. Robertson claimed that in these talks the two men (and Bain, recently deceased, could not gainsay it) had worked out an arrangement of benefit to both. For its part the Library would provide "a room for an historical exhibit of Canadian pictures covering the period from about 1758 to the present time…."[7] From Robertson was to come the big prize that Bain must have patiently sought those 25 years and which few library boards could have resisted: "Eventually all my Canadian collection, in portfolios, embracing about 20,000 pictures, all relating to Toronto and Canada, will come to the Public Library …."[8] This plan of action had apparently been set aside until a new building could be constructed to house his donations properly.

Robertson waited nearly a quarter of a century, but by 1910 his chief condition had been met, at least theoretically. The year before, a beautiful new reference library had opened at College and St. George streets. In order to prod the board into immediate action, he took the initiative of offering "about one hundred pictures, all framed, as a beginning of what should be a good collection…."[9]

He laid down conditions to ensure that the library made room for his donations. The pictures, he stipulated, were to be exhibited in rooms satisfactory to him, properly cared for, insured and catalogued. Most importantly, they were neither to be lent to anyone for any reason nor to be removed from the library building on College Street. To the library board, this latter condition must have seemed rather inconsequential at the time, especially in light of what they hoped would follow: Robertson's priceless collection of Canadiana. If any of the board members had concerns that Robertson's generosity might eventually create space problems at the new building, they did not register them. The board did not have to debate the offering long. The next day it passed a resolution accepting Robertson's gift and thanking him for his "generous offer and the splendid public spirit which prompted it...."[10] His conditions, they assured him, would be faithfully adhered to.

Community response to the news of Robertson's offer was quick and positive. The *Toronto Globe*, otherwise a bitter editorial foe of Robertson's *Telegram*, praised the gift enthusiastically on May 11, 1910, calling it "a matter of very great interest, not only to the people of Toronto, but to the people of Canada. The historical value of the collection can hardly be calculated, even at the present time, and with the passing years it will be tremendously enhanced."[11]

Why did he make such a generous offer? Robertson expressed a concern for Torontonians and maintained that a good historical collection would enhance their awareness of their heritage — a long and glorious tradition of loyalty to the Crown. Such a collection as he envisaged would "Be appreciated not only by the older generation of Torontonians, but by the descendants of the pioneers of this Dominion who fought for the flag from 1758, and later, when in 1812-15 the ancestors of many who are to the fore today shouldered the musket and did their duty."[12]

In addition, there was the requisite amount of Toronto boosterism, second nature to the Toronto entrepreneur who had made his fortune in this energetic and expanding city. It was important to Robertson that Toronto take its place among the great cities of Great Britain and the United States which "all have historical exhibits of this kind, and there is no reason Toronto should not in a few years have a collection that will compare favourably with other collections of similar character."[13]

Finally, Robertson's concern for the preservation of Canadian history cannot be discounted. He saw in this task a particular urgency, in that no one else had undertaken to do it; this work, he wrote, "must begin at once if the material out of which the history of Upper Canada in general and Toronto in particular is made is to be rescued from oblivion."[14]

It was only with the gifts of succeeding years that the library staff must have come to realize the full extent both of Robertson's generosity and of the implications of his requirement that the material not be moved from the College St. building. At first there had been no problem. By 1911, room had been made for the pictures already given. Even then, however, the board reported monthly additions to the collection and recommended the purchase of a series of movable screens to accommodate the overflow.[15] By the time of the collection's public opening on January 29, 1912, it already numbered 588 pictures.

Then, it seems, Robertson's giving began in earnest: in 1912, the Library received 400 more pictures. By the end of 1913, the collection numbered 1,900 works. Both the building and its staff were further constrained by the fact of the collection's immense popularity, and provision had to be made for the large numbers of people who came to view the works: 26,890 in 1912 and a staggering 36,000 the following year.[16] Still, at this point there is no evidence either from the board minutes or from the annual report that those responsible for administering the library were anything but thrilled with the now rapidly expanding collection. In 1913, for example, Chief Librarian Locke reported that the Historical Collection "is the largest public collection of its kind in Canada, and constitutes a comprehensive pictorial history of the development of the Dominion."[17]

Because of the wide public interest shown in the collection, the library found itself with a great opportunity to teach its patrons something about Canada's past. According to Locke, one of the collection's principal virtues was that, in addition to the historical education of adults, the library was able to enhance the popularity of its "National Story Hours" for children through illustrations from the collection:

> During these weekly offerings the stories of the pioneers were told by librarians to groups of fifty children at a time in the presence of the portraits of the early explorers, pioneers and statesmen, and where the scenes of their early lives and exploits are portrayed in picture form. It has at once become a great educational factor which we may use to develop in the boys and girls of Canada an interest in the history of their country, and foster in them a pride in its pioneers ....[18]

In 1914, as well, the gratitude of the library board was very much in evidence. Nearly 400 pictures were added to the Historical Collection and, from the public pronouncements of the chief librarian, at least, it was apparent that everyone was most pleased with the progress of the acquisitions. And, indeed, it would have been difficult to complain in the face of Robertson's munificence. In addition to his donations, he initiated at his own expense projects which increased the collection's educational and functional value. Reports in 1914 suggested, for example, that Robertson was enhancing the Military Collection by "having painted a representation of a captain and a private, in full uniform of the time, of every regiment which has served in Canada."[19]

By the end of 1915, however, the relationship between the John Ross Robertson Historical Collection and the Toronto Public Library had reached a turning point. Robertson's donations kept flowing in apace — 500 pieces during that year alone — but by then the staff and administration were growing increasingly alarmed at the space the collection was eating up at the College St. branch. Its 2,872 pieces were threatening to overwhelm the Children's Department, the Reading Room and the Circulation Department. This growth led Locke to report to the board that:

> There is no more room .... We are facing a serious problem in the great growth of this Collection .... We thought the gallery was almost filled a year ago, but now it is crowded, much too crowded in fairness to the pictures, and is practically closed. It is a pity to have this great work halted on account of lack of space.[20]

As a remedy to this situation, Locke suggested building a two-storey extension to the library north on St. George St. This addition, he suggested, could accommodate the Robertson Collection on the upper floor, and the Children's Room, Circulating Library and Reading Room on the lower one. His report to the board received full and, on the whole, approving coverage from Toronto papers, with Robertson's *Telegram*, the *Mail and Empire*, and the *Globe* devoting at least a full column each to the chief librarian's proposals.

By this time Robertson had abandoned himself completely to his collecting instincts. Indeed, he had adopted the practice of sending his latest acquisitions directly from his buying agents to the library. He pursued his quarry, suggests his biographer, "with the acquisitive eagerness of a questing crow."[21] He regularly made buying trips to Great Britain and the United States that lasted as long as three weeks at a time. European booksellers were alerted to the arrival of the man, and museum curators knew him by sight. For Robertson, gathering materials for his collection had all the thrill of the chase: "'You have to hunt for these pictures.... I have, as the small boy would say in Hide and Seek, been hot and cold in my hunt for pictures.' He followed the trail of some of them 'month after month and year after year, like a detective.'"[22] Robertson was clearly well suited to such a pastime, and his efforts brought remarkable successes, including his purchase of 213 superb ornithological paintings by the English artist William Pope. He was all the more proud of his find when he was informed that buyers in Boston were prepared to pay three or four times what he had paid for the works.

Yet, in the midst of his collecting frenzy, Robertson was becoming less satisfied with the manner in which his collection was being housed. In a letter to Locke dated March 13, 1916, Robertson revealed anxiety about the state of the collection and reasserted his long-expressed desire to have proper facilities built for it. To this end, he was not above dropping a hint or two to the chief librarian. Expressing his belief that the Royal Ontario Museum would dearly love to buy the Pope Collection, he wrote, "but I am resolved that whatever I give in the picture line of either Canadian pictures including these birds and game shall go to the library in the idea that some day perhaps after I am deade [sic] and gone, the Trustees may erect a new building, an addition to the present one ...."[23]

For his part, George Locke was completely convinced of the need for the new addition and, together with the chairman of the board, had opened a campaign to convince the board that added space was needed as soon as possible. The results were neither impressive nor immediately forthcoming. Such inactivity must have been foreign to Robertson's nature, for on May 12, 1916, he and his allies in the cause tried a frontal approach to the board. Robertson took the highly irregular step of attending a board meeting to lobby for new premises himself, although ostensibly he attended in order to release to the library his invaluable collection of maps and plans of the town of York from 1792 to 1834 and of Toronto from 1834 to 1916, as well as an additional 100 maps of the American continent and of Canada showing territories under all the treaties from 1713 to 1896.

Announcing to the board that this collection could now be transferred to the library, he addressed what must have been the major reason for his personal appearance. The collection, he said, now numbered 3,329 pictures, and more room was needed with better lighting. He also expressed hope that some day a room at least twice the size of the present gallery would be provided for displaying the collection. The board accepted the gift and agreed to abide by the conditions Robertson had set down earlier for the care of the materials. These conditions did not expressly include the construction of a new room, however, and there is no evidence that the board was prepared to authorize one.

That year, 1916, saw numerous attempts to move the collection into a more congenial environment. Because of Robertson's initial conditions, however, these efforts could not include the movement of any pieces of the collection outside the College St. building. Chief Librarian Locke's frustration with this increasingly unworkable situation and with the failure of his efforts to alleviate it are evident in his report for the year 1916. The collection, he said, "has completely filled the Historical Room, and the collection of Canadian prints must now cease. The matter was brought to the attention of the Board in my report of last year as a possibility which needed to be considered. It is no longer a theory; it is now a condition to be faced."[24] He recommended exactly the same solution he had the year before, but again with no result.

Meanwhile, of course, Robertson did not stop collecting Canadian prints. He continued the quest for materials upon two continents, and there was seemingly no limit to the effort he was prepared to expend upon his collection, short of financing a new addition to the library himself. Between 1915 and 1917 he conceived, financed, edited, had printed, and distributed a complete catalogue for the collection. Just to put the first draft into typed form, he noted, had cost $2,000 and the efforts of two secretaries for a year. He foresaw a total cost per volume of $5, but did not expect to make any money on the production. He had the first 500 copies printed and sold at $2 per volume.

This was clearly a labour of love, and Robertson entertained little hope for the catalogue's commercial success: "I don't suppose," he wrote to Locke, "that in the entire Dominion there are 500 people interested enough in Canadian history to buy such a volume."[25] Nevertheless, he considered it worth the effort: "As it [the Collection] is, however, the second, if not the first and best collection of its kind in the world, I think it deserves the best I can do for it because it will be there long after I am gone and for that matter as long as time lasts."[26] There was little disagreement among any of the parties involved as to the value of the collection — only as to how it should best be cared for and at whose expense.

For its part, the board, it seems, had its own solution in mind: that Robertson provide new quarters himself. And in case Robertson had missed their line of thinking, Norman B. Gash, chairman of the library's Board of Management, made it plain. During a ceremony in which Robertson presented the Pope Collection to the library in 1917, Gash suggested, none too delicately, "Perhaps Mr. Robertson may be gracious enough to present us in a few years an art gallery designed to display to advantage such pictures as these ...."[27] If board members cherished visions of palatial new premises for the collection falling from Robertson's gracious hand, however, they would be greatly disappointed.

That same year, seemingly out of exasperation with the intransigence of the board, Robertson set out on his own to provide some more space for his collection. He sought two estimates from the Pedlar People of Ottawa, dealers in sheet metal buildings, for a crude metal structure to house the overflow. Robertson's inquiry had been made without the knowledge of either the board or the chief librarian, and the latter was clearly shocked to find such a proposal on his desk, complete with quotations from the hopeful contractor. His response to Robertson was quick and definite: "On taking the matter up we find that it is impossible for us to put up such a building in the public park at the rear of our Library. It would be an eyesore to the community, and the Board would not allow of it."[28]

His further assurances to the newspaperman were tinged with frustration at the tight spot he must have found himself in with the board, and would have been slight consolation to Robertson: "I shall have to take care of the matter in some other way, and as I told you, it will be arranged all right when the time comes. If you will give me a fortnight's warning I shall see to it that things are put into shape."[29] Whatever Locke might have meant by "when the time comes," there was no addition immediately forthcoming.

The library board, despite its unwillingness to move on the repeated requests of either Robertson or Locke, recognized the loss of a great benefactor in the passing of John Ross Robertson on May 31, 1918. Although deadlock had lasted for nearly three years over the collection, there was no disagreement about either its worth to the public library or the generosity of the man who had gone to such efforts to develop it. In a letter of condolence to Robertson's widow, the board acknowledged itself "deeply indebted to him for the magnificent collection known as the John Ross Robertson collection..." and observed that "the citizens of Toronto have... lost a public spirited citizen, and the Public Library a true friend."[30]

Robertson's death also ended what must have been a special relationship between Chief Librarian Locke and the newspaperman, one from which both patron and recipient must, despite the occasional misunderstanding, have derived satisfaction. This is evident in Locke's touching eulogy: "I feel a real loss today," he writes, "when I think that the most frequent visitor to my office will not again appear in that unheralded, enthusiastic manner, which could hardly wait a moment in the eagerness to tell me of a new discovery he had made in regard to some person who had to do with the early life of our country."[31] And of Robertson's role in establishing the collection, Locke wrote:

> The historical collection is one of his undying monuments, not a static, but a dynamic monument, which will give pleasure and patriotic profit to hundreds of thousands of coming Canadians, many of whom will doubtless echo the saying of the bare legged boy of ten years, who, after wandering among the pictures with his companions was heard to say: "Wasn't it awfully decent of John Ross to do all this for us?"[32]

Yet, even more through his death than in life, Robertson, it seemed, was determined that his collection should be cared for under better conditions at the College St. Library. And the conditions of his will, sworn on February 6, 1918, seemed designed to force the board, through the sheer number of pieces added to the collection if nothing else, to acquiesce to his long-expressed desire for it. The main stipulation was that relevant material "be deposited and kept in a room in the Chief Public Library building in College Street, to become their property and not to be removed therefrom...."[33]

The list of Robertson's accessions was staggering. It included all his engravings illustrative of Canadian life, men, subjects, or history (framed or unframed) and all his extra volumes related to Canada, Canadian history, the Town of York, Toronto, and Governor and Mrs. Simcoe; all manuscripts written and typed relating to Canadian history; 13 volumes of Simcoe's papers and correspondence and 11 volumes of the personal correspondence of Simcoe and his wife; and his 1,000-volume Masonic library. As if to emphasize his desire that his collection be properly cared for, Robertson included the explicit warning that "anyone taking any step to set aside or alter this will or any portion thereof ... shall forfeit all benefits hereunder."[34]

Curiously, despite the pressure that this flood of new arrivals at the public library undoubtedly must have created, a sort of truce emerged after Robertson's death between library management and the board, for no mention of the overcrowded conditions was made in the reports of the chairman of the board or of the chief librarian for either 1918 or 1919. There are two possible reasons for the temporary truce: either the proponents of the new addition judged that it would be in bad taste to follow Robertson's death by crass appeals for money — although Robertson himself would probably have approved this course of action — or they judged that nothing was likely to be accomplished and let the matter rest.

The former was probably the case. In 1920 Locke renewed his assault upon the previously unyielding board in order to gain new accommodations for the Historical Collection. His address reveals both his rising frustration at the board's inactivity and his concern about the effect the huge collection was having upon the rest of the services at the public library. Using a favourite tactic, Locke read successive quotes from his addresses to the board of 1916 and 1917. Noting that the collection was already crowding out the Children's Services and Circulation departments, he observed, "I desire to bring the matter again before the board, as it is likely the part devoted to the Reading Room in the College Branch, now ridiculously small, will be still further curtailed and perhaps abolished before the end of the year ...."[35]

Clearly, by this time the Historical Collection was beginning to pose problems that even the board could not overlook. Besides the threat it posed to the other departments in the College St. branch, it was beginning seriously to affect the level of service that the library was able to provide to the public. Furthermore, because of the collection's cramped viewing conditions and poor lighting, public interest was declining rapidly: the number of visitors, as high as 36,000 in 1913, had shrunk in 1919 to 4,000, and further declines were forecast.

The following year Chief Librarian Locke found an important new ally in W.T.J. Lee, incoming chairman of the board, who had no patience for the subtle diplomacy of the Chief Librarian on behalf of the new addition. Lee was a savvy political operator and reached for whatever levers he felt might be necessary to propel the unmovable board into action on this matter. His address to the board for 1921 was a stinging assault which worked to the fullest possible extent upon both the august memory of the founder of the collection and the civic pride of those listening. "I sometimes wonder," he mused,

> whether the City considers it is fulfilling its obligations to the late Mr. John Ross Robertson while it fails to provide suitable accommodations for the Historical collection of pictures upon which he spent upwards of $300,000. ... Up to the present time the City Council has done absolutely nothing to recognize the great generosity of this public-spirited citizen of Toronto. You have had your attention called at various times during the past two years to the crowded conditions of this Collection, and I am sure I am voicing the sentiments of the Board and of the citizens of Toronto generally when I say that I am ashamed that something has not already been done by this great City to perpetuate the donor's name ....[36]

As a remedy for the situation he called for an infusion of both city and provincial funds for the long-sought-after addition. By using such a blunt approach, Lee must have done as little to ingratiate himself with the individual board members as he did to win support for the cause of a new addition.

During this period, though, it had become apparent that the need had at least been recognized. In 1922, for example, some of the pressure had been relieved by the purchase of the property north of the library and the establishment of Boys and Girls House. Although this action helped, it was only an interim measure to deal with the crowded conditions, and Locke continued to call for the new addition, though in less strident tones.

With the administrator's rhetoric scaled down in the mid-1920s, the only consistent voices calling for expanded space seemed to be those whose job it was to make do in the still-crowded conditions. In her report on the collection for 1925, librarian Margaret McElderry observed, not without a note of despair, "We are still hoping against hope that a gallery befitting this grand gift of Mr. John Ross Robertson's may materialize at no distant date."[37] The following year she reported:

> While many persons express themselves on leaving the Gallery as being delighted with the Collection, others air their views about hanging the pictures in too close proximity, making it difficult to get the proper perspective. One person remarked: "It would be better to put only half the number in." Query: What would be done with the other half? We are all waiting for a solution of this problem.[38]

It was not until 1929 that the long-desired addition was finally authorized and built. The new wing, to the north of the original structure, contained rooms for the display of the Historical Collection and had special facilities for the storage of pictures that were not being exhibited. This addition, concluded a relieved Locke, "has eased up matters very much." Not only the library staff appreciated the change in 1929: visitors to the collection increased to 6,000, and this number increased dramatically to 11,619 in 1931, 13,000 in 1932, and 13,500 in 1933. For the time, the John Ross Robertson Historical Collection could be shown to better effect, although problems remained with the classification, storage and display of the collection until the completion of the Metropolitan Toronto Reference Library in 1977.[39]

Conclusion

The development of Canada's foremost collection of visual Canadiana had finally achieved what its founder had desired since its inception. John Ross Robertson, accustomed as he was to having his own way regardless of the cost, had been battled to a stalemate by the library board. This situation continued beyond his death and was only resolved (partially) 19 years after he had first founded the collection. Despite having loyal allies in the chief librarians and successive chairmen of the board, Robertson had clearly not taken into account the actions — or, perhaps, more correctly, the inaction — of a board that was at times as individualistic as it was just plain stubborn. Some curious questions remain to be answered: why, for example, in light of the great expense to which Robertson went to build up the collection, did he not finance the construction of adequate facilities (the steel shed notwithstanding) himself? He was certainly financially capable of doing so.

Perhaps it was mostly due to the nature of the man; once he had determined that the library board ought to finance an addition to house the collection, it would have seemed a defeat for him to do so. And in his dealings with the board, as in his dealings at the *Telegram* and the Hospital for Sick Children, Robertson was not about to settle for a defeat. Rather, he seems to have adopted the only course of action that he knew would eventually see his aims accomplished and which did eventually prevail: he gave so generously to the library and built up such a massive collection that it threatened to undermine the very purpose for the library's existence. Left with such a tradition of benevolence on the one hand and the sheer volume of the collection on the other, the library had eventually no recourse but to build the long-requested facility. And so perhaps the wily old publisher in the end accomplished his main goal over and against what proved to be the most determined and effective opposition he had ever faced.

Notes

[1] Ron Poulton, *The Paper Tyrant* (Toronto: Clark, Irwin, 1971), 173.

[2] Ibid., 162. According to Poulton (1971), the Hospital for Sick Children had received over $16 million both from Robertson directly and through the trust fund he established for it. In 1971 the trust was worth $8.5 million.

[3] These included a copy of the *Daily Telegraph*, July 6, 1849, and a copy of the *Courier of Upper Canada*, September 19, 1831 (Toronto Public Library Third Annual Report, 1885).

[4] Typed excerpt from library board minutes of May 8, 1896, John Ross Robertson file, Baldwin Room, Toronto Public Library.

[5] Figures taken from Annual Reports, 1904-1912.

[6] *Toronto World*, March 20, 1910.

[7] John Ross Robertson, letter to Toronto Public Library Board, May 12, 1910, John Ross Robertson file, Baldwin Room, Toronto Public Library.

[8] Ibid.

[9] Ibid.

[10] Board minutes, May 13, 1910.

[11] *Toronto Globe*, May 11, 1910.

[12] Robertson to library board, May 12, 1910.

[13] Ibid.

[14] Ibid.

[15] Board minutes, September 15, 1911.

[16] Annual Reports, 1912, 1913.

[17] Ibid., 1913.

[18] Ibid., 1912.

[19] Ibid., 1914.

[20] Ibid., 1915.

[21] Poulton, 148.

[22] Ibid., 155.

[23] Robertson to Locke, March 13, 1916.

[24] Annual Report, 1916.

[25] Robertson to Locke, March 13, 1916.

[26] Ibid.

John Ross Robertson

[27]Poulton, 151.

[28]Locke to Robertson, October 30, 1917.

[29]Ibid.

[30]Board minutes, June 15, 1918.

[31]*Toronto Evening Telegram*, June 3, 1918.

[32]Ibid.

[33]Will of John Ross Robertson (photocopy) in Baldwin Room, Toronto Public Library.

[34]Ibid.

[35]Annual Report, 1920.

[36]Annual Report, 1921. While Lee obviously represents a partisan voice in the debate, his address gives some solid clues as to where resistance was strongest to the building of expanded facilities. The library board to which he spoke consisted of two members appointed by the separate school Board, three public school board representatives, the current mayor and three representatives — usually councilmen — appointed by Toronto City Council. Lee's remarks suggest that he believed this latter group was the major impediment to any expansion proposals.

[37]Annual Report, 1925.

[38]Ibid., 1926.

[39]Curiously, library officials could provide no record of how the conditions of Robertson's bequest were adapted to meet the new situation. By 1977, it appears, Robertson's insistence that his collection reside in the College St. building "and not ... be removed therefrom" had become a non-issue.

W.W. Francis: Scholar and Showman
of the Osler Library

Faith Wallis

Abstract

For the first three decades of its existence, the Osler Library of the History of Medicine at McGill University was directed by Sir William Osler's second cousin, William Willoughby Francis. Francis' deep personal attachment to Osler converged with his own scholarly and bibliographical talents to produce *Bibliotheca Osleriana*, the justly famous catalogue of the Osler collection. But his correspondence with members of the Library's board of curators, and the minutes of that body, reveal his stubborn unwillingness to augment the collection or to envisage the Library's vocation as anything other than a shrine to Osler's memory. To scholars, Francis provided a unique kind of highly erudite reference service; to medical students, he transmitted an Oslerian enthusiasm for medical history and medical bibliography. Part scholar, part showman, W.W. Francis unconsciously translated his own complex personality into a style of librarianship which has left a permanent imprint on this institution.

Résumé

Dans les trois premières décades de son existence, la Bibliothèque Osler sur l'histoire de la médecine de l'Université McGill fut dirigée par le cousin de Sir William Osler, William Willoughby Francis. L'attachement profond de Francis à Osler, son érudition et ses talents pour la bibliographie sont à l'origine de la *Bibliotheca Osleriana*, le fameux catalogue de la collection Osler. La correspondance de Francis avec les administrateurs de la bibliothèque et les procès-verbaux de l'organisme révèlent son entêtement à ne pas accroître la collection et à consacrer la bibliothèque exclusivement à la mémoire de Osler. Francis offrait aux lettrés un service de référence de haute érudition tout à fait unique. Aux étudiants en médecine, ils transmettait l'enthousiasme « oslérien » pour l'histoire de la médecine et la bibliographie médicale. En partie lettré, en partie vedette, W.W. Francis imprima inconsciemment sa personnalité complexe au style de bibliothéconomie qui a toujours marqué l'institution.

The Osler Library of the History of Medicine at McGill University is a place rife with ghosts. On quiet days, with nary a reader in sight and half the staff on holiday, the immortals distinctly outnumber the mortals.

These are the folk whose last resting place is the Osler Library and whose ashes repose behind the bronze portrait plaque of Sir William Osler in the niche of the Osler Room. They include Sir William Osler himself (1849-1919), in his day the pre-eminent physician in the English-speaking world and in our day still a potent symbol of the ideal qualities, intellectual and moral, of a doctor. At his own request, he is buried amongst the books on the history of medicine and science which he loved to collect and which he bequeathed to his old medical school. At his side is his wife, Grace Revere, granddaughter of the Boston patriot. The two sons of their union are not here: Paul, who lived a bare few weeks, is buried in his birthplace, Baltimore, where his father was Professor of Medicine at the Johns Hopkins University and Physician in Chief at the Johns Hopkins Hospital. The second boy, Edward Revere, died in August 1917 of shrapnel wounds, and rests in a military cemetery in Belgium.

The children of Sir William's body, parted from him in his own lifetime, lie far from him now in death. But the child of his heart is right by his side: William Willoughby Francis, Osler's second cousin (although Osler always called him his nephew), Osler's *alter ego* and *redevivus* and, from the inception of the Osler Library here at McGill on May 29, 1929, until his death on August 10, 1959, Osler's Librarian (as Francis liked to call himself).

For 30 years, Francis presided as the privileged guardian and interpreter of this remarkable collection and of the man who had made it. Francis' specialty was showing visitors and students about the place, talking about the books, talking about Osler. This talk, studded with scholarly anecdotes about the precious volumes and with personal anecdotes about Sir William, he humorously dubbed his "showman's patter," and late in life he was persuaded to record and transcribe this oral catalogue of the Osler Library.

"Showman's Patter" has never been published and probably never could be, but it stands as a fitting companion piece to Francis' unique scholarly monument, the printed catalogue of Osler's collection, *Bibliotheca Osleriana*.[1] Francis published hardly anything besides *Bibliotheca Osleriana*, and his life was to an extraordinary degree bound up in that single book. He belonged, heart and soul, to the library that embodied the human being he loved beyond anything else. Behind his jocular, easy-going, unambitious and somewhat disorganized façade, he shielded a fierce and jealous attachment to the Library, an attachment which overlapped almost totally with his devotion to Osler. This subterranean passion occasionally emerged in Francis' stubborn unwillingness to extend the Library beyond the frontiers defined by Osler in his lifetime and, more evidently, in a deep anxiety that he might be compelled, by the university or by his own health, to retire.[2] For Francis, the Osler Library was not just the place where he worked; it was his expression of himself, as close to him as his own clothes.

The analogy of clothing is more than metaphorical. Francis inherited Sir William's mantle in the literal as well as the figurative sense, for he wore Sir William's old suits, and even his fur coat, all his life. Clothing was a code for the deep and complex love that bound uncle to nephew, and an incident involving a waistcoat was one of Francis' earliest memories of Osler:

> He was my godfather, I was called after him, and I was always his special pet. One of my earliest recollections is of his going off for a while, and I was weeping at seeing him pack up, and he threw me a waistcoat, said "Here now: you take charge of that and keep it until I come back." He was gone for some months, but I never let that waistcoat out of my hand. Then, another recollection. We always tried to induce him (he was sometimes a little shy about it, especially if the table was laid) when he came in, to get him to vault over the dining-room table. He would put his left hand in the centre of the table and vault right over it, laid or not, and it was a good big table because there were nine of us children.[3]

Francis and Osler

William Osler was a part of Billy Francis' life from its beginnings. His mother, Marion Osler, William's cousin, was married to a Montreal businessman named George Grant Francis. In the 1870s, when Osler was a medical student and later a young professor at McGill, the Francises lived at the top of University Street in a house which still stands, now directly across from the Strathcona building, which housed the Osler Library for many decades. The Osler family was very close, and Osler loved young children. Being then a bachelor, he spent many of his leisure hours at the Francis home, where there were children galore: Grant, Marion ("Maisie" or "May"), Gwyn, Britton ("Brick"), William Willoughby, Gwendolyn, Beatrice and James.

Vaulting over the dining room table was one of the tamer things Osler did to amuse his little cousins, for his strong sense of mischief was exercised by devising pranks and practical jokes he and the young ones could spring upon their parents. In 1884, the family moved to Toronto and, although Osler visited frequently (Francis' waistcoat memory is probably a recollection of one such visit), his relationship with the children was sustained by letters. Osler's favourite medium was the postcard, and he invented dozens of amusing postcards for the lad who was rapidly becoming his favourite "nephew," the boy he also called "the little doctor."[4]

321

William Francis was Osler's godson and namesake (the Willoughby being the name of another godfather, a wealthy business associate who apparently played no role whatsoever in Billy's life[5]) and, as it soon appeared, his shadow and acolyte, and his informally adoptive son.

Francis was educated at Trinity College School in Port Hope, Ontario, where Osler had been head boy under the school's founder, W.A. Johnson. But if Osler's career at Trinity College School was marked by Father Johnson's passion for natural history and the world of the microscope, Francis' took a different turn: languages, classical and modern, were his strong suit, and he loved literature.

Francis was an extraordinary Latinist. Edmund Simpson (MD McGill 1936) recalls "watching and listening one day as [Francis] read a passage from a Latin book. The Latin went in the eye but it came out the mouth in English as fast as reading a native tongue."[6] The foundations for this linguistic and literary facility were laid at Trinity College School and then cemented by early exposure to Uncle Willie's burgeoning library.

The centre of Billy Francis' world was "Uncle Willie," and Uncle Willie reciprocated by taking Billy on his travels and vacations with him, even after Osler moved to the United States, first to Philadelphia (1885-89) and then to Baltimore. On one of these vacations, when he was 11, Billy Francis was taken to meet a lady, the widow of a famous Philadelphia surgeon named Gross. Her maiden name was Grace Revere. It was plain, even before he proposed marriage to Grace Revere Gross, that Osler intended to maintain this special close relationship with his godson and "nephew."[7] After Osler and the widow Gross were wed, Francis was a frequent visitor to their Baltimore home and later a boarder, for Osler paid for his education, first in arts and later in medicine, at Johns Hopkins. Even after Osler's own son Revere came along, Francis retained his special place in Osler's affections, for the two spoke the same language, especially when it came to books.

The two Williams shared a robust appetite for reading and for trading and delighting in the kind of erudition that comes from reading: detailed, curious, anecdotal, and verbally elegant. One of young Billy's daily tasks was to read for ten minutes every evening to Osler as he took his bath. Osler recognized Francis' love of books and his extraordinary talent for absorbing that special kind of bookman's scholarship. As his own historical library grew, and with it his plans for its cataloguing and eventual disposition, so did his explicit conviction that Francis would be designated its caretaker.

Francis graduated from Hopkins with his medical degree in 1902, interned for two years at the Royal Victoria Hospital in Montreal, and returned to Baltimore as a fellow in pathology. The year he spent in this post coincided with Osler's final year at Hopkins before he became Regius Professor of Medicine at Oxford. Francis then went on to do post-graduate study in paediatrics in London, Berlin and Vienna. In 1906 he returned to Montreal to set up practice. Concurrently he held the post of Demonstrator in Anatomy from 1907 to 1911, assisting Dr. Maude Abbott. The two got along very well, sharing as they did a boundless devotion to Osler. The only source of friction was that Dr. Abbott obliged Francis to take the 8:00 a.m. sessions with the students in the pathological museum. Francis was a notoriously late riser; "Never mind, Bill," Osler used to say to him in Baltimore. "You'll be in time for the afterbirth."[8]

Francis' letters to "Maudie" are deeply affectionate and funny. For reasons unknown, he addressed her as "the Dutch Rabbit" as well as "ma chère amie," and he joked with her about her boundless energy and enthusiasms. He remained one of her closest friends and staunchest allies to the end of her life, and he raised the money to print her *Atlas of Congenital Heart Disease*. Every day of his working life as Osler Librarian, Francis ate his sandwich lunch from noon to one o'clock in Dr. Abbott's medical museum.

In 1911, Francis discovered he had apical pulmonary tuberculosis. He was obliged to renounce his practice, and he retreated to a sanitarium in Ste.-Agathe for 18 months. A letter from John McCrea, written to Francis shortly before his departure to the Laurentians, wished him a speedy recovery and thanked him for his work at the Royal Victoria Hospital Clinic: "... you have always done it most satisfactorily, and I hope you will be back soon to continue it. I don't hesitate to say this about your work, because it is a satisfaction to a man to know that he has done his work well: and most of all at a time like this ...."[9] But it is doubtful that Francis felt so positively about his career as a physician. Unlike Uncle Willie, he never published a paper on a medical subject, and he showed little enthusiasm for clinical work or scientific curiosity.

Francis never resumed practice after his discharge from Ste.-Agathe. Instead, he entered into a more congenial line of work for someone of his unambitious character and literary tastes: assistant editor of the *Canadian Medical Association Journal* and secretary-treasurer of the Canadian Medical Association. When he went overseas in 1915 with No. 3 Canadian General Hospital (the McGill unit), it was as registrar. One of his companions at No. 3 was Archie Malloch, son of an old Hamilton colleague of Sir William's, a McGill medical graduate of the class of 1913, and a special protégé of Osler's. He and Francis shared a bent for literary work and libraries and a devotion to Osler; Malloch later became librarian of the New York Academy of Medicine, a medical historian of some note, and joint editor with Francis of *Bibliotheca Osleriana*.

Francis was one of the few members of No. 3 to remain with the unit throughout World War I. We hear very little of his experiences in No. 3, but much more of his visits, while on leave, to 13 Norham Gardens, the Oxford home of Uncle Willie and Aunt Grace. In 1919, Francis returned briefly to Canada for demobilization and promptly returned to England, a bare two weeks before Osler died. He was with Osler at the end, and in the final days he became once more the adoring lad who read aloud to his beloved uncle:

> The night before [he died], I read to him for quite a long time, things he asked for out of the "Spirit of Man", and we finished with the last verses of "The Ancient Mariner". I thought at the time how well it fitted him, and afterwards, what an appropriate valedictory for this lover of men and books:
> He prayeth best who loveth best
> All things, both great and small ....
> When I took leave of him, he said to me, as though I were still a child, "Nighty-night, a-darling!"[10]

It was Osler's wish that his library be catalogued before it went back to Canada, but, with the estate to be wound up, the work could not commence immediately. Hence Francis took up a post in Geneva with the League of Red Cross Societies as editor of all four editions — English, French, Italian and Spanish — of the *International Journal of Public Health*, a striking indication of his facility for languages. He greatly enjoyed Geneva, and he formed fast friendships with bibliographers and medical historians such as Arnold Klebs and the young Henry Sigerist.

On March 14, 1921, he married an Englishwoman, a secretary with the journal, named Hilda Colley. It is interesting to note that both Osler and Francis were in their early forties when they married, and both committed matrimony suddenly and surreptitiously. Both men were also, to all appearances, fortunate in finding very compatible mates, although Mrs. Francis and Lady Osler bore not the least resemblance to each other.

Where Lady Osler was a Victorian *grande dame*, proud of her vocation to manage aggressively the well-being of her husband and his extended family, Hilda Colley came from an ordinary English provincial bourgeois family and was a thoroughly modern young woman. She was in her thirties when she met Francis; she had worked as a medical secretary (one of her employers was Sir James Mackenzie), and she had driven an ambulance during the war. Where Lady Osler was a matriarch and a social animal, Hilda valued privacy and independence. Her temper was a perfect fit for Francis; she loved literature (and apparently wrote, but never published, poetry herself), played tennis and golf with zest, hated entertaining, and was a highly intelligent woman. When the journal ceased publication in 1921 and the call came from Lady Osler to return to Oxford and commence cataloguing the books, Hilda crossed the English Channel with Francis in January 1922. She was very pregnant at the time, and their first and only child, Marion Grace (known as Maisie), was born in Oxford a bare few days later.

Bibliotheca Osleriana

Francis now applied himself full time to cataloguing Osler's library, a task that consumed 7 years of 12- to 14-hour working days. He was assisted throughout by Reginald Hill of the Bodleian Library, who had served as Osler's bibliographical assistant in his latter years; less continuous help was afforded by Archibald Malloch (who shared with Francis the responsibility of being Osler's literary executor) and Leonard Mackall, with assistance from Arnold Klebs for the incunabula. Francis, however, was the chief and final editor. His pace governed the production of *Bibliotheca Osleriana*, and his scholarship shaped its perfection of detail. Given the somewhat spotty and unproductive nature of Francis' early career, his achievement in producing *Bibliotheca Osleriana* seems quite extraordinary.

Osler was the most important thing in Francis' life, but Francis was also sensitive to the differences between himself and his adored namesake. He had tastes that Osler did not share — for instance, music — but above all he lacked Osler's strong purpose, serious ambitions, focused energies, and healthy egotism. Francis was well aware of his lack of moorings and motivation. In a letter to Maude Abbott written on board the ship that was carrying him and No. 3 Canadian General Hospital to Europe, he stated:

> I am too sleepy to put into this the affection I feel & which your letter and all your devotion deserves. I cannot see what I have done to inspire this devotion in you and my other dear friends. But to me my friends and my music are an infinite consolation. Success in a worldly or professional way is not, & never will be, for me. But as Stevenson says — ["]so long as we love we serve... no man is useless who has a friend."[11]

It is in this light that Francis' work on *Bibliotheca Osleriana* must be seen, for here for the first and, as it transpired, the only time in his life he knew that he was doing something that was both important and utterly suited to his tastes and talents. To catalogue Osler's books was to fuse his profound devotion to "the Chief" with his own deep predilection for historical, philological and bibliographical erudition. The result was an extraordinary outburst of concentrated and intense energy. From January 1922 until 1929, Francis took hardly a day's vacation from his task, to which he brought a degree of painstaking meticulousness and a passion for accuracy and thoroughness that astounded some and infuriated others.

Chief amongst the infuriated was Lady Osler,[12] who had hoped to have the library catalogued and shipped off to McGill in a matter of months. Her impatience was compounded by the presence of the Francis family at 13 Norham Gardens. She grew increasingly hostile to Hilda Francis, whose origins she considered common, and whom Francis had had the effrontery to marry without the match having been contrived or approved by herself. Mrs. Francis' modern manners in dealing with the servants and in raising little Marion offended Lady Osler, adding to her sense of depression, grief and futility, and tainting her letters to Archie Malloch and Harvey Cushing (the famous neurosurgeon and Osler's biographer) with an uncharacteristic bitterness and self-pity. Caught between Hilda and Aunt Grace, Francis withdrew into silence, which only irritated Lady Osler. Finally, Lady Osler expelled the Francises from her house. Hilda and Maisie were exiled to Boar's Hill, and Lady Osler's frustration focused on Francis himself and his incomprehensible slowness in producing the catalogue.

Francis' dilatoriness was not due to laziness; quite the contrary, it was the unproductiveness of the perfectionist, who refuses to relinquish a single word to the printer that has not been checked and corrected, proof-read and checked again. Osler long before had recognized this editorial fastidiousness as a salient characteristic of his nephew. "His meticulosity," he said, "exceeds anything you ever met with."[13] This meticulosity was compounded by the fact that the production of *Bibliotheca Osleriana* also dovetailed with at least two other important labours of medical historical bibliography — Geoffrey Keynes' bibliography of Sir Thomas Browne and Arnold Klebs' catalogue of medical and scientific incunabula. Keynes and Klebs supplied information to Francis, but they also demanded information from him, so that Francis spent much of his day unravelling complex inquiries from his collaborators. His correspondence with these two, preserved in the Osler Library, is a record of interactive bibliographical detective work that reveals Francis' dogged pursuit of truth down to, and particularly in, the smallest detail.

But ironing out every particular of the publishing history of *Religio Medici* or collating the signatures of every incunabulum took a long time. The months stretched into years, and the more work Francis did on the catalogue, the more there was to check and revise. John Fulton, professor of the history of medicine at Yale and himself a close friend and collaborator with Francis on several later bibliographical projects, recalls that

> ... Dr. Francis was averse to having anything go to the Press until he himself had verified every comma on every card. His corrections in proof were numerous and disturbing to the printers; they, how-ever, were equally exasperating to him, and each correction

strengthened his own conviction that nothing must pass for the press without his personal verification. Months passed, the Press meanwhile clamoring for cards, but Dr. F. refused to send them until he saw fit. Some felt insulted that their work was not allowed to stand, but Hill took a broader view. Malloch's letters imploring dispatch rested on the consulting room table unanswered. Lady Osler was beside herself and at times could seem to talk about little else — this despite letters from Dr. Cushing urging her to let the careful scholar set his own pace. Still Dr. Bill refused to be moved or hurried and he would often remark casually to a few who were sympathetic that he had never done anything with his life, his opportunity to accomplish something worthwhile had now come, and he intended to make the best of it. Hurry meant inaccuracy, and everything must be sacrificed to his ideal.[14]

The result was a library catalogue which, to say the least, is like no other. To Osler, proclaimed on the title page as the author, is due primarily the collection of the books themselves as well as the unusual division of the catalogue into its constituent parts: *Bibliotheca prima*, the works of the greatest names in medicine and science, chosen for their eminence and ranged in chronological order, and conceived as a curriculum for a course, formal or personal, on the history of these subjects; *Bibliotheca secunda*, the other authors of less than "superstar" status, arranged in conventional alphabetical order; and *Bibliotheca litteraria*, being literary works by physicians, or what Francis called "medicated" literature by laymen. These three are followed by the form-divisions *Historica, Biographica, Bibliographica*, Incunabula, and Manuscripts.

Many of the annotations are also by Osler, but most of them are Francis'. The notes and descriptions are copious and to the bibliographical purist undoubtedly excessive, but few who wander into the pages of *Bibliotheca Osleriana* would wish them away. Countless readers and reviewers have commented on the charm and readability of *Bibliotheca Osleriana*, but few have also detected its genuine greatness. One of these was Lloyd Stevenson, who wrote:

> It is a great book — the record of a happy lifetime of collecting, informed by the highly personal taste and opinion of Osler, enriched by the scholarship of Hill, Malloch, Mackall and Francis. It was Francis, above all, who made it what it is, an accurate work of reference, oddly and delightfully combined with paragraphs of agreeable book talk. The effect is surprising. It is as if the apples and oranges of a school Arithmetic had the look, the feel, and the scent

of real fruit, as if a tarry Trade Wind sprang from the pages of a Geography, or the shouts and trumpets of battle from a manual of historic dates. These old medical books, some of them at least, are unaccountably alive. It occurs to the catalogue browser that they are not merely *rariora*, interesting bibliographical specimens, *objets d'art*; that they were written and published by real men in real life, with definite objects, under specific circumstances, and now and again with definable results. They were meant not merely to be collected but to be *read*.[15]

Part of Francis' success in conveying this living quality was due precisely to the fact that he *did* read the books. Lady Osler noticed, and disapproved, for, as she rightly saw, it added immeasurably to the delays in producing the catalogue. So did others, like John Fulton, whose views of Francis' "besetting sin" were more tolerant: "Having found what he wanted bibliographically, the lure of the printed page led him always onwards. He had no idea of time, and if the text of some old medical work interested him, he would be likely to retire at three or four in the morning."[16]

But another element in the success of *Bibliotheca Osleriana* as (if you will) romantic bibliography was Francis' fine literary style and his justly famous wit. Consider his note on the disputed death date of the seventeenth-century Italian physician and poet Francesco Redi:

> Death is almost a habit with Redi — in books of reference. He died, perhaps for the first time, in 1676 (cf. no. 5789 [J.F. Dannemann, *Die Naturwissenschaften in ihrer Entwicklung...*, 1910-13]), again in 1694 (De Renzi; Haeser; S.G.L., etc.), and then more frequently. Autopsied in 1696, he was found dead in March 1697 and made his will the following December — a Gilbertian sequence given in a recent biography ... without comment! His final dissolution occurred in 1698 (see no. 5387 [the introduction to the 1702 ed. of his *Sonetti*]) and the Crusca Academy held a memorial meeting in 1699. The contradictory evidence is in favour of 1697, which is also said to be the date on his monument.... The last of his autograph letters... is dated 20 Nov., 1696.[17]

In a genre not renowned for whimsy, Francis' little footnote on Redi is a miniature masterpiece, but one that sprang, as Lloyd Stevenson observed, from his rigorous "meticulosity."

Almost in spite of Francis, *Bibliotheca Osleriana* did finally emerge from the Oxford University Press. The editors dedicated it to Lady Osler, a homage to her patience and determination to see this, her husband's dearest project, to fruition. Lady Osler herself, gratified at the issue and perhaps loath to witness the departure of the books for Montreal and the empty shelves that would result, died in 1928.

One can well imagine how complex her relationship with Francis must have been. Francis was a living reminder of Osler's attachments before he met the widow Gross, and in an emotional sense he was Osler's son, one more after his own heart than his much fussed over but inarticulate and unintellectual Revere. By marrying without consultation, Francis also silently defied Lady Osler's determination to arbitrate her extended family's personal lives, and in the end he successfully usurped her role as manager of Sir William's reputation and residual legatee of his charisma. The tension between the two was quite explicit in the years of the *Bibliotheca*'s making, and yet there were deep wells of mutual respect and affection. Their correspondence is tender and often touching, as when Francis wrote to her at Christmas 1920, addressing her by Revere's favourite term of endearment, "Dearest Muz."[18] In the end, each acknowledged and accepted Sir William's love for the other, Francis by the dedication of *Bibliotheca Osleriana* to her, and Grace by leaving Francis the largest individual bequest in her will as well as £10,000 as an endowment for the Osler Library.

"I am Osler's Nephew and Librarian"

The books and Dr. Francis arrived in Montreal in November of 1928. Unpacking began on March 1, 1929, and the sorting and shelving were completed a bare nine days before the official opening on May 29.

Francis was installed as Osler Librarian, or, as he occasionally preferred it, Osler's Librarian, but the governance of the library was not his alone. By the provisions of Osler's deed of gift, the library was to be directed by a board of curators, modelled after the Curators of the Bodleian Library, of which Osler himself had been one. The curators in the first years of the library included Dean C.F. Martin as *ex-officio* chair (the Dean of Medicine is still the *ex-officio* chair of the Curators), Mr. Henry Osler as representative of the Osler family, and Archie Malloch as elected curator. The minutes of their meetings, kept by Francis himself as *ex-officio* secretary, make for interesting reading, not least because they reveal some of the tensions between Francis' views on the nature and destiny of the Osler Library and those of the curators.

If there is a single constant theme that resurfaces meeting after meeting, year after year, it is that Francis was not doing enough to build the library's collections. At the meeting of June 25, 1930:

> Dr. Malloch thought the Library should take all medical and scientific historical periodicals and procure the back numbers. The Librarian objected that there is no room to display current numbers,

that the complete sets would take up too much of the small space available for expansion, and that the three or four important journals taken by Osler himself would probably suffice for the present.[19]

As a sop to Malloch, Francis took out subscriptions to *Sudhoffs Archiv* and *Janus*, two journals to which Osler had subscribed. Malloch, however, was not to be appeased, and in 1931

produced a list of thirty-two periodicals in the history of science and medicine, which are being received by the New York Academy of Medicine. It was decided [the passive voice in the minutes is always a code for Francis' disapproval] that some journals might be purchased for the Osler Library, and that these should be made available on the tables for visitors.[20]

In 1933, the topic came up again:

Dr. Francis reported that of the 35 periodicals dealing with the history of science or medicine on Dr. Malloch's list of December 1931, nearly one-half were available in our McGill libraries. This, with the addition of the Leipsic "Mitteilungen" (formerly received) was thought sufficient for the present.[21]

What is remarkable about this little exchange is Francis' resistance to expanding the library beyond the parameters set by Osler and the singularly obtuse positions he was ready to take in order to avoid doing so. Money was certainly no object; indeed, throughout his tenure, Francis consistently turned back surpluses, year after year, to be re-capitalized in the endowment. Sometimes these surpluses were very substantial — over $5,000 in the middle of the Great Depression.

Certainly no true-born librarian has ever let lack of space stand in the way of the relentless drive to build a collection, and Francis' assertion that about half of Malloch's titles were already at McGill begs the question of why he was not subscribing to the other half. Evidently Malloch felt that Francis was passively, but inflexibly, refusing to expand the collection, and he let the matter of periodicals drop. In 1935, however, he tried another tack: "... it was felt that the accumulated surplus was too large, and it was suggested by Dr. Malloch that more money should be spent on books. It was recommended that the Librarian should consult with Dr. Malloch about the purchase of expensive books, some of which he had under consideration."[22]

Again Francis successfully evaded the issue. When it came up again in 1938, he claimed that the shelf space was inadequate and that "he was not tempted to add more books than seemed necessary. He systematically bought all new historical and biographical books listed by the New York Academy and the College of Physicians of Philadelphia."[23] This of course was pure obfuscation; what Malloch was referring to was not current works on medical history, but rare books. Why was Francis not continuing to build Osler's collection of old primary works?

Malloch brought the matter up again in 1941,[24] specifying that rare books would be a suitable way of investing the annual surplus. In 1942 the subject came up again, and Francis as usual dodged it with a specious rationalization: "It was pointed out that this surplus gave opportunity of spending more on old books. The Librarian explained that orders for several old books had arrived after they were sold, and that he had not yet got the habit of cabling for ordinary desiderata."[25] This must have left the curators scratching their heads long enough for Francis to change the subject. Of course, one does not cable ordinary desiderata; one cables orders from catalogues. But was Francis doing even this? His financial report contains a rubric for postage and telegrams, but his acquisition statistics show him buying only between nine and fifteen or so old books each year. Indeed, in dollar figures his book purchases actually declined over the period of his tenure, and he persisted in turning back large surpluses. When the ailing Malloch was replaced on the board by John Fulton, Fulton inherited Malloch's duty of pressuring the reluctant librarian to buy more books, and with about as much success.

Francis was similarly resistant to the idea of building up the endowment of the Osler Library. At the very first meeting, Dean Martin suggested that a campaign be mounted to build an endowment of about $50,000. Francis, in a move which no librarian, indeed no administrator of any breed, can look upon with anything other than appalled disbelief, replied that the current annual income of $1,900 was more than sufficient for the library's needs and that he deprecated any appeal to the Osler family or to Osler's old associates.[26] Subsequent efforts to galvanize Francis into fundraising met with silent resistance, despite the evident interest of the Osler family in donating to the library. It was not until the arrival of Lloyd Stevenson and the election of Wilder Penfield to the Curators in the early 1950s that foundation money was actively sought and a Friends organization planned.[27] Francis recorded these events without comment in the minutes, save to protest, a few years later, that all this additional income was a terrible burden to him because he could not keep up with the ordering.[28]

What are we to make of this curious unwillingness to build the collection? To be sure, Francis had not himself the instincts of a collector, as he freely admitted on numerous occasions. Many librarians who are not themselves personally interested in collecting can sympathize with him. What they will find harder to comprehend is that Francis could not even conceive of building the library up for the sake of stimulating study and research in the subjects Osler hoped to promote. This was certainly Malloch and Martin's vision of what the library could be, and Malloch tried to bring Francis around both to the endowment campaign and to an expanded acquisitions programme by using precisely this logic:

> I think [Malloch wrote to Francis] a short statement should be prepared setting fort[h] the present endowment and income, how the money is spent, and what the new $45,000 or $50,000 new endowment is for. The Bibl. Osler. should be the centre for the study of the hist[ory] of med[icine] (& science) in Canada. That is why nearly all the mag[azine]s devoted to that subject should be taken .... Also the Lib[rary] should not stand still. Important new books are coming out all the time.[29]

But Francis does not seem to have seen the Osler Library as Canada's centre for medical historical research at all. For him, it was always, as he half-facetiously called it, "the shrine," a particular monument to Sir William Osler, and he obstructed every change that might deflect attention from the founder to the foundation. For instance, he and Malloch skirmished on and off throughout the 1930s over the card catalogue of the library. Francis used a card catalogue strictly for new accessions. At one Curators' meeting Malloch suggested integrating *Bibliotheca Osleriana* entries into this card catalogue. Francis snapped back: "The Librarian, having an un-American faith in the superiority of a printed catalogue (especially ours) over any card catalogue, objected to any plan that would divert readers from consulting the Bibliotheca Osleriana."[30]

Malloch wrote to Francis after the meeting and tried to explain himself: he did not wish to set the printed catalogue aside, but merely to have all the titles in the library available in one handy alphabetical reference so that Francis could verify whether or not he had a certain book when he was placing orders.[31] Francis in turn defended his obduracy in terms which reveal, once again, his determination to maintain the spotlight on Osler:

> Frankly, without blowing my own horn, I think I have had enough experience with catal[ogue]s and cataloguing to be allowed a librarian's right to manage this one myself — which is not, however, to say that I am not open to advice and suggestions from the curators and others.

I cannot consent to have the "B.O." superseded by a card-cat[alogue]. The pr[inted] book embodied W.O.'s collection, his notes and, I believe, his spirit, and is much handier, quicker and more instructive than any card-cat[alogue] could be.[32]

Whether Francis really believed the latter — and Lloyd Stevenson has gone on record saying that in his later years at least he was quite frank about how awkward *Bibliotheca Osleriana* was to consult[33] — he certainly believed the former. Osler was the primary focus of the library, and the history of medicine was of interest only because it was of interest to Osler. It is noteworthy that Francis in his annual reports justified the acquisition of every rare book on the grounds that it "filled a gap" in Osler's collection or was a volume that Osler had expressed a wish to acquire. And when he came to teach a course in the history of medicine, Francis lectured first on the life of Osler, then on the Osler Library, and only thereafter began a chronological survey of medical history.[34]

Bibliotheca Osleriana was, of course, Francis' special achievement, and perhaps he suspected that he had shot the bolt of his creative energies on it. Although he professed to be planning other publications, such as an edition of the correspondence of the seventeenth-century Italian physician Giorgio Baglivi from a unique Osler Library manuscript, he actually published little more than a few pieces about the library, a handful of short notes, and some reviews and obituaries.[35] He had but small motivation towards original research, and even projects one would think would have inspired him, such as a new edition of Osler's essays, never saw the light of day. His scholarship during the Osler Library years was what one might call reactive. Lloyd Stevenson describes it thus:

Year after year he sat at his desk, tracing references, deciphering manuscripts, pouncing on errors in proofs, and working out the answers to historical questions with endless patience — all for the benefit of the writings of others, of the physicians and historians of two continents. His name appears in a thousand prefaces and notes of acknowledgement. Of these he was justifiably proud.[36]

His major activity, and to all appearances major source of pleasure, was working out historical and linguistic problems posed by other researchers, or, in flat parlance of librarians, answering reference inquiries. In Francis' day, the Osler Library was a clearing-house and consulting service for every conceivable kind of medical historical and bibliographical information. Many of these inquiries came from afar and by mail, and Francis' answers were often so detailed, thorough and well written that they were incorporated into the printed works of the inquirer as appendices or extended notes.[37]

Translation was another common task: one of his first projects as Osler Librarian was translating Vesalius' letter to his printer Oporinus as part of the preparatory work for Malloch's splendid album of Vesalius' illustrations, *Icones Anatomicae*[38]; one of his last was translating the Edinburgh thesis of one of the founders of the Faculty of Medicine, John Stephenson.[39] Closely related to translation was the furnishing of apt quotations and phrases for inscriptions, be they for the new annex to the New York Academy of Medicine or the Montreal Neurological Hospital. As the world's leading medical philologist, he was also consulted by Penfield and others to assist them in coining legitimate new medical terminology from Greek and Roman roots (centrecephalic, epileptogenic, discoidectomy...).[40]

Another avocation was editing the works of others, his major achievement in this line being Harvey Cushing's bio-bibliography of Vesalius, left unfinished at his death in 1937.[41] He also served as *éminence grise* in a number of important bibliographical projects, such as Fulton's bibliography of Fracastoro[42] and Keynes' of Harvey.[43] And if he had no proofs of his own to correct, he scratched his itch for perfection in print by ferreting out typographical errors in other people's books. I confess that when I first took to reading Francis' correspondence I found this particular trait quite offensive; when someone sends your library a copy *gratis* of their book, to reply with a two-page list of errata seems in bad taste. Miss Desbarats, his secretary, thought it so rude that she would occasionally refuse to type his letters![44]

But if one steps back a pace, one can perhaps understand, if not condone, this apparently inconsiderate pedantry. All these qualities — the attention to detail, the editorial instincts, the passion for perfection at any price, the generous expenditure of time and thought on work that would always remain unnoticed or even anonymous — were exactly the qualities which, when for a season they found their privileged focus and motivation, had produced *Bibliotheca Osleriana*. Detached from the grand project that had sustained them in the 1920s, these same talents dissipated themselves in half-hearted projects, unfulfilled commitments, and the routine of reference work. Only in his very last years did Francis start to publish substantial original articles in scholarly medical history journals, but he did so as co-author with Lloyd Stevenson, who very evidently provided the active and designing intelligence behind these essays.[45] As a result, Francis received little recognition from the learned world of his day, although he patently cherished the recognition he did receive, particularly his Honorary Fellowship in the Royal Society of Medicine.

Showman's Patter

As the years wore on, Francis' friends and admirers became anxious that his vast reserves of erudition, particularly concerning the Osler collection, were very likely to perish unrecorded. Charlie Martin in particular began to badger Francis at Curators' meetings to put his "showman's patter" down on paper. Year after year, Francis swore that progress was being made on this project, but at the end of a decade he had only 17 typed pages to show for it. Martin forced the issue by purchasing out of his own pocket a dictaphone machine so that Francis could tape his spiel; Martin also paid Francis' secretary overtime to transcribe the tapes. Francis loathed the machine and, according to Miss Desbarats, attempted sabotage by more or less deliberately pushing the wrong buttons and erasing instead of recording.[46]

Nonetheless, at the end of another decade, "Showman's Patter" was complete — or as complete as it would ever be. It is a curious companion piece to *Bibliotheca Osleriana*, chatty, full of jokes, and peppered with one or two tall tales. Francis, the preternatural proof-reader and passionate perfectionist, thought it best not to consider publishing the patter because so many of his assertions would need to be verified, and "it would be a shame to spoil a good story for the sake of a few facts."[47] Nonetheless, the patter is also a superbly rich lode of facts, as well as fun. Consider this description of the oldest item in the Osler Library, an Assyrian medical tablet (*Bibliotheca Osleriana*, 53):

> The oldest thing in the Library is the Assyrian medical tablet no. 53. It is the first medical one to be found at the site of ancient Assur, the capital of Assyria. It was obtained from some Arabs who had raided the German workings by a padre in the French army in 1918, who sent it to his brother, Professor Scheil of the Académie des Inscriptions in Paris. The text was written on soft clay, in the cuneiform (wedge-shaped) script of Babylon, and afterwards baked …. The front or obverse of the tablet is the one that shows the most cracks. In the upper lines, which are so chipped away that they cannot be read, there is apparently a description of some eye disease. The lines below are nearly all prescriptions, such as this, "The plant cummin thou shalt take and grind up and give him to drink thereof in the best beer… and he will live". Probably the best beer had more to do with it than the cummin! The last lines on the back are the colophon giving the name and address of the medical student for whom this copy was made about 700 B.C. perhaps in the reign of Sennacherib. His father and grandfather were officials in the temple of Assur, the goddess who gave her name to Assyria. He is probably the first medical student whose name as such we know. It describes itself as the 32nd extract from an old work. There may

well have been as long an interval between the original and this copy as between this and us. The last line is the catch-line, the first of the next tablet, and the sequence is hardly scientific, passing from eye disease to "If a man's insides rise up and gripe him".[48]

Or the following remarks on *Bibliotheca Osleriana* 2795-2809, a collection of the pamphlets by the eighteenth-century quack, James Graham: "At the end of no. 2803 I have inserted a copy of a letter from the *Lancet*, 1847, which gives the name of the druggist whose inscription is on the fly-leaf and 'who refused to sell [Graham] Ether for the purpose of immoderately sniffing it up his nose, & thereby affecting his brain.'"[49]

The patter is also an index of how completely inseparable Francis was from the library. Access to this collection had to go through Francis, who in his subtle and genial way kept an iron grip on his role as its interpreter. Not only was *Bibliotheca Osleriana* to be its premier catalogue, but, as a complaint registered in the Curators' minutes reveals, one had to have the Librarian present in order to find anything at all because of the eccentric shelving system. The curators pleaded with Francis to have the cases marked, which Francis promised to do and never did,[50] and Malloch even had to instruct him to keep an accessions register.

Francis' tours, or, as he called them, "lecture-demonstrations," were performances, and any visitor at the fringes of a group whose attention wandered from the patter and who began browsing independently along the shelves would be brusquely told that if he was not interested in the tour, he should leave.[51] But many were utterly captivated by Francis' talk and also by his body language — the evident sensuous pleasure with which he caressed the precious volumes.[52]

They were also seduced by his wit, which ran to the facetious, with atrocious puns, allusive riddles, and a dash of Chaucerian ribaldry. Francis collected limericks, and he tossed bits of homemade doggerel at colleagues, family, and even onto the margins of his correspondence. A single example must suffice here. In 1933, as an economy measure in the Depression, the university letterhead was redesigned by architecture professor Ramsey Traquair, so that it could be printed entirely in black, instead of black and red. Traquair also refashioned the coat of arms, with the "martlets" — the chubby heraldic birds which are the symbol of McGill — now elongated, thin and almost vertical on the shield. This prompted the following Franciscan epigram:

Alas, poor Martlets, once so plump and red,
Now like black beetles pendant, shrunk and dead;
Crushed in the TRACK-WHERE slipped a cubist pen!
Oh for fat times (with room for you) again![53]

If Francis left little in the way of a written memorial, he nonetheless made a deep mark on several generations of McGill medical students. This influence was only marginally connected to his teaching. His course on the history of medicine for second-year students was only ten lectures (reduced to eight during the war) and was not, as the history of medicine course is now, obligatory. Francis was fairly casual about preparing his lectures (his lecture notes are extremely jejune), and he seems to have regarded the classes as essentially an extension of his tours of the library. "Gosh!" he wrote in 1937 to Archie Malloch, "You don't think I ought to *write out* my lectures?? That would take from now till Domesday. I'll see what I can do with notes and readings.... If the lectures are not a success, I'll try to arrange to have the 100 or so men split into groups that can be handled in the Library."[54] Miss Desbarats recalls following Dr. Francis into the classroom, carrying the stack of twenty or so books around which he would weave his lecture.[55] Francis craved the academic cachet this teaching appointment brought, especially as it had been Osler's wish that his librarian also be professor of the history of medicine,[56] but he was apparently an indifferent lecturer, and there were no essays or assignments given in his course.

Where Francis really did his teaching was through the Osler Society. This club had been founded in 1921 by medical students who desired to perpetuate Osler's memory and ideals. They met, often at the homes of professors in the early days, to read papers on medical historical topics. With the arrival of Francis and the Osler Library in 1929, meetings were held in the library itself. Dr. Francis presided as perpetual honorary president, and he never missed a meeting save during his hospitalizations for heart attack in the 1940s and 1950s.

His role went far beyond that of academic adviser and ceremonial patron. Francis actively directed the students towards subjects for their Osler Society papers and closely supervised their research and writing. In fact, he behaved more like a professor with the Osler Society than he did in his formal course. Dr. Eleanor McGarry recalls that when the time came for her to give a talk, Dr. Francis *told* her that she was going to work on Maude Abbott, placed in front of her Maudie's original diaries and letters, and instructed her in how to undertake historical research.[57] The experience was deeply formative, and many of the Osler Society presentations from the Francis years won the Osler Medal of the American Association for the History of Medicine awarded to outstanding student essays or found their way into print. Francis was intensely proud of the Osler Society, whose voluntary and non-competitive atmosphere brought out his natural talents as a teacher in a way the classroom never could.

Francis also demonstrated extraordinary and unobtrusive kindness towards those students who exhibited an interest in medical history. His correspondence in the 1930s makes frequent reference to Mordecai Etziony, an impecunious and scholarly Jewish immigrant whose early career as a medical student was dogged by his poor English but whose talent for historical research Dr. Francis zealously endeavoured to advance. Under Francis' guidance, Etziony wrote an essay on the Hebrew allusions in Vesalius. With an energy he hardly ever applied to his own efforts, Francis endeavoured for years to get Malloch to accept Etziony's essay for inclusion in *Icones Anatomicae*. Etziony eventually did publish on historical and bibliographical subjects, and he remained an *habitué* of the library.[58] Another beneficiary of Francis' generosity was Robert Fortuine (MD 1941), whom Francis actually boarded in his own house. Fortuine now practises in Alaska and produces very competent medical histories of the arctic regions. Another admirer, Edmund Evan Simpson (MD 1936), was so infected by the physical beauty of the Osler Library books that he began to buy type and print broadsides and pamphlets, and he produced a loving tribute to Francis' influence from his own Blackwood Press.[59]

Francis' final decade in the Osler Library was a slow ebbing of the tide of his influence and control. As coronary after coronary confined him for months to hospital, his list of activities in the annual reports shrunk to a few routine "lecture-demonstrations" for the students of the Library School or the nurses. Unable to bend over, even to take off his own galoshes in winter, Francis would struggle up the hill from his apartment on Milton Street by eleven o'clock and often left for home at three o'clock.[60]

The arrival of Lloyd Stevenson and the election of Wilder Penfield to the Curators in 1956 marked the beginning of a new and more active era for the Osler Library. Stevenson, brought in by the Faculty as Assistant Osler Librarian and evident heir-apparent, took over the teaching of medical history (though he tactfully left the biographical lecture on Osler to Francis). Elected dean and hence chair of the Curators a few years later, Stevenson spearheaded with Penfield a whole series of new initiatives, including the negotiation of the Wellcome Trust endowment (which to this day pays for most acquisitions of current works) and the inauguration of the Osler Lectureship. If Francis was saddened by the decline of his own powers, he was also reassured by the university's decision in 1943, when he turned 65, that he should remain in office as long as he was competent. He was treated with tender reverence by the new generation of curators and Miss Desbarats took care of business, so that he had the satisfaction of dying in harness, on August 10, 1959.

A few years later, Cécile Desbarats, who somewhat after the manner of Lady Osler kept open house long after the master had gone, wrote to Edmund Simpson:

Yes, you are perfectly right, somebody should write a biography of Dr. Francis, well-peppered with his own epistles. I don't think he ever realized what a great influence he exerted over so many — students and doctors alike. He was often reproached for not having written mighty tomes of erudition himself, but nobody will ever know how much of his time was spent helping others, who picked his brain, and claimed his brain-children as their own! Nevertheless, I think he did more in his own quiet way for the history of medicine — and mankind in general — than the many prolific writers whose articles appear in our slightly stuffy journals. He was perfectly contented just to be at his desk, at the beck and call of whoever dropped into the library, perpetuating the Osler tradition which was so close to his heart.

Who could handle this job is another matter. Perhaps in a few years' time, one of the students who came under his spell, may attempt such a thing. Like Osler, his warm and magical personality would be hard to put down in black and white, and perhaps he might prefer to live on in the thousands of notes tucked away in this library which we bless every day or by the letters which are treasured all over the world.[61]

All that William Willoughby Francis did and wrote and said defies summary treatment, and it is extraordinarily difficult to know where and how to end this brief introduction to the scholar and showman of the Osler Library. There is so much more that deserves discussion. His correspondence with the great medical historians and bibliographers of his day — Cushing and Fulton, Malloch, Keynes and Klebs — would make a meaty essay in itself, and the history of the Osler Society merits a whole book. His delightful patter could be excerpted for hours, and his ordinary correspondence is a bottomless store of minutiae on medical history and bibliography, laced with shameless gossip. In a more philosophical, or sociological, mood, one could likewise use Francis as a case study of how academic institutions shape themselves around the eccentricities and obsessions of individuals. But were Francis here today, he would doubtless prefer to ring down the curtain with a laugh, and one at his own expense.

My epilogue, then, is Dr. E.H. Bensley's reminiscence of how Francis' humour could parody even his own preoccupation with Osler and his renowned tendency to bring Osler into every conversation:

Never happier than when he was making fun of himself, [Francis] knew what his friends expected and he did not disappoint them ....
On February 6, 1956, the Osler Society was holding one of its

regular meetings. Dr. Harry Ballon was the Honorary President and that evening he was the speaker. His subject was "Sir James Hector, the Hannibal of the Rockies". At the conclusion of his presentation, all heads turned towards Dr. Francis. As usual, he was sitting in the big leather arm-chair reserved for him and, as usual, he was asked to open the discussion. I can remember wondering idly how he would go about establishing a connection between Sir James Hector and Osler. I soon found out. Dr. Francis gave his characteristic chuckle and then he spoke. "Osler", he said, "Osler had a dog called Hector."[62]

Notes

[1][W.W. Francis, R.H. Hill and A. Malloch, eds.], *Bibliotheca Osleriana: a Catalogue of Books Illustrating the History of Medicine and Science, Collected, Arranged, and Annotated by Sir William Osler, Bart., and Bequeathed to McGill University* (Oxford: Clarendon Press, 1929). A revised edition with a new introduction by Lloyd G. Stevenson, addenda and corrigenda was published by McGill-Queen's University Press in 1969, and reprinted in 1989.

[2]His former assistant, Miss Cécile Desbarats, recalls his distress during one of his frequent hospitalizations at being away from the library; when she came to visit, he was almost rude, pumping her for every detail of the small doings at the Osler Library, and then peremptorily packing her off, saying, "Hadn't you better get back to the Library?" (Cécile Desbarats, personal communication to the author.)

[3]Transcription of interview with W.W. Francis for "Sir William Osler: the Beloved Physician," Canadian Broadcasting Corporation, ca. 1957, from a recording in the Osler Library; cf. Osler Library Board of Curators, Annual Report of the Librarian, May 8, 1958, Osler Library Archives and MSS Acc. 388. Incidentally, there were not nine children in the Francis family, but nine persons, seven children and their parents.

[4]Childhood letters from Osler to the Francis children are preserved in the Osler Library as part of the Osler Papers, Archives and MSS Acc. 326, file 1.6.

[5]Personal communication from Dr. Marion Francis Kelen to Dr. E.H. Bensley.

[6]Edmund Evan Simpson, *William Willoughby Francis* (Sacramento, Calif.: Blackwood Press, 1981), [1].

[7]George T. Harrell, foreword to *The Twilight Years of Lady Osler* by Frederick B. Wagner (Canton, Mass.: Science History Publications, 1984), xii.

[8]Recorded by Lloyd Stevenson, "W.W. Francis," *Bulletin of the History of Medicine* 34 (1960): 378.

[9]John McCrea to William Willoughby Francis, January 16, 1911, Francis Correspondence, Osler Library MSS and Archives Acc. 381.

[10]Recorded by Harvey Cushing, *The Life of Sir William Osler* (Oxford: Oxford University Press, 1926): 1370-71.

[11]William Willoughby Francis to Maude Abbott, May 6, 1915, Francis Correspondence, Osler Library MSS and Archives Acc. 381.

[12]The relationship between Francis and Lady Osler is chronicled by Wagner, *Twilight Years*, based on Lady Osler's letters to Malloch, now in the Osler Library, Archives and MSS Acc. 573.

[13]Quoted by Lloyd G. Stevenson, prologue to second edition of *Bibliotheca Osleriana*, xi.

[14]"The Story of the Osler Catalogue, 1922-1929, by a Somewhat Prejudiced Observer," in *W.W. Francis: Tributes from his Friends* (Montreal: Published by the [Osler] Society [of McGill University], 1956), 33.

[15]"W.W. Francis," 376-77. Emphasis in original.

[16]Fulton, 32.

[17]*Bibliotheca Osleriana*, 481.

[18]Cited in Wagner, 36.

[19]Osler Library Board of Curators, Minutes, June 25, 1930.

[20]Osler Library Board of Curators, Minutes, December 30, 1931.

[21]Osler Library Board of Curators, Minutes, January 23, 1933.

[22]Osler Library Board of Curators, Minutes, January 28, 1935.

[23]Osler Library Board of Curators, Minutes, May 16, 1938.

[24]Osler Library Board of Curators, Minutes, October 20, 1941.

[25]Osler Library Board of Curators, Minutes, November 23, 1942.

[26]Osler Library Board of Curators, Minutes, June 25, 1930.

[27]Cf. Osler Library Board of Curators, Minutes, February 27, 1956.

[28]Osler Library Board of Curators, Minutes, October 7, 1958.

[29]Francis Correspondence, Osler Library Archives and MSS Acc. 381.

[30]Osler Library Board of Curators, Minutes, January 22, 1934.

[31]Francis Correspondence, Osler Library Archives and MSS Acc. 381.

[32]Francis Correspondence, Osler Library Archives and MSS Acc. 381.

[33]"W.W. Francis," 376. Its very awkwardness, however, served one of his purposes, as the necessity of consulting a multitude of catalogues was one of the reasons Francis invoked most frequently for not buying more books.

[34]Dr. Eleanor McGarry, personal communication to the author.

[35]See the appended bibliography of Francis' publications.

[36]Stevenson, 378.

[37]Cf. the appended bibliography of Francis' publications, "Notes on Plate V."

[38]Andreas Vesalius, *Icones Anatomicae*, New York Academy of Medicine Library History of Medicine Series 3. ([New York]: Academia Medicinae Nova-Eboracensis et Bibliotheca Universitatis Monacensis, 1934).

[39]See the appended bibliography of Francis' publications, "Repair of Cleft Palate."

[40]Wilder Penfield, "A Cock to Asclepius," in *W.W. Francis: Tributes from his Friends*, 52-55.

[41]Harvey Cushing, *A Bio-Bibliography of Andreas Vesalius* (New York: Schuman, 1943).

[42]With Leona Baumgartner, *A Bibliography of the Poem "Syphilis sive Morbus Gallicus" by Girolamo Fracastoro of Verona* (New Haven: Yale University Press, 1935).

[43]*A Bibliography of the Writings of Dr. William Harvey* (Cambridge, Mass.: Cambridge University Press, 1928). Cf. 2d ed., 1953, Preface, p. vi.

[44]Personal communication from Cécile Desbarats to the author.

[45]See the appended bibliography of Francis' publications.

[46]Personal communication from Cécile Desbarats to the author.

[47]Osler Library Board of Curators, Minutes, March 5, 1951.

[48]W.W. Francis, "Showman's Patter" (unpublished MS in the Osler Library, Archives and MSS Acc. 381), 18-19.

[49]Ibid., 225.

[50]Osler Library Board of Curators, Minutes, January 23, 1933.

[51]Personal communication from Cécile Desbarats to the author.

[52]Personal communication of Elaine Yarosky to the author, corroborated by Harry Ballon in an untitled contribution to *W.W. Francis: Tributes from his Friends*, 7.

[53]This poem, with its riposte from the Principal's secretary, Dorothy McMurray, is preserved in the research files of Dr. Edward Bensley, housed in the Osler Library, in the file "Francis — Black Martlets."

[54]William Willoughby Francis to Archibald Malloch, Francis Correspondence, Osler Library Archives and MSS Acc. 381. Emphasis in original.

[55]Personal communication of Cécile Desbarats to the author.

[56]Osler Library Board of Curators, Report of the Librarian, May 16, 1938.

[57]Personal communication of Dr. Eleanor McGarry to the author.

[58]Cf. Mordecai Etziony, "My Introduction to the Osler Library," in *W.W. Francis: Tributes from his Friends*, 65-68.

[59]See note 5 above.

[60]Personal communication of Cécile Desbarats to the author.

[61]Cécile Desbarats to E.E. Simpson, November 29, 1962, Francis Correspondence, Osler Library MSS and Archives Acc. 381.

[62]E.H. Bensley, "W.W. Francis: Patron of the Osler Society," *Osler Library Newsletter* 8 (Oct. 1971): [3].

Publications by W.W. Francis

The following list of Francis' publications is representative, but not necessarily exhaustive. It is presented in chronological order arranged in the following sections: articles and chapters in collected works, obituary notices and tributes, and book reviews. Unless otherwise indicated, all items are by W.W. Francis.

Articles and chapters in collected works

"The Osler Library." *McGill News*, Supplement, September 1929. 3p. [Francis' address on the opening of the Library.]

"The Osler Library." *Canadian Medical Association Journal* 21 (1929): 137-39. Reprinted in *The First Memorial Osler Celebration of the Canadian Medical Association*, 13-15. [Toronto: Canadian Medical Association], 1929.

McGill University. Museum of Human Anatomy. *Exhibition of the History of Anatomical Illustration*. Montreal: Renouf, 1930. "Prepared by John Beattie and H.E. MacDermot with the assistance of W.W. Francis." Reprinted in 1947.

"The Osler Library." In "The William H. Welch Medical Library of the Johns Hopkins University. An Account of its Origin and Development ...." *Bulletin of the Johns Hopkins Hospital* 46 (1930): 74-82.

"The Osler Day at Hamilton." *Canadian Medical Association Journal* 32 (1935): 468-69.

"Margaret Charleton and the Early Days of the Medical Library Association." *Bulletin of the Medical Library Association* 25 (1936): 58-63. [Francis' presidential address to the Association.]

"Sir William Osler and his Library." *D.C. Libraries* 8 (1937): 25-38.

"'Apologia' from an Unfinished Bibliography of Vesalius by the late Harvey Cushing with an Introductory Note by W.W. Francis." *Bulletin of the History of Medicine* 8 (1940): 381-91.

"Notes on Plate V, by W.W. Francis." In "Copernicus, Polish Astronomer, 1473-1543," by W. Carl Rufus. *Journal of the Royal Astronomical Society of Canada* 37 (1943): 129-42.

"Titles and Blurbs." *Bulletin of the Medical Library Association* 34 (1946): 320-23.

"Osler and *Religio Medici*." *Journal of the History of Medicine and Allied Sciences* 4 (1949): 116.

"The Osler Family." In "Sir William Osler Centenary. Some Recollections." *British Medical Journal* (July 9, 1949): 109-10.

"Osler and the Reporters, with an Unpublished Note on 'The Fixed Period'." *Canadian Medical Association Journal* 31 (1949): 68-69

"A Message from the Osler Library, McGill University." In *Congress Handbook for International Congress of Medical Librarianship*, 1, 1953.

"Linacre and Aldus." *Journal of the History of Medicine and Allied Sciences* 8 (1953): 329-30.

"Erasmus Darwin on Nicholas Robinson." *Journal of the History of Medicine and Allied Sciences* 9 (1954): 110-11.

"Osler's Catalogue." *Journal of the History of Medicine and Allied Sciences* 9 (1954): 464-65.

[with Lloyd G. Stevenson]. "Three Unpublished Letters of Edward Jenner." *Journal of the History of Medicine and Allied Sciences* 10 (1955): 359-68.

"Osler, Arms and the Man." *Journal of the History of Medicine and Allied Sciences* 10 (1955): 432-33.

"On the Death of Harvey: a Premature Threnody by Nikolaas van Assendelft." *Journal of the History of Medicine and Allied Sciences* 12 (1957): 254-55.

"Redi's Renal Calculi." *Journal of the History of Medicine and Allied Sciences* 13 (1958): 85.

"Repair of Cleft Palate by Philibert Roux in 1819: a Translation of John Stephenson's *De velosynthesi*." *Journal of the History of Medicine and Allied Sciences* 18 (1963): 209-19. With Introductory note by Lloyd G. Stevenson. Reprinted in *Plastic and Reconstructive Surgery* 47 (1971): 277-83.

Obituary notices and tributes

"Sir Andrew Macphail." *Bulletin of the History of Medicine* 7 (1939): 799-800.

"Harvey Cushing." *Canadian Medical Association Journal* 41 (1939): 496.

"Maude Abbott." *Bulletin of the History of Medicine* 10 (1941): 305-8.

"Rabelaesius Mariopolitanus." *Journal de l'Hôtel-Dieu de Montréal* 2 (1944 for 1943): 359-61. [Memorial issue to Léo Pariseau]

W.W. Francis

"Books and the Man." In "Tributes to Colin Kerr Russel 1877-1956, at the Montreal Neurological Institute, October 10, 1956, by W. Penfield, W.W. Francis and F. McNaughton." *Canadian Medical Association Journal* 77 (1957): 716-18.

Reviews

Review of *A Treatise on the Canon Medicine of Avicenna*, translated by O. Gruner. *Canadian Medical Association Journal* 24 (1931): 856-57.

Review of *Short Years: the Life and Letters of John Bruch MacCallum, M.D., 1876-1906*, by Thomas Archibald Malloch. *Canadian Medical Association Journal* 38 (1936): 312-14.

Review of *John Ferriar; Public Health Work, Tristram Shandy, Other Essays and Verses*, by Edward Mansfield Brockbank. *Journal of the History of Medicine and Allied Sciences* 8 (1953): 109-10.

Review of *The Life and Times of Gaspare Tagliacozzi, Surgeon of Bologna, 1545-1599*, by Martha Teach Gnudi and Jerome Pierce Webster. *Journal of the History of Medicine and Allied Sciences* 9 (1954): 123-24.

Review of *Halsted of Johns Hopkins; the Man and his Men*, by Samuel James Crowe. *Bulletin of the History of Medicine* 31 (1957): 582-83.

Sydney B. Mitchell and the
Establishment of Graduate Education
for Librarianship

Robert E. Brundin

Abstract

Sydney Bancroft Mitchell, founder of the School of Librarianship at the University of California, Berkeley, was an early promoter of graduate university education for librarians. Recognizing the need for this level of training before many of his contemporaries, he established the master's degree program at Berkeley in 1926. It was the third graduate program west of the Mississippi River. Genuinely interested in people, he enjoyed talking with and listening to others, and he took a great personal interest in his students. He had a strong influence on the careers of his graduates, many of whom became leaders in the profession.

Résumé

Sydney Bancroft Mitchell, le fondateur de l'École de bibliothéconomie de l'Université de la Californie à Berkeley, fut l'un des premiers à promouvoir l'éducation supérieure pour les bibliothécaires. Il en reconnut la nécessité avant la plupart de ses contemporains et mit sur pied un programme de maîtrise àBerkeley, en 1926. C'était le troisième programme d'études supérieures à l'ouest du Mississippi. Très préoccupé par les gens, Mitchell aimait parler aux autres et les écouter. Il s'intéressait beaucoup à ses étudiants et influença grandement les carrières de ses diplômés. Plusieurs d'entre eux devinrent des « leaders » dans la profession.

Sydney Bancroft Mitchell, founder and for twenty years the Director and Dean of the School of Librarianship of the University of California, Berkeley, is sometimes more remembered as a horticulturist and breeder of iris than as a library educator. Nonetheless, his contributions to librarianship

Reprinted with amendments from *Libraries & Culture*, Vol. 29, No. 2, Spring 1994
Copyright © 1994 by the University of Texas Press, P.O. Box 7819, Austin, TX 78713-7819

were significant, and he was one of the early initiators and promoters of graduate education for librarianship in the North American West.

Though Canadian by birth and education, Mitchell, like many of his contemporaries, was unable to find opportunities for professional advance-ment in Canada and went as a young man to the American West, where his work in California was of influence up and down the Pacific Coast, irrespective of international boundaries. In this paper, the major portion of his career will be traced, with emphasis on his efforts to establish graduate training for librarians in the 1920s and 1930s when, in both the Canadian and American West, such training was in only rudimentary stages of devel-opment.

Sydney Mitchell was born in Montreal, Quebec, on 24 June 1878, St. Jean Baptiste Day, feast day of the patron saint of French Canada. "This was," he later wrote, "more appropriate for a little French Canadian than for me,"[1] as he was of Scotch-Irish ancestry.

His father ran a cleaning and dyeing business patronized largely by French Canadians, and their home on Rue St-Hubert was in the heart of a French Canadian residential district. Thus young Mitchell grew up in a bilingual atmosphere, and he remained fluent in French throughout his life.[2]

Mitchell's interest in gardening developed long before his interest in libraries. His earliest recollection of planting anything was when he buried a chocolate bar at the suggestion of an older boy who assured him that chocolate grew in that fashion! Before he was nine, his interest in gardening had grown to the extent that what little money he could obtain he spent on seeds of annuals, particularly sweet peas, and monopolized the small back yard, seeking to get rich by selling radishes to his family.[3]

Proceeding through the Montreal Protestant school system, Mitchell entered McGill University in 1896, and, after losing one year due to illness, received the Bachelor of Arts degree in 1901 with honors in English and history. His father wished him to become a lawyer, but Mitchell thought he would rather teach. Because McGill University at that time had no courses in education, he followed the advice of a friend and obtained an interview with Charles H. Gould, the university librarian, to discuss possibilities in librarianship.

Gould, who was to remain a friend and advisor of Mitchell's throughout the latter's career, encouraged the young man to become a librarian. He offered him an unpaid apprenticeship in the university library, which Mitchell accepted, thus beginning a forty-five-year career in the profession. In 1901, he was the first male graduate of McGill to become an apprentice in the library.[4]

Mitchell was rapidly advanced to a paid position in charge of the reading room and of circulation, for which he received forty dollars a month.

He had decided by this time that in order to advance he must go to library school, so he retained the above position just long enough to earn sufficient money to cover his expenses. Then, in September 1903, he entered the New York State Library School at Albany, directed at the time by Melvil Dewey, and graduated with a library certificate in 1904. Throughout this period he had been studying for the Master of Arts in English and history at McGill, and he received this degree the same year.

In later years Mitchell was quite critical of his library school experiences at Albany, remarking on the lack of any scholarly or academic atmosphere and the trivial nature of most of his courses.[5] These experiences, coupled with his interest in teaching, probably played a part in motivating him to enter library education later in his career.

Indeed, some weeks before Mitchell finished library school, Charles Gould wrote to offer him a position as cataloguer in the McGill University Library, but what really interested Mitchell was the prospect that an endowed library school might be started there. Gould intimated that if the school were established, he wished Mitchell to be on hand to take charge of it, "… an alluring prospect to one then filled with ideas as to how — and how not — a library school should be run."[6]

As it turned out, the library school at McGill was not fully developed until a later date. Even so, Mitchell, during his time with the library as a cataloguer, had opportunity to teach reference service, loan procedures, bibliography, and a course on library buildings during the annual sessions of the Summer School for Librarians held on the campus.

He was particularly impressed with the teaching methodology of one of his McGill colleagues, Mary Imogene Hazeltine, later director of the Wisconsin Library School. In her reference course, which Mitchell audited, Hazeltine concentrated on standard titles which she knew her students would find in their own libraries, instead of trying to impress them with her knowledge of obscure materials which they would never encounter in their own work.[7] It was Mitchell's firm belief that it was not "… a function of professional schools to turn out graduates in the image of their makers, but rather to encourage that variety and vigour which means life."[8]

In 1908, with his salary still at sixty dollars per month after almost four years' experience, and the work, in his own words, becoming "more routine," Mitchell obtained a position with the Bay State Nurseries in North Abington, Massachusetts. He had applied unsuccessfully for two library positions in Canada, become discouraged, and thought to enter the nursery business in which he had become "… an enthusiastic and knowledgeable amateur."[9]

Mitchell thought at the time that he had left librarianship permanently, and, after obtaining some experience, would return to Montreal to open his

347

own nursery. However, a letter from his former roommate at Albany, Jack Goodwin, changed his plans. Goodwin, then librarian in charge of circulation at Stanford University in California, wrote that the position of head of the order department would shortly be open, and inquired if Mitchell were interested. Mitchell replied in the affirmative and Stanford Chief Librarian George T. Clark employed him sight-unseen on Goodwin's recommendation.

Mitchell spent three pleasant and profitable years at Stanford. His salary of one hundred dollars per month permitted his fiancée, Rose Frances Michaels, to come to California from Montreal, and they were married in 1908. He liked his work in the order department and, though he characterized Clark's administration as a "benevolent autocracy,"[10] he thoroughly enjoyed his working relationships with his chief librarian, and they remained personal friends throughout their lifetimes, to the extent that Clark wished Mitchell to succeed him on the former's retirement from Stanford in 1927.

During this period Gould, at McGill, had mentioned Mitchell's name to the administration at the Toronto Public Library as a good candidate for the position of assistant librarian for acquisitions. Nothing materialized of this, though, as the chief librarian chose to employ a bookseller without library training for the post. "They say he is a very nice fellow," wrote Gould to Mitchell, "and has a good knowledge of books from a bookseller's point of view, but I do not imagine that his knowledge of technical matters will ever be likely to put his chief to the blush. Perhaps Mr. Locke [the chief librarian at Toronto] himself thought of this when the appointment was in view."[11]

Though Mitchell was, at the time, not actively seeking a different position, he was approached in 1911 by a classmate from Albany, Harold L. Leupp, then associate librarian at the University of California, Berkeley, with an invitation to become head of the accessions department. Mitchell was getting a bit restless at Stanford; the salaries were low, and under Clark's style of administration there was no call for a second or third person in command, and therefore little opportunity for advancement. Thus he accepted Leupp's invitation and began a career at Berkeley which was to last thirty-five years.

At the time Mitchell joined the staff at Berkeley, Harold Leupp, though associate librarian, was actually in charge of the library. During Leupp's first year of service at the university, President Benjamin Ide Wheeler had been greatly impressed by his administrative ability and had given him the major responsibility for the day-to-day running of the library.[12]

Chief Librarian Joseph Rowell, who had been in office since 1875, thereafter devoted himself primarily to book selection, collection development, and archival work. This new division of duties, which might have led to conflict between the two men, actually proved to be a situation which both accepted amicably, each respecting the other's strengths and contributions.[13]

Leupp's style of administration was quite different from that of George Clark at Stanford. Leupp believed in gathering about him a group of colleagues whose advice he would seek and who would work with him rather than under him.[14] He also was a perfectionist, and demanded this perfection in those who worked with him. Though he delegated authority to others, he sometimes had difficulty in completely relinquishing that authority,[15] but, as Mitchell later wrote, "... if you had the guts to stand up to him, ... you could work with him and have more opportunity to get your ideas adopted than with most of the administrators of his time."[16] In Sydney Mitchell, Leupp obtained a very able colleague indeed.

Mitchell was physically not an impressive man. He was short of stature and somewhat overweight. Born with a congenital hip dislocation, he walked with a decided limp. His hair was tousled and he tended to look a bit rumpled and unkempt. But what he lacked in physical attributes he made up for in temperament. Determined to succeed, he rarely avoided challenges. When the McGill University Library had been "... reluctant to employ a cripple [as a student assistant], he set a record for climbing the stack staircase from bottom to top and back again. Thenceforth, no one questioned his ability to get around fast on his own legs."[17]

Mitchell liked people and liked talking with them. He was genuinely interested in others and in what they had to say, a quality which was to stand in his favor in his later administrative work. He rapidly gained the friendship, confidence, and respect of his colleagues at Berkeley.[18]

Mitchell had an excellent sense of humor, and employed it to best advantage when giving a public address. While a student at McGill, he had won a contest in the Arts 1900 class for giving the best rendition of Napoleon's address to his army after the Battle of Austerlitz. According to a classmate at the time, Mitchell had "brought down the house" when, in his speech accepting the prize, he had ended with, "Nous avons passé Austerlitz, mais en avant je vois Waterloo," referring to the fact that although the "Napoleon contest" was over, the class was still anticipating a very difficult final examination![19]

This, then, was the man who, in 1911 and at the age of thirty-three, came to the University of California as head of the accessions department. Though Mitchell, as noted, had developed a particular interest in library education, he had little opportunity in his initial years at Berkeley to do much teaching. The library did, however, offer summer courses in "library methods." These had been started in 1901 for the benefit of librarians in the area, and in the summer of 1912 Mitchell had an opportunity to teach a course on "book buying."[20] This experience started him thinking about the possibility of establishing a library school at the university, but it was to be several years before he would be able to achieve this goal.

In the meantime, the advent of United States' participation in World War I in 1917 and Harold Leupp's receipt of a commission in the army left Mitchell as the associate in charge of the library. He was appointed by the university president, and remained in that position until Leupp returned in February 1919.

Although his administrative duties were heavy, Mitchell found the time in 1918 to draft a plan for undergraduate instruction in library science, which was presented to the Committee on Courses of the Academic Senate in April of that year and was accepted. It provided for four year-long, six-credit courses open to upper division students during the regular terms, with the twenty-four units of credit to be applicable to the Bachelor of Arts degree. The four courses were Bibliography, Cataloguing, Library Administration and Study, and Selection of Books.[21]

Although Mitchell had contacted Leupp for permission to begin the courses, when the latter returned to the library following the war he showed no interest in the new program. He let it be known that he did not particularly appreciate "Mr. Mitchell's library school," as he felt it was occupying too much of his assistant's time,[22] though he later gave Mitchell full responsibility for the courses as an adjunct to his other duties.

Two difficulties with the program soon emerged, in Mitchell's view. One was the fact that it was an undergraduate program and tended to attract "immature" students ill-prepared to undertake professional courses together with their other university work. Secondly, it proved difficult for Mitchell and Edith Coulter, the head reference librarian, to teach the courses in addition to performing their regular functions in the university library.[23] Mitchell's solution was to propose the formation of a graduate school which would be independent of the library, with its own staff and budget.[24]

The year was 1919, and only two library schools existed in the United States west of the Mississippi River, one at the University of Washington, established in 1911, and a school at Kansas State University, Emporia, begun in 1902. In Canada, summer schools were offered at McGill University beginning in 1904 and in Toronto beginning in 1911. Moreover, most schools offered their courses at the undergraduate level. Thus Mitchell was somewhat ahead of his time in submitting his proposal for a school offering graduate courses only, and it was not accepted by the university administration.

In June 1919 Rowell retired, Leupp became chief librarian in title as well as in function, and Mitchell was appointed to Leupp's former position of associate librarian, with added administrative duties beyond the running of the order department. The result, of course, was even less time for the running of the library science program, which was Mitchell's real interest.

350

A partial solution to the problem was achieved in 1922, when Mitchell persuaded the university administration to create a separate undergraduate Department of Library Science within the College of Letters and Science, with himself as chair, at the rank of associate professor. This new department continued to occupy quarters in the main library building, and its instructors, including Mitchell, continued with their dual functions, but administratively the department became a separate entity with its own budget. Mitchell was also able to persuade Leupp to transfer Della Sisler, a cataloguer in the university library, to the department full-time, with the title "Associate in Library Science."[25] Thus, almost single-handedly, Mitchell had established a library school.

Though working relationships between Mitchell and Leupp had been very good in the beginning, by this time the two had become, in many respects, rivals. With the appointment of Leupp to the chief librarianship in 1919, Mitchell realized that he had little chance of succeeding to the top position, as the two were only a year apart in age.[26] Jealousies developed as Mitchell sought new outlets for his administrative ambitions. Though Mitchell was still technically associate librarian in Leupp's library, the latter maintained, according to a former student and library assistant, that he was not operating a "finishing school" for Mitchell's program, and refused to employ its graduates.[27] He was later to change his opinion in this matter, however.

Competition between the two developed on other levels, as they were of quite different temperaments. Mitchell was a humanist, with the "common touch" always about him; Leupp was something of an elitist who, in the words of a colleague who knew both men, "... should have lived as an aristocrat in the eighteenth-century French court."[28] Thus, Leupp probably welcomed the partial separation of Mitchell's school, as this lessened somewhat the potential areas of conflict between the two.

Complicating matters was the fact that Mitchell really did not wish to leave Berkeley to seek a position elsewhere.[29] He had already made a name for himself as an authority on the growing and breeding of iris, an avocation which continually threatened to become his vocation. In 1922 he had acquired three acres of land in the Berkeley hills on which to expand his gardens and where, in 1923, he and his wife had a Spanish-style home built to their specifications. His first book on horticulture, *Gardening in California*, was published by Doubleday in 1923 and included a frontispiece photograph of one of the Mitchell gardens. There was little incentive for him to depart the San Francisco Bay area.

Apparently, up to this time, Mitchell only once had seriously considered taking a position elsewhere. In 1914 he had applied for the position of Librarian of the University of British Columbia, and had his friend and former employer George T. Clark write him a letter of reference.[30] He had at that time not yet become an American citizen (he was naturalized in 1922) and thought to return to Canada. However, the administration at British Columbia decided, due to "fund shortages" occasioned by World War I, to appoint an acting librarian from the staff,[31] and nothing came of Mitchell's application.

Nonetheless, by 1925 Mitchell had become quite unhappy with his circumstance at Berkeley. His duties as associate librarian were taking up most of his time and he found it extremely difficult to administer the Department of Librarianship as well as teach many of its courses. Therefore, he told Leupp that he intended to ask the university to establish librarianship as a graduate school beginning with the university year 1926-1927. If this were done, he would leave the library and administer the school on a full-time basis. If he were turned down, he intended to seek employment elsewhere.[32]

Thus it was that on 17 December 1925, Mitchell appeared before the Graduate Council of the university with a proposal for "... the establishment of a Graduate School of Librarianship, with a fixed curriculum of two years; the work of the first year to consist of training in the required technique; the work of the second year to develop the broader aspects of library administration, including cooperation with departments of instruction and research in the University..."[33] A committee of six was appointed to investigate the proposal and make recommendations.

On 1 February 1926 the committee reported back to the Graduate Council with a resolution to establish a Graduate School of Librarianship, with a certificate to be awarded on completion of the first year of work, and a master's degree on completion of the second year.[34] This resolution was accepted by the Council, which then asked the committee to draw up a curriculum for the School of Librarianship and submit a second report.[35]

However, it proved necessary to speed up the process, as the proposal for the School needed to reach the President in advance of the adoption of the budget for 1926-1927, scheduled for the March meeting of the Board of Regents.[36] Therefore, Mitchell was asked to present the proposed program of the School of Librarianship verbally to the Graduate Council at its meeting of 15 February 1926. Mitchell, always able with words, convinced the Council to pass the program "in principle," with the understanding that there would be a detailed, formal presentation to the University Council at its next meeting.[37]

The Academic Senate's approval of the new curriculum followed in March, and on 8 June 1926 the Board of Regents authorized the School to award the degree of Master of Arts.[38] As Mitchell recounted in retirement, this was indeed a proud moment in his career. The School of Librarianship had been approved through the appropriate administrative machinery of the university; "... we weren't getting in by the back door, or through a hole in the fence, or anything of that kind."[39] He had always been somewhat apologetic that the original Department of Librarianship had been created essentially by administrative fiat, and tended to be overlooked or sometimes resented by the academic "regulars." The approval of the Regents "regularized us," as Mitchell later said.[40]

As approved by the Regents, the first year's program consisted of courses in "Cataloguing and Classification," "Reference Materials," "Trade Bibliography and Book Buying," "Book Arts and Selection," "The American Public Library," and two choices of elective courses dealing with particular types of libraries. Upon satisfactory completion of the twenty-four units of work involved in this first year, the student received a Certificate in Librarianship.[41]

The second year allowed for a more flexible program. The student chose two courses from Group I: "History of Libraries," "History of Printing," and "Paleography." From Group II courses — "Bibliographic Cataloguing," "History and Philosophy of Classification," "Bibliography," and "Evaluation of Books" — the student picked two to three courses, depending on unit value. Finally, he or she picked one "type of library" course, selected from "University Libraries," "School Libraries," or "Public Libraries." A thesis, worth two units, and six units of courses from outside the School were also required,[42] and the graduate received the Master of Arts degree. This curriculum remained basically the same until Mitchell's retirement in 1946.

Although terminology used to describe the Berkeley program, together with its content, have been changed markedly, the structure and broad subject coverage as planned by Mitchell has remained constant, testifying to the sound, pragmatic manner in which he approached this task. His work was grounded not only on a thorough knowledge of what was being done in other parts of the country, but on what he felt to be basic to the profession, based on twenty-two years of experience. Mitchell also pioneered the concept of graduate library education in his part of the country; up to this point, the training offered was primarily through short courses offered by public libraries.

During the early years of the school, Mitchell himself taught many of the courses, in addition to administering the program. His particular interests were the courses "Book Arts and Selection," "Trade Bibliography and Book Buying," "University Library Administration," and "Book Collecting for Large Libraries," all areas in which he had had extensive experience. Assistant Professors Coulter and Sisler, now both full-time with the School, taught most of the other courses.[43]

Mitchell called on nearby librarians to teach part-time, mostly with respect to the offering of courses on the administration of various types of libraries. His most notable assistant in this regard was Carleton B. Joeckel, later to gain prominence at the University of Chicago, who taught public library administration and the course "The American Public Library."[44] At this time, Joeckel was chief librarian of the Berkeley Public Library, though he had earlier served with Mitchell on the library staff at the university.

Due to his vigorous efforts to establish graduate library education west of the Mississippi River, and to his activities from 1924 to 1927 as head of the Carnegie Institution Committee for the study of college library problems, Mitchell's name had come to the attention of several persons prominent in librarianship at the time, one of them being William Warner Bishop, then university librarian at the University of Michigan. In the spring of 1926, Bishop was seeking a suitable candidate for a full professorship at the newly formed library school of that university; the plan was that the person selected would in time assume the directorship of the school from Bishop, who would continue in his position as university librarian.[45]

In a report to several administrative officers of his university, Bishop spoke of his search efforts and in extremely candid terms compared the credentials of thirteen distinguished librarians under consideration, among them Sydney Mitchell. Of Mitchell he wrote: "There seems substantial unanimity of opinion that Mr. Sydney B. Mitchell ... possesses more nearly the qualifications which we require than any other person."[46]

Bishop's high opinion of Mitchell was confirmed by his good friend and colleague James Ingersoll Wyer, Director of the New York State Library, who ". . . feels very strongly that Mr. Mitchell ... is the best man for the post."[47] The result was that "out of a clear sky," as Mitchell later put it, he received an offer to go to Michigan as a full professor at a fifty percent increase over his California salary.

Mitchell was suddenly placed in a very difficult position. The time was late May of 1926, and the University of California Board of Regents had, as mentioned, recently given approval for the formation of a Graduate School of Librarianship, with Mitchell as head. Yet the offer from Michigan was quite tempting.

Although Mitchell did not really wish to leave California, he realized that the Michigan position had great potential, whereas, at the time, he had doubts that California would ultimately finance its new School. He solved his dilemma by requesting a year's leave of absence to go to Michigan.

The university had originally offered him sabbatical leave, feeling that experience in another institution might be beneficial for all parties.[48] However, generous as this seemed, Mitchell, as he recalled later in his memoirs, looked on the agreement "with a cold, fishy eye."[49] By requesting a leave of absence, he left himself free either to stay at Michigan or to negotiate the terms of his return to Berkeley. Under provisions of the sabbatical leave, he would have been obliged to return at the level of associate professor, with a salary of $3,900, as contrasted with the full professorship and $6,000 salary offered by Michigan.

The University of California granted Mitchell the leave of absence he sought, and he spent the 1926-1927 academic year at Michigan, teaching courses in book selection, academic library administration, and national and regional bibliography to forty-seven first-year and six advanced students. In addition to gaining experience in a different locale and under different teaching conditions, Mitchell took the opportunity to visit many midwestern and eastern gardens, and developed an interest in the growing and breeding of daffodils,[50] more common there than in western gardens.

Throughout the year, however, he played what he termed "a game of poker" with the administrators at California. As late as December 1926 he was in correspondence with the comptroller at California with regard to the possibilities of withdrawing his pension funds and investing them in the Michigan scheme.[51] Indeed, the records are clear that he was highly thought of by Bishop, who wished him to stay on at Michigan and take charge of the school when he had become more familiar with the library scene in that state. Mitchell even went so far as to contact his colleague Carleton Joeckel in Berkeley regarding the latter's interest in assuming the directorship of the California School.[52] (The School was being administered on a part-time basis by Harold Leupp during Mitchell's absence; the rivalry between the two had lessened considerably upon Mitchell's departure for Michigan.)

Mitchell's "game of poker" ended in his favor. With the Michigan offer in hand, he again approached the administration at California with regard to their long-range plans for the new library school, and was able to gain a permanent appointment as Director of the School of Librarianship ". . . with every assurance now from the administration that it will be developed into a two-year graduate school along the lines I had proposed."[53] As part of the agreement, Edith Coulter was to be placed on full-time assignment with the school. Mitchell later called these events ". . . the greatest break the School ever had . . .",[54] and most certainly it represented a great achievement in his efforts to promote graduate library education on the West Coast of the United States. Mitchell had long felt that the education of librarians should be conducted at universities[55] rather than by public libraries, as was often the practice, and particularly at the graduate level, and this 1927 agreement fulfilled both of these requirements.

Thus, in September 1927 Mitchell began what was to be a nineteen-year tenure as director/dean of the Berkeley library school.

Undergraduate courses in library science were eliminated, and a bachelor's degree was required for admission. In requiring the baccalaureate for admission, Mitchell placed Berkeley at the forefront of a movement to upgrade North American library education, a movement which was not to see complete fruition until some forty to fifty years later.

The number of those admitted each year was increased from thirty to fifty and, according to plan, the second-year curriculum leading to the master's degree was begun in 1928. A certificate, rather than the customary Bachelor of Library Science, was given upon completion of the first year of the curriculum. With minor modifications, this curricular structure was retained until shortly after Mitchell's retirement in 1946.

Mitchell worked hard during the late 1920s and early 1930s to consolidate the new program and to achieve recognition of it by library employers, including Harold Leupp of the university library. He established a close working relationship with the California state librarian James L. Gillis; the State Library had for many years conducted a training program for librarians, but this was ceased by mutual agreement and aspirants for professional library training were directed to the university.

In the 1930s Mitchell began offering the first semester of the Berkeley curriculum at the University of California at Los Angeles, using the Berkeley and visiting faculty to serve the needs of southern California.[56] This was one of the earlier efforts at extension work in library education.

He achieved the cooperation of neighboring public and school librarians in setting up "field work" situations in which students could involve themselves in practical work experiences,[57] though he was not a pioneer in this regard. He also consolidated subjects in the curriculum under four headings — "Cataloguing and Classification," "Bibliography," "Library Administration and Extension," and "Study and Selection of Books" — thus giving emphasis to major rather than to minor divisions in the curriculum.[58] In this, Berkeley did pioneer a structure which was to be widely emulated by other North American library schools in later decades.

Recognizing the need to give attention to the fields of children's literature and library work with children, Mitchell obtained the services of Jessie E. Boyd, a high school librarian and 1929 master's degree graduate of the school, to teach in these areas. Miss Boyd, in Mitchell's words, "... proved to be about the best person we have ever had in this field...",[59] and went on to become supervisor of libraries for the Oakland, California, public school district.

Once the program had been consolidated and had been awarded some recognition in the profession,[60] Mitchell worked toward regularizing the standards of admission, which had been somewhat flexible in the early years. In 1930 the age limit for entrance was reduced from forty to thirty-five, as, in Mitchell's opinion, experience had indicated that those admitted at ages above thirty-five tended not to complete the program or to do poorly in it when compared with younger students.[61] Candidates were advised to gain at least two years' experience in libraries before attempting the second year of the master's degree program.

Though strict in terms of maintaining what he considered to be desirable standards of quality for his library school program, Mitchell was at heart a great student of human nature, and extremely tolerant of the eccentricities of those around him. He took a great personal interest in each of his students, and took the time to make himself familiar with the background of each one, and of his or her career interests and potentialities.[62] One graduate of the school later remarked that Mitchell knew him better than did his parents![63]

Together with the personal interest he took in his students, Mitchell possessed a remarkable ability to judge people and their strengths and weaknesses. Thus, he was consulted by many librarians seeking candidates for vacant positions. Mitchell enjoyed this type of involvement with his students, and during the 1930s and early 1940s he was frequently called on to provide references for persons seeking employment up and down the West Coast of the United States and Canada. Always forthright in his judgements, if he thought the job was not right for the person, or the person was not right for the job, no recommendation was forthcoming.[64] His suggestion to Ray Lyman Wilbur, president of Stanford University, of Nathan Van Patten for the post of university librarian in 1927[65] resulted in the employment of an expert bibliographer and bookman who was to double the size of that library and its collections during his twenty-year tenure.

It should be noted at this point that Sydney Mitchell was not a man completely without prejudice, and these prejudices sometimes influenced the recommendations he made with regard to employment. However, his prejudices were very common to his time, and in acting on them he was choosing to follow, rather than challenge, the status quo.

As an example, Mitchell often favored men candidates for positions over their women counterparts, particularly with respect to administrative posts.[66] His stated belief was that the investment made in training a capable man was a better one than that made in training a capable woman, "for the simple reason," as he wrote, "that a much larger proportion of them will spend the rest of their lives in the profession."[67]

He was also realistic concerning some of the racial and ethnic prejudices of his time, although, on a personal level, he did not accept these prejudices. He once told a graduate that since she was Jewish her job opportunities would be limited, and that in particular she should not try to seek employment in a small town library. She took his advice and stayed in the San Francisco Bay area.[68]

Mitchell had a photographic memory for people; he could recall every graduate of the school, his or her academic and personal history, and details of employment. On occasion, in this era prior to the advent of the curriculum vitae and the personal data file, an individual would be employed sight unseen, on Mitchell's recommendation alone.[69] As graduates of the School grew in number and traveled to other parts of the continent, his advice was increasingly sought with regard to appointments in the Midwest and East.

In his report for the biennium 1942-1944, two years before his retirement, Mitchell noted that the school had been involved in the placement of 130 individuals in full-time positions during that period. He noted that he and his secretary did most of this work, and that most librarians "… seem to prefer to deal direct rather than through general university placement services."[70]

Although Mitchell was a strong promoter of the School within the university and the state, working always to ensure that proper standards of entrance were maintained and that graduates were well-placed, he did not attempt to promote himself or the School on a nationwide basis. His personality was such that he preferred to maintain a fairly low profile among his colleagues, and to exert his energies toward influencing his students to become the leaders in the profession which he expected them to be. In this regard, one writer has called him "… perhaps one of the most influential advisors of Western [American] librarianship."[71]

Thus, Mitchell, in his own way, had, in the words of one of his students, "… a more profound and far-reaching influence in California in his time than any individual except James L. Gillis."[72] (James Gillis was state librarian for many years, and developed the county library system, which maintains its importance today.) And through the careers of his students, his influence extended well beyond the borders of the state. Prominent graduates such as Seymour Lubetsky, Herman Henkle, Blanche McCrum, Mortimer Taube, Lawrence Clark Powell, Edwin Castagna, and Robert Vosper, the latter two serving as presidents of the American Library Association, acknowledged their indebtedness to Mitchell for the sound advice he gave them in their early years in the profession.[73]

Mitchell never forgot graduates of the School who showed promise. When Henkle was appointed chief of cataloguing at the Library of Congress and asked Mitchell to send him a "brain," Mitchell remembered Lubetsky, who was at the time classifying parts in the Oakland, California, shipyards,[74] and who, at the Library of Congress, was to make significant contributions to the development of modern descriptive cataloguing theory.

Later in their careers, students could identify with Mitchell when they were dealing with frustrating problems in administration, and could remember his advice on helping them cope with problem situations in their work.[75] It was this ability to empathize with his students on a personal level that was probably one of Mitchell's greatest talents, but it was not a talent that would necessarily lead to recognition beyond those who were in immediate contact with him.

In all of his activities, Mitchell's personality and ability to understand and deal effectively with those around him was of tremendous assistance. If humanly possible, Mitchell liked to deal personally with his colleagues, rather than by telephone or mail. They appreciated his "... certain human qualities, unassuming nature, and approachable manner; there was always an opportunity to talk to him about anything."[76]

Mitchell thrived on this type of direct contact. His home and gardens in the Berkeley hills were the frequent setting for informal gatherings of students and alumni, and a kettle was always on the stove to serve up tea to the unannounced visitor. Students, former students, and colleagues came to him and told of their hopes and fears, their successes and failures, because they liked and trusted him.[77]

One of the precepts which Mitchell advanced to students in his classes on library administration was that individuals should never get so involved in work that they could not fall back on a hobby.[78] He himself was probably the best example one could find of a person who lived by that precept. His "hobby" of gardening in general, and raising and breeding iris in particular, was often in danger of becoming his profession. It was said that during the depression years of the 1930s he made more money from his books and articles on gardening and from selling new breeds of iris bulbs than he did as director of the School of Librarianship.[79]

In any event, he became internationally known as a breeder of iris and daffodils, and founded, and for ten years edited, the quarterly journal of the California Horticultural Society. He wrote articles on gardening for *Sunset Magazine* from 1929 until his death in 1951, and, for fifteen of those years, edited a regular gardening column for that journal. Mitchell also found time to publish five books on gardening which sold very well. He was and remains the only individual to have served as president of both the California Library Association (1938-1939) and the California Horticultural Society (1933-1945).

If he was not a scholar in librarianship, it was by his own choice. His greatest achievements were with people, and people were always one of his greatest interests. A colleague has described him as "... a natural politician, a realist, capable of motion forward, backward, sideways, and circular when necessary to achieve his goals," but also a man who had "principles, courage, and loyalty. The example he set for me and others was of what librarians and educators are capable of achieving."[80]

Mitchell did have some thirty articles and numerous book reviews published in library periodicals, but he never found time to write the book on university librarianship for which purpose he had taken a sabbatical leave, and he failed to finish writing his memoirs; they were completed and published posthumously, from notes he had left and from an interview taped a few months before he died. However, he found the time to become outstanding in the two fields he loved the best — teaching and horticulture.

By 1946, when Mitchell retired, the School of Librarianship at Berkeley was well-established, with a reputation for producing graduates qualified to assume leadership positions in the library world. Mitchell himself was known and respected in the profession, called on frequently as a consultant or conference speaker. In 1945 he had been granted the honorary degree of Doctor of Letters by Occidental College in California for his contributions to librarianship.

Sydney Mitchell died in Berkeley on 22 September 1951 at the age of seventy-three, surrounded by the beautiful gardens he had lovingly tended for so many years. The gardens have long since disappeared, but Mitchell lives on in the halls and classrooms of the School which he founded and painstakingly built into a position of eminence in the field of North American graduate library education. And this is probably the best memorial a library educator could ever have.

Notes

[1] Sydney B. Mitchell, *Mitchell of California: the Memoirs of Sydney B. Mitchell, Librarian—Teacher—Gardener* (Berkeley: California Library Association, 1960), 9.

[2] Lawrence Clark Powell, "Mitchell, Sydney Bancroft (1878-1951)," in *Dictionary of American Library Biography*, ed. Bohdan S. Wynar (Littleton, Colo.: Libraries Unlimited, 1978), 366.

[3] Rose Mitchell, letter to Mrs. Burges [not further identified], 19 July 1940, in Sydney B. Mitchell, Correspondence and Papers, ca. 1925-1951, Manuscript Division, Bancroft Library, University of California, Berkeley, box 1.

[4] Mitchell, *Mitchell of California*, p. 103.

[5] Sydney B. Mitchell, "The Pioneer Library School in Middle Age," *Library Quarterly* 20 (October 1950): 272-88.

[6] Mitchell, *Mitchell of California*, 140.

[7] Ibid., 141.

[8] Ibid., 140.

[9] Mitchell, "The Pioneer Library School," 288.

[10] Mitchell, *Mitchell of California*, 205.

[11] Charles H. Gould, Librarian, McGill University, letter to Sydney B. Mitchell, 2 December 1909, in Letter Book, McGill University Library No. 16: 19 October 1909 to 11 April 1910, McGill University Archives, Montreal, file no. 267, box C58.

[12]Kenneth G. Peterson, *The University of California Library at Berkeley, 1900-1945* (Berkeley: University of California Press, 1970), 51.

[13]Ibid.

[14]Mitchell, *Mitchell of California*, 207.

[15]Peterson, *The University of California Library at Berkeley*, 57.

[16]Mitchell, *Mitchell of California*, 207-8.

[17]Powell, "Mitchell, Sydney Bancroft," 366.

[18]Monroe E. Deutsch, Provost and Vice-President, University of California, letter to Morse A. Cartwright, Director, American Association for Adult Education, 13 April 1937, in University of California, School of Librarianship, Correspondence, 1926-1946, University of California Archives, Berkeley, President's Files, box 1.

[19]A.S. McCormick, M.D., 1901 Arts graduate, McGill University, letter to G.C. Papineau-Couture, K.C., 19 January 1952, in Sydney B. Mitchell, Correspondence and Papers, ca. 1925-1951, box 1.

[20]Mitchell, *Mitchell of California*, 208.

[21]Harold L. Leupp, "Excerpts from the Report on the University Library for the Year 1918-1919, Submitted by Harold L. Leupp, Librarian, July 1, 1919," in University of California, School of Librarianship, Reports, 1918/19-1959/60, University of California Archives, Berkeley, 1-2.

[22]May Dornin, Class of 1922, Department of Library Science, interview with William Boletta, June 1978, tape recording, School of Library and Information Studies, University of California, Berkeley.

[23]Harold L. Leupp, "Excerpts from the Report on the University Library for the Year 1919-1920, Submitted by Harold L. Leupp, Librarian, July 1, 1920," 3-4.

[24]Ibid., 4.

[25]Harold L. Leupp, "School of Librarianship—Excerpts from the Report on the University Library for the Academic Year 1921-22, Submitted by Harold L. Leupp, Librarian, Printed in the Annual Report of the President of the University," in University of California, School of Librarianship, Reports, 1918/19-1959/60, University of California Archives, Berkeley, p. 2.

[26]May Dornin, taped interview.

[27]Ibid.

[28]John Dale Henderson, Class of 1930, School of Librarianship, interview with William Boletta, June 1978, tape recording, School of Library and Information Studies, University of California, Berkeley.

[29]May Dornin, taped interview.

[30]George T. Clark, Librarian, Stanford University, letter to F.F. Wesbrook, President, University of British Columbia, 3 July 1914; and, George T. Clark, letter to Sydney B. Mitchell, 30 July 1914; both in Sydney B. Mitchell, Correspondence and Papers, ca. 1925-1951, box 1.

[31]Charles H. Gould, Librarian, McGill University, letter to Sydney B. Mitchell, 4 October 1915, in Letter Book, McGill University Library No. 26: 28 September 1915 to 17 May 1916, McGill University Archives, Montreal, file no. 25, box C60.

[32]Mitchell, *Mitchell of California*, 213.

[33]University of California, Graduate Council, "Minutes: Graduate Council: December 17, 1925," in Minutes: August 1923-May 1932, University of California Archives, Berkeley, vol. 52, p. 351.

[34]Ibid., "Appendix A to Minutes: Graduate Council: February 1, 1926," 355.

[35]Ibid., "Minutes: Graduate Council: February 1, 1926," 353.

[36]Ibid., "Minutes: Graduate Council: December 17, 1925," 352.

[37]Ibid., "Minutes: Graduate Council: February 15, 1926," 359.

[38]University of California, Academic Senate, "Minutes of the Academic Senate: Meeting of August 23, 1926," in Minutes: 1925-28, University of California Archives, Berkeley, vol. 24 [vol. 5 on original binding], 78.

[39]Mitchell, *Mitchell of California*, 213.

[40]Ibid., 214.

[41]University of California, Academic Senate, "Minutes of the Academic Senate: Meeting of May 10, 1926," vol. 24 [vol. 5 on original binding], 72-73.

[42]Ibid., 73.

[43]University of California, School of Librarianship, *Announcement for 1926-1927*, and *Announcement for 1928-1929* (Berkeley: University of California Press, 1926, 1928).

[44]Ibid.

[45]Mitchell, *Mitchell of California*, 215.

[46]William Warner Bishop, "Report to the President, to the Dean of the Graduate School, and to the Dean of the College of Literature, Science, and the Arts, on a Possible Faculty for the Department of Library Science, May 5, 1926," in University of California, School of Librarianship, Records, 1926-1960, University of California Archives, Berkeley, box 1. (This is a photocopy; the original document is in the archives of the University of Michigan.)

[47]Ibid.

[48]Mitchell, *Mitchell of California*, 214.

[49]Ibid.

[50]"Notes on S.B.M.," in Sydney B. Mitchell, Correspondence and Papers, ca. 1925-1951, box 4.

[51]Sydney B. Mitchell, letter to Robert Gordon Sproul, Comptroller, University of California, 7 December 1926, in University of California, School of Librarianship, Records, 1926-1960, box 1.

[52]Sydney B. Mitchell, night letter to Carleton B. Joeckel, Librarian, Berkeley Public Library, n.d., in University of California, School of Librarianship, Records, 1926-1960, box 1.

[53]Sydney B. Mitchell, letter to Bertha Gunterman, Editor, Longman's, Green and Company, 25 February 1927, in University of California, School of Librarianship, Records, 1926-1960, box 1.

[54]Mitchell, *Mitchell of California*, 214-15.

[55]Sydney B. Mitchell, letter to C.C. Williamson, Director, Columbia University Library, 24 November 1926, in University of California, School of Librarianship, Records, 1926-1960, box 1.

[56]Lawrence Clark Powell, Class of 1937, School of Librarianship, and Dean Emeritus, Graduate School of Library and Information Science, University of California, Los Angeles, letter to the author, 24 May 1982.

[57]University of California, School of Librarianship, "Report of the School of Librarianship for the Biennium 1928-30," in Reports, 1918/19-1959/60, University of California Archives, Berkeley, 2.

[58]Ernest J. Reece, *The Curriculum in Library Schools* (New York: Columbia University Press, 1936), 86.

[59]University of California, School of Librarianship, "Report of the School of Librarianship for the Biennium 1928-30," 3.

[60]In 1933 the Board of Education of the American Library Association established a new system of accreditation providing for three levels of schools — types one, two, and three. California was designated a type one school, as it offered the master's degree in library science, which type two and three schools did not. At this time, only four other schools in North America were designated as type one programs.

[61]Sydney B. Mitchell, letter to Monroe E. Deutsch, Provost and Vice-President, University of California, 23 April 1935, in University of California, School of Librarianship, Correspondence, 1926-1946, box 1.

[62]Helen A. Kearney, Class of 1924, Department of Library Science, interview with William Boletta, May 1979, tape recording, School of Library and Information Studies, University of California, Berkeley.

[63]John Dale Henderson, taped interview.

[64]J. Periam Danton, Dean Emeritus, School of Librarianship, interview with the author, 9 February 1982.

[65]Sydney B. Mitchell, letter to Ray Lyman Wilbur, President, Stanford University, 17 May 1927, in University of California, School of Librarianship, Correspondence, 1926-1946, box 1.

[66]Betty Ruth Koudayan, "Blanche P. McCrum," in *Leaders in American Academic Librarianship: 1925-1975*, ed. Wayne A. Wiegand (Chicago: American Library Association, 1983), 188.

[67]Sydney B. Mitchell, "Ways and Means of Limiting Library School Output," *American Library Association Bulletin* 26 (July 1932): 429.

[68]Thelma Percy, Class of 1942, School of Librarianship, letter to Dean Michael Buckland, 28 November 1979, in an unclassified file of materials relating to Sydney B. Mitchell in the files of the School of Library and Information Studies, University of California, Berkeley.

[69]Dorothea Dudley Nelson, Class of 1932, School of Librarianship, letter to Rochelle P. Schmalz, Newsletter Editor, 7 April 1979, in an unclassified file of materials relating to Sydney B. Mitchell in the files of the School of Library and Information Studies, University of California, Berkeley.

[70]University of California, School of Librarianship, "Report of the School of Librarianship for the Biennium 1942-44," in Reports, 1918/19-1959/60, University of California Archives, 4.

[71]Rudolf Englebarts, *Librarian Authors: a Bibliography* (Jefferson, N.C.: McFarland, 1981), 50.

Sydney B. Mitchell

[72]John Dale Henderson, taped interview.
[73]See Wiegand, ed., *Leaders in American Academic Librarianship*, pp. 192, 281.
[74]Lawrence Clark Powell, letter to the author.
[75]John Dale Henderson, taped interview.
[76]Helen A. Kearney, taped interview.
[77]Lawrence Clark Powell, *A Passion for Books* (Cleveland, Ohio: World Publishing Company, 1958), 141.
[78]Bertha Hellum, Class of 1934, School of Librarianship, interview with William Boletta, 5 July 1979, tape recording, School of Library and Information Studies, University of California, Berkeley.
[79]Ibid.
[80]Lawrence Clark Powell, letter to the author.

From: "Sydney B. Mitchell and the Establishment of Graduate Education for Librarianship" by Robert E. Brundin in *Libraries & Culture*, vol. 29: 2 pp 166-185 By permission of the author and the University of Texas Press.

Helmut Kallmann: Pioneer Canadian Music Historian/Librarian

Dawn L. Keer

Abstract

Helmut Kallmann is among the foremost music historians and music librarians in Canada. He has been the pioneering force behind the collection and preservation of Canadian musical material in all its forms. His publication *A History of Music in Canada 1534-1914* (1960) is a standard reference work. His co-editorship of the *Encyclopedia of Music in Canada* (1981, 1992), as well as numerous articles on the history of music in Canada, established his name as the leading authority in that field. Kallmann was the founding chief of the Music Division of the National Library of Canada (1970-87). From 1950 to 1970 he was librarian of the CBC Music Library in Toronto. Kallmann's efforts led to the establishment of the Canadian Music Library Association in 1956 (now the Canadian Association of Music Libraries). This paper draws largely from Kallmann's own words about his life and work recorded during lengthy interviews with the author.

Résumé

Helmut Kallmann est parmi les historiens de la musique et les bibliothécaires de musique les plus connus au Canada. Il est le pionnier de la cueillette et de la conservation du matériel musical sous toutes ses formes. Son livre l'*Histoire de la musique au Canada 1543-1914* (1960) est un ouvrage de référence essentiel. Sa participation comme co-éditeur à l'*Encyclopédie de la musique au Canada* (1981, 1992) et la publication de nombreux articles sur l'histoire de la musique canadienne ont fait de lui une autorité dans le domaine. Kallmann a été le directeur fondateur de la Division de la musique de la Bibliothèque nationale du Canada (1970-1987). De 1950 à 1970 il était bibliothécaire à la musicothèque de Radio-Canada à Toronto. C'est grâce aux efforts de Kallmann qu'a vu le jour la *Canadian Music Library Association* en 1956, connue aujourd'hui sous le nom d'Association canadienne des bibliothèques musicales. Cet article cite abondamment des extraits d'entrevues que Kallman a accordées à l'auteur et dans lesquels il parle longuement de sa vie et de son oeuvre.

Helmut Kallmann is acknowledged as an editor, essayist, biographer, bibliographer, archivist, music historian and music librarian. He is active in the fields of research and publishing. This is so now, in his retirement, as it has been throughout his long and extremely productive career. As F.D. Donnelly points out in *The National Library of Canada* (1973), Helmut Kallmann championed the need for a national music library for the use of all Canadians as early as 1953.[1] He doggedly pursued this vision to its realization. Along the way, in advance of becoming the founding chief of the Music Division of the National Library of Canada (1970), he joined with like-minded individuals to co-found the Canadian Music Library Association (1956), now the Canadian Association of Music Libraries.

Although many of the contributions of Helmut Kallmann are readily recognizable and have been documented, the life of this Canadian librarian/ historian has not been recorded anywhere apart from brief biographical entries in a number of sources.[2] Most often the biographical entries read the same, that is, as lists of Kallmann's accomplishments. Just how much one can find out is limited possibly to what Kallmann wants to tell about himself. Well before I met him, I tried to conjure an image of Kallmann while reading the scholarly materials he had written. Kallmann's essay "Music Librarianship" in *Careers in Music* (1986) is a wonderfully informative piece written in an almost conversational tone. It made me wonder how much of Kallmann's own story was being told there. I wondered if he was describing himself when he wrote about the qualities a person should possess in order to be a librarian.

Since no single extensive account existed that chronicled the life, life's work and major contributions of this important Canadian figure, I found that getting to the root of the question "who is Helmut Kallmann?" seemed very much to be a matter of talking to Kallmann himself.[3] I therefore undertook lengthy personal interviews with Helmut Kallmann as well as shorter interviews with many of his colleagues.[4]

As a result of this research I discovered that the circumstances of Helmut Kallmann's personal life and background have combined to create a person who is not only a scholar in his own right but has also been instrumental in furthering the scholarship of others. Certainly, his pioneering work in the field of Canadian music history, the *Catalogue of Canadian Composers* (1952) and *A History of Music in Canada 1534-1914* (1960), enabled scholars to pursue a field of study which barely existed before Kallmann's efforts to collect and consolidate this body of knowledge. His encyclopedic knowledge was put to use as he co-edited the first comprehensive encyclopedia of music in Canada.

As a refugee from Nazi Germany when only a boy, Helmut Kallmann eventually found his way to Canada. During internment in Great Britain and then in the camps of New Brunswick and Quebec, and, finally, after his release and eventually as a student in Toronto in the 1940s, Kallmann sought to read and write and explore the history of music. In his new-found home, he discovered his curiosity about Canadian music history could not be satisfied easily. No one had written authoritatively and definitively about Canadian music history, or so it seemed to Kallmann. Numerous trips to libraries and exhaustive research showed an abundance of materials which only needed collecting, assimilating and presenting. Slowly and methodically, Kallmann began what became a lifetime commitment. In his own words:

> I think the best thing Canada offers to anybody who comes from Europe is that wide-open field for pioneer work. There's always something that the European will find that hasn't been done yet in Canada. Certainly music history was one of those fields.
>
> And I've been extremely lucky in having a career that just started at the bottom and went up in a gradual but straight line. I haven't had any reverses. And I've had the luck of having the sort of key positions in this particular field. First in the CBC, I was in the nerve centre of music broadcasting. Then at the National Library, I again was in a central position of being able to set up this documentation centre and collection of the musical memory of the country. But in addition, I was invited to work on the *Encyclopedia [of Music in Canada]*. Then when the Musical Heritage Society came about in 1982, again, I was right there. So I've been extremely fortunate in being able to do all this pioneer work.

Within the purview of Canadian music history and music librarianship, Kallmann's name is both known and respected. Helmut Kallmann has been linked to numerous pioneering endeavours in both fields. However, Kallmann did not miraculously appear on the Canadian cultural stage as a native son. In fact, he brought with him a heritage and formative education from another time and place.

Formative Years

Helmut Kallmann's upbringing in Berlin between the wars was largely influenced by the fact that his parents were educated, professional middle-class people. Fanny Paradies (his mother) was a professional social worker, and Arthur Kallmann, a lawyer. On the August 7, 1922, they welcomed the birth of their son, Helmut, a brother for 16-month-old Eva.[5] From a very early age, Helmut took a keen interest in the music he heard in his home. Arthur Kallmann documented Helmut's musical progress in his "children's diary." For example, at the age of four:

367

> 27 February 1927 — H. comes to me at the piano and, as he did recently, tries to follow the notes I play, standing now on my right, now on the left, paying attention to fast or loud or soft passages; then he plays himself and asks that the book stay open on the piano until next Sunday when we'll continue.[6]

Helmut began his study of the piano at the age of seven, supervised by his father, who tutored him in a gentle manner, never forcing him to practise, having him progress as he was ready. Kallmann remembers: "What my father did teach me was values …. I learned that the purpose of playing the piano was to get to know these wonderful, great compositions, the melodies, harmonies, and so on, and it wasn't to win an award in a competition or to get so many marks." With music stacked to the left and right of the piano, Helmut explored everything he could put his hand to, including vocal scores, operas, and string quartets: "taking up music and reading books was not just entertainment or a hobby. It was really a commitment. It was education."

Helmut's roots were Jewish, but he considers his ethnic background as "95 per cent German." Even though there were many Orthodox Jews in German society, his upbringing had been only marginally religious. However, with the rise in power of Hitler and the upsurge of anti-Semitism, "in order to find a source of spiritual strength," people went back "a little bit" to their roots. Times became increasingly more difficult for Jews, who were forced to carry identification cards. Helmut was only 16 years old when he carried this card, made of "a sort of canvas or oil cloth." Arthur Kallmann was 65 years old, placing him over the age limit of the Jewish males being rounded up by the Nazis in November 1938. Helmut was slightly under the lower age limit and together they initially escaped being sent to concentration camps. However, the concern remained that this eventually could become a reality.

One of Helmut's teachers had left Berlin with a list of names of children who had no relatives in England and therefore few prospects of being able to emigrate. His efforts to find a placement for Helmut were evident the day the Kallmanns received a letter from a refugee committee in London. It was March 1939, and Kallmann remembers:

> I still see my mother coming in and saying, "Here is a letter" and, "You've got a chance to go to England," and my mother was beaming with joy. My father was absolutely devastated. "We are going to first of all lose our son. Secondly, he's just in his last year before the senior matric, and what's he going to do there without a matric, and why can't he at least stay here and finish the matric?"

Feeling as if enough had already been done against the Jews, Arthur Kallmann was unwilling to accept that his only son should have to leave the country. Kallmann recalls his father's thinking at the time reflected the sentiments of other older German citizens: "'Well, the Nazis have gone so far, what else can they do to us? Nothing! They've taken away our jobs, but they can't destroy us!'" Nevertheless, some children were sent away. And so, preparations began to ready Helmut for the trip. Whatever the future was to hold, there was a sense of optimism:

> When you are a teenager you don't really understand the seriousness of things. It was bad enough for me to go to school and know that people could call dirty names after you and you couldn't really do anything about it, and the teachers might make anti-Semitic remarks, and they did, too! It was pretty grim. But at the same time, when you are a teenager, you have that optimism, that zest for life.

Even with all the packing and farewell visits, the night before Helmut was to leave his home for what was to be the last time, he sat at his desk writing compositions and copying the opus numbers for Beethoven works into a reference list to take with him. The next morning he and his father walked to the offices of the Gestapo to get Helmut's passport. "I still remember my father saying to the official there — he was a Gestapo man, I suppose— 'Don't you think my son should stay here and finish his matric?' And the man said, 'Be glad he can go!'"

In June 1939 Helmut's family and friends bid him farewell. They all stayed behind:

> My sister stayed behind. And as a matter of fact, if you define close relatives, those people who have no other ancestors than you have, in other words, your siblings, your parents, your grandparents, great-grandparents, your aunts, uncles, great aunts and so on; every one of my closest family stayed in Germany... and eventually the war picked up and they were taken to various concentration camps.... My aunts, my parents, my sister... perished in concentration camps.

Relocation

Helmut Kallmann came to London on what was called a children's transport. On a large ship with 200 children and several adult supervisors, he arrived at Southampton, then took a train to Waterloo Station in London, and there the group divided up.

London held some positive experiences for Kallmann. The availability of public libraries where one might freely browse through the shelves was a new and thrilling adventure for young Helmut. The libraries in Berlin were closed stack, requiring that patrons select from a catalogue the materials they were interested in reading. But in London, Kallmann was able to explore each library's holdings of music materials: "Usually I loved to browse, and I read a lot of books on music appreciation, music history. I didn't read the whole books, but I would stay there and nibble on the books." Music he heard on the radio also led Kallmann to the library to investigate: "I was so impressed by some of the tunes, I just had to look them up. These are the instruments that are playing and these are how the instruments are arranged and so on. That was just marvellous, and all this for free!"

The variety of pleasant and unpleasant circumstances during his "waiting period" of relative freedom in England ceased entirely in May 1940, when Helmut Kallmann was interned. Kallmann was just 17 years old:

> One morning the hostel father came up to me [and one other boy] and said, "You are wanted to come along to the police [for] a couple of weeks. Take along your toilet things and a change of shirt." Well, we had suitcases but you didn't need that much, so he gave us a wooden box and the two of us marched along. He took us to the local police station and then [next day] they took us in the van up to what was a race course [Kempton Park] outside London, and there they had over 1,000 people.

Numerous subsequent relocations finally ended when Kallmann boarded the Polish ship *Sobieski* bound for Canada.

Canadian Internment and the First Library Job

On July 15, 1940, the *Sobieski* landed at Quebec City. From there, the men and boys were taken by train first to Trois Rivières, then on to Camp B outside Fredericton, New Brunswick. Kallmann remembers that "there [they] were in the middle of the forest." An account of camp life, from the organization of groups and daily routines to the details of the lives of individuals, is documented in volume 1 of New Brunswick author Ted Jones' *Both Sides of the Wire: The Fredericton Internment Camp*. In it, many excerpts of Kallmann's camp diary appear as well as some reminiscences taken from Kallmann's letters to Ted Jones, such as: "The officers' attitude was that a prisoner should spend his days working, that is, doing physical work, whereas many of us would have preferred to stay in the camp to read, study, write, or similarly spend the time."[7] Kallmann's camp diary, written in German and then later translated, records many aspects of the educational opportunities for the young internees who wished to study for their junior and senior matriculation examinations.

What Kallmann now acknowledges as his first library job occurred in Camp B in the fall of 1940: "... A job I recently got is helping at the camp library."[8] Werner Lewin, a fellow internee studying Restoration drama, had the responsibility of running the camp library, with Kallmann's help: "That was the kind of work I enjoyed. So I volunteered and of course, I was nobody, I was just a clerical assistant."

Kallmann's boyhood friend Peter Ball had fled from Nazi Germany to the United States shortly before the outbreak of World War II. He was Kallmann's link to the outside world. In letters to Peter Ball, Kallmann kept him informed about his library work and about musical life in camp, critiquing the works he listened to on radio: "Yesterday I heard *Don Pasquale* which is not too strong. It lacks the sharp contrast between recitative and aria as Mozart has."[9]

Kallmann recalls the dawning of this interest in library work began in Berlin. His fascination with all the volumes of music in his home led him to attempt to classify or at least categorize the materials:

> I still can tell you what we had in the way of operas. There was *Figaro*, *Don Giovanni*, and I think the *Magic Flute* was together with the *Missa Solemnis* by Beethoven. These are piano vocal scores. And there was the *St. Matthew Passion* in the brown volume... and I guess there was a B minor mass. There was probably Weber's *Der Freischütz*, and there was an old volume of the *Flying Dutchman*. That was the extent of the operas. But my father, as a pianist, had practically all of the Beethoven, Mozart, Bach, Chopin, Schumann, Weber, Mendelssohn piano music.... And piano duets, Haydn symphonies, Beethoven symphonies, Mozart, and so on.... I still remember some of the colour and the beauty of the volumes.

Peter Ball, on violin, and Kallmann, on piano, had begun to play Mozart and Schubert violin sonatas while in high school. Their musical interests and explorations were, in retrospect, what Kallmann feels "fed into music librarianship":

> We got very interested in Mozart. We loved to compile information, so it was just natural that we were playing Mozart and there were these Köchel numbers. Probably, E major Sonata, 301, or something. So we made up pages and pages where we numbered from 1 to 627. And whatever Mozart his father had, my father had, we looked through where the Köchel numbers were. The old Peters editions and any other nineteenth-century ones didn't have

the Köchel numbers, but the newer ones did. And then there were biographies, catalogues, and we got to three-quarters of the Köchel numbers.

By doing that we got to know exactly how many concertos Mozart had written and how many masses and how many organ sonatas, how many operas and so on, and we learned the fun or the necessity of cataloguing.

And when he [Peter Ball] left for New York in, I would think, September 1938, our correspondence says, you know, "I found three more Köchel numbers: 443 is such and such a song, and this divertimento has two oboes, two horns, and two bassoons." And so we had a long discussion and we made tables on Mozart's life, when he went on his third trip to Italy and whatever, Vienna, Munich ....

In February 1941, Lewin was released from camp, and Kallmann took over the library until the break-up of Camp B in June. Shortly before leaving Camp B, Kallmann wrote to Ball:

I sometimes forget the outside world at all, it is a thing hard to imagine. Yet I regard camp life as a better type of life than hostel life .... Besides running our library I have got much time for studying. I am learning a bit of harmony and town planning. I am not able to compose anything because of the lack of piano playing. Besides, there is a lack of any books regarding history of music or town planning. There hardly seems a possibility of getting a practical, professional, and definite training.[10]

Kallmann had left his home in Berlin before his seventeenth birthday and had not seen his family since, nor was he to see them again. By mid-summer 1943, Kallmann had been interned for over three years. He was just turning 21 when he emerged from internment camp a free man into a land that he would eventually consider his home.

At the University of Toronto

Relocated to Toronto, Kallmann began a meagre life as an auditor's assistant and then a book store assistant until he registered at the University of Toronto in 1946, the year he became a Canadian citizen. "I suppose I had saved 100 or 200 dollars and I got one semester of a scholarship" to study for his Bachelor of Music degree. Even though Kallmann's main interest was in musicology or music history, there were no programs offered in these fields, so "as the lesser of two evils" he took the school music course. This was the first music education course offered in Canada and its purpose was to train musicians to go into the schools to teach music at the elementary level and to start choirs, orchestras and concert bands at the secondary level.

> I was afraid of writing quadruple counterpoint and that kind of thing and difficult harmony. I had been through too many harmony text books — it was so complicated, these sliding inner voices and harmonies, the 9th chord on the 3rd step with a flattened 6th and whatever — so [with] the school music course, at least harmony, counterpoint was down to manageable sizes. Anyway that's why I took that course, but mainly I was interested in music history.

Throughout his studies in music history, Kallmann dedicated his energies to meticulous note-taking: "I enjoyed compiling information and comparing different viewpoints to such a degree that I had sort of found my own element." Four months before his final examinations, at Christmas 1948, Kallmann sat down to document what he could of Canadian music history:

> I took a few sheets of paper. I wrote down all the names of Canadian performers and composers that I knew, and that wasn't very much. And then I looked at some books like the *International Cyclopedia of Music [and Musicians]*, which at that time had more Canadian musicians than any other encyclopedia, I think, more than *Baker's [Biographical Dictionary of Musicians]* and certainly more than *Riemann [Lexikon]*, more than the old *Grove's [Dictionary]*.
>   In 1947 the CBC brought out the *Catalogue of Canadian Composers* ,[11] which I saw in the library, and there was another bit of information compiled. It had people that I knew from seeing. Harry Freedman was a student at the same time (not in my class); [so was] Harry Somers. Sam Dolin was teaching, John Weinzweig was teaching, Barbara Pentland was there. These were people that I knew, and here was information about them.
>   Before I knew it, I had a dozen pages of notes and I decided that they should be organized in some way: composition, performance, education, church music. So I bought myself a binder and I put things in there alphabetically.[12]

This compiling of notes, which originally began when Kallmann was a youth in Berlin and continued throughout his internment years and then while he was a student at the University of Toronto, was the ground work for what would become a lifetime of research and scholarly contributions in the field of Canadian music history.

Music Librarian for the Canadian Broadcasting Corporation, Toronto

After graduating from the University of Toronto, Kallmann took a position in the CBC Toronto Music Library. "I started to work on the first of May, in 1950. That was really where I belonged, and in a way it was a free education because for those 20 years I met just about every musician who had a CBC program." The CBC Music Library was the ideal place for Kallmann to apply the research he had done, in music generally and in Canadian music specifically. Within weeks of arriving at the CBC, librarian Erland Misener requested that Kallmann begin working on a revision of the *Catalogue of Canadian Composers*, which was a major source of information for the CBC:

> Right after 1945, Canadian composers just popped up like mushrooms. Every year, every month, there was another one: Barbara Pentland, Godfrey Ridout, Bob Fleming, John Beckwith, Harry Somers, Harry Freedman, Jean Papineau-Couture, Clermont Pépin. They all came to public attention at the same time. Well, I suppose Weinzweig had been there a few years before, but it was just terrific, and all these great talents, like Lois Marshall, Elizabeth Benson Guy, Patricia Rideout, you know, we could go on and on, they were students at that time, right after the war.

The music library was a sort of nerve centre for music producers, musicians, conductors, announcers, all requiring the services of library personnel. However, a number of events conspired to lead to a dramatic change in the role of the CBC Music Library and the responsibilities of library staff. Gradually, with the advent of television in 1952, live radio programming declined and by 1957 virtually all the major radio musical variety shows had come to an end.[13]

In 1962, Kallmann was appointed supervisor of the Music Library. Within a few years, he had bought "all the [orchestral] Mozart, Haydn and Beethoven and whatever was in the public domain," building a large collection in the Music Library.

Kallmann's commitment to the collection, preservation and dissemination of musical materials had not declined, but the lack of growth and activity in the CBC Music Library by the end of the 1960s was a factor leading to his lack of enthusiasm: "The library was built up, the programming went down. It was no longer a challenge, so I became a bit restless." While he had made no conscious decision to leave the CBC, when the opportunity to move to the National Library presented itself, Kallmann accepted.

In 1970, Helmut Kallmann was considered *the* person to establish the Music Division at the National Library of Canada. This position, however, was not simply handed to him. In many ways and for nearly two decades, while he was a librarian at the CBC in Toronto, Kallmann had pursued his vision of a national music library. He assumed roles and accepted numerous responsibilities which garnered him a respected position in the national and international community of music librarians and musicians/composers. He established his authority as a scholar of Canadian music history with the publication of *A History of Music in Canada 1534-1914* (1960). Kallmann's intensive and extensive research into the history of music in Canada resulted in an immense and growing body of materials, the foundation for a future encyclopedia, and several decades of his own periodical articles as well as the basis for the revision of the *Catalogue of Canadian Composers* (1952).

A National Representative

In the early 1950s, Sir Ernest MacMillan invited Kallmann to be an individual member of the Canadian Music Council. The *Canadian Music Journal*, the scholarly publication of the Canadian Music Council, was launched in 1956, one year after MacMillan's *Music in Canada*, an anthology of essays, was published.[14] Kallmann was a contributor to both publications, as well as a member of the editorial board for the *Canadian Music Journal*. Kallmann remembered the excitement at that time when "the Canadian Music Council was trying to get all the national [music] organizations together, was trying to be an umbrella organization. It was also trying to establish contacts between Canadian and international organizations." The International Association of Music Libraries (IAML) was one such international organization.

The IAML had started the *Répertoire International des Sources Musicales* (RISM) project:

> the census of music before 1800 anywhere in the world. In my travels, especially to Quebec City, but also in Toronto and in Halifax, I had seen some pre-1800 music and so I thought we ought to participate. After all, I was interested in something which concerned Canada as a whole, not just me as an individual researcher.

Kallmann asked the Canadian Music Council for a formal endorsement, received it, and established contact with IAML.[15] Libraries reported their holdings of pre-1800 music to Kallmann who for years relayed this information on to the RISM project.

Another reporting responsibility undertaken by Kallmann involved Canada's new music publications. The journal of the International Association of Music Libraries, *Fontes Artis Musicae* (established in 1954), included in each issue a *liste internationale sélective*,[16] which reported new music publications by country. Kallmann was the "obvious person to do this for Canada" as he was on the receiving end at the CBC of many of the new publications in Canada. He submitted lists to *Fontes Artis Musicae* for many years.

The Canadian Music Library Association

Reporting the pre-1800 music and the new publications of Canadian music to an international music library network was not a task that Kallmann intended to carry out in isolation. He acknowledged that contact with fellow Canadian music librarians was essential: "And who are these people? If I want to have some information about Vancouver, who do I write to and what do they have? Do they collect local materials, and so on? And who in Canada has [for example] a good collection of French music?"

Kallmann turned to his contacts within the library and university communities to discuss finding those Canadians working with music materials in Canadian libraries and bringing them together into a music section within the Canadian Library Association:

> I spoke to [music librarian] Ogreta McNeill[17] at the Toronto Public Library who was very enthusiastic. As a matter of fact, the Canadian Library Association had already on its own talked about a music section. You know, [they had] a children's library section, public library section, research sections, and whatever. So they wanted to create a music section. Then I had made contact with [Laval University music professor] Lucien Brochu.[18]

Letters signed by Sir Ernest MacMillan and librarian Jean Lavender as well as McNeill, Brochu and Kallmann were sent to all interested persons and all libraries whose collections might include music.[19] Gradually, membership lists were assembled.

The efforts of Kallmann and a group of equally enthusiastic individuals led to the establishment of a music section of the Canadian Library Association. Ogreta McNeill became the first chairperson. Kallmann took the chairmanship next, 1957-58, and again in 1967-68.

Advocating a National Music Library

A first project for the new music section "undertaken during 1956-57 was the gathering of opinions concerning the kind and extent of musical services to be offered by the National Library when it [was] formally opened for use."[20] This project held considerable importance for Kallmann, as he had already begun to address this concern three years earlier. In a note to himself, January 19, 1953, Kallmann outlined some major points to consider — a brief review of libraries and archives, coverage of the importance of musicological research to provide historical documentation of Canadian music history and literature, government activities in this regard, the need for the gathering of history while the pioneers were still alive — the tasks of the national music library.

Six months later, June 16, 1953, in a letter to the first national librarian, Dr. William Kaye Lamb, Kallmann expressed an interest in the activities of the new National Library in the field of music. In three concise paragraphs he presented his case, ending with: "I believe that the function of a National Music Library as archives for such documents [of the Canadian musical past] is one of its most urgent ones and should be taken into consideration in the planning of the library as early as possible."[21] Lamb's response was prompt and positive, saying, "If you care to send me an outline of some of the things you think a Music Division should do, I shall be very glad to have it."[22] As an interested individual, Kallmann sent off his recommendations to Lamb. Correspondence between the two librarians continued until submissions by Kallmann came under the aegis of the Canadian Music Library Association (CMLA).

The CMLA completed its survey (1957) and made contact with the National Library to present its membership's suggestions of what categories of materials were to be given priority in the National Library's acquisition program. Top priority was to be given to Canadiana. In the non-Canadian field, explicit guidelines were given regarding acquisition. Recommendations for services and additional suggestions were forwarded along with a three-page addendum from Kallmann covering specific suggestions concerning the Canadiana collection.[23]

W. Kaye Lamb had purchased the Percy Scholes[24] library (1957) and, in Kallmann's view, "that was reason, in a way, to start a music division. But he didn't." In his article "The Percy Scholes Collection: Nucleus for a National Music Library" (1958), Kallmann fully described the acquisition and lauded the National Library for taking the initiative of acquiring the material which was to form the nucleus for further additions. He expressed optimism that the National Library "may soon be looked upon as the nation's foremost source of musical literature."[25]

A Step Towards Standardizing Music Collections

Submitting recommendations for the establishment of a national music library was a major focus for the CMLA. Another task which needed to be addressed, however, was assessing the music collections of already existing libraries and recommending standards. Under the chairmanship of Helmut Kallmann, a committee developed a set of standards for collections of music materials in medium-sized public libraries. The final publication included sections on books, periodicals, printed music and recordings, suggested children's recordings and a list of French books and periodicals.[26] *Standards for Music Collections in Medium Sized Public Libraries* (1960) gave public librarians some direction and guidance for creating and developing unified music collections within their libraries.

The initial core of CMLA executive members, Kallmann being one of them, set the tone for years of continued commitment to service to the music library community through the pursuit of worthwhile projects and the publication of useful materials for music librarians. Taking the initiative in another CMLA project was Kallmann's way of taking personal responsibility for developing and preserving an important historical source of musical literature.

The Data Sheet Project
"This is one of the main projects of my life." (Kallmann 1990)[27]

In 1963, Kallmann suggested to the CMLA that a bibliography of Canadian sheet music should be compiled. He pointed out that the material was disappearing fast and should be located and listed before it disappeared altogether and made the task impossible.[28] Kallmann was in a position to know precisely how difficult the situation had become, as he had begun collecting early Canadian sheet music in the 1950s. He attempted to include as much of this early Canadian music as he could in his *Catalogue of Canadian Composers* (1952), but, as he explains, "I hadn't actually seen much of it, [as] I got my information out of dictionaries, lists, and so on." When the opportunities to purchase these materials presented themselves, he began his collecting.

From its humble beginnings in Kallmann's private collection, this CMLA-sanctioned project eventually expanded to achieve the official status of National Union Catalogue of Printed Music up to 1951, with its home in the Music Division at the National Library of Canada.

Maria Calderisi Bryce joined the Music Division in 1973 with the dual qualifications, unique at that time, of a degree in music and a library science specialization in music librarianship. Her comments, reflecting an involvement with the Data Sheet project spanning almost two decades, indicate the value of this long-term undertaking:

> We call it a union catalogue. It is a tremendous tool for access to that kind of material that would never ever have been catalogued officially by the National Library and has still not been to this day. There are various ways of using it. The date and now more recently a place index have been set up which allow Canadians to pick out a body of material that may have been popular in Canada, popular enough to have been published in Canada, in a certain decade or in

a certain part of the country. And then a subject index to the sheet music allows people to identify special publications to honour a prime minister, or to commemorate a certain event.[29]

In retrospect, Canadian composer and writer John Beckwith, a long-time friend and colleague of Kallmann's, recognizes a pattern in Kallmann's activities within the International Association of Music Libraries and the Canadian Music Library Association, later the Canadian Association of Music Libraries[30] and the commitment he brought to their varied projects:

> He came into organizations like those and he could see potential, particularly organizational things, logical things that the organization could do, could be responsible for. With the Canadian Music Library Association he was responsible in the 1960s for some of their publications. This idea of making available historical material (beyond what was in his book) that librarians could use as resource materials was very much typical of his way of doing things.[31]

Chief of the Music Division, National Library of Canada

> During Canada's Centennial on June 20, 1967, the new 15-floor building at 395 Wellington Street was officially opened .... The new building brought together collections of the National Library that had previously been stored in various buildings in the Ottawa-Hull area. Researchers, writers and students could now use books, documents, pamphlets, microfilm and sound recordings under one roof. The National Library could now become a recognizable national institution.[32]

National Librarian William Kaye Lamb was nearing the end of his career when the National Library took up residence in its new home. Over the years, he had accepted recommendations for the establishment of a music division and he had made the major acquisition of the Percy Scholes collection, which stood as the basis for a national music collection. He did not, however, establish a music division before he retired. This task fell to his successor, Dr. Guy Sylvestre, Canada's second national librarian (1968-83). Kallmann had had the experience of going from library to library to conduct the research for his *History of Music in Canada,* and he felt very strongly about the need for one central library which would serve researchers. When Sylvestre became National Librarian, Kallmann once again pushed for the formation of a national repository for music and music materials.

One project Sylvestre became involved in was the acquisition of the Healey Willan collection. However, once this was accomplished, Sylvestre was faced with finding someone to take care of this and future acquisitions and materials. After all applicants were heard, the position of Chief of the Music Division fell to Helmut Kallmann. "With the hiring in 1970 of Helmut Kallmann ... the Music Division was created. Dr. Kallmann[33] was the first subject specialist hired by the Library, and the Music Division, its first subject division."[34]

> I didn't have a library degree, all I had was a Bachelor of Music, in school music of all things, and I've never been in library school for a single day, you know. But he [Sylvestre] wanted somebody who had this background in Canadian musical history, who would know what was important, where the materials were and who had published what and, also [someone] who had a bit of a name.

Kallmann brought some very definite ideas to this new position: "My main idea was looking at it from the point of view of the researcher. The National Library must be able to offer a one-stop music collection that embraces all types of musical Canadiana, whatever they are, as long as they document the musical life of Canada."

Upon arriving at the National Library, Kallmann recognized that the collection of music materials needed to be sorted and unified: the historical copyright deposits, the copyright deposits of primarily sheet music from 1953, and the sound recordings only from 1969 on, the current production of publications in Canada, music periodicals, the books on music, scores, materials from the library of Percy Scholes, the Healey Willan collection, and odds and ends from the Library of Parliament.

"And we set up vertical files," recounts Kallmann. He could not have known then that this simple beginning would blossom so successfully. Over 20 years later, these vertical files have grown immeasurably, in both size and value. Kallmann's successor as Chief of the Music Division, Timothy Maloney, relates: "Those vertical files which Helmut has built are a treasure trove, absolutely a treasure trove. And there is no other such gold mine in the country to which people can come and find as much information on all aspects of the music in Canada."[35]

Collections, Acquisitions and Exhibitions

By 1972, almost all the music collection was located on 3M, the third mezzanine, at the National Library, where Kallmann's office remained for another 15 years. It was there that he would at times speak with members of the public who wished to leave their own, or their relatives', musical estates. In 1990, the Director of the Public Services Branch, Flora Patterson, noted, "If you have a high profile, like Dr. Kallmann did, who is well known in the music world, then people are apt to think about leaving their material to the National Library."[36]

Two major acquisitions awaited Kallmann's organizational skills when he came to the National Library: the Percy Scholes collection, acquired in 1957, and the Healey Willan papers, 1969. With the support of the National Librarian, Kallmann acquired the collections/papers of Alexis Contant, Claude Champagne, and "all kinds of other people."

The Glenn Gould acquisition was completed even though Kallmann knew he did not have sufficient staff to deal with it at the time. Timothy Maloney acknowledges the importance of this collection:

> He had to handle the whole Gould acquisition, for example, which was immense. It's huge, over two hundred boxes. Typically a big archival acquisition is forty, fifty boxes. It was four or five times that. It really was a major *coup* for the Music Division and continues to be the single biggest acquisition for a manuscript collection and arguably the single most important archival collection in terms of the importance of the person to whom it belonged. There's only one Glenn Gould and he was absolutely a giant in Canadian music circles.[37]

Due to the enormous size of the collection, Kallmann continued on, even after he had officially retired, to organize an exhibition and to publish an exhibition catalogue. The exhibition opened in Ottawa at the National Library on April 14, 1988.

The Encyclopedia of Music in Canada

Kallmann had barely begun the massive undertaking of building the Music Division for the National Library when he was called upon to assume the critical role of content editor for Canada's first encyclopedia devoted to music in Canada. Starting as a major undertaking in the 1970s, but with its roots in the 1950s, the *Encyclopedia of Music in Canada* occupied Kallmann for over 20 years. The work on the *Encyclopedia of Music in Canada* occupied a tremendous amount of Kallmann's time when, at the same time, he was responsible for the Music Division at the National Library:

> I did the encyclopedia work evenings, weekends .... Dr. Sylvestre sooner or later gave me permission to attend meetings, make phone calls during the day and, later on, I think, to take a certain

proportion of my time off because it was so much in the interests of the National Library to have this information and to get the acknowledgement that the National Library was the source of so much of the material.

The project was completed and the landmark *Encyclopedia of Music in Canada* was published in 1981. Two years later, in 1983, the French edition appeared. The *Encyclopedia of Music in Canada* quickly became an indispensable guide to all aspects of music in Canada, current and historical. In 1988, Kallmann, with co-editor Gilles Potvin and associate editors Robin Elliott and Mark Miller, began work on the second edition of the *Encyclopedia of Music in Canada*. It appeared in 1992 as an extensively revised and expanded edition, including full coverage of jazz and pop music in Canada and information on a whole new generation of composers and performers.

Retirement

While Chief of the Music Division, Kallmann maintained an almost unbelievably demanding regimen. His philosophy behind the Music Division did not change dramatically over the years. When he began, as when he retired in 1988, he thought of the Music Division "as a mixture of a library, an archives, a documentation centre, where you document current events and that sort of thing, clippings, programs, and photos, and so on, and, fourthly, as a sort of museum, a music museum."

It was an awesome mandate for most, but a necessary, even an only, way for Kallmann:

> I admit it was very much for the staff to cope with all that, and usually they didn't cope entirely. You know, we want to organize a photo collection, we want to organize the concert programs, and the sheet music should be in better boxes, and there should be a better system for this and that, and a lot of that is not in the narrow sense in the mandate of the National Library.
>
> And very often the staff said, "No, you just have to give up collecting the newspaper clippings. It just takes so much time." But my argument has always been that if you don't collect it now, it'll be gone. Even if you collect your photos, if you just throw them in a box and wait for happier days when you have somebody to organize them, it's still better than [not collecting at all].

In the notice of his retirement in the *National Library News*, these words summed up his contribution:

Dr. Helmut Kallmann was Chief of the Music Division from 1970 to 1987 .... He has overseen the development of the Music Division since its inception, and it is now the largest collection of Canadian music in the world. The National Library and the Canadian music and academic communities have benefited immeasurably from Dr. Kallmann's work.[38]

Accolades and Acknowledgements

Helmut Kallmann's humility is characteristically evident when he speaks of his past accomplishments in terms not of what he has done for Canada, but of how fortunate he has been to have had the opportunity to be in Canada to pursue his dreams:

> If I had stayed in Germany or in England, there wouldn't have been that challenge to be the pioneer music historian of that country because they had dozens before, for a century, who knew much more than I, and there was no need for someone to do it all over. But Canada was just the marvellous opportunity for pioneering. And I found out when I came to Toronto and I started university that everybody had their eyes on the future. They were going to start the school music, all my classmates, they were going to start orchestras, bands and choirs and various schools, and other people were going to establish opera and new university departments. Maybe they would introduce musicology. That was still five, six years away. And I was the only one who sort of looked backwards, into the rear-view mirror.
>
> I was lucky because, I guess, even in my childhood, I was always looking for something others weren't doing — also something where I could compile facts. But in Germany would I ever have become a musicologist or music historian? Probably a librarian in the end. Probably it would have worked out that way. Or some kind of editorial person, you know, where you do editing and proof-reading and compiling facts.

The connection between being a new Canadian and making a major contribution to Canada surfaced as a common point for consideration with a number of Kallmann's colleagues and acquaintances during many of the research interviews I conducted. What follows are some excerpts which illuminate this theme.

A contemporary of Kallmann's, the late Henry Kreisel, Canadian author, had this to say:

It's always fascinated me that it was people like ourselves [he and Kallmann], who were really not Canadian, certainly not born here, who were accidentally, in one sense, dumped here and then made the country our own (and the country accepted us, obviously), who should have recognized the value and the interest in the Canadian culture. When I came to Toronto, my schoolmates didn't know anything. Nothing. I asked them, "What should I read?" My friends and colleagues in English language and literature in Toronto didn't know much about Canadian literature. There was a general sort of feeling of denigration: it wasn't very important, there was nothing very good anyway, all the good stuff is written somewhere else.

It's not uncharacteristic that Kallmann should have been the person who then became a pioneer in the study of Canadian music — someone from outside. Maybe that's how it had to be. Maybe it was people from the outside who could see better, with a clearer view and with a better kind of perspective than people who were born and raised here.[39]

Words from Kallmann's long-time colleague and friend, the late Keith MacMillan:

It was [*The Catalogue of Canadian Composers*], I think. I can't think of anything else that almost proclaimed Helmut's seriousness as a student of this kind of thing. I think it took a European or somebody from outside the country to start a study of this kind — the story behind the people and the listing of the kind of works that these people were writing and Helmut's own intimate knowledge. Practically all of his work at that time and even since has [come from] sort of "root" sources, not other people's publications.

But I think it took a European to bring a fresh look at us. One takes oneself for granted. I was always very fond of Marshall McLuhan's phrase about "fish can see anything but the water." Which means you're least sensitive to your most immediate environment because you take everything for granted. Well, Helmut didn't when he came here. He began to be curious about the musical history of this country and could learn very little about it. Most people said, "Oh, we don't have any."[40]

The University of Toronto acknowledged Kallmann's achievements and contributions by awarding him an honorary Doctor of Laws in 1971. In 1977, Kallmann was presented with the Canadian Music Council Medal for outstanding service to music in Canada at the Canadian Music Council

Conference in Vancouver. Again, in 1982, the Canadian Music Council recognized Kallmann with a special citation for the editors of the *Encyclopedia of Music in Canada.*

"In 1987 I was almost overwhelmed with recognition," Kallmann recalls of the year that began with an announcement of the recipients of the Order of Canada. Later in 1987, Kallmann was made an honorary member of the Canadian Association of Music Libraries. At the joint conference of the Canadian University Music Society and the Canadian Association of Music Libraries (now independent of the Canadian Library Association) in May 1987, a reception was held in honour of Kallmann, where he was presented with a citation in tribute to his achievements in music librarianship.

Helmut Kallmann's old-world values and his charm and grace acquired through an early twentieth-century European upbringing have endured the ravages of war, the separation from family, the years in internment camp, and survived. The late twentieth-century Kallmann, a slight yet hardy gentleman, enjoys many simple pleasures of life: going for walks, working a bit in the yard, playing chamber music at his piano with an ensemble of fellow musicians. By contrast, Kallmann is also perfectly at ease at formal public occasions, in a large crowd of academics or dignitaries, or having a casual chat with colleagues and friends. His quick wit and subtle sense of humour enhance the excellent conversational skills he has and which he is not reticent to use, in English, in German, or in French.

Many of Kallmann's colleagues have described his quiet demeanour and certain shyness as "self-effacing." However, while Kallmann does not solicit flattery from others, he graciously acknowledges praise when it is given. Kallmann maintains a healthy scholarly pride in himself and all his accomplishments, and by no means purposefully works at being inconspicuous, but, as he would explain it, he has some difficulty in "blowing his own horn."

Helmut Kallmann is now retired but is as active as before. Work with the Canadian Musical Heritage Society continues, as does writing, reviewing and generally keeping in touch with the "heart beat" of music in Canada. The incredible energy with which Kallmann goes about his life and his work seems to well from an inner source of strength and resolve. He has applied this energy unstintingly throughout a career that seems to show no signs of diminishing. The magnitude of his accomplishments has assured his place in the forefront of Canadian music research and music librarianship. Even so, with an optimistic eye on the future, Kallmann plans to continue to write, to research, and to explore and develop his ideas. Indicative of this great spirit, the last words are Kallmann's: "I've never in my life run out of things to do. I've never been bored and I don't think I ever will be. There will be always something else to do, even if it's just putting my papers in order and making lists of my correspondence."

Notes

[1] F. Dolores Donnelly, *The National Library of Canada: A Historical Analysis of the Forces which Contributed to its Establishment and to the Identification of its Roles and Responsibilities* (Ottawa: Canadian Library Association, 1973), 129.

[2] Examples of some biographical entries: *Baker's Biographical Dictionary* (New York: Schirmer Books, 6th ed., 1978: 852; 7th ed., 1984: 1152), *The Canadian Encyclopedia* (2d ed., vol. 2. Edmonton: Hurtig, 1988: 1125), *Dictionary of Library and Information Professionals* (vol. 1. Listings. Woodbridge, Conn.: Research Publication, 1988: 623), *Encyclopedia of Music in Canada* (Toronto: University of Toronto Press, 1981: 488), *International Who's Who in Music and Musician's Directory* (Cambridge, U.K.: Melrose, 1988: 470; 1985: 458; 1980: 372).

[3] This I undertook to do in the summer of 1990 as part of the research for my Masters in Library and Information Studies thesis (University of Alberta, 1991). "Helmut Kallmann: An Account of His Contributions to Music Librarianship and Scholarship in Canada" covers Kallmann's early life in Berlin, relocation to England and internment in Canada, and his education and his life's work in Canada. In August 1993, I conducted another series of interviews with Kallmann and others in preparation for the writing of "Creating History: Helmut Kallmann and Music in Canada," for a CBC Radio "Ideas" documentary (aired as "Ideas Profile: Helmut Kallmann," April 20, 1995).

[4] Although publicly known details of his life and work have been meticulously collected from a variety of secondary sources, it is from the personal interview with Helmut Kallmann that the first-hand facts have been gathered. I say interview, instead of the plural, because I think of our many meetings as one long conversation. Unless otherwise indicated, quotations to follow will be the words of Helmut Kallmann, July 9, 10, 11, 13, 14, 23, 24, 25, 1990.

[5] Eva Kallmann was born March 20, 1921.

[6] Arthur Kallmann, "Children's Diary," February 27, 1927.

[7] Ted Jones, *Both Sides of the Wire: The Fredericton Internment Camp*, vol. 1 (Fredericton, N.B.: New Ireland Press, 1988), 162.

[8] Helmut Kallmann, letter to Peter Ball, November 23, 1940.

[9] Kallmann, letter to Ball, December 23, 1940.

[10] Kallmann, letter to Ball, June 13, 1941.

[11] In 1951, as librarian of the Canadian Broadcasting Corporation Music Library, Toronto, Kallmann edited a revised and enlarged edition of this original publication.

[12] This single binder was the beginning of a collection of materials which now occupies several dozen binders and several metres of shelf space in Kallmann's private study. Their contents provided some of the core material for the *Encyclopedia of Music in Canada*.

[13] Gordon Richardson, "The Music and Record Libraries of the Canadian Broadcasting Corporation," *Fontes Artis Musicae* 34, no. 4 (October - Dececember 1987): 211.

[14] Kallmann, "Canadian Music Council/Conseil canadien de la musique," *Encyclopedia of Music in Canada* (Toronto: University of Toronto Press, 1981), 148.

[15]William Guthrie, "New RISM Representative," *Canadian Association of Music Libraries Newsletter* 17, no. 1 (March 1988): 3.

[16]Vincent Duckles, *Music Reference and Research Materials* (London: Collier-Macmillan, 1964), 110.

[17]Ogreta McNeill, at that time the head of the music collection of the Toronto Public Library, was the first Canadian to hold degrees in both music (1952) and library science (1953) (*Encyclopedia of Music in Canada*, 549).

[18]On two or three previous visits to Université Laval, Kallmann had been assisted by music professor Lucien Brochu in finding copies of old music. Kallmann remembered: "This old music was stored in a little room in some beautiful old cupboards with glass windows, where the cleaning staff kept their supplies, and so that was the room where nobody had ever looked at it [the old music] in years."

[19]"The Canadian Music Library Association — L'Association canadienne des bibliothèques musicales," *Canadian Library* 17, no. 6 (May 1961): 320.

[20]"The Canadian Music Library Association," *Canadian Library* 17, no. 6 (May 1961): 320.

[21]Kallmann, letter to W.K. Lamb, June 16, 1953, in Kallmann's private papers.

[22]W.K. Lamb, letter to Kallmann, June 19, 1953, in Kallmann's private papers.

[23]Lorna D. Fraser, Secretary, CMLA, and Kallmann, letter to W.K. Lamb, April 7, 1957, in Kallmann's private papers. (Original in the National Library of Canada.)

[24]Scholes, an English scholar "of the widest interests, one of the few who are more interested in writing for the layman than for other scholars ... never sacrificed accuracy and attention to detail." From Kallmann's "The Percy Scholes Collection: Nucleus for a National Music Library," *Canadian Music Journal* 2, no. 3 (Spring 1958): 43.

[25]Kallmann, "The Percy Scholes Collection," 45.

[26]Helen Sinclair, "Canadian Music Library Association." In *Annual Reports of Officials, Projects, Sections, Committees for 1958-1959. Feliciter* 4, no. 9 (May 1959, Part 2): 4.

[27]During the July 1990 interview, Kallmann made this assessment, looking back over a lifetime of commitments to numerous worthy projects.

[28]"Canadian Music Library Association," *Proceedings: 18th Annual Conference* (Ottawa: Canadian Library Association, 1963), 71.

[29]Maria Calderisi Bryce, telephone interview, Edmonton to Ottawa, July 9, 1991.

[30]In 1972, the Canadian Music Library Association (CMLA) became the Canadian Association of Music Libraries (CAML), the Canadian branch of IAML, and moved its headquarters into the Music Division at the National Library.

[31]John Beckwith, personal interview, Toronto, July 18, 1990.

[32]"Twenty Years After: The National Library Building, 1967-1987," *National Library News* 19, no. 11 (Nov. 1987): 2.

[33]Kallmann received an honorary LLD from the University of Toronto in 1971.

[34]Ian Wees, *The National Library of Canada: Twenty-Five Years After*, a retrospective overview by Ian Wees published on the occasion of the silver anniversary of the National Library of Canada (Ottawa: Minister of Supply and Services Canada, 1978), 32.

[35]Timothy Maloney, personal interview, Ottawa, July 25, 1990.
[36]Flora Patterson, personal interview, Ottawa, July 24, 1990.
[37]Maloney, July 25, 1990.
[38]"Retirements," *National Library News* 20, no. 1 (January 1988): 6.
[39]Henry Kreisel (1922-1991, personal interview, Edmonton, May 29, 1990.
[40]Keith MacMillan (1920-1991), personal interview, Toronto, July 19, 1990.

Contributors

Biographical entries supplied by the contributors

Charles Acland teaches cultural and media studies in the graduate programme in Communication Studies at the University of Calgary, where he is an assistant professor. His work on popular taste, national culture, and Canadian cultural history has appeared in *Communication, Journal of Communication Inquiry, Wide Angle*, and the *Canadian Journal of Film Studies*, among other scholarly and popular publications. His book *Youth, Murder, Spectacle: The Cultural Politics of "Youth in Crisis"* was published in 1995 by Westview Press.

Lorne Bruce has worked as a chief librarian for smaller public libraries at Hanover and King Township in Ontario. Currently he is in collection development at the University of Guelph Library. He is the author of a number of articles and book reviews on public library service. His major publications include *Public Library Boards in Postwar Ontario 1945-1985* (with Karen Bruce) and *Free Books for All; the Public Library Movement in Ontario 1850-1930*.

Robert E. Brundin is Professor Emeritus at the School of Library and Information Studies, University of Alberta. He taught in the areas of reference, Canadian materials, rare book librarianship, and facilities planning, among others. He continues to teach a course on facilities planning. Prior to university teaching, he was a reference librarian and college library director for many years.

William J. Buxton is Professor of Communication Studies at Concordia University. Author of *Talcott Parsons and the Capitalist Nation-States* (Toronto, 1985), he is currently editing (with Charles R. Acland) a collection of writings on Harold A. Innis, and he is doing research on the Communications Program of the Rockefeller Foundation.

Claire England teaches collections and reference materials at the Faculty of Information Studies, University of Toronto. Her interest in fire and water damage to library collections came about because of the problems of prevention, recovery and control in damage-affected materials and collections. She and a colleague, Karen Evans, wrote *Disaster Management for Libraries: Planning and Process* (Canadian Library Association, 1988).

Elizabeth Hanson has been on the library faculty of Indiana University Libraries, Bloomington, since 1977 and is currently Head of the Medical Sciences Library and Acting Head of the Biology Library. In 1994 she received her PhD from Indiana University (School of Library and Information Science); her dissertation focused on the Westmount Public Library (Westmount, Que.). Her primary research area is Canadian library history with a second specialty in the history of British libraries and librarianship.

Dawn Keer holds a BA in Music History and Literature and a BEd in Secondary School Music. For over 15 years she was an instrumental music teacher before receiving a master's in Library and Information Studies at the University of Alberta (1991). Dawn Keer is now a teacher-librarian/technology coordinator for the Edmonton Catholic Schools. Experience as a freelance broadcaster with CBC Radio (Edmonton) includes interviews, commentary, and the writing and production of a radio documentary.

Marcel Lajeunesse has taught at the École de bibliothéconomie et des sciences de l'information of the Université de Montréal since 1970. Full professor since 1985 and director from 1987 to 1994, he is now Assistant Dean for Planning and Assistant Dean responsible for the Humanities sector of the Faculty of Arts and Sciences. Dr. Lajeunesse is the author or co-author of eight books and has published over sixty articles.

Bertrum H. MacDonald is the Director of the School of Library and Information Studies in the Faculty of Management at Dalhousie University, Halifax, Nova Scotia. He is the editor of *Épilogue*, a bilingual scholarly journal devoted to exploration of the history of print culture in Canada. His primary research interest focuses on the history of the diffusion and use of scientific information amongst Canadian scientists.

Peter F. McNally is Associate Professor with the Graduate School of Library and Information Studies at McGill University (Montreal, Quebec), where he lectures and publishes on reference, bibliography, and the history of books, printing, and libraries. In 1980, he founded the Library History Interest Group of the Canadian Library Association, serving as its first convenor and since 1995 as its co-convenor. During 1995-96, he has been a Fellow of the National Library of Canada.

Elizabeth Mitchell obtained an Honours BA from the University of Toronto (Trinity College) and taught for three years, after which she returned to the University of Toronto for a Master of Library Science degree. She has been Information Services Librarian at Belleville Public Library since 1973, and she is currently President of the Hastings County Historical Society. Her paper grew out of research originally undertaken in 1976 for a booklet celebrating 100 years of library service in Belleville.

Darrel R. Reid completed undergraduate studies at the University of Regina and master's degrees in history and library science at the University of Toronto. Thereafter, he served as an information specialist with two public policy studies organizations at Queen's University: the Institute of Intergovernmental Relations and then the School of Policy Studies. In 1994 he completed a PhD in history at Queen's. He is currently Director of Research for the national caucus of the Reform Party in Ottawa.

Maxine K. Rochester (BA (University of Sydney), MLS (University of Western Ontario), PhD (University of Wisconsin)) is Associate Professor in Library and Information Studies at the School of Information Studies, Charles Sturt University-Riverina, at Wagga Wagga. She edits *Education for Library and Information Services: Australia.* Her major research project in the library history area is a study of the impact of Carnegie Corporation of New York grants for library development to Canada, South Africa, New Zealand and Australia in the 1920s and 1930s.

Basil Stuart-Stubbs was a reference librarian at McGill University Library from 1954 to 1956, a catalogue, serials and special collections librarian at the University of British Columbia (UBC) from 1956 to 1964, University Librarian at UBC from 1964 to 1981, and the Director of its School of Library, Archival and Information Studies from 1981 to 1991.

Faith Wallis received a BA and MA in History and an MLS from McGill University and her doctorate in Medieval Studies from the University of Toronto in 1985. She joined the staff of the Osler Library in 1985 and the following year became its director. In 1992 she left the Library to take up full-time teaching in the Department of History and the Department of Social Studies of Medicine at McGill University.

Index

Monographic titles and material in footnotes not indexed